Buck Shaw

Buck Shaw

*The Life and Sportsmanship
of the Legendary Football Coach*

KEVIN CARROLL

McFarland & Company, Inc., Publishers
Jefferson, North Carolina

LIBRARY OF CONGRESS CATALOGUING-IN-PUBLICATION DATA

Names: Carroll, Kevin, 1950– author.
Title: Buck Shaw : the life and sportsmanship
of the legendary football coach / Kevin Carroll.
Description: Jefferson, North Carolina : McFarland & Company, Inc., Publishers, 2022 |
Includes bibliographical references and index.
Identifiers: LCCN 2022003533 | ISBN 9781476686905 (paperback : acid free paper) ∞
| ISBN 9781476644318 (eBook)
Subjects: LCSH: Shaw, Buck (Lawrence Timothy), 1899–1977. |
Football coaches—United States—Biography. | San Francisco 49ers
(Football team)—History. | Philadelphia Eagles (Football team)—History.
| National Football League Championship Game—History. | Football players—
United States—Biography. | Notre Dame Fighting Irish (Football team)—
History. | BISAC: SPORTS & RECREATION / Football
Classification: LCC GV939.A429 C37 2022 | DDC 796.332092 [B]—dc23/eng/20220215
LC record available at https://lccn.loc.gov/2022003533

BRITISH LIBRARY CATALOGUING DATA ARE AVAILABLE

ISBN (print) 978-1-4766-8690-5
ISBN (ebook) 978-1-4766-4431-8

Front cover: Santa Clara head coach Buck Shaw (Archives
and Special Collections, Santa Clara University)

Printed in the United States of America

*McFarland & Company, Inc., Publishers
Box 611, Jefferson, North Carolina 28640
www.mcfarlandpub.com*

To all Albuquerque Academy football players,
coaches and trainers, 1985–2018

Acknowledgments

The author is especially indebted to Sara Perez Webber, whose meticulous editing and insightful suggestions were invaluable in finalizing this project. A major salute to the helpful and kindly college and university archivists who acted upon my appeals for help with both alacrity and expediency. This includes Laura E. Rocke at the University of Nevada, Reno, and Summer Shetenhelm at Santa Clara University as well as Jessica Guardado, Loyola Marymount University Special Collections; Stephanie Plowman, Gonzaga University Archives and Special Collections; David Crawford, Creighton University Archives; and Mary Ruwell and Ruth Kindereich at the United States Air Force Academy Archives and the Public Affairs Office of the United States Air Force Academy.

Thanks also to curator Katherine Crowe and her friendly staff at the Denver University Archives. Kate Johnson, Northern Colorado University; Mary Safell, Texas Christian University Mary Couts Burnett Library; Germain Bienvenu, Louisiana State University Special Collections; Rebecca Baker, University of Washington Libraries, Special Collections; and Kenneth Johnson and Tomeka Meon Myers, Library of Congress, also provided valued assistance.

Mr. Robert Wayne Cook of Stuart, Iowa, shared a wealth of information about Buck Shaw's childhood and coaching career during the initial stages of my research. At the eleventh hour, Buck Shaw's grandchildren, Pam Hammer, Gary Piers and Sue Healey, graciously offered numerous family photos for publication. A list of people interviewed for this project appears in the Bibliography.

I'd also like to thank Mr. John Purcell and my daughters, McKinnon and Letitia, for guiding me through the whitewaters of a computer's workings. Finally, thanks to my supportive and loving wife, Linda, who spent seemingly endless hours proofreading manuscript pages. I love you!

Table of Contents

Preface

While researching my previous book, *Dr. Eddie Anderson: Hall of Fame College Football Coach*, I kept coming across the name Buck Shaw. Anderson and Shaw both hailed from Iowa and were Notre Dame teammates, who from 1919 through 1921 played next to one another—Anderson at right end and Shaw at right tackle—for famed coach Knute Rockne. Both earned All-American honors as seniors and entered the coaching ranks immediately upon graduating from college.

Several laudatory articles about Shaw's Santa Clara University teams during the '30s further piqued my interest. Although Santa Clara's student body numbered about 500, Shaw's squads played the likes of Stanford, Michigan State, Oklahoma and Louisiana State—and, more often than not, beat them. During his seven-year head coaching tenure at Santa Clara, the Broncos won 77 percent of their games, including two Sugar Bowls.

Having coached high school football for 40 years—30 as a head coach, often competing against larger schools—I appreciate Shaw's skill in taking on formidable rivals. Even more so, I admire his wholesome approach to the game. Shaw was an excellent teacher of football fundamentals with a firm command of the game's Xs and Os, and his greatest coaching strength was his unique ability to relate to young men and mold them into a team. Shaw often had his players believing that they were not only teammates but family, a sentiment his appreciative players embraced. He modeled genuine sportsmanship, earning the respect of players, officials and opposing coaches alike.

During his 39 years in the profession, Shaw coached at five schools. His groundbreaking efforts as the first varsity football coach of the United States Air Force Academy led to the academy achieving an undefeated season against Division I opponents in only its fourth year of existence. Shaw also served two winning stints as a professional coach—first as the inaugural coach of the San Francisco 49ers, then a three-year stint with the Philadelphia Eagles that culminated in winning the National Football League (NFL) Championship. In 1960, the Associated Press (AP), United Press International (UPI) and the NFL honored Shaw as "Coach of the Year." His esteemed coaching legacy earned him induction to the College Football Hall of Fame, the Iowa Sports Hall of Fame, and the San Francisco Bay Area and San Jose halls of fame.

Surprisingly, however, Shaw has never been mentioned as a possible candidate for admission into Canton's Pro Football Hall of Fame—even though his .621 winning percentage over 12 seasons surpasses that of current Hall of Fame member coaches Weeb Ewbank (51 percent), Sid Gillman (54 percent), and Marv Levy and Jimmy Johnson (56 percent). Shaw's winning percentage is almost identical to Hall of Fame coach Bill Cowher's .623.

A fierce competitor as a player, Shaw possessed the same intense desire to win as a coach. Yet his gentlemanly demeanor debunked famed baseball manager Leo Durocher's theory that "nice guys finish last." He'd build up his players rather than berate them. "A player doesn't get better by a coach telling him how ineffective he is," Shaw once told reporters. "Start making them believe they are champions and pretty soon they'll be playing like champions."

A class act throughout his coaching career, Shaw himself went out as a champion, retiring after clinching the NFL's top prize for the Eagles. Today, Buck Shaw could serve as a role model for coaches in any sport at any level. While many newspaper articles have been written about the "Silver Fox," as sportswriters nicknamed Shaw, most have virtually ignored his early coaching years at North Carolina State and Nevada. Like many of the pro players he mentored throughout his career, Shaw's efforts and skills helped make the NFL the multi-billion-dollar business it is today. This book aims to bring wider recognition to Buck Shaw, his admirable coaching philosophy and his role in shaping the game of football.

Introduction

The temperature was a brisk 28 degrees as Lawrence "Buck" Shaw reconnoitered the gridiron of Philadelphia's Franklin Field on December 26, 1960. As he buttoned up his stylish overcoat, the bespectacled 61-year old, silver-haired coach hoped that the afternoon's bright sunshine would dry the stadium's grass field before kickoff. Several days of light snow and rain had left the field with soggy, slippery footing that could hinder his team's passing game.

Despite the field conditions, Franklin Field was a classic football venue. Franklin Field boasts many "firsts," underscoring its importance to the sport—first college stadium to add a scoreboard and upper deck, increasing seating capacity to 70,000 in 1925; site of the first radio broadcast of a football game, when Cornell defeated Penn 9–0 in 1922; and the first television broadcast of a football game, when Penn crushed Maryland 51–0 on October 5, 1940. And in 1958—the same year Shaw assumed the team's coaching reins—Franklin Field became the home of the Philadelphia Eagles.

On this particular afternoon, the venerable stadium would host a game that drew more fanfare than it had in years. Over 67,000 fans would watch Buck Shaw's Philadelphia Eagles battle Vince Lombardi's Green Bay Packers for the championship of the National Football League.

Only two years before, in 1958, both teams finished in the cellar of their respective conferences. It took Lombardi two and Shaw three years to lead their teams to this championship game. Both were excellent coaches with contrasting styles. Volatile and imperious, Lombardi was known for leading through fear. Soft-spoken and low-keyed, Shaw of the Eagles was regarded as a player's coach. Green Bay's offense was predicated on a powerful ground game exemplified by its "Packer Sweep," while Philadelphia's high-octane offense relied on its pinpoint passing game. Prior to Lombardi's landing in Green Bay, his coaching jobs were limited to New York and New Jersey. Shaw's coaching resume included stints across the entire breadth of America. Yet both had played football at Catholic universities under renowned coaches. In the '30s Lombardi had been one of Jim Crowley's famed "Seven Blocks of Granite" at Fordham, while Shaw had earned All-American honors playing for Notre Dame's legendary Knute Rockne. Their careers were on divergent paths on this momentous day, with Lombardi on the threshold of an illustrious but tragically short head-coaching career, and Shaw at the twilight of his. The Eagles coach had announced that 1960 would be his last season on the sidelines.

Nicknamed the "Silver Fox" because of his prematurely gray hair and football sagacity, Shaw had molded both college and professional squads for nearly 40 seasons. The media and Philly fans viewed it as fitting that Shaw's last game coaching the Eagles would be the pinnacle of his coaching career.

How would the retiring coach handle the pressure? Shaw seemed calm and quietly confident while exchanging pleasantries with the opposing coach during the pregame warm-up. At the season's start, most football pundits believed Cleveland's Browns and the New York Giants had more talent and depth than Philadelphia. Yet it was Shaw's Eagles under the on-field generalship of 34-year-old Norm Van Brockin and 35-year-old center/linebacker Chuck Bednarik that now assembled on the sidelines of the championship game. Following brief words of encouragement with a wink and a nod, Shaw sent the Eagles' kick-return team onto the field to face the "Young Turks" of the NFL—Vince Lombardi's Green Bay Packers.

Given the name recognition of each coach in the 21st century, today's reader might assume the outcome of he 1960 NFL title game. Yet Buck had a decades-long history of quietly leading his underdog teams to victory.

ONE

The Early Years

Lawrence Timothy Shaw was born on March 28, 1899, in Mitchellville, Iowa. "Buck," as he came to be called at a young age, was one of five children born to cattle ranchers T.J. and Margaret Shaw. Buck had two older brothers, William and John (often called "Jack"), a younger brother, Jim, and a sister, Mary. When Buck was 10 the family moved to Stuart, about 39 miles west of Des Moines, where the Shaws became pillars of the community.

Raising Hereford cattle and breeding Percheron horses, T.J. Shaw was also a prominent land dealer. He continually bought and sold parcels of land around Stuart until he and Margaret moved to Des Moines in 1934. In 1915, the civic-minded Shaw became vice president of the town's Commercial Club, an organization devoted to stimulating business and commerce in the area. Shaw also served eight months as a city councilman and numerous terms as an elected school board member. He accepted the vice presidency of the Stuart Savings Bank, a position he held until becoming president of the Fidelity Loan and Trust Company in 1918.

While his dad was establishing himself as a pillar of the community, young Buck was gaining recognition for his athletic prowess. As an eighth grader, the strapping youngster earned a spot on the high school baseball team as a pitcher. In a 1915 photo of the Stuart High baseball team, Shaw, only a freshman, is easily mistaken for an adult. Hauling hay and other ranching chores undoubtedly led to Buck's early physical maturity. When the Shaws moved to Stuart in 1910, the local high school didn't offer football. A fatality several years earlier caused the school to drop the sport. Although Buck was a year older than his brother Jim, both were in the same high school class. Both pitched for the baseball team and played basketball, Buck as a center, Jim as a guard. In an era before "slam dunks" and the three-point line, when a dozen or more passes were the prelude to a two-handed set shot, Buck scored 19 points against Anita High School in January 1917. In his senior year, local papers touted Buck as the star of the Simpson Southwest Iowa hoops tournament. However, Buck's first love was track. Shaw competed in almost every track event and demonstrated his versatility at a meet in Adair in May 1916, when he finished second in the discus, won the 440 yard dash, and won the shot put with a throw of 38 feet, 1 inch.

Young Buck had a unique training regimen for the shot put. Living on a farm south of Stuart he walked to school carrying a 12-pound shot in his hip pocket. As he walked, he would throw the shot ahead of himself.[1] A Stuart old-timer recalled Shaw's track meet performance at nearby Guthrie Center: "He threw the discus all the way off the track into the creek. The referee said, 'Ah, hell, I'm not going to measure that; give him first place.'"[2]

Buck's halcyon high school years took a serious tone in April of 1917, when the United States declared war on Germany. Buck's two older brothers, William and Jack,

1915 STUART HIGH SCHOOL BASEBALL TEAM

Manager, Dunnigan. Back row, left to right: George Zenor, "Buck" Shaw, Rolland Smith, "Whitey" Maline, Jim Doud, Lloyd Gettys. Front row: Wayne Belden, Brinton Knox, Joe Gettys, Glen Caskey, Jim Shaw.

Seated at the far left of the second row in a dark sweater, high school sophomore Buck Shaw was often mistaken for an adult at first glance (courtesy Robert W. Cook).

enlisted in the Army at Fort Dodge, Iowa. T.J. and Margaret Shaw proved to be just as patriotic as they were civic-minded. With two sons in the Army, T.J. served on the local draft board, while Margaret led women's sewing groups knitting socks and hospital shirts and rolling bandages for the Red Cross. Margaret was pleasant, but adamant, in requesting that all volunteer knitters use needles no finer than #13, but that #14 needles were preferable. Furthermore, all socks were to be finished with a rounded toe. When not knitting, Margaret enjoyed holding literary club meetings. She especially enjoyed discussing the writings of O. Henry.

During his senior year in high school, Buck contributed to the home front effort by serving as secretary of the Patriotic Service League. The League was comprised of 34 boys who each pledged to raise and give $10 to the YMCA before May 10, 1918. Each boy raised the money himself, with no help from parents. All funds collected were to benefit Allied war prisoners.[3]

Largely due to the efforts of Dr. Elbert Taylor Warren—Stuart town leader, Drake University football alum and direct descendant of President Zachary Taylor—Stuart High School reintroduced football in the autumn of 1917. Coach Robert "Rusty" Armstrong led Stuart High School's gridiron squad and introduced Buck to the game of football. However, it didn't happen immediately. Because Buck had pitched for the high school team as an eighth grader, he was ineligible to participate in interscholastic sports his senior year. Fortunately, that autumn a rule change was implemented allowing students to compete until age 18. As a result, Shaw became eligible for football after missing the first three games of the season. Buck joined his brother Jim in the lineup for the first time in a 12–7 win over Winterset on November 10. Splitting time between tackle and halfback, Buck scored Stuart's first touchdown on a four-yard run. Buck assumed most of the team's kicking chores in the season's final three games against Dexter, archrival Guthrie Center and Adair, all Stuart victories.

What kind of student was Buck in high school? Most classmates agreed that he was very quiet. Years later, when Buck was in the national spotlight coaching at Santa Clara, a former classmate, Mrs. Victor Miller, reflected on Buck's academic interests: "Buck studied only enough to be eligible; that is every subject except Physics, and he led the class in that." (Though it's safe to assume there were no future physicists in Buck's class, as his physics grade for the year was only 77 percent.) Miller also recalled that Buck was not interested in girls but read everything he could find on football.[4] Buck earned mostly C's in English, history and plane geometry, achieving his best academic performance in a farm shop class, where he consistently earned B's in his junior and senior years.

As late as May 31, 1918, the hometown *Stuart Herald* reported that Lawrence Shaw would attend Notre Dame University in the fall. However, with two sons in the Army, T.J. and Margaret Shaw wanted their two younger boys to go to school closer to home. So Buck and brother Jim enrolled at Creighton University in Omaha that September, which was only 100 miles from Stuart.[5] Despite his limited football experience Buck opted to try out for coach Tommy Mills' football squad.

Unfortunately for Shaw, Creighton and the nation, the Spanish Influenza pandemic reached its pinnacle in October of 1918. In that month alone over 195,00 Americans succumbed to the dreaded disease, resulting in a national casket shortage.[6] On October 5, the Omaha Health Commissioner issued a formal order closing theaters, schools, churches, dance halls and other public places as a precaution against the spread of disease. However, the ban didn't yet apply to open area events and on October 12, Creighton opened its season with a 60–0 pummeling of visiting Nebraska Wesleyan. While Buck didn't start the contest, he played and made the most of his limited appearance. However, as the deadly flu continued spreading across America many colleges— including Creighton—canceled their remaining football games for October.

After a three-week hiatus, Creighton resumed play on November 2, by defeating the University of South Dakota 13–0. Buck Shaw started at right tackle and again the following Saturday in a 37–7 victory over Haskell Indian. In its summary of the game *The Omaha Daily Bee* reported, "Tackle Nemzek scored three of Creighton's five touchdowns. His running mate, Buck Shaw, was in every play and often threw his man for a loss."[7] Though Shaw's previous football experience consisted of four high school contests, he'd cracked Creighton's starting lineup as a freshman and proved his worth.

That fall, like most Creighton students, Buck and Jim Shaw joined the Student Army Training Corps (S.A.T.C.). With the country immersed in the Great War, the United States' armed services had an insatiable demand for recruits. In an attempt to satisfy this need Secretary of War Newton D. Baker announced the creation of the S.A.T.C. program to all college and university presidents on May 18, 1918. Institutions of higher learning with enrollments of 100 or more were eligible. Student corpsmen received a small monthly stipend. They were also issued uniforms, subjected to military discipline and given about a dozen hours a week of military drill and related courses. The program served as a pre-induction center where young men could be temporarily held prior to call-up for active military duty.[8]

While the Shaw brothers drilled on campus, their parents continued supporting the war effort back in Stuart. Margaret Shaw presided over volunteer sewing centers for the Red Cross, while T.J. coordinated and led several liberty bond drives, one of which raised

$42,400—three times its original goal.[9] While the oldest Shaw brother, William, was stationed at Iowa's Camp Dodge, Jack Shaw was serving with the 168th regiment in France. The regiment was eventually assigned to the famed "Rainbow" Division, so named by then Maj. Douglas MacArthur, who claimed that the division's makeup stretched like "a rainbow from one end of America to the other."

During the war, a letter took weeks, if not months, to reach its intended party. An undated letter by Stuart's Otto Spangler, written from the Western Front to his younger sister, Ada, indicated that Jack Shaw was in the midst of the fighting. An excerpt from the letter appeared in the November 29, 1918, issue of the *Stuart Herald*: "Sergeant Wilkinson and Corporal Tolson of Winterset, both fine fellows, were killed. Glover, Bower, Hoop and Benge were wounded. Shaw, Hamm, Fred and I are left now." In the 164 days of fighting at the Champagne-Marne, Aisne-Marne, as well as the Meuse Argonne offensive, the 168th suffered 700 killed and 3,100 wounded. When word of the armistice arrived on November 11, two days after Buck's strong showing against Haskell, the town of Stuart went wild. Mayor McKee declared a "Day of Rejoicing." Streets were roped off for dancing. The Earlham and Stuart High School bands blared music on the sidewalks. The Kaiser was hanged in effigy before its head was cut off and its body dragged through the streets.[10]

* * *

Creighton's next football game was scheduled for November 16, against the Kansas Aggies (Kansas State). However, Dr. Fred Langdon, the physician for the Creighton S.A.T.C., refused to let the Creighton men play as the corps had been in quarantine for over a week, and he feared the rain and wet field would result in a serious outbreak of influenza.[11] Although disappointed, Shaw and company looked forward to their last game, a Thanksgiving date with the Colorado School of Mines. Unfortunately, the influenza miasma persisted. Colorado Mines canceled at the eleventh hour when a new flu outbreak struck the Centennial State. Scrambling to find a last-minute replacement, Creighton coach Tommy Mills contacted Morningside College, Iowa State, Northwestern and Missouri. All declined. Mills briefly thought he rectified the situation after contacting Notre Dame's Knute Rockne. Rockne, whose Ramblers were in Lincoln to play the University of Nebraska on Thanksgiving, indicated that he might be willing to meet Creighton in Omaha, two days later, on Saturday, November 30.

On Thanksgiving, Notre Dame and the Cornhuskers played to a scoreless tie in a quagmire. The muddy slugfest saw both of Notre Dame's traveling squad quarterbacks suffer knee ligament tears. Injuries to three other Rambler backs added to Rockne's woes. Viewing discretion as the better part of valor, Rockne wired Mills that it would be inadvisable for his depleted squad to meet Creighton.[12] With a record of three wins and no losses, Creighton's abbreviated 1918 season ended.

It was Buck Shaw's first and last season at Creighton. Buck had wanted to attend Notre Dame since he had watched their track team compete in the Drake Relays in high school. When the war ended, he wrote his father asking if he could attend school there. Because of the war, not only were freshmen eligible for varsity competition, but rules regarding transfer eligibility at colleges maintaining S.A.T.C. programs were also relaxed. Creighton and Notre Dame both had S.A.T.C. programs. As a result, Buck and his brother opted to transfer to Notre Dame in the spring of 1919. In doing so he'd be eligible to play football that fall.

1. T.Mills, Coach   2.   3. Condon   4.   Lammers   5. Rev. J. McWilliams
6. L. Rater   7.   8. J. Hall   9.   10. T. Dorwart.
11.   Serr   12. P. McGoMan.   13. B. Kenney   14. P. Boland   15. D. Manley   16. J. Dorwart
17.   Keane   18.   Lucas   19. M. Harmon.   20. E. Leahy.   21. J. Condon   22. N. Hall   23. F. Comol
24. P. Emery   25.   Shaw.   26. M. Healey   27. E. Hulbolland.   28   Little   29. W. Kemzer.   30. F. Shevlin.   31. J. Broz
Creighton University   1918
Creighton U.   1918

Just as COVID-19 affected the 2020 college football scene, the Spanish Flu pandemic of 1918 forced colleges to play abbreviated schedules. Creighton won all three games it played. Shaw (#25) is seated second from the left on the bottom row (courtesy Creighton University Archives).

* * *

Good news reached Buck in South Bend in April of 1919. He learned that his brother Jack and the 168th regiment would be sailing from Brest, France, to New York aboard the *Leviathan*. After taking the lead in planning a welcome home celebration for Iowa's returning doughboys, T.J. Shaw traveled with a party of Stuart citizens to New York. Once there the group chartered a tugboat and steamed out to meet the *Leviathan* as it arrived in the harbor. T.J. recalled that from a distance the ship and its crowded occupants resembled a big cake of honey with bees swarming over it.[13] After the *Leviathan* docked, father and son visited for an hour. The next day T.J. Shaw traveled to Camp Upton, about 65 miles north of New York City, where the 168th bivouacked. There he once again visited with Jack as well as a half-dozen other boys from Stuart.

Buck couldn't make it back to Iowa to see the 168th regiment parade through downtown Des Moines on May 15. Nor could he make it to Stuart on May 20, when the town threw a lavish, all-day bash for 35 returning soldiers and sailors from the local area, for Buck was now cutting a new trail at Notre Dame.

Two

Rockne's Ramblers

Shaw had his work cut out for him upon his arrival at the South Bend campus in January 1919 as a member of the Class of '22. The "good fathers" at Notre Dame refused to accept most of the first semester credits Shaw had earned at Creighton. To make up the lost credits and graduate on time, Buck found himself attending classes on most days from 8 a.m. until nearly five o'clock in the afternoon, as well as on Saturday mornings.[1] While the school's dynamic football coach, Knute Rockne, was known to recruit talented players from other school's freshman teams, this wasn't the case with Shaw.[2] Throughout his career, Shaw continually maintained that his motivation for transferring was a desire to compete on Notre Dame's track team—a squad comprised of several world class athletes. Since the Iowa native had enjoyed his previous gridiron participation, and Rockne served as head coach of both track and football, Shaw decided to give football a shot. Rockne didn't know who Buck was until another student took him up to the coach and introduced him. Unfortunately, an injury caused Shaw to miss most of spring football practice. He'd have to wait until the fall to show what he could do.

Heartley "Hunk" Anderson was one of Buck's famed teammates, who later played pro ball before enjoying a lengthy coaching career. "I remember the first day that Buck showed for practice," Anderson recalled. "Rock fitted him in Ray Eichenlaub's old pants. He didn't look like much. Until we saw him play."[3] Eichenlaub had been a 6-foot, 210-pound stud fullback and four-year starter from 1911 to 1914. While Shaw also stood at six feet, he only weighed 175 pounds. Struggling to keep his pants up, Shaw must have been an amusing and sympathetic sight to many at that first practice. Shaw, however, had the last laugh when in 1920, Father Bernard Lange, the university's director of physical culture, awarded Shaw a medal for being the "best built man" on campus. Shaw won out over 300 contestants. When the honor was announced, teammates Edward "Slip" Madigan and Maurice "Clipper" Smith began addressing Shaw as "Adonis."[4] The self-effacing Shaw, whose association with both men would continue long after graduation, took their razzing in stride.

Despite Shaw's limited playing experience, the newcomer's blocking ability and work ethic greatly impressed Rockne and assistant coach Gus Dorais. Shaw had already left an indelible impression on his former coach at Creighton, Tommy Mills. When Notre Dame visited Nebraska in 1919, Mills told the *Omaha World Herald* on October 17, "Shaw is one of the most natural football players I've ever seen." Although Shaw didn't crack Rockne's starting lineup as a sophomore, the *Notre Dame Scholastic*'s recap of the 1919 season indicates that he saw considerable game action:

> Shaw played the role of "Minute Man" throughout the season … called on frequently to jump into the tackle position, where he acquitted himself so strikingly that even the taciturn Rockne

was wont to point him out with a "That's-him!" Shaw was impenetrable. Possessed of impressive physique and a "football'" disposition, he has the making of a champion. Willing, anxious and industrious, the big fellow should during his two remaining years develop into an All-American.[5]

The *Scholastic's* laudatory assessment was prescient, for Shaw would earn All-American honors at tackle during his senior season. As an understudy in 1919, he helped the Ramblers (the nickname "Fighting Irish" had yet to be adopted) go undefeated in nine games, including victories over Nebraska, Indiana, Army, Michigan State and Purdue. Shaw's successful sophomore season, however, nearly ended before it began. In his first semester on campus, several of Buck's' classmates opted to visit the Palace Vaudeville Emporium in South Bend rather than attend the mandatory 3 p.m. Sunday vespers service on campus. Having attended mass daily since his arrival on campus (something Buck would do throughout his three years at Notre Dame) and speculating that perhaps Notre Dame's Fathers of the Holy Cross weren't as stringent on such matters as their Jesuit counterparts at Creighton, the usually dutiful Shaw accepted his classmates' invitation to join them. It was the wrong move. On Monday morning, the revelers found themselves in the president's office begging not to be sent to another small Catholic college where they did not have vespers service on Sunday afternoon. The miscreants only escaped expulsion when Coach Rockne intervened on their behalf. However, the "pardoned" students left with a clear understanding that any future behavioral mishaps would result in immediate expulsion.[6]

At the same time as he was coming to the aid of misguided youth, Rockne was on the verge of becoming one of the nation's premier coaches. The immigrant son of a Norwegian carriage-maker who migrated to America in 1893, Rockne fell in love with the rough-and-tumble game of football growing up on Chicago's sandlots. After graduating from high school, Rockne worked as a postal clerk while continuing to play football and running track for various athletic clubs around the Windy City until saving enough money to enroll at Notre Dame in 1910. Despite a frustrating freshman season spent "riding the pine" in football, the 22-year-old freshman enjoyed immediate success that spring in track and field. Rockne's persistence on the gridiron earned him a starting role his sophomore year, and his determination and leadership skills resulted in his election as team captain as a senior. It was at this time that Rockne's name first appeared in the sports sections of American newspapers. The catalyst was his performance in Notre Dame's 35–13 upset of mighty Army on the plains at West Point on November 1, 1913. That overcast afternoon saw Coach Jesse Harper's visitors unleash a passing attack never before witnessed. Quarterback Gus Dorais completed an unheard of 14 passes for 243 yards. Several spirals covered a distance of 35 yards, including a 40-yard touchdown pass to Rockne, who—along with halfback Joe Pliska—caught most of the 145-pound Dorais' passes. Notre Dame's aerial performance that day not only popularized the forward pass, it also vaulted the small Indiana school onto the national sports scene.

* * *

With most of his undefeated 1919 squad returning, Rockne anticipated the 1920 season as eagerly as a child looking forward to Christmas. However, Rockne's expectations crashed that spring when the university expelled the team's star, George Gipp. The Laurium, Michigan, native had proven himself to be a gifted triple-threat halfback and fierce tackler since arriving on campus in 1916 as a 21-year-old freshman. A spirited and gifted competitor on game days, Gipp was a prima donna during the week. He often skipped practices. When he did show, Rockne occasionally banished him to work with the scrubs, which he did halfheartedly. But on game days, Gipp would again be in the starting lineup.[7]

Reflecting on his temperamental halfback years later Rockne recalled:

> You couldn't get him to exert himself any more than he had to, and if the games in which he played had happened to go Notre Dame's way, without much of a struggle, I doubt if Gipp would ever have been more than an average player. But let the game threaten to get out of hand, and there was no stopping Gipp. He played like a man possessed, and he played until he had expended every ounce of his great reserve power, if the situation warranted. Such an exhibition was the one he gave in the Army game of 1917.[8] [Gipp's triple-threat performance was instrumental in the Ramblers' 7–2 victory.]

In *Rockne of Notre Dame*, Ray Robinson wrote, "Gipp continued to receive special treatment from Rockne. A lesser player would have had a tongue lashing administered to him by the head coach and probably would have been thrown off the team. Instead, Rockne pampered his star pupil…."[9]

Off the field Gipp refused to let studies interfere with his late-night pool hustling and card playing. He seldom attended classes, preferring to ply his craft at Hullie and Mike's pool hall on Michigan Avenue. His substantial winnings allowed Gipp to quit his dining hall job after only one semester. He moved off campus and spent most of his South Bend years living at the lush Oliver Hotel where he often drank heavily. By March 1920, the Notre Dame fathers had had enough of Mr. Gipp. Publicly citing "excessive absences" as the reason for the decision, but privately fed up with his incessant disobedience of university rules, the "powers that be" expelled him.[10]

The news stunned Rockne and teammates alike. Gipp, however, took the news with his characteristic nonchalance. Rockne's bewilderment quickly turned to panic when he learned that rival schools were feverishly recruiting the exiled Gipp. Rockne responded by pleading Gipp's case for readmission. Rockne also took his case to sympathetic downtown businessmen, who over the next few weeks continually petitioned Notre Dame president Father Burns to rescind Gipp's expulsion. With his patience at an end and afraid of alienating many of the school's financial boosters, Father Burns finally agreed to reinstate Gipp in April 1920.[11]

As Murray Sperber writes in *Shake Down the Thunder*: "When President Burns acted in 1920, no doubt he hoped and even assumed that the incident would soon be forgotten. He had no way of knowing that within nine months George Gipp would become Notre Dame's first consensus All-American, would die, and then, twenty years later, would be sanctified in a Hollywood film."[12]

When the 1920 season kicked off Gipp was again starting at left halfback and junior Buck Shaw was making his first start at right tackle. Teaming with fellow Iowan Eddie Anderson, who played right end, the duo consistently opened huge holes for teammates over the next two seasons. After lopsided wins over Kalamazoo and Western Michigan, Rockne's lads met the season's first major challenge at Nebraska.

It was the sixth year in a row that Notre Dame made the trip to Lincoln. After World War I, the Ku Klux Klan experienced a resurgence across America, and it had a strong contingency in Nebraska. Since the series' inception in 1915, the animosity between the two schools had subsided significantly, but in 1920, 9,000 rabid Cornhusker fans greeted the South Bend visitors with vitriolic anti–Catholic jeering and catcalls. Rockne endured the abuse for two reasons. First, the game continually sold out, yielding the small Indiana school a significant payday. Second, because of a strong anti–Catholic bent across much of the Midwest, including Indiana, Notre Dame had difficulty scheduling prominent football schools, and Rockne wanted the notoriety that came from playing the big boys.

Shaw made his presence felt early in Notre Dame's 16–7 win by blocking a Nebraska punt as described in *The Lincoln County Register*'s post-game summary: "A safety in the first period was responsible for Notre Dame's first points. Weller, Nebraska's right tackle, had his punt blocked by Shaw and in the scramble that followed the Cornhusker recovered the ball, but was downed behind the goal for a safety."[13] Blocking punts became a specialty for Shaw, who repeated the feat later that season in games against Army, Indiana, Northwestern and Michigan State. The *Omaha World Herald* added: "Buck Shaw, who played a sterling game for Rockne's crew at right tackle, is a former Creighton man having been on the Blue and White squad in 1918. He was vociferously cheered by Omaha rooters. Buck so far enjoys the universal distinction of never having played in a game in which his team was defeated, either in high school or college."[14]

After defeating Valparaiso 28–3, Rockne's Ramblers journeyed to West Point in late October. Since the series' inception in 1913, the Army–Notre Dame game sparked the interest of New York City's working-class Catholics. Many, who never attended colleges themselves, now professed loyalty to the small Midwestern Catholic school, and rode the train 50 miles north to cheer their "adopted" school to victory. When the rivalry later moved to New York City, many local blue-collar Notre Dame fans rode the city's subways to the game—thus, the origin of Notre Dame's so-called "subway alumni."[15]

Both teams entered the 1920 contest undefeated before a capacity crowd of 10,000 at Cullum Hall Field. This game more than any other may have been a true reflection of the legendary George Gipp's personality and athleticism. In a prelude to the afternoon's performance, Gipp engaged in a drop-kicking competition with Army's Russell "Red" Reeder during the pregame warm-up. When Reeder dropped out at the 40-yard line, Gipp walked to the 50-yard line and called for four footballs. He then drop-kicked two over the north cross-bar before turning and nonchalantly kicking the remaining two over the south cross bar.[16]

Soon after the kickoff, the game resembled a street fight. Behind the flashy performance of former Rutgers All-American Walter French, who returned a punt 60 yards for a touchdown and drop-kicked an extra point and field goal, Army took a 17–14 halftime lead. An irate Rockne spent much of the intermission reaming Eddie Anderson, whom he blamed for French's long scoring run. The coach then continued his tirade upon spying Gipp leaning against a wall calmly smoking a cigarette. "What about you, Gipp? I don't suppose you have any interest in this game?"

To which Gipp indignantly replied, "Look, Rock, I've got $400 of my own money bet on this game, and I'm not about to blow it."[17]

In the second half, Gipp proved to be true to his word by playing like a "man possessed." After a scoreless third quarter, Gipp's runs and accurate passing led to John Mohardt's second touchdown run. Gipp then drop-kicked the extra point giving Notre Dame a 21–17 lead. Later, Gipp again demonstrated his versatility by returning a punt 50 yards to set up his team's last touchdown. Playing the greatest game of his career in Notre Dame's 27–17 win over Army, Gipp personally accounted for 332 total yards in rushing, passing and kick returns. The 6-foot, 185-pound halfback also kicked three extra points and threw a touchdown pass. Viewing Gipp's performance as a godsend, Eastern newspapermen zealously transferred Gipp's Herculean deeds to paper. While pounding their typewriter keys to meet their respective deadlines, sportswriters began the process of chiseling the name of George Gipp forever into the Golden Age of American sports.[18]

In Notre Dame's inaugural homecoming game before 12,000 fans at Cartier Field on November 6, Gipp lived up to his press clippings. Despite playing only half the game, Gipp—with Shaw and Eddie Anderson opening a huge hole off tackle—ran 80 yards for a touchdown and passed for another 171 in a 28–0 victory over Purdue.

Rockne's lads had a tougher time of it the next week in eking out a squeaker over Indiana at Indianapolis. Subjected to a severe physical pounding, Gipp exited the game early with what was initially diagnosed as a separated shoulder and possible broken collarbone. Nevertheless, with his team trailing 10–0 late in the second quarter, a heavily taped Gipp returned to score a touchdown and led Notre Dame to a 13–10 win.

On the jubilant trip back to South Bend, Gipp, although severely battered and bruised, departed the team train in Chicago to help his friend and former teammate, Grover Malone, coach a high school football team for a few days.[19] Somehow, the coaching sojourn turned into a three-day drinking binge. When he boarded the train to return to South Bend, Gipp had developed a nasty cough. By kickoff the following Saturday, the cough was worse, with the halfback suffering from a fever and sore throat as well. Rockne had no intention of playing his ailing star at Northwestern.

Gipp watched as his teammates built a 21–7 lead. Almost 1,100 Notre Dame students had ridden the South Shore electric train to Evanston. In the middle of the third quarter, most began yelling, "We want Gipp!" Northwestern fans joined in, and by the quarter's end the chanting by the crowd of 20,000 reached a crescendo. Usually indifferent to the cheering throngs, Gipp left his seat on the bench and gradually inched closer to Rockne, who was standing on the sideline. Early in the fourth quarter, Rockne looked over his shoulder and spotted Gipp bundled in blankets, standing near his elbow. He asked Gipp if he felt like playing, to which the halfback nonchalantly shrugged before replying, "Sure, let's go."[20]

To the fans' delight, Gipp entered the game and on the first play dropped back and tossed a 35-yard touchdown pass to Eddie Anderson. On Notre Dame's next possession, Gipp decided to spread the wealth and completed a 54-yard scoring pass to Norm Barry, giving Rockne's gang a 33–17 win. Considering Gipp's deteriorating condition, it was an amazing and gutsy performance.

As his teammates were blanketing Michigan State 25–0 on Thanksgiving Day to give the Irish an undefeated season, Gipp lay gravely ill at South Bend's St. Joseph's Hospital, diagnosed with pneumonia and strep throat. The streptococcus infection quickly spread through Gipp's body. The dying 25-year-old's supposed deathbed request to Rockne to have his boys "win one for the Gipper" has been exhaustively covered in print and immortalized in the 1940 Hollywood movie *Knute Rockne: All American*.

Gipp died in the early morning hours of December 14, 1920. Over 1,500 Notre Dame students and townspeople attended the funeral in a blinding snowstorm and later escorted the coffin to the train carrying Gipp's body back to northern Michigan. The pallbearers included teammates Hunk Anderson, Ojay Larson, Joe Brandy and Norm Barry. The coffin was transported by sled the last six miles to the cemetery in Laurium. In his book *The Notre Dame Story*, Francis Wallace described the scene most poignantly when he wrote, "And the snows of Christmas powdered the grave of Thanksgiving's hero."

* * *

In its review of the 1920 football season, the *Notre Dame Scholastic* wrote: "Shaw is a type of college man very seldom seen on any campus. Modest, unassuming, friendly, always a gentleman; we wish him unbounded success in his last year of varsity competition."

Besides gaining notoriety for his gridiron performance and overall demeanor, Shaw was also realizing his aspirations in track. The 1921 Rambler track squad included stellar performers Gus Desch, the world's champion in the 40-yard low hurdles; Johnny Murphy, a former national champion high-jumper; and Chet Wynne, the national record holder in the 40-yard high hurdles. Shaw contributed to the team's success as a shot putter. After performing admirably at the Penn Relays, Shaw won the shot at the Western Conference meet on June 2, with a throw of 44 feet, 7.5 inches. Then at the first NCAA Championship meet on June 18 in Chicago, Shaw placed fifth. Gus Pope of Washington won the event with a toss of 45 feet, 4.5 inches.

Shaw (top row, second from left) was the 1921 Western Conference shot put champion. Chet Wynne (top row, third from left) was a football teammate and Carlinville Eight cohort. Wynne later served as head football coach at both Auburn and Kentucky (courtesy Greg Piers).

Although Shaw's original motivation for transferring was to compete on Notre Dame's elite track squad, by his senior year it was becoming apparent that Shaw's dedication to the game of football may have surpassed his passion for track. When Rockne learned that his athletic tackle had kicked in high school, he sent Shaw home with a suitcase full of footballs to kick over the summer. The conscientious Shaw spent many humid Iowa evenings practicing the skill. His efforts paid dividends, for Shaw would make good on 39 of 40 extra-point attempts for Notre Dame in 1921—a remarkable feat for that era.

That year Notre Dame adhered to Western (Big Ten) Conference rules, which prohibited coaches from supervising or conducting team practices before September 15.

Another example of Shaw's commitment occurred when team captain Eddie Anderson, intent on extending Notre Dame's two-year undefeated string through 1921, called for "voluntary" practices in South Bend beginning shortly after Labor Day and running to the official start of practice. Among the 30-plus aspirants who heeded the call, Shaw and Anderson were the only returning starters to attend the daily practices.[21]

The 1921 campaign began with fire works when Johnny Mohardt, replacing the soon-to-be immortalized George Gipp at left halfback, returned the opening day kick-off for a touchdown en route to a 56–0 shellacking of Kalamazoo. After defeating DePauw 57–10 the next week, it was a confident Notre Dame squad that boarded the train for Iowa City on October 7. Howard Jones coached a University of Iowa team spearheaded by quarterback Aubrey Devine and tackle Duke Slater, who both would earn All-American honors. The Hawkeyes jumped to an early 10–0 lead before Mohardt's 50-yard touchdown pass to Roger Kiley cut the lead to 10–7 just before halftime. Notre Dame threatened to score numerous times in the second half, but several Iowa interceptions kept the Ramblers from reaching paydirt. The 10–7 loss—Notre Dame's first and only loss in three seasons—was agonizing for Shaw, who had never before played in a football game in which his team was defeated. Adding insult to injury, Shaw's parents and siblings made the trip from Stuart to see it.

Notre Dame's 1921 homecoming game versus Nebraska on October 22, would draw over 20,000 fans, the largest crowd ever to witness a game at Cartier Field. At halftime, Rockne and his squad assembled at midfield to pay tribute to the memory of George Gipp. A bugler blew taps and the crowd stood with reverential bare heads. Buck Shaw played superbly that afternoon, which not only further endeared him to Rockne and teammates, but also drew raves from prominent Midwestern sportswriters. *The South Bend Tribune* reported on the selfless Shaw:

> Notre Dame is late in discovering the real value of Buck Shaw; and this failure is due to the absolute lack of any attempt upon his part to secure recognition. Everybody has always admitted that Buck was good—and let it go at that; but the form shown by the big tackle in his last few games has been of such a superlative character that an appreciation of it has swept the campus as no other movement for any man has swept it since George Gipp flashed into fame. Buck Shaw is of All-American timber if any man on the squad draws that recognition.[22]

Anchoring a defensive line that yielded Nebraska only two first downs, Shaw was a tackling machine both on punt coverage and at the line of scrimmage. Three of his tackles threw Cornhusker ball carriers for losses of nine yards or more. On offense, the "moving company" of Shaw and Eddie Anderson continually opened holes on an off-tackle play; on one such play, Mohardt scored the game's only touchdown in a 7–0 win. For extra measure, Buck Shaw kicked the point after.

Notre Dame's visit to Army was chaotic and controversial. The chaos started when some of the 8,000 fans in attendance, jostling for seats, impeded West Point's Superintendent Gen. Douglas MacArthur's access to his customary box seat. The unruly behavior not only delayed the opening kick-off but resulted in America's most highly decorated World War I officer calling for additional military police to clear a path to his esteemed perch.

A major reason for Notre Dame's gridiron success was Rockne's implementation of the so-called "Notre Dame Shift" or "Rockne Shift." Rockne didn't invent the shift. He had learned it from his predecessor at Notre Dame, Jesse Harper. Harper, in turn, had picked it up during his days at the University of Chicago. While other schools employed the shift, none had mastered it as proficiently as Rockne's squads. The shift entailed the entire backfield changing alignment as the quarterback called the signals. The ball was often snapped before the backs came to a complete stop. Critics of the shift railed that it gave the offensive backs an unfair momentum at the start of the play and denied the defense a fair chance to adjust to the new formation.

As General MacArthur's gendarmes were restoring order in the stands, another confrontation was occurring at midfield, where Army coach Charles Daly was voicing the above objections to both the game officials and Rockne. At one point, there was a threat of canceling the game if Notre Dame's backs did not come to a dead stop before hiking the ball. With rule book in hand, Rockne diplomatically argued that Daly's interpretation of a dead stop did not comply with the written rules. The officiating crew agreed with Rockne.[23]

When the teams returned for the second half with the Ramblers leading 14–0, Army coach Daly resumed vehemently challenging the legality of Notre Dame's shift with the officials. Overhearing Daly's urgent pleas and possibly sensing he wouldn't need it, Rockne, wanting to keep good relations with West Point, informed referee Ed Thorp that his team would not employ the shift for the rest of the game. The coach was true to his word.[24] In the end it didn't matter, as Notre Dame added two more touchdowns for a 28–0 win. Shaw kicked all four extra points.

After the game Rockne's gang traveled to Deal, New Jersey, to spend the remainder of their Eastern sojourn as guests of Mr. Joseph Byrne. An active and generous alumnus, Byrne readied the team for the Rutgers game by hosting several dinner parties and arranging for Broadway show tickets, including a performance by the incomparable Ziegfeld Follies at the Globe Theater.[25] The experience must have been an eye-opener for a kid who grew up in Stuart, Iowa.

The Rutgers game was played on Election Day—Tuesday, November 8—at New York's Polo Grounds. Like Army coach Charles Daly, Rutgers coach George Foster Sanford also protested to officials about the legality of the Notre Dame shift during the pregame talk. Although Notre Dame was penalized a total of 75 yards for their backs not coming to a complete stop after shifting, it had little effect on the game's outcome, as Notre Dame cruised to a 48–0 win before a disappointing crowd of only 12,000. Although the game was not the financial payday Rockne had hoped, his team's superb performance garnered extensive and glowing newspaper coverage along the Eastern seaboard.

Notre Dame hosted Haskell Indian from Lawrence, Kansas, the following week before a slim crowd at Cartier Field. Regarding Haskell as a lightweight opponent, Rockne turned the game-day coaching over to assistant Walter Halas, and traveled to Milwaukee to scout their next foe, Marquette. Notre Dame's easy 42–7 win confirmed Rockne's assessment of Haskell.

It was cold and snowy the following week when Rockne returned to Milwaukee with his team in tow. Coach John Ryan's Marquette squad was game, but Notre Dame jumped to an early 14–0 lead.

Bundled and shivering in a blanket on the Marquette bench for most of the game was a reserve halfback named Pat O'Brien. Making the most of his brief fourth-quarter appearance, O'Brien ripped off a 30-yard run against the Irish second team. O'Brien eventually became a popular Hollywood actor and, nearly two decades later, starred in the lead of the movie *Knute Rockne: All-American*. It didn't help on this day, however, as Notre Dame prevailed 21–7.

Buck Shaw closed out his collegiate career when he and his teammates rolled to a 48–0 Thanksgiving win over Michigan State at Cartier Field. Notre Dame finished the 1921 season with a record of 10 wins and one loss. Buck's sterling play earned him a spot on several All-American teams, including famed sportswriter Grantland Rice's Hall of Fame Team. Lawrence Perry, a so-called college football expert of the day, assessed Shaw's play in this colorful but confusing description: "Shaw was a 'berserker' in the line, as well as a ranger of indomitable mold. His play against West Point and Rutgers was a proclamation to Eastern critics or should have been."[26] Wisconsin sportswriter Roundy Coughlin also selected Shaw as well as teammates Eddie Anderson and Johnny Mohardt, to the All-Western Team. Nine of the 11 starters on Rockne's 1921 squad earned some type of All-American recognition.

When Shaw arrived home in Stuart for Christmas vacation, a throng of family, friends and well-wishers met his train at the station. The welcoming committee then ushered Shaw to the local Catholic church for a grand reception in his honor. Stuart's old-timers said that Shaw's welcome equaled the 1898 celebration the town held for returning Spanish-American War veterans and Congressional Medal of Honor winner Osborne W. Deignan.[27]

* * *

By the early '20s Rockne's "Notre Dame System" of football had caught the fancy of universities and colleges nationwide. Many wanted to emulate Notre Dame's gridiron success. To achieve that, they needed to hire coaches who were well versed in Rockne's style of play. Who better than the players who executed it every autumn Saturday? By 1921, Rockne was receiving dozens of letters from colleges across America, asking if he could recommend someone capable of successfully implementing Rockne's System at their schools. Rockne soon became a conduit for many of his players to enter the coaching profession. Just as he identified players who would excel on the gridiron, Rockne had a talent for recognizing players who had the makings of successful coaches. Among those Rockne's recommendation launched on successful and lengthy coaching careers included Shaw's blocking partner Eddie Anderson, who would win over 200 games coaching at four schools, with his longest stints at Holy Cross College and the University of Iowa. In 1939, Anderson was named the college Coach of the Year while coaching Heisman Trophy winner, Nile Kinnick. One of Anderson's unique accomplishments occurred in the 1920s, when he earned a medical degree from Chicago's prestigious Rush Medical Center, while coaching DePaul's football team in the afternoons, and playing pro football for the NFL's Chicago Cardinals on Sundays. Anderson was a practicing physician for 30 seasons out of his 39-year coaching career.

Center Harry Mehre, the ringleader of the ill-advised scheme to miss Sunday vespers during Shaw's first semester at Notre Dame served as head coach at the University of Georgia from 1928 to 1937, compiling a record of 59 wins, 34 losses and six ties. In 1938, he assumed the coaching reins at the University of Mississippi, where his teams won 31 games, lost eight and tied one. After retiring from coaching, Mehre (pronounced Meer) became a popular Atlanta sportswriter and television personality. Today, a beautiful athletic complex at the University of Georgia in Athens bears his name.

Frank Thomas was another of Shaw's teammates to gain coaching fame. After enjoying a successful reign at the University of Chattanooga, Thomas took the head job at Alabama. During his 15 years at Tuscaloosa, Thomas coached four undefeated teams and compiled an enviable record of 114 wins, 24 losses and seven ties. Due to poor health, he stepped down from coaching in 1947 to concentrate on his duties as Alabama's athletic director before retiring in 1952.

Rockne's 1921 fullback and champion hurdler, Chet Wynne, also found coaching success in Alabama. His 1932 Auburn team, featuring All-American halfback Jimmy Hitchcock, was undefeated. Wynne's years at Auburn were sandwiched between coaching stops at Creighton and the University of Kentucky. Licensed to practice law in three states—Nebraska, Alabama and Illinois—Wynne also served as a state legislator in Nebraska.

The fiery Hunk Anderson served as an unpaid assistant on Rockne's staff until taking the head coaching job at the University of St. Louis in 1927 and 1928. He then returned to Rockne's Notre Dame staff. When Rockne was killed in a plane crash in 1931, Hunk took over as head coach. A three-year record of 16 wins, nine losses and two ties resulted in his firing. Anderson then served as head coach at North Carolina State and a Detroit Lions assistant before finishing his career as a Chicago Bears assistant from 1940 until his retirement in 1951.

After grabbing his sheepskin from Notre Dame, Buck Shaw would go on to have a long association with both Ed "Slip" Madigan and Maurice "Clipper" Smith, the two upper class men who had nicknamed Buck "Adonis" in 1920. Madigan, who earned a reputation as one of the game's greatest showmen while coaching at St. Mary's College between 1921 and 1939, squared off against several of Shaw's Santa Clara teams. After retiring from coaching Madigan became a successful home builder in northern California.

Another classmate, Roger Kiley, became head coach at Loyola University in Chicago before the school dropped the sport. He later served as an assistant to Chet Wynne for three years during Wynne's successful stint at Auburn. After which Kiley became a Chicago alderman, practiced law, and eventually became an Illinois appellate court judge.

Shaw's teammate, Tom Lieb, who was two years behind him at Notre Dame, became the national collegiate discus champion in 1922 and 1923. He won the bronze medal in the

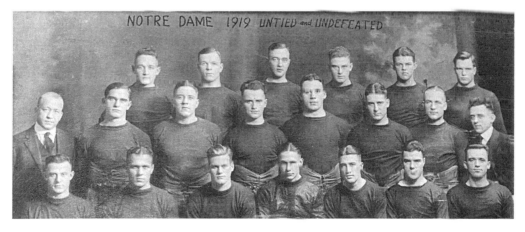

Buck Shaw (third from right, top row) lettered on Notre Dame's 1919 squad. Coached by Knute Rockne (far left, second row) and Gus Dorais (far right, second row), several players later became major college coaches including Maurice "Clipper" Smith (second from left, first row) at Santa Clara and Villanova, Ed "Slip" Madigan (fourth from left, second row) at St. Mary's, Heartley "Hunk" Anderson (second from left, top row) at Notre Dame and North Carolina State and Eddie Anderson (far right, top row) at Holy Cross and University of Iowa (courtesy Pam Hammer).

event at the 1924 Summer Olympics in Paris. Lieb began his football coaching career as an assistant at Wisconsin before returning to assist Rockne at Notre Dame in 1929. The Irish won the national championship that year, and much of it could be attributed to the hard-working Lieb, as Rockne spent most of the season sidelined with phlebitis. Lieb later served as head coach at Loyola University in Los Angeles from 1930 to 1938. He quit in 1939 to take care of his terminally ill wife. After her death, Lieb took the head coaching job at the University of Florida from 1940 until 1945. He finished his coaching career as an assistant at the University of Alabama before retiring in 1951.

Buck Shaw's 39-year coaching career would begin in 1922, and his success would exceed that of most of his Notre Dame teammates. Buck Shaw, however, had one more football game to play.

THREE

Carlinville and Getting into Coaching

Buck Shaw "stepped in it" during his first semester at Notre Dame and he'd do it again during Thanksgiving weekend of 1921. Some of the very classmates who anxiously sweated out their fate for skipping Sunday Vespers with Shaw two years earlier also shared in the 1921 gaffe. Known as the "Carlinville Eight," the participants suffered consequences more severe than the stern lecture issued them in 1919.

By the early 1920s, the college gridiron was propelling the game of football to new heights of popularity. Many who were too young to serve in "the Great War" now viewed the donning of helmet and shoulder pads as the ultimate test of one's manhood. They wanted the challenge of the gridiron even if they lacked the finances, aptitude or desire to attend college. For these spirited young men semi-pro football afforded a salve for their football itch.[1]

Semi-pro teams sprouted throughout the Midwest, and many small towns were proud of their teams and wholeheartedly supported them. Intense rivalries developed between neighboring hamlets and towns that sometimes resulted in heavy betting. One such rivalry emerged between the central Illinois towns of Taylorville and Carlinville. Founded in 1839, Taylorville is the county seat of Christian County. Carlinville, located about 80 miles to the southwest, was established as the county seat of Macoupin County in 1825. When Standard Oil of Indiana opened two new coal mines in the area in 1917, Carlinville's population mushroomed from 4,000 to 6,000 nearly overnight. Organizing its first semi-pro team in 1920, Carlinville filled its ranks with many of the area's hard-nosed miners.

Taylorville's semi-pro team, the Independents, were organized in 1914 and coached by Grover Cleveland Hoover. Well versed in the game and a stickler for conditioning, the burly Hoover conducted practices nightly during the season. Under Hoover, Taylorville dominated "down-state" semi-pro football for the next six years. Upon his premature retirement from coaching in 1919, Hoover had compiled an incredible record of 45 wins and two losses.

In 1920, Lionel Moise coached the upstart Carlinville team that finished its inaugural season undefeated with a 10–7 victory over Taylorville. The Independents vowed revenge if Carlinville visited Taylorville in 1921. Having played the 1920 season without the benefit of a coach, the Taylorville players coaxed Hoover out of retirement to again coach the Independents.[2]

The two teams scheduled a rematch for November 27. As the contest approached, rumors spread that avid Carlinville fans had wagered $30,000 on the game's outcome. With so much at stake and Taylorville entering the contest undefeated in six games, Carlinville officials decided to hedge their bets by bringing in talented "ringers." Frank

Seyfrit, a Carlinville resident and reserve end on the Notre Dame football team, had often played for Carlinville on Sundays. Team officials now persuaded Seyfrit to recruit more players for the Taylorville contest. Acting as the "roper," Seyfrit convinced seven Notre Dame teammates to play. The "ringers" included team captain Eddie Anderson, Buck Shaw, Harry Mehre, Roger Kiley, Chet Wynne, Bob Phelan, Earl "Nails" Walsh and Seyfrit. Each received $100 plus another $38 for traveling expenses.[3]

Taylorville first suspected something might be afoot when Coach Hoover received an anonymous letter warning that Carlinville was loading their squad with ringers. Hoover sent a man named Carroll Hill to Carlinville to eavesdrop around the town to verify the rumors. Hill reported back that the rumors were indeed true.[4]

Deciding to fight fire with fire, Hoover apprised a Taylorville player, Dick Simpson, of the Carlinville caper. Simpson telephoned his brother, Roy "Dope" Simpson, who was a reserve end on Bob Zuppke's University of Illinois squad on Saturdays and a starter for Taylorville on Sundays. "Dope," in turn, "roped" eight of his Illini teammates into the Taylorville camp. The interlopers included Illinois team captain Laurie Walquist, Vern Mullen, Joey Sternaman, Jack Crangle, Harry Gammage, Don Murray, R.T. Green, John Teuscher, and of course, the "Dope." Each would receive $100, a suit of clothes, a pair of shoes and a hat for doing battle against Carlinville.[5]

On November 26, Shaw and cohorts arrived by train in Springfield where they spent the night under the watchful eye of Carlinville coach Lionel Moise. Wearing their game uniforms the next morning, the eight traveled by car to nearby Taylorville. In anticipation of the much-ballyhooed rematch, the town had assumed a carnival atmosphere. Vendors hawked food from dozens of colorfully decorated wagons that surrounded the stands, and calliope music filled the air. The Baltimore & Ohio Railroad ran a special 15-car train from Carlinville that disgorged hundreds of excited fans, who expected to soon be counting their winnings.[6]

Over 4,000 exuberant fans jammed into Hoover Field with 1,800 customers paying a whopping $3 per grandstand seat while others paid $5 to park a car packed with fans around the field's perimeter. The weather was ideal for football as the visiting team trotted onto the field to warm up. By kickoff rumors floated throughout the grandstands that Carlinville fans had now wagered up to $100,000 on the game's outcome. Seeing so many strange faces among the squad, Carlinville fans initially refused to applaud because they mistakenly thought it was Taylorville running onto the field.[7]

"What are you yelling for? That's the Taylorville team," said a Carlinville woman.

"Oh, no, that's Carlinville," replied a Taylorville policeman.

"I guess I know our boys and not one of those fellows is from Carlinville," the woman replied indignantly.[8]

Adding to the confusion was the fact that both teams wore blue jerseys, with Taylorville's a slightly lighter shade.

Attempting to hide their identities, several of the Carlinville Eight wore tape across the bridge of their noses or partially smeared their faces with shoe polish. A few resorted to wearing phony mustaches, which were quickly knocked askew once the game started. Having forgotten his blue jersey, Notre Dame fullback Chet Wynne played in a white sweatshirt that made him stand out like a pelican dropping on a navy pea coat.[9]

Opting to gamble, Taylorville's Coach Hoover decided not to start his Illini ringers. Instead, he kept them hidden in cars around the field from which they could watch the game while warmly bundled in blankets. Carlinville Coach Moise would also take a gamble. He decided to let Eddie Anderson start at quarterback. Anderson had never played quarterback in his life. Moise, however, had little choice. Years later, Tom Lieb, a Notre Dame teammate who didn't participate in the Taylorville game, shed light on the decision. "Frank Thomas was supposed to play quarterback," Lieb said. "But he didn't wake up on time—we called him Sleepy, you know—and Eddie Anderson had to play. That messed up the offense."[10]

Notre Dame ringer Bob Phelan took the game's opening kickoff for Carlinville. "I nearly scored when I took the game's opening kickoff, and if I had the game may have ended differently. I reached Taylorville's 15-yard line then tripped over Roger Kiley who was making a block."[11]

A penalty set the visitors back, and three plays later Taylorville's Vern Mullen blocked Chet Wynne's punt. Lightning later struck twice to set up the first half's only score, when Mullen again blocked Wynne's punt at midfield. With Wynne and several Independents in hot pursuit, the pigskin bounced to the Carlinville one-yard line, where Andy Newman recovered it for the home team.

Three running plays failed to gain an inch. That's when Taylorville's 5-foot, 6-inch, 145-pound quarterback Charlie Dressen, who would later manage Major League Baseball's Brooklyn Dodgers and Detroit Tigers, skirted around end to score standing up. Taylorville took a 7–0 halftime lead.

Realizing that his Taylorville regulars had probably accomplished all that they could, Coach Hoover played his trump card by starting the Illinois ringers in the second half. The Carlinville team, resting on the east side of the field during halftime, sensed something was up when a fresh Taylorville squad began running plays to warm up. Carlinville ringer Roger Kiley approached Eddie Anderson shortly before the second-half kickoff. "Eddie," Kiley said, "one of those Taylorville guys looks real familiar."[12]

Kiley, in fact, recognized Jack Crangle, an All-Western Conference end for Illinois. Shortly after the kickoff, the Carlinville Eight realized that this fresh Taylorville 11 was as skilled and well conditioned as any college team. The Illini ringers controlled the second half action. On three occasions they drove deep into Carlinville territory. Joey Sternaman, the starting quarterback for the University of Illinois who had replaced Charlie Dressen at the half, capped each drive with a drop-kick field goal to give Taylorville a 16–0 win.

The defeat left Carlinville rooters crestfallen. Those who had bet heavily on the game wandered the streets in a daze. One Carlinville merchant, realizing that the had lost his fruit and vegetable store on the game's outcome, openly wept.[13]

It was a different story for those who had bet on Taylorville. Immediately after the game, one fan embraced Coach Hoover while sobbing, "You wonderful man. You saved my home for me." He had mortgaged his home and business for $2,000 to bet on Taylorville.[14]

A spontaneous parade of ecstatic Taylorville fans marched down Walnut Street. A donkey wearing a sign labeled "Carlinville" led the marchers. With a band playing "Under the Double Eagle," the revelers reached East Main and headed past Milligan's Smokehouse, Taylorville's number-one hangout. Many celebrants left the parade to enter the Smokehouse and collect their winnings being held by the stakeholder, Charlie Milligan. The parade finally ended at the Antlers Hotel on Market Street, but the drinking and celebrating continued well into the night.

In his 1967 copyrighted manuscript *Touchdown Taylorville!*, Scott Hoover, the son of Taylorville coach Grover Cleveland Hoover and an 11-year-old spectator on that day, described the following post-game scene. "The Notre Dame boys showered and dressed and stood out in the street watching the small town celebrate…. One of them approached an Illinois boy and said, 'We know who you are and I guess you know us. We won't say anything and hope you won't.' The Illini assured him that they didn't want any trouble and that 'mum' was the word."

Shaw and his teammates rode the train back to South Bend, hoping to put the escapade behind them. Notre Dame officials were unaware of the Taylorville episode when school closed for Christmas vacation. With the secret still safe when classes resumed in January, the eight breathed easier in hopes that the incident was buried forever. However, external forces were at work.

In her 1989 article for the *Taylorville Breeze Courier*, "The Game That Never Was," Johanna Tinnea described how the scandal began to unravel: "Shortly after the New Year the University of Wisconsin protested that Laurie Walquist, a star basketball player for Illinois, was ineligible because he had participated in a semi-pro football game on November 27, 1921, at Taylorville, Illinois. Walquist denied the charges but Wisconsin had proof."

On January 27, 1922, the Taylorville incident exploded onto the national scene when the University of Illinois declared nine of its athletes ineligible for further intercollegiate competition because they had played in a semi-pro football game on November 27, 1921, at Taylorville, Illinois.[15]

On January 30, the other shoe dropped in South Bend. With overwhelming evidence against them, the eight sullen athletes confessed to school officials that they had played for Carlinville on the date in question. The Associated Press reported, "They insisted that they received no pay and agreed to play simply as a Thanksgiving holiday lark, and without knowledge that the affair was an outgrowth of a town rivalry which became so acute that about $100,000 was said to have been bet on the game." All also denied having any prior knowledge of any Illinois athletes playing for Taylorville.

Rendering a swift decision, Notre Dame's athletic committee banned all eight from further intercollegiate competition. "We will stand for no taint or hint of professionalism here," declared committee chairman Father William Casey, "not even if it wrecks our teams forever."

Father Casey went on to lament, "Anderson, Wynne and Shaw are three of the most popular players in the school. All are described by students as the 'finest and fairest fellows who ever lived.' Shaw told a fellow student that this was the first time in his life he had ever played a football game in violation of team rules."[16]

On January 31, Buck Shaw mournfully confessed his role in the "phantom" game:

At first only two of the Notre Dame men planned to go, but at the last minute eight decided to make the trip.

When we got to Taylorville and saw how big the game really was we were going to back out. At a meeting though, we were told that the townspeople had a lot of money [on] the game and would probably lose it unless we played, so we decided to go through with it. We were sick of the whole thing before we got into the game.

We played to win, but didn't use the shift and ran most of our plays from the kick formation. Eddie Anderson played quarterback for the first time in his life and we used a sub on his end [Seyfrit]. The man who did our passing had never passed in a game before.[17]

Reflecting on his Carlinville experience years later, center Harry Mehre joked, "I guess you could say it was the first senior bowl."[18]

Notre Dame's teams weren't, as Father Casey described "wrecked forever," but their 1921 sports teams took a major hit. Eddie Anderson, Harry Mehre and Roger Kiley were dismissed from the basketball team on which Kiley served as captain. Anderson and Kiley were also both banned from baseball and Mehre from track. Shaw, the Western Conference shot put champion, who came to Notre Dame primarily to compete in track, would lose his last semester of eligibility; so would star hurdler and track team captain Chet Wynne. Robert Phelan of Madison, Iowa; Earl Walsh of Adrian, Iowa; and Frank Seyfrit were all banned from future participation in football.

Notre Dame souvenir photograph of 1921 letter men includes seven members of the "Carlinville Eight" (courtesy Sue Healey).

* * *

In a 1970 interview Buck Shaw recalled:

I'd never really thought about coaching until Rock [Rockne] came to me in the spring of my senior year with a couple of letters from schools seeking coaches—one from Auburn, another from the University of Nevada.

A friend of mine at school was from Nevada and he told me American football was new out there. They'd been playing rugby before.

It seemed like an interesting challenge, so I took the Nevada job as line coach.[19]

Heeding Horace Greeley's words, "Go West, young man," Shaw ventured to the Silver State. However, he didn't go alone. At the ungodly hour of 6:30 a.m. on Thursday, August 24, Buck married the love of his life, Marjorie Bowerman, at St. Mary's Church in Niles, Michigan. Buck's teammate, Clipper Smith, had been dating Marjorie's friend. One day Clipper brought Buck around to meet Marjorie. The two hit it off immediately. "I wasn't a football fan then," recalled Marjorie 38 years later, "but I became one in a hurry."[20] The newlyweds then traveled to Des Moines, and on to Stuart, where the Shaw family hosted an informal reception for the couple. After a short stay, Buck and Marjorie headed to Reno, where Buck would serve as an assistant football coach to Raymond O. Courtright.

As a four-sport letter man at the University of Oklahoma, Courtright, not only tossed a no-hitter against Missouri, but once pitched all 20 innings of a 1–1 tie against Oklahoma State. In 1912, an ailing Courtright rose from a sickbed to kick two fourth-quarter field goals in a 6–5 victory over Kansas. After coaching at a high school for a year, Courtright took the position of athletic director and head football coach at Kansas State Normal School (today's Pittsburg State). In April 1919, Nevada hired the versatile Courtright to coach the football, basketball, baseball and track teams. To facilitate his handling it all, they also made "Corky," as he was soon nicknamed, athletic director. Courtright's 1919 squad finished with eight wins, one loss and a tie. His 1920 team finished with seven wins, three losses and a tie. When the 1921 squad slipped to four wins, three losses and a tie, Corky decided to implement the Notre Dame system—thus, his letter to Rockne and subsequent hiring of Shaw.

With roughly a dozen full-time assistants, a handful of graduate assistants, strength coach and coordinators for video, recruiting, offense and defense, today's Division I head coach would guffaw at the prospect of only one coach running the entire operation. Yet "Corky" Courtright coached the Nevada Wolf Pack solo for three seasons. Buck Shaw was his first assistant. The game of football has evolved dramatically in the last century, becoming highly specialized, more intricate and played by bigger and faster men, often on artificial turf. In the early '20s the game was in its toddler stage, not yet influenced by television and a playoff system that guarantees tens of millions of dollars. Many schools could only afford to hire one coach.

Seventy-five candidates showed for Nevada's first day of practice in 1922, but that number dwindled to 50 by the third day. Nevada gave neither athletic scholarships nor provided players with on-campus jobs. All the players were "walk-ons." Often referred to as the "Sagebrushers," Nevada lacked the kind of talented linemen who had played with Buck Shaw at Notre Dame, such as "Hunk" Anderson, "Clipper" Smith and "Slip" Madigan. However, Nevada linemen "Horse" Hobbs, "Fish" Fisher, "Pix" Pierson, and "Spud" Harrison were a match in the nickname department.

Shaw's masterful teaching of blocking and tackling paid immediate dividends as the Wolf Pack won their first three games. One came against Saint Mary's College, coached by Buck's former Notre Dame teammate Ed "Slip" Madigan. Madigan was in his second year of an extremely successful 19-year tenure at the school. The Illinois native had matriculated at Notre Dame in 1915 but left school after the 1917 season to join the Navy. Reenrolling after the war, Madigan became Shaw's teammate in 1919. A gifted coach, Madigan was also a dynamic showman who guided St. Mary's football to soaring heights. In one of Madigan's many firsts, he arranged for a radio broadcast of the October 7, Nevada-St. Mary's contest from Reno. The entire St. Mary's student body gathered in the campus gymnasium back in Oakland, listening in anguish to the play-by-play of Nevada's 21–13 win over their beloved Saints.[21]

The season literally heated up for Nevada's Sagebrushers after their 35–7 Homecoming win over Whitman College. On the night of November 13, a fire gutted the entire upper floor of the Mackay Field training quarters building. Quick thinking by volunteer students and the rapid response of the Reno Fire Department, whose firemen fought the

flames in oxygen helmets obtained from the Mackay School of Mines, saved the building from complete destruction. Alert students entered the flaming building and carried
almost all of the training apparatus to the football field, including many trophies and
photographs of famous teams and athletes.[22]

Mr. Clarence Mackay had donated the building, the field and the Mackay School
of Mines building to the University of Nevada as a memorial to Mr. John Mackay, his
father. John Mackay was born into dire poverty near Dublin, Ireland, in 1831. In 1840, he
migrated with his parents and younger sister to the slums of New York City. When his
father died two years later, the 11-year-old quit school and began hawking newspapers
on street corners to support his mother and sister. At age 17, he acquired a position as an
apprentice ship's carpenter at the William H. Webb shipyard on New York's East River,
where he learned skills that proved to be invaluable when he sailed to San Francisco in
late 1851 to mine gold. After years of working the Sierra foothills, Mackay crossed the
Sierras and arrived at the Comstock Lode in 1859 without a dime in his pocket. Through
hard work, expert use of heavy machinery, and shrewd investments, Mackay's silver min-
ing operations were earning him between $248,000 and $303,000 per month in cash by
1875. He became known as a "Bonanza King."[23]

Nevada's football fate suffered yet another blow the following weekend at the University of California. A San Francisco newspaperman had dubbed Coach Andy Smith's
California Golden Bears "the Wonder Team." The appellation was fitting. Led by 6-foot,
200-pound Harold "Brick" Muller and 132-pound quarterback Charley Erb (remember
the name), California would compile a record of 27 wins, no losses and a tie, amassing 1,220 points while allowing just 81 for the opposition between 1920 and 1922. As the
Nevada State Journal reported on November 19, "Coach Courtright pulled the most unexpected bit of strategy ever witnessed in the case of a small college pitted against a larger
one, by starting a team composed of second-string men with but two exceptions, 'Spud'
Harrison and Captain 'Horse' Hobbs." Courtright's strategy failed miserably, as California raced to a 41–0 lead before Nevada returned a blocked punt 70 yards for a touchdown. When the contest mercifully ended, the final score read: California 61, Nevada 13.
Despite the lopsided loss, Nevada was one of only three teams to score on Cal's "Wonder
Team" that season. In the season's finale the following week, the Sagebrushers scored in
the fourth quarter to salvage a 7–7 tie with Santa Clara.

The Wolf Pack's other losses were to powerhouse University of Southern California
(7–0) and Stanford (17–7). With a final record of five wins, three losses and a tie, Nevada
fans were optimistic about the future. "Beat California in 1923" became the off-season
rallying cry for the city of Reno.

* * *

Nevada's football picture continued to brighten in February of 1923, when the
Mackay Field training building was fully restored after fire had gutted it the previous
November. February also saw 40 prospective linemen heed Coach Buck Shaw's call for
help. With "Corky" Courtright's blessing, Shaw conducted individual and group training sessions for the recruits in basic line play. The sessions ran throughout the spring
semester.

With several first-string backs returning, Courtright optimistically declared, "I
see no reasons why Nevada will not have the strongest team in her history."[24] When
November 3 was announced as the date of the 1923 Nevada-California game, Wolf Pack

captain-elect Chester Scranton proclaimed, "We're going to do more than score this time. We're going to win."[25]

Despite the Mackay family's philanthropy, the university's athletic department often operated on a shoestring. In April, school officials informed Courtright that the 1923 athletic budget had no funds to retain his one and only assistant, Buck Shaw. When word leaked around campus that the popular coach might not be retained, the university's student body sprang into action. Spirited students scheduled a number of vaudeville acts at the local Rialto theater as a fund raiser to pay Shaw's salary. For a week preceding the April 27 curtain call, students waged a vigorous ticket-selling campaign, with sales exceeding Shaw's $1,800 yearly salary. By all accounts, the acts drew rave reviews, and a grateful Shaw welcomed the opportunity of coaching another season on Nevada's sidelines.

Buck and Marjorie Shaw spent most of that summer in Stuart, Iowa, visiting family and friends before returning to Reno on August 15. When practice officially began for the 1923 campaign on September 10, Buck had 35 linemen from which to mold a starting front seven. The former Golden Domer's competitive juices must have been boiling over that autumn, for not only did he want to coach, but he also wanted to don the helmet and pads again as a player. He scratched his itch by joining a Sacramento football club comprised of "ne'er-do-wells" and "has-beens." The team played its games on Sundays. Besides Buck, one of the few talented Sacramento players was Hal McCreery. After graduating from high school, McCreery played for Sacramento on Sundays while working weekdays to save money for college. He and Shaw bonded, as Shaw taught the younger McCreery a few tricks of a tackle's trade. The 170-pound McCreery later captained the 1927 Stanford team. In club Sacramento's 14–0 loss to the Olympic Club of San Francisco on October 7, the *Nevada State Journal* reported, "Shaw at his old position was said to be the only redeeming feature in an otherwise farcical contest."[26] How many games Shaw played for Sacramento in 1923 is uncertain.

Nevada opened the 1923 campaign against the Olympic Club team of San Francisco on September 22. (Yes, the same team Buck's Sacramento Club would play on October 7.) Founded in San Francisco in the early 1860s, the Olympic Club originally fielded swimming and golf teams. The club added football to its activities in 1892. With the exception of 1897, they annually provided needed gridiron competition for colleges in the Bay Area. However, when more West Coast colleges began fielding better teams in the late 1920s and early '30s, teams like California and St. Mary's stopped scheduling the "Flying-O's," as the Olympic Club came to be known. The loss of these big money games led to dwindling revenues for the club as well as difficulty scheduling a full slate of games and an overall decrease in support for the program. As a result, the Olympic club stopped fielding football teams in 1935.[27]

Nevada's early season optimism suffered a jolt when the Olympics, with two wins already under their belt, thrashed Nevada 27–3 on a muddy Mackay Field. However, Nevada's 41–0 pasting of Cal-Davis the following Saturday rejuvenated both the players' confidence and the fans' expectations. On the evening of October 4, hundreds of students and community businessmen jammed into the school's gymnasium to give the Wolf Pack a raucous send off to Stanford. When the team entered the gym it received a tumultuous 10-minute standing ovation to the recurring chant, "It's Nevada's Year!"[28]

Several hundred zealous Wolf Pack fans made the trip to Palo Alto and, shortly after the opening kickoff, launched into the ditty "Stanford University, she ain't what she used to be." They were right.

Led by Ernie Nevers and a strong supporting cast, coach Andy Kerr fielded the strongest Cardinal squad in years. In its season opener Stanford blanked Nevada 27–0. Things got worse the following week as USC stomped Nevada 33–0 in Los Angeles. When the heavily favored Sagebrushers only managed a 7–7 tie in their Homecoming game against Santa Clara two weeks later, prospects for their November 3 encounter with California's "Wonder Team" at Berkeley seemed abysmal.

In what would be one of the first of his many public speaking engagements throughout his career, Buck agreed to address a group of 40 boys at a Reno YMCA dinner on the eve of the game. Shaw limited his remarks to the essentials necessary for making a football team. He cited aggressiveness, obedience, confidence, harmony, and concentration. So taken by Shaw's affable and personable demeanor, the boys accompanied him to the train depot to see the team off.[29]

Days before the contest, Jack James, a sportswriter for the *San Francisco Examiner* wrote that the California-Nevada game would be a "glorified scrimmage" for the home team.[30] On the day of the game the *Examiner's* only mention of the supposed impending massacre was a headline on the sports page declaring, "Nevada Wolves Not Expected to Trouble Bruins Much." (One of Cal's early nicknames was the Bruins. However, the school eventually dropped that moniker and UCLA adopted it.) Instead, the paper devoted most of its sporting news ink to the opening of the horse racing season at Tanforan, the highlight being the $2,000 purse of the inaugural Tanforan Handicap.

Although entering the fray with only one win in five outings, Nevada was showing signs of improvement. That, combined with California's extreme over-confidence, would yield an unexpected outcome. Since his Bears had outscored their opponents 151 to 0 in six previous contests, California coach Andy Smith viewed the Nevada game as merely a light workout for his "Wonder Team." Confident of victory, Smith skipped the contest to scout Stanford at Palo Alto, even though the "Big Game" was three weeks away. Not only did Smith bail on the Nevada game, but he took several key players along with him to help scout. Among them were team captain Don Nichols (a 1922 All-American) and center "Babe" Horrell (a 1924 All-American). Other factors also influenced the game's outcome. During a bye week earlier in the season, Courtright and Buck scouted the Bears and decided to focus their team's defensive efforts on stopping three of Cal's base plays. The decision would pay off. Having attended Smith's coaching clinic that summer, Courtright now possessed a greater understanding of Cal's offense. Furthermore, with several injured starters returning to the lineup, the Wolf Pack would be at full strength for the first time in weeks.

In the early '20s colleges often conducted preliminary contests before the main event in an attempt to bolster attendance. On November 3, the Cal-USC freshman game preceded Cal's varsity tilt with Nevada. Because the freshman game ran unusually long, and Berkeley's field lacked lights, both schools agreed just before the kickoff to play 10-minute quarters instead of the usual 15 to avoid darkness.[31] The game quickly turned into a punting duel with both teams kicking on second and even first down to gain field position. Just before the half, Nevada advanced the ball to Cal's 10-yard line when a penalty and a sack forced Nevada's "Little Bill" Gutteron to attempt a field goal that fell short. In the second half, Gutteron missed a second three-point attempt. For California, a poor snap to drop-kicker Bill Blewett on Nevada's 15-yard line resulted in a low kick that hit one of his own lineman in the back. Those were the game's only scoring chances. The stunning news of Nevada's scoreless tie with powerful California ricocheted across the country.

"You weren't football players that last half," one California player told a Nevada player after the game. "You were a bunch of raving maniacs."[32]

California and Nevada sportswriters agreed that the Sagebrushers had outplayed the Bears, particularly in the second half. "California was outplayed," wrote Miles York, sportswriter for the *San Francisco Journal*. "Nevada did not win the game technically, but if there was ever such a thing as a moral victory, that victory belonged to the lads of Reno yesterday."[33]

When the train carrying the victors pulled into Reno's Southern Pacific station at 7:10 a.m. the following Monday, most of Nevada's student body was there to greet them. With the school band playing "Hail, Hail, the Gang's All Here," the players piled into a student-drawn wagon and paraded to the Golden Hotel for breakfast. Courtright and Shaw used the stop to quietly slip away from the day's remaining activities. During a rally later that morning at Mackay Field, university president Walter Clark paid tribute to the players. Clark also lauded coach Corky Courtright as the man "whose hope, faith and methods had fruited after four years of service." He then added, "I don't know who selected line coach Buck Shaw, but whoever made the selection made it well. I want to say a very honest word of gratitude for the manliness of both men. They are both clean, straight and honest. Every man of the university would do well to pattern themselves after them."[34]

The momentum carried into the next week, when Nevada steamrolled Fresno State

Action from Nevada's 7–7 Homecoming tie with Santa Clara on October 23, 1923. The next week Nevada (in striped sleeves) stunned the football world by playing California's "Wonder Team" to a scoreless tie (courtesy Nevada University Reno Special Collections and Archives).

46–3. Even a 10–10 tie with Slip Madigan's vastly improved St. Mary's team in the season's finale couldn't cool the embers of Nevada's miraculous showing against California. Despite a final mediocre record of two wins, three losses and three ties, the 1923 scoreless tie with Cal had all of Nevada feeling like world-beaters.

Nevada's November football euphoria began to dissipate in December, when head coach Courtright announced he was looking into coaching opportunities elsewhere. Rumor had it that Courtright claimed that interference of "downtown interests" made it impossible for him to continue coaching at Nevada.[35] On December 28, Reno papers reported that he had applied for the football job at Oregon. The next day similar reports had Courtright a candidate for Kentucky's top spot. Rumors grew rampant as to where Corky would land. Speculation continued well into the new year, leaving Shaw in a precarious position. If Courtright left, Buck might be named his successor, but there were no guarantees. If Courtright stayed, Buck's $1,800 assistant's salary would still have to be raised by the student body and/or local boosters. Shaw's integral role in Nevada's scoreless tie with California had garnered him national attention. As he and wife Marge were expecting their first child soon, Shaw needed not only a stable income but also a raise. January came and went with Courtright still casting job feelers near and far. Uncomfortable with the Nevada situation, Buck decided to make a move.

FOUR

Trading Wolf Packs Twice

February 1924 was an exciting month for Buck and Marge Shaw. On February 13, the day before Valentine's Day, Marge gave birth to a daughter, Joan, in Reno. Three days later North Carolina State athletic director John F. Miller announced the hiring of L.T. "Buck" Shaw as the school's new football coach. How did Buck make the connection to the Raleigh, North Carolina, school? Miller had sent a letter to Knute Rockne asking if he could recommend a former player as a coach. Rock forwarded the letter on to Shaw and told State officials he was doing so. Shaw would also serve as head track coach and be trading schools nicknamed the Wolf Pack. On February 22, Shaw told the *Nevada State Journal* that while his connections with Nevada's coaching staff had made him many friends and he was confident about the future of Nevada football, as a new father, he just couldn't reject N.C. State's $4,000 salary offer.

Shaw's unexpected departure left Nevada's administrators in a quandary. Several university officials had tabbed Shaw as Coach Courtright's possible successor, which seemed imminent as it was public knowledge that Corky had spent over two months shopping for another head coaching gig. Nevada's coaching haze cleared somewhat on March 24, when Courtright accepted a three-year contract and substantial raise to assume the coaching reins at the Colorado School of Mines. Both Shaw and Courtright continued to conduct their coaching and physical instruction roles at Nevada until the end of the school year. Shaw's family then spent the summer in Chicago before heading to North Carolina in late August.

On April 30, Nevada named Charley Erb, a three-year starting quarterback and captain of California's 1921 "Wonder Team," as its new head coach. During Erb's three seasons as the Golden Bears' trigger man (1920–22), Cal had thumped Nevada by scores of 79–7, 51–6 and 61–13. Nevada officials probably reasoned, "if you can't beat 'em, join 'em." However, Erb's tenure at Nevada would be brief.

Shaw and assistant Gus Tebell welcomed over 30 candidates to Raleigh for the start of practice in early September. During the hot, sultry 16 days of two-a-day practices, the Wolf Pack players donned full pads daily, with the only concession to the stifling heat being cotton sweatshirts in lieu of the customary woolen jerseys of that period. The coaches conveyed that every position was up for grabs. Even North Carolina State captain Cleve Beatty found himself battling two underclassmen to keep his starting guard position. From day one Shaw diligently set about installing the "Notre Dame" system. At the heart of the system was the backfield shift from the T formation to the Box formation. The shift had two major aims. First, it was intended to get off to a flying start, to get a jump on the opposition. Second, the shift attempted to get the right men in the right place at the right time, throwing the opposing players—the line especially—off balance.[1] If well executed it would outnumber the defense at the point of attack.

Shaw's Wolf Pack opened the 1924 season at home against Trinity University from Durham, North Carolina. Trinity's Blue Devils began playing football in 1888 but discontinued the sport from 1895 through 1919. The school re-instituted the game in 1920 with a different head coach serving yearly through 1926. In 1924, it was Howard Jones' turn. Jones came to Durham from the University of Iowa, where in 1921 his Hawkeyes dealt Knute Rockne's Notre Dame squad its only loss in three years (and Shaw his first loss ever as a player). Shortly after the '24 season Trinity changed its name to Duke University, and Jones departed to become head coach at the University of Southern California (USC).

Heavy rain left Raleigh's Riddick Field a quagmire, which hampered Carolina's newly installed offense. However, Trinity unveiled a unique shift of its own which proved to be a formidable obstacle for Shaw's squad in the first half. Howard Jones called it the "Bird Cage" shift because, after breaking the huddle, the initial formation resembled a bird cage. Initially, only four players aligned on the line of scrimmage, with a second line of four players a yard or two behind them, and the three remaining players positioned in a third line a yard behind the second four. Except for the center, who had one hand on the ball, Trinity players assumed two-point stances upon breaking the huddle. On the quarterback's command, three players from the second line shifted to a designated spot on the line of scrimmage. The fourth man in the second row then shifted somewhere in the backfield, along with the three players originally stationed in the last line. This shift allowed Trinity to go unbalanced either right or left, giving the defense little time to adjust before the ball was snapped. It bewildered Carolina's defense. Yet somehow Trinity didn't score, and the first half ended scoreless. At halftime State's coaches diagrammed adjustments that ended the Wolf Pack's confusion. State rallied for two fourth-quarter touchdowns while stifling Jones' "Bird Cage" shift to earn a 14–0 win.

Years later, in 1936, when Shaw was a rookie head coach at Santa Clara and Howard Jones had brought USC to national prominence, Bay Area reporters were impressed to learn of Shaw's win over Jones' 1924 Duke squad. When asked to recount the contest Shaw downplayed it, saying that Jones didn't have much talent that year. What the humble Shaw didn't say was that he didn't either.

Immediately after the contest, players from both teams complained of having itchy, burning skin. At first, Trinity's coaches thought it to be "lime burn." However, as Riddick Field hadn't been lined with lime, officials deduced that the players' suffering resulted from dye poisoning caused by their mud-and water-soaked jerseys.[2]

The Wolf Pack experienced a harsher discomfort the following week at State College, Pennsylvania. Confident of victory, Penn State coach Hugo Bezdek brayed days before the game that he would be able to substitute freely against the visitors. Averaging 185 pounds per man, an exceptionally large team for that era, the Nittany Lions rolled up 51 consecutive points before N.C. State scored late in the game. Stunned by the 51–6 loss, in which Bezdek's boys amassed 580 yards of total offense to the Wolf Pack's 50, many N.C. State fans realized that a winning season wasn't in the cards. A 10–0 loss the following week at South Carolina confirmed those suspicions.

For North Carolinians the greatest football game staged annually is the clash between the University of North Carolina and North Carolina State. Only 25 miles separate the campuses. The 1924 contest was scheduled for the Thursday of State Fair Week in Raleigh, when over 100,000 tourists would visit the Capital City. Since resuming athletic relations in 1919, the Tar Heels had prevailed in three of the five bitterly fought contests. Prognosticators viewed the game as a toss-up. Playing before 15,000 fans on a hot afternoon that drained the energy of both squads, the Wolf Pack dropped another one. Despite 110 yards in Tar Heel penalties, State couldn't sustain any consistent drives and suffered its second consecutive 10–0 loss. State's season reached its halfway mark the following week with a 17–7 loss to the Virginia Military Institute (VMI).

Despite only one win in its first five outings, the young, inexperienced Wolf Pack had demonstrated significant improvement in the preceding weeks. Through Shaw's patient mentoring and calm encouragement, State would see a silver lining in the weeks ahead. In their first-ever meeting, North Carolina State tied a Davidson College team that had won five of its first six games. Rallying in the fourth quarter the following week, Charlie Shuford's 20-yard scoring run gave State a 6–3 win over Virginia Tech. Then, although outplayed for most of the game, Shaw's boys managed a scoreless tie against a superior Maryland squad. However, the season ended on a sour note, with both Wake Forest and Washington & Lee earning shutout wins at State's expense.

Despite finishing the '24 season with a record of two wins, six losses and two ties, players and university officials seemed pleased with the coaching staff's performance. The following appeared in the school's November *Alumni News*: "L.T. 'Buck' Shaw knows the Notre Dame football system. He can teach it to our men. He made an excellent start this fall and he will spend the better part of two months this spring in another long session with the squad." The article then asked fans for patience and their support by directing local high school talent to the university.[3]

* * *

While North Carolina State may have been confident about its football future with Shaw at the helm, Shaw wasn't happy in Raleigh. Whether Buck couldn't get acclimated to the weather or as a native "Iowa Yankee" he couldn't adjust to living in the South, who knows? Perhaps he felt he couldn't produce a winner at State or may have just missed living in the West. But when the University of Nevada contacted him in late autumn about possibly returning to Reno, Buck expressed keen interest. It seemed that Charley Erb, who had succeeded Corky Courtright as Nevada's football coach a year earlier, was dissatisfied with the situation in Reno. Apparently, the "powers that be" in Reno were also unhappy with Erb and the school's three-win, four-loss and one-tie season. When Erb informed Nevada athletic director J.E. Martie that he wouldn't return in 1925, Martie knew where to turn—to Raleigh, North Carolina.

On January 15, 1925, North Carolina State athletic director John Miller announced that Buck Shaw had resigned as head coach to accept a similar position at the University of Nevada. Shaw's willingness in taking a pay cut to return to Reno evidenced his desire to leave Raleigh.

Carrying baby Joan in his arms, Buck Shaw stepped with wife Marge off the train in Reno late in the evening of August 20, 1925. The next morning, he told a reporter from the *Reno Journal-Gazette*, "It's like getting back home, for it was like being in exile to spend a year in North Carolina."

Upon arriving he learned that the university had re-sodded Mackay Field and purchased new equipment for the first team, with new uniforms to be issued shortly. Seventeen letter men from the 1924 team were returning. Although practice couldn't officially start before September 15, coaches could hold "chalk-talks" with players, and team members could work out on their own. Wasting no time, Shaw arranged for team captain "Fighting Tom" Roach to supervise workouts for linemen. Roach, who had spent the summer swinging a pick at a Comstock mine, was more than ready for the task. Meanwhile, the backs trained under the direction of returning quarterback "Little Bill" Gutteron.

Buck hired his former Notre Dame and "Carlinville Eight" teammate Bob Phelan as an assistant. Phelan had spent the previous two seasons playing professional football for the Rock Island Independents in Illinois. After spending August attending Knute Rockne's Notre Dame coaching clinic, Phelan joined Shaw on September 15, when the pair greeted nearly 100 football candidates for the official start of practice. With only 10 scheduled practice days before the season opener, the two Rockne disciples had their work cut out for them.

Nevada opened the season at home in an inaugural meeting with St. Ignatius, a Jesuit school that would shortly change its name to the University of San Francisco. Halfback Harry Frost's five-yard touchdown run and Max Allen's conversion earned Shaw a 7–0 victory in Shaw's head coaching debut in Reno. As an experienced grid coach from any era can attest, the slide from the winner's penthouse to the depths of the loser's outhouse is often only a week away. Such was the case for Buck Shaw when Nevada traveled to Berkeley for their annual clash with California. Unlike 1923, when the heavily favored Bears suffered a humiliating tie with the Wolf Pack—because Coach Andy Smith and several of his key players skipped the Nevada game to scout Stanford—Cal now had all hands on deck. Blessed with more speed, strength and depth, and bent on revenge, the Golden Bears trounced Nevada 54–0. Sporting scribes reported that Nevada's offense looked out of sync. That happens when a squad encounters a vastly superior athletic team. Unfortunately, Nevada athletic director J.E. Martie consistently scheduled similar heavyweights throughout Shaw's tenure, frequently early in the season when the squad was least prepared. Besides the humiliating losses, playing powerhouse programs often left Shaw's out-manned squads with numerous injuries. Such was the case after the '25 Cal game, when Nevada lost several starters for weeks and quarterback Bill Gutteron for the season.

Fortunately, an open date allowed Nevada's walking wounded time to heal before hosting and blanking a surprisingly tough College of the Pacific squad 14–0. It looked like the Wolf Pack might keep it rolling the following week against St. Mary's College at San Francisco's Ewing Field. Buck's former Notre Dame teammate, Slip Madigan, had molded the Saints into a West Coast juggernaut en route to an eight-win and two-loss season in '25. After a scoreless first period, Nevada self-imploded. A solemn Shaw addressed his team's 35–0 loss in a post-game interview: "Nevada actually threw the game away. During the first quarter we had it all over the Oakland team…. We slumped either physically or mentally after the first quarter. What caused it I can't tell but it may have been the unusually warm weather. It was like a midsummer day. The fact remains that we threw away the game when we should have fought the last three quarters as we started."[4]

Hosting a strong Santa Clara University squad for its Homecoming game on Halloween, the largest crowd in years turned out at Mackay Field to cheer on the Wolf Pack. Adam Walsh was in his first year as Santa Clara's head coach. Captain of the 1924 Notre Dame team, Walsh was the center on the Irish line tabbed the "Seven Mules," who blocked for Knute Rockne's famed "Four Horsemen." Walsh's Irish squad had defeated Stanford in the Rose Bowl the previous January. As a senior at Notre Dame, the Churchville, Iowa, native etched his name in the annals of Irish football lore by making a last-minute, game-saving interception against Army with two broken hands. According to teammates, Walsh broke his right hand early in the game. Rather than leave the field, he had a trainer splint it during a time out. Several series of plays later he fractured his left hand. Rockne continually sent in substitutes to get Walsh out of the game, but Walsh refused to leave.

All three previous meetings between Nevada and Santa Clara had ended in ties. This one would not. It ended with Nevada's first-ever Homecoming loss, 20–7. Disappointed but not disheartened with the outcome, Shaw and assistant coach Phelan continued to focus on basic fundamentals and offensive timing in preparing for Fresno State. Their patience bore fruit in their home finale, as the Wolf Pack vented their frustrations over their last two losses by exploding for a 60–6 win against a mediocre Bulldog squad.

Then, in their best performance of the season, Nevada blanked Cal-Davis 19–0. The following Tuesday Harry Standerwick, a former Reno resident with long-time ties to the *Reno Gazette,* wrote the following appraisal of Nevada's showing against the Aggies:

> In defeating the University of California Agricultural College team the boys gave us the first real football we have had from Nevada in at least six years....
>
> We were treated to a spectacle wherein we saw a well organized team prove that it was versed in every department of the game, relying not on individual stars for prominence, but upon perfect team work, upon a well planned attack, a knowledge of football, and a team showing a spirit that was characteristic of Nevada in the earlier days.... Our hats are off to Coach "Buck" Shaw, who undoubtedly has developed the most perfect football team that Nevada has ever had in its history.[5]

The letter went on for several columns gushing over Nevada's mental toughness and resilience.

The Wolf Pack traveled to Tucson the following week to be the Homecoming opponent of the University of Arizona. Although controlling the game's tempo, the Wolf Pack managed only a scoreless tie. Viewing Nevada's 1925 season record of four wins, three losses and a tie as a sign of fortuitous things to come, university officials signed Shaw to a new two-year contract.

* * *

Shaw welcomed the degree of stability the new contract offered, for on September 3, 1926, Buck and wife Marge were blessed with the birth of their second daughter, Patricia. The former Notre Dame tackle seemed to confirm the university's show of confidence in him when his Sagebrushers won their first three games of the 1926 season. The victims were St. Ignatius (the future University of San Francisco), College of the Pacific, and Fresno State. Up next was a trip to Palo Alto to meet Stanford. Elated by their team's undefeated record and encouraged by Stanford coach Pop Warner's assessment that "this is the poorest team I have coached in 15 years," several hundred Nevada fans planned to make the trip to support their team. The slogan around Reno during game week was "Over the Hump, and Back the Pack."[6] Realizing that Warner must have subjected his Cardinals to a severe tongue-lashing as well as a hellish week of practice, Shaw anticipated an extremely rugged game. With that in mind, he increased the size of Nevada's traveling squad from the customary 22 players to 27.

Nevada drew first blood in the contest on a scoring happenstance that left Shaw in stitches. Playing center for Stanford was none other than Hal McCreery, Buck's younger teammate from his brief playing days with the Sacramento football club in 1923. During their time together, Buck occasionally aligned over the center in a staggered stance on obvious punting situations. As the center's fingers tightened on the ball just before snapping it, Buck would stealthily kick the ball sending it on an erratic path to the punter. Shaw performed the feat so furtively that officials never caught him at it, believing it to be merely a poor snap from the center.

Now, three years later and unbeknownst to McCreery, Shaw had taught the trick to several Nevada linemen. With Stanford's Mike Murphy aligned in punt formation in the shadow of his own goalpost, McCreery readied to snap by tightening his grip on the ball when a Nevada lineman kicked it, rocketing the ball well over Murphy's head. Murphy won the ensuing scramble to recover the ball in Stanford's end zone, but Nevada was awarded a safety and took a 2–0 lead. Realizing he had been the victim of Shaw's tactic, McCreery turned to the Nevada bench, raised his fist and yelled loudly enough for the whole stadium to hear, "Damn you, Buck Shaw!"[7] On the sidelines Shaw doubled over with laughter. For the rest of his playing days Stanford teammates often referred to McCreery as "Bad Pass."

The comedy of errors continued for the home team in the second quarter, when Stanford's seemingly cursed Mike Murphy fumbled, and Nevada's "Red" Pierce recovered the ball in mid-air and rumbled 60 yards with it for a touchdown. Nevada led 9–0 at halftime. However, Stanford had the last laugh. An irate Pop Warner blistered his team in the locker room and started a new lineup in the second half that played inspired football. When the final gun sounded, Stanford had tallied 28 first downs to Nevada's five en route to a 33–9 win.

Returning to Reno the following week, the Wolf Pack hosted St. Mary's College for Homecoming. Anticipation for the contest ran high throughout the city, and officials predicted a record-setting crowd. Having previously upset the University of California, St. Mary's was a solid favorite. Addressing the student body at Thursday night's pep rally Shaw's remarks conveyed a guarded optimism: "Nevada has a fighting chance to win, and that is all Nevada ever asks for."[8] Because both teams utilized the "Notre Dame System," many believed that since Shaw was well versed in it, he knew how to defend it, which increased Nevada's chances of victory.

As was customary at Nevada games during the period, the Wolf Pack freshmen played a preliminary game before the main event. By the end of the freshman game, the stands were overflowing with fans and autos jam-packed with spectators surrounded part of Mackay Field. After the opening kick off, 10,000 boisterous fans found St. Mary's coach "Slip" Madigan's sideline antics to be just as entertaining as the on-field action. With both teams deadlocked in a scoreless tie for the better part of three quarters, the stress seemed to be too much for Madigan. In an era when coaches watched their charges from the team bench, Madigan—who stood 5 feet, 6 inches tall and weighed just a few pounds more than his 156-pound Notre Dame playing weight—hopped and scurried along the sidelines like a bantam rooster. He bellowed to players, yelled at officials, gesticulated frantically, swung his arms as if he were hitting an imaginary heavy bag, cursed, prayed and threw his Italian-imported Borsalino hat to the ground several times, often following it with a swift kick. "The hat was on the field as much as we were," recalled Andy Marefos, who later played fullback for St. Mary's.[9] While such theatrics were alien to Nevada fans, they were part of Madigan's regular game-day routine.

Madigan's prayers were answered late in the third quarter when St. Mary's recovered a fumble on Nevada's 10-yard line. On the next play, Saint quarterback Leo Rooney ran for a score. In the fourth quarter a long pass put the ball on Nevada's four-yard line, from where St. Mary's Johnny Farrell hit paydirt. Red Watson's extra-point kick gave the visitors a 13–0 lead and Coach Madigan enough breathing room to feel it safe to finally take a seat on his team's bench. That's the way the game ended. Always gracious in defeat, Shaw hugged his former Notre Dame teammate at midfield, shook his hand and wished him luck. It would be years before Buck got the better of Slip Madigan on the gridiron.

Automobiles and 10,000 fans surround Mackay Field during Nevada's 13–0 Homecoming loss to "Slip" Madigan's St. Mary's squad in 1926. Nevada fans found Madigan's sideline histrionics to be just as entertaining as the game (courtesy Nevada University Reno Special Collections and Archives).

Nevada next headed to San Jose to meet Santa Clara. Although Nevada was rated a slight favorite, Santa Clara outplayed the Wolf Pack in every aspect of the game to earn a 25–0 win. The *San Francisco Examiner* reported, "Mentor 'Buck' Shaw's charges seemed at a loss to fathom Santa Clara's brilliant wide end runs."[10] Bronco halfback Len Casanova inflicted most of the damage on those runs and was equally effective with his passing. The Wolf Pack bounced back the next week with a 45–7 victory over Cal-Davis to give Nevada a record of four wins and three losses entering the season's finale against California at Berkeley.

For the first time since 1919, Nevada would not be facing an Andy Smith-coached team. From 1920 through 1924, Smith's Cal "Wonder Teams" went undefeated, amassing an amazing record of 44 wins, no losses, and four ties. His 1925 squad slipped to a six-win and three-loss record. In December of that year, Smith traveled to Philadelphia where he contracted pneumonia. When his condition worsened, the 42-year-old Smith was hospitalized on Christmas Eve. He never recovered and died there on January 8, 1926. Smith's ashes were later spread over the field at Berkeley's Memorial Stadium.

When Shaw brought his Wolf Pack to Berkeley in 1926, California, under first year head coach Clarence "Nibs" Price, was coming off a five-game losing streak. Price had served as Smith's assistant since 1919 and had been responsible for recruiting significant high school talent to the Berkeley campus. But now Cal was experiencing its first losing season in over a decade. Less than three minutes into the game Cal halfback Earl Jabs brought the 35,000 spectators to their feet with his 46-yard touchdown run. Dick Blewett's extra-point kick gave the Bears an early 7–0 lead. Nevada retaliated quickly on Mike Lawlor's beautiful 40-yard scoring pass to "Spud" Murphy. The extra-point attempt failed and the score remained 7–6 for three quarters. Substituting freely at the start of the fourth, the Bears wore down undermanned Nevada. Earl Jabs scored two more touchdowns and Cal won its third game of the season 20–7. In reviewing the game the *San Francisco Examiner* reported, "In spite of the superiority in power executed by the Bears, Nevada put on a good fighting exhibition of football. Coach Shaw yesterday put a determined team on the field and they were a credit to him."[11]

It was the media's second laudatory comment about the character of Shaw's Wolf Pack in as many days. On November 13, the day of the Nevada-Cal clash, the *Reno Gazette-Journal* quoted football referee J. Rufus Klawans, who had officiated several Nevada games, "There are no more sportsmen-like men to be found on any football team than members of the Wolf Pack." By all accounts, Nevada's "classy" gridiron conduct was a reflection of its head coach, Buck Shaw.

* * *

While emphasizing sportsmanship, clean play and football fundamentals were earning Shaw the admiration and respect of the media, opposing coaches and his own players, those qualities alone didn't directly correlate to wining games. For Buck Shaw the first half of the 1927 season was a nightmare in blue and white, Nevada's team colors at the time. Bound by Far Western Conference rules the Wolf Pack couldn't begin official organized practice until September 15. Athletic Director J.E. Martie did Shaw no favors in scheduling the season opener on September 24. (Despite the official starting date of September 15, Martie customarily scheduled the Wolf Pack's opener for the last weekend of September.) Nine days of practice were insufficient to effectively evaluate 85 football candidates, install the kicking game, and hone a starting 11 into a cohesive unit ready for 60 minutes of football. But an even greater obstacle was the fact that Nevada gave no athletic scholarships but continued scheduling opponents that did.

The previous spring Shaw's assistant, Bob Phelan, resigned his post to accept a coaching job in the East. Shaw hired former Notre Dame fullback Harry O'Boyle to replace him. Despite the best efforts of both men, Nevada's early games were a seemingly endless cavalcade of lost fumbles, intercepted passes, holding penalties, kicking game miscues and injuries to key personnel. The Wolf Pack looked inept and listless in a season opening loss to St. Ignatius, 19–0. Hopelessly outclassed the following week, Coach "Nibs" Price's California squad pummeled Nevada 54–0.

Nevada's third game of the year pitted them against Stanford at Palo Alto. Stanford's legendary coach, Pop Warner, thought so little of Shaw's charges that he delegated assistant coach "Tiny" Thornhill to oversee the anticipated rout while he traveled to Los Angeles to scout Stanford's next opponent, USC. Given his marching orders, Thornhill started and played the second team for most of the contest. The Cardinals' second-stringers had no trouble handling the mistake-prone Wolf Pack. Nevada, however, scored their first points of the season on a blocked Stanford punt that resulted in a safety. The final score read Stanford 21, Nevada 2.

The Wolf Pack looked better against Fresno State the next week but lost 10–7 when the Bulldog's Elwood Mitchell kicked a late game 15-yard field goal. Traveling to San

Francisco's Kezar Stadium on October 22, fans once again witnessed St. Mary's coach Slip Madigan's demonstrative antics as Nevada battled his Saints to a scoreless tie at half-time. However, St. Mary's doused any hopes of a Nevada upset by exploding for six touch-downs in the second half to win 38–0.

With five losses in five outings and the injury list the size of a bath towel, things looked abysmal for Nevada's Homecoming game with Santa Clara. Jake Lawlor, a 1927 team member, who later went on to coach Nevada's football, basketball and baseball teams, and serve as the school's athletic director from 1951 until 1969, recalled Buck Shaw's pregame remarks to the decimated squad.

"It looks like you people [the starting 11] will have to play the whole game. There won't be any substitutions unless some of you just have to come out of there. We just have too many injuries."[12]

The starting 11 rose to the challenge. Trailing 7–0 in the second quarter, Nevada halfback Jim Bailey made lemonade out of lemons on fourth down when he scooped up a low snap from center, faked a punt, then took off running. He only stopped when he crossed the Santa Clara goal line 65 yards later. Bailey's extra point boot tied the score at 7. Late in the game, a gutsy Nevada goal line stand preserved the 7–7 tie. The Wolf Pack's starting 11, including Jake Lawlor and his older brother Mike, played the entire game with no substitutions. Their valiant effort earned them the respect and admiration of the entire student body. With the 7–7 Santa Clara tie, the Wolf Pack seemed to hit its stride. Over the next two weeks Nevada defeated the College of the Pacific at Stockton 19–13, and the Young Men's Institute (YMI), 13–7. Coached by ex-Nevada football star Jimmy "Rabbit" Bradshaw, YMI's lineup consisted of former players who had graced the West Coast college gridirons a year or two earlier. Nevada's season, however, ended with a dull thud when Gonzaga thumped the out-classed Wolf Pack 41–6 at Spokane.

Nevada's disappointing two-win, five-loss and one-tie 1927 season was an omen of things to come.

* * *

On January 24, 1928, Shaw signed a contract to again serve as Nevada's head foot-ball coach—this time, however, with a new set of conditions. First, he asked to have com-plete control of the football squad. Managing the football team's training would be Shaw's sole responsibility, independent of the physical education department. Second, he would remain in Reno only for the playing months and no longer spend the second semester as a regular instructor in the physical education department. At the time, Shaw planned to enter business in Des Moines, Iowa, during the off-season, possibly in the bond busi-ness with his brother Jim, and return to Reno for the start of football. Third, his sal-ary of $2,400 would continue to be paid from the proceeds of the student body's annual Wolves' Frolic, not the physical education department. Finally, he would have no varsity assistant.[13]

Obviously, the contract's terms indicate Shaw believed that J.E. Martie, in his dual role of athletic director and physical education department chair, was making unwar-ranted and uninvited overtures into Shaw's daily coaching operation. A claim later Nevada coaches echoed. The ink was hardly dry on the contract when Martie told report-ers that the physical education department would hire a new faculty member who might help Shaw with his coaching.[14] Furthermore, being a part-time Reno resident strongly hinted that Shaw was not only considering pursuing endeavors outside of coaching, but perhaps leaving the profession altogether—a theme that persisted throughout his coaching days.

Despite the contract's terms, Shaw had a varsity assistant at the start of football. The physical education department hired one of Shaw's former Nevada players, Chester "Chet" Scranton, as a faculty member. Shaw was agreeable to Scranton serving as his assistant. Unfortunately, for both men, the 1928 schedule was just as daunting as the '27 slate, but Nevada had less talent and depth to cope with it. In the season opener at San Francisco's Kezar Stadium, St. Ignatius' "Grey Fog" blanked the Wolf Pack 12–0. Nevada then returned home to take a 32–7 trouncing at the hands of the University of Utah. The following week at Santa Clara, the undermanned Wolf Pack battled the Broncos to a scoreless first half before losing 19–6. Against the undefeated College of the Pacific in week four, the Wolf Pack had a chance to chalk up its first win, but Jim Bailey had his field goal attempt blocked with three minutes remaining and Pacific beat Nevada for the first time, 7–6. The Associated Press best described the gutsy Wolf Pack effort in their Homecoming game against St. Mary's on October 20: "A powerful St. Mary's football squad, outfought and outwitted in the first three quarters here today, sent forward passes speeding to all corners of the lot in the fourth period and defeated the Nevada Wolves 23–0."

When things seem like they can't get any worse, they always can. That's what happened to Nevada in the week leading up to the Cal-Davis game. Buck Shaw suspended team captain Jim Bailey and starting guard "Nig" Newton for breaking team training rules. Ironically, a pencil sketch portrait of Jim Bailey graced the sports page of the *Reno Gazette-Journal* just days earlier. Addressing the issue Shaw declared, "If any more instances of players breaking training rules come to my attention, those involved will receive the same treatment without respect to their position or experience."[15]

The university's board of athletic control took no action, declaring that Coach Shaw was well within his rights in suspending the two players. However, the board also said it would meet when the season was over on November 17 to thoroughly investigate the situation. Neither Bailey nor Newton made the trip to Sacramento to play in the 6–0 loss to Cal-Davis. Still in search of its first victory, Nevada suffered a heartbreaker the following week at Fresno. The Wolf Pack were nursing a 12–6 lead late in the game when Bulldog quarterback Joe Renna threw a 40-yard touchdown pass with only 90 seconds remaining. Fortunately, Renna's extra-point attempt skidded under the crossbar and Nevada escaped with a 12–12 tie.

The season concluded with Nevada's annual visit to Berkeley to take on the California Golden Bears. Knowing that Shaw's decimated Wolf Pack posed no real threat, Cal coach "Nibs" Price started his second team. Loaded with talent, Cal's second stringers could have started on most other squads. The return of Jim Bailey and "Nig" Newton to Nevada's lineup after serving their suspensions didn't help. Cal scored almost every way possible in amassing a 33–0 lead by the end of the third quarter. Coach Price stepped on the accelerator in the fourth by inserting the first team into the one-sided fray. Desperate and frustrated, and in a rare loss of composure, Nevada tackle Jake Lawlor slugged California guard Joe Pitto. A fistfight ensued and both combatants were ejected. With the ball on Nevada's 31-yard line and leading 54–0, Cal's first team halfback "Dutch" Clymer opted to rub salt in the Wolf Pack wounds. Dropping back to pass just as the gun sounded ending the game, Clymer lofted a long pass to teammate Van Tagen in the end zone to make the final score, California 60, Nevada 0. One wonders what words, if any, Shaw had for Bear coach "Nibs" Price during their post-game handshake. The Sagebrushers finished the '28 season winless, with seven losses and a tie.

Two days later, on November 19, Buck Shaw submitted his resignation as head coach of Nevada. He stated his intention of going to Des Moines to enter the bond business. Buck attributed the Nevada team's failure to win games to a lack of sufficient depth, stating the team had no reserve strength after a first team was picked. Shaw explained the major obstacle to Nevada's winning was the university's failure to offer athletic scholarships and offering few athletes a crack at on-campus jobs. Yet Nevada continued competing against schools where athletic scholarships played a vital role in securing outstanding athletes for those teams.[16]

Athletic Director J.E. Martie responded to Shaw's critique by saying that he did not favor establishing athletic scholarships at Nevada regardless of what happened on the football field. "As long as I am head of this department I will not favor men being paid to go to school."[17] He elaborated that he did not think it right to give scholarships to athletes when they had not earned them through their scholastic standing as well as their athletic record.

University officials declared that the school's finance control committee which consisted of Martie, Professor Charles Haseman and three student officers would have the final say in selecting a new coach. However, no new coach would be named until after an intense review of the entire athletic situation on campus. Shaw's resignation was a hot topic in Reno. The general consensus of most campus talk was that the Nevada players regretted Shaw's leaving. They felt that Shaw knew football from alpha to omega, and that the team's poor showing over the last two seasons was due to a lack of material.

On December 13, the *Reno Gazette-Journal* reported that the Nevada student body had voted to deny the granting of athletic scholarships and against helping to pay coaches' salaries in the future. After a two-month search, the Nevada student body and university officials announced the hiring of George Philbrook to succeed Shaw as head football coach. Philbrook, like Shaw, was a Notre Dame graduate who was coming to Nevada from Whittier College where he served as both head football and track coach.

The University of Nevada football program would remain in upheaval and discontent for years.

Philbrook coached the Reno school from 1929 through 1931, compiling a record of six wins, 15 losses and five ties. Clarence "Brick" Mitchell followed him from 1932 through 1935, achieving a record of 10 wins, 20 losses and three ties. Utterly frustrated with the Nevada situation, Mitchell told the *Reno Gazette-Journal* on December 20, 1934: "I will not resign, nor will I sign a new contract until conditions which have prohibited any coach in the past 20 years from making good are remedied." He further indicated that Nevada Athletic Director J.E. Martie was a perennial source of friction throughout the coaching regimes of Courtright, Erb, Shaw and George Philbrook.

In October 1938, discontent with the football program's operation came to a head when the Nevada players petitioned the school's regents to have athletic director Martie, head football coach Doug Dashiell and assistant coach Duane Keller resign. During the height of the furor, the *Reno Gazette-Journal* ran an article reflecting on Shaw's coaching tenure at the school. It opined that the 1927 Nevada schedule was entirely too ambitious for the material on hand, and that Buck had even less material in 1928 when the Wolf Pack went winless: "They were perhaps the most improperly equipped team ever to play football. At the end of the year Shaw resigned, thoroughly disgusted and glad to resign. He said he hoped he never saw another football."[18]

While coaching at Santa Clara in the mid–'30s, all Shaw would say about his four-year stint as Nevada's head coach was "It sure was a tough spot."[19]

Seeing no way around the demoralizing dissatisfaction within the football program, the university's board of regents canceled Nevada's last three games of the 1938 season. The entire athletic department was redesigned and the school hired James Aiken from Akron University to assume the newly created position of athletic director/head football coach. While Nevada football was undergoing this trauma, Buck Shaw was making national headlines as the head coach at Santa Clara University.

Shaw (second from left, top row) with his 1926 Nevada team. Assistant coach Bob Phelan (first on left, top row) was Shaw's Notre Dame teammate and Carlinville Eight cohort. Athletic Director J.E. Martie (second from right, top row) was a source of friction for Shaw and numerous other Wolf Pack coaches (courtesy Nevada University Reno Special Collections and Archives).

FIVE

The Apprentice Years
at Santa Clara

The Shaw family returned to Des Moines after Buck resigned as Nevada's football coach. Shaw also dove into the bond business. However, as the heavy snows blanketing Iowa's barren cornfields began to thaw, Shaw's coaching itch returned. Buck's decision to scratch the itch was fortuitous, for with the stock market crash and the Great Depression only months away, few folks would soon be in a position to buy bonds. With so many former Notre Dame teammates and alumni coaching on college campuses across America, there were bound to be opportunities for Shaw to again drape a lanyard and coaching whistle around his neck. The chance came sooner than expected.

Joe Boland, a former Golden Domer, resigned as Adam Walsh's line coach at Santa Clara University to accept the head coaching reins at St. Thomas College in St. Paul, Minnesota. Walsh, one of Notre Dame's heralded "Seven Mules," knew of Buck's All-American play at South Bend as well as his propensity for molding good linemen out of mediocre athletes while at Nevada. Believing that he and Shaw would collaborate as smoothly as devout nuns "working the beads" during a Rosary, Walsh encouraged Santa Clara officials to hire him as line coach. Buck didn't need much persuading. On April 11, 1929, Santa Clara officially announced Shaw's hiring.

However, while Walsh welcomed working with Shaw, he wasn't thrilled about another season at Santa Clara. Two months earlier Walsh had applied to replace his former Notre Dame teammate, Tom Lieb, as line coach at the University of Wisconsin. Lieb was returning to his alma mater to join Knute Rockne's staff. When Bay Area reporters queried him on the matter, Walsh candidly admitted that he'd accept a better coaching position if one were offered.[1] Despite media rumblings about his future at the school, Walsh conducted a productive spring practice throughout March and April.

On May 8, what many anticipated happened. Walsh resigned as Santa Clara's head football coach. What no one anticipated, however, was Walsh's leaving to accept the position as line coach at Yale. This set a precedent at the Ivy League institution, for previously it had only hired alumni to serve as football coaches. Concurrently, Santa Clara announced that Buck Shaw would still serve as an assistant coach. Ten days later, Santa Clara hired Maurice "Clipper" Smith as its new head coach. Yet another Golden Domer, Smith was thrilled that his old buddy and former teammate—whom he'd nicknamed "Adonis"—would serve on his staff.

Since leaving South Bend in 1921, Smith had spent four years coaching football at Columbia College in Portland, Oregon, which later became the University of Portland; and another four as head coach of Gonzaga University in Spokane, Washington, where he amassed a record of 23 wins, nine losses and five ties. "Clipper" arrived at Santa Clara on June 2, but not before announcing his engagement to Miss Charlotte Louis Jones of Spokane. Smith had earned reputation as a stickler for discipline as evidenced by an event that occurred the previous season. While his Gonzaga squad was en route to Portland one of the regulars—a key man—broke training. At the next station, 100 miles from Portland, Clipper bought a one-way ticket back to Spokane and gave it to the errant player.[2] Smith also brought a clipboard of new ideas with him to Santa Clara. First, he invited the public to visit practices and announced that except on rare occasions, when secrecy was vital, the public was always welcome. Breaking with tradition, he opted not to have a team captain, declaring: "Elect a man a captain and you lose a good football player. The psychological effect is too great in the wrong direction."[3] Instead, team captains would be named on a game-to-game basis, and after the season the team would elect an honorary captain based upon the season's play. In another first, Smith taught a law class at the university.

When a sportswriter asked, "Do you plan to practice law?" Smith replied, "You never can tell when I may have to,"[4] an answer that showed Smith had no illusions about the stability of the coaching profession.

Arriving from Des Moines on September 16, "Adonis" immediately set to work. Smith and Shaw met daily establishing plans and tactics for the upcoming season. Joining their meetings was George Barsi, who had played halfback for the Broncos the previous three seasons. Barsi would serve as freshman coach. Nearly 100 candidates reported for the first day of practice. In an era when that many candidates turned out, cuts were gradually made to trim the squad to a more workable number. Smith, however, announced another novelty. He would keep all 97 players on the team, explaining, "Think of the experience they'll gain from chalk talks and scrimmaging. It will fit them for battle next year."[5]

In the vernacular of the '20s and '30s, the term "Goofs" applied to non-scholarship football players, who—while on the team—never made the traveling squad, rarely dressed for home games or lettered. They did, however, take daily poundings as scout team players scrimmaging the first team. The Broncos carried a lot of Goofs on its '29 squad. On college campuses today, such players still exist—though "Goofs" has been replaced by the vividly descriptive appellation of "Slap Dicks."

In the weeks of practice leading to the season opener against California, Buck continually drilled his charges on both the tackling dummy and blocking sled. When not training the backs on fundamentals, Maurice Smith was choreographing a new backfield shift. Called both the "Clipper" or the more regal "King Alphonso" Shift, it began in the huddle, with the seven linemen aligned in a straight line with their backs to the line of scrimmage and three to four yards from the football. Three backs, also in a straight line and further back from the football, faced the linemen from a distance of two yards. The quarterback, who called the signals, positioned himself between the lines, from which he gave the play and snap count. When ready, he waved his arms to break the huddle. On this signal, the seven linemen performed a military whirl and double-timed it to the line of scrimmage on the quarterback's cadence. The shift's aim was to speed up the offense while concealing the formation until just before the ball was snapped. The shift caught the fancy of fans and sportswriters. Many coaches believed it similar to the shift Coach Chick Meehan used at New York University, but more complicated and flamboyant in its mechanics.[6] While showy and impressive, the extraordinary amount of time invested in mastering the "Clipper Shift" led Smith to jettison it after a couple of seasons.

Four games into the 1929 season, Santa Clara had defeated St. Ignatius 20–7 and West Coast Army 20–0, while losing to California 27–6 and the Olympic Club 20–0. To Pacific Coast football fans the annual "Big Game" was, and still is, the matchup between the University of California and Stanford. Clipper Smith and Buck Shaw were now introduced to what West Coast fans tabbed the "Little Big Game"—the gridiron contest between Santa Clara and St. Mary's. Today neither school fields a football team, but both schools were gridiron powers in the 1930s. Both are Catholic schools. Santa Clara is run by the Jesuits, and St. Mary's by the Christian Brothers. In the '20s and '30s, both were also all-male institutions. Santa Clara was founded in 1851, St. Mary's in 1863. From 1922 through 1928 the two schools had met annually, with the Gaels of St. Mary's winning six of their seven hard-fought encounters.

In 1929, the annual battle became more than an internecine struggle of the Catholic Church. It became personal. As previously mentioned, St. Mary's coach "Slip" Madigan and "Clipper" Smith and "Buck" Shaw had been friends and teammates at Notre Dame in 1919. All three blocked on the same offensive line and had learned the Notre Dame System at the knee of the revered Knute Rockne. Now, ten years later, they were squaring off as opposing coaches. The scenario enthralled the Bay Area media and fans alike.

Maurice "Clipper" Smith pictured here during his coaching years at Gonzaga University, succeeded Adam Walsh as Stanford's head coach in 1929 (courtesy Gonzaga University Archives and Special Collections Department, Rg_1925_1926_1927).

The "three amigos" and their respective squads met at Kezar Stadium before 35,000 fans on Sunday, November 10 (so much for the Sabbath being a day of rest). If any Gael or Bronco player turned a cheek that afternoon, it was probably because it was on the receiving end of a right cross. The "Clipper" or "King Alphonso" Shift made little dent on St. Mary's defense. The game's decisive play came late in the fourth quarter, when the Gaels' Mack Stennett connected on a 62-yard touchdown pass to Bud Toscani, giving St. Mary's a 6–0 win. The gritty, "balls out" struggle was a prelude to the fierce, tightly contested battles that characterized the "Little Big Game" for Shaw's remaining years at Santa Clara.

Santa Clara's major win that season came on the heels of a team tragedy the following week. On November 12, one of the team's best linemen, Hank Louma, underwent surgery for peritonitis, which resulted from an appendectomy performed the previous week. For several days after the operation, he drifted in and out of consciousness before dying on Friday, November 15. Whether Louma's death inspired his teammates to strive for greater heights is unknown, but the Broncos upset Pop Warner's heavily favored Stanford Cardinals the next day, 13–7.

After defeating Loyola at Los Angeles' Wrigley Field 37–0, Santa Clara's coaches and players boarded the SS *Maui* and steamed to Hawaii on December 4 for the season's finale against the University of Hawaii. The two schools met at King's Street Honolulu Stadium, an edifice neighbors endearingly called the "termite palace." Introducing the "Clipper Shift" to the islanders, Santa Clara blanked the Deans (as they were then nicknamed) 25–0 to finish the season with five wins and three losses. Shortly after the team returned home, a tragedy erased the Hawaiian trip's pleasant memories. On January 2, the coaches and team attended the funeral of Bronco halfback Johnny Casanova, who died on New Year's Eve from injuries sustained in an automobile accident on Christmas night.

Introducing the "Clipper Shift" to the Hawaiian Islands, an unidentified Santa Clara back carries the ball in the Broncos' 25–0 win over the University of Hawaii in 1929 (courtesy Archives and Special Collections, Santa Clara University).

Johnny was the younger brother of Len Casanova, a star halfback at Santa Clara—who played an integral role in defeating Shaw's 1926 Nevada team. Len Casanova later served as head coach at Santa Clara from 1946 through 1949. However, he is mostly remembered as the highly successful head coach at Oregon from 1951 through 1966.

* * *

Because his assistant's job at Santa Clara was not full-time, Buck had to find off-season employment to feed his family. With the country buried under the economic avalanche of the Great Depression, this was no easy task. Fortunately, Buck found work with the Standard Oil Company, a job he would keep for six years. The job's flexible hours permitted Buck to attend all of Santa Clara's spring practices.

Always looking for new ways to generate public interest in Santa Clara football, Clipper Smith introduced the annual "Bronco Round-Up." Held on a weekend after the final day of spring practice in late April, the Round-Up was a free outdoor athletic show the likes of which Santa Clara had never seen. Its inaugural year, the day began with a "bronc-busting" event featuring popular local cowboys. The Western theme continued with mounted riders engaging in a stake race. Events then became sport-specific, with Santa Clara players competing in punting for both placement and distance, a fumble recovery contest, one-on-one blocking by position, tackling and blocking demonstrations, a 120-yard obstacle run, and a four-mile run by position. After the four-mile participants caught their breath, Smith divided the squad into two teams that competed in a 30-minute scrimmage dramatically billed as the "blood and iron" football game. The day's final event was a greased pig chase followed by a barbecue in the campus gardens for students, alumni, faculty and guests. While the events changed, the annual pigskin Round-Up drew thousands of spectators during Smith's years at Santa Clara.[7]

The Broncos opened the 1930 season with a 27–0 win over Cal-Davis followed by two losses—a 19–7 loss to powerhouse California, and a 20–0 defeat at the hands of Pop Warner's Stanford Cardinals. For Buck Shaw personally, the season's most challenging contest came when Santa Clara traveled to Reno to battle Nevada. No matter the circumstances of one's departure, returning to coach against one's former school is a mixed bag emotionally. Yes, one wants to win, but one can't forget the fine people one worked with and coached at the previous institution. Nor can one dismiss the opportunity and paychecks the former school provided. Shaw undoubtedly experienced similar feelings on October 11, when he once again set foot on Mackay Field.

Matching wits across the field from Smith and Shaw was Coach George Philbrook. Another former Notre Dame lineman, Philbrook had roomed with Knute Rockne as a student in 1910. That same year the University of Michigan canceled its scheduled football game with Notre Dame, claiming that Philbrook and another Domer were ineligible because they were in their seventh year of playing college ball. The claim was true. Philbrook had indeed played four years of college ball in Washington, three at Whitman College, before enrolling at Notre Dame. Philbrook was in his third year at the South Bend campus when Michigan cried foul.[8] A superb athlete, Philbrook competed in both the shot and discus at the 1912 Olympics. While Buck didn't know Philbrook, he had coached and appreciated many of the Sagebrushers on the opposing sideline, including Jake Lawlor, who now served as Philbrook's line coach.

Santa Clara was favored to win, but several key Bronco players were still hobbling from physical poundings they sustained at both Cal and Stanford. Nevada had lost to Utah but looked significantly improved in a tie against Brigham Young. Despite numerous turnovers by both teams, Nevada—hoping to impress if not beat their former coach—gave a gutsy effort. Neither team seriously threatened the other's end zone and the game ended in a scoreless tie. From a psychological perspective, it may have been the best mutual outcome for both Shaw and his former Wolf Pack players. Obviously, Clipper Smith and Santa Clara didn't view it that way.

Focusing on line play for nearly two weeks before meeting the Olympic Club paid dividends, as the Broncos handled the strong Flying-O squad 14–2. In that contest the Bronco backfield looked better than it had all season. Speaking of looks, to protect his broken nose fullback Bob Stockton wore a specially designed helmet that gave him the appearance of a masked Hannibal Lecter.[9] The win restored the players' confidence and raised their spirits for the upcoming "Little Big Game" against archrival St. Mary's. They'd need more than confidence as Slip Madigan brought another strong Gael squad into Kezar Stadium.

Clipper Smith introduced the Bronco Roundup to promote Santa Clara football during his coaching tenure at the school (courtesy Archives and Special Collections, Santa Clara University).

Nearly 45,000 fans saw St. Mary's take a 7–0 lead on a 48-yard touchdown pass from Mack Stennett to Dick Boyd. Undaunted, the Broncos retaliated with a long drive of their own. With only 45 seconds remaining in the half and the crowd going berserk, Santa Clara halfback Chris Machado tossed a pass toward Gil Dowd in the end zone. Unfortunately, Gael defender Bob Patterson stepped in front of Dowd, intercepted the pass, and returned it 96 yards for a St. Mary's touchdown. Neither team scored in the second half.

The Gaels' 13–0 victory was their seventh consecutive win in the brutally physical series. Game hero Bob Patterson emerged from the contest with a fractured ankle. Someone's cleat caught Santa Clara's Al Tassi, leaving a severe gash across his forehead and down the side of his face. Playing with a blood-soaked bandage around his head, Tassi was the afternoon's leading tackler. When he finally exited the game, the crowd gave the bloodied Tassi a standing ovation. Bronco scatback Chris Machado unknowingly sustained a life-threatening injury during the contest but continued playing. After the game, the gritty Machado was hospitalized with a ruptured spleen and bruised kidney.[10] His season over, he spent two weeks recuperating in St. Mary's Hospital.

The Broncos rebounded from the tough loss by shutting out their last three opponents of the season: the West Coast Marines 58–0, Loyola 32–0 and the University of San Francisco 14–0. Finishing the season with five wins, five losses and a tie, Santa Clara was building a program to be reckoned with in the future.

* * *

The Shaw family enjoyed living in Northern California and on March 5, 1931, Buck happily signed another contract to again coach football at Santa Clara. However, his joy turned to heartbreak on March 31, when he learned of Knute Rockne's death. The tragic news stunned Buck, Clipper, college football, and the entire nation. The famed 43-year-old Notre Dame coach was killed when the Fokker Trimotor plane in which he was a passenger crashed in a remote Kansas cornfield. The crash killed all eight people on board. Catching the flight in Kansas City, Rockne was en route to Hollywood, where he had recently signed a contract with Universal studios to make several two-reel talkies about football. Rockne was to meet with production people to finalize the start of filming.

Presidents Hoover and Coolidge, as well as King Haakon VII of Rockne's native Norway, all eulogized America's renowned coach. Telegrams of condolence poured in from the likes of Gen. Douglas MacArthur, Secretary of War Patrick J. Hurley, Will Rogers, Lou Gehrig, Babe Ruth and Jack Dempsey. New York City Mayor Jimmy Walker interrupted his return trip from California to the Big Apple to pay his respects to the grieving Rockne family, who received thousands of telegrams and phone calls of condolence. With pictures of the plane's twisted and scattered wreckage splashed across the front pages of the nation's newspapers, the tragedy spawned banner headlines. For weeks, sports columnists wrote about Rockne's life—lauding his impact on American youth and society.

Numerous schools that had battled Rockne's Notre Dame squads also paid tribute to the native Norwegian. Purdue University President Edward C. Elliot ordered the university's campus flag to be flown at half staff declaring: "It is a tragic climax of an extraordinary career. Knute Rockne was more than an athletic coach. He was a great leader of men, whose influence was nationwide. A genius has passed from us. We at Purdue are stunned."[11]

Georgia Tech coach Bill Alexander praised his coaching adversary, "Rockne was above all else a sportsman in the truest sense of the word. His life is an example that present day youth would do well to model."[12]

Thomas S. Gates, President of the University of Pennsylvania, professed: "His passing removes from the field of intercollegiate athletics a man whose ability, high ideals, capacity for leadership and influence for good served to justly earn for him the respect and affection of all those with whom he came in contact."[13]

His former players now coaching in the Bay Area were crestfallen. St. Mary's coach Slip Madigan told the *San Francisco Examiner*, "Rockne has joined the immortal George Gipp. At Notre Dame we used to say of Gipp, 'Everything he touched turned to gold—he was the perfect football player.' Rockne has joined the immortals. Everything he touched turned to gold. He was the master strategist, the great psychologist."[14]

At Santa Clara, Clipper Smith and Buck Shaw released the following joint statement: "He [Rockne] was as near to us as any member of our families would be. His success was our success. We tried as all Notre Dame men do, to emulate his deeds and his success."[15]

Notre Dame assistant coaches Hunk Anderson and Jack Chevigny took on the grim task of traveling to Kansas to retrieve Rockne's body. The loss of his best friend and mentor left Hunk Anderson so distraught that he lost nearly 40 pounds over the next three months.[16] Funeral rites for Rockne were held at Sacred Heart Church in South Bend on April 4, 1931. The church could only accommodate 1,500 of the 4,000 mourners who came to pay their respects. After the service all 4,000 followed the bronze casket, which was covered with a Notre Dame football blanket, to Highland Cemetery where Rockne was laid to eternal rest.

On the evening of April 8, Clipper Smith and Buck Shaw gave a tribute to Rockne before the Santa Clara alumni association. The next morning both the Santa Clara and St. Mary's football teams and coaches attended a solemn high mass for the soul of Knute Rockne at the Old St. Mary's Church in San Francisco.

* * *

Like most college teams, Santa Clara lost key players to graduation from its 1930 squad. Unfortunately, during the off-season several solid underclassmen became academic casualties while another handful left school due to the realities of the Great Depression—namely, no money. Although roughly three dozen players matriculated to the varsity from the freshman squad, when reporters asked Buck Shaw about the team's chances for the upcoming season he could only respond, "Fair."

The Broncos kicked off the 1931 campaign against California at Berkeley. Bill Ingram had replaced "Nibs" Price, who resigned as head coach after the '30 season. Ingram had played football at the Naval Academy and returned to his alma mater as head coach in 1926 to lead the Middies to an undefeated season, with the only blemish on the record being a 21–21 tie with Army at Chicago's Soldier Field before 111,000 spectators. Ingram first met Knute Rockne that weekend. In a rare coaching faux pas, Rockne had sent his undefeated and heavily favored Irish squad to Pittsburgh to face Carnegie Tech under the guidance of assistant coaches Hunk Anderson and Tommy Mills (Buck's old coach at Creighton), while he scouted Notre Dame's future opponent, Navy. Furthermore, because Rockne had contracted the previous year to watch and write an article on the '26 Army-Navy game for his syndicated column, he felt obligated to attend.[17] Skibo coach Wally Steffen made psychological hay of Rockne's absence by ranting to his squad that the famed Irish coach regarded Carnegie Tech so lightly that he didn't even deem it necessary to be in attendance. The fired-up Skibos responded by playing their best game of the year and upset the Irish 19–0. Despite the egg on his face, Rockne graciously telephoned

Carnegie athletic director Clarence "Buddy" Overend that evening to congratulate him on Tech's victory.[18]

As Navy and Notre Dame battled over the next four years, Rockne and Ingram became close friends. When Ingram was one of numerous candidates interested in Cal's coaching vacancy in 1931, Rockne's glowing recommendation won him the job. Only a month before his tragic death Rockne visited the Berkeley campus while touring as a pitchman for Studebaker Motors. Addressing Cal's student body Rockne declared, "Bill Ingram, a Prince of Blood, and one of the best coaches, should please everyone at California but the alumni, and no one will please them."[19]

On March 31, 1931, the day Rockne was killed, Ingram and Stanford's Pop Warner flew from San Francisco to Glendale, California, looking forward to reuniting with Rockne that evening. When informed of the coach's death after stepping off the plane, the ashen-faced Ingram replied, "Knute Rockne can't be dead. I don't believe it."[20] Ingram remained silent for 10 minutes before offering, "The best friend I ever had. Without doubt Rock was the greatest figure of intercollegiate athletics. He leaves a great work unfinished, for as much as he had done for football, he had greater plans to bring it even to higher standards."[21]

The Bay Area media, harboring national championship aspirations for the Golden Bears, soon tagged the popular Ingram with several titles including "Navy" Bill, "Sailor" Bill and "Barnacle" Bill. Santa Clara gave "Navy" Bill's squad all it could handle in the season opener, drawing first blood when Doug Murray tackled Cal quarterback Hank Schaldach for a safety. Santa Clara's minuscule 2–0 lead looked like it might hold up until Schaldach scored on a two-yard run with seven minutes remaining, giving Cal a 6–2 win. A disgruntled Ingram's post-game comments could not have pleased either Smith or Shaw. "I almost feel as if we had been licked. Santa Clara has a nice football club—and it played a brilliant game. But a team like that should not be serious for California."[22]

The Broncos had a similar encounter against Pop Warner's Stanford squad the next week. After a scoreless first half, Stanford's depth asserted itself in the second stanza. The Cardinals mounted several threatening drives only to see each fizzle deep in Santa Clara territory. Finally, in the fourth quarter, Stanford captain Harry Hillman's four-yard touchdown run gave Stanford a 6–0 win. A bright spot for Santa Clara was Joe Paglia's punting. Just as he had done the previous week against Cal, Paglia placed several "coffin corner" punts inside Stanford's 10-yard line.

Santa Clara broke into the win column the following week by thumping the San Diego Marines 34–0. They then defeated the Olympic Club 19–6, with Broncos Fritz Danz and Johnny McGuire each scoring a "pick-six" touchdown. Playing West Coast Army at San Francisco's Seal Stadium on a rainy Friday night, the steady downpour made the field a slippery mess and an equalizer as the local Presidio "Jar Heads" battled the heavily favored Broncos to a scoreless tie.

The game had a painful outcome for Santa Clara fullback and punter Joe Paglia. As it turned out, the Seals Stadium field had been lined with lime. The chemical reaction of lime with water from Paglia's drenched jersey left his back itching and burning. With his back looking like someone had taken a steam iron to it from his hips to his shoulders, Paglia spent several days in a hospital bed lying on his stomach. Although doctors and coaches advised him not to play, nothing could keep him from lining up against St. Mary's.

A few days before the annual Little Big Game the *New York Sun* published the All-Time Notre Dame football team. Buck Shaw was selected as first team tackle and

Clipper Smith as a second team guard. The *Sun's* columnist wrote, "Buck Shaw was a Greek god come back to life." He wrote of Clipper Smith, "Morrie Smith, who weighed only 155 pounds exemplified the power of mind over matter. Smith was as tough as a whale bone."[23] Santa Clara fans hoped the *Sun's* plaudits for the coaches might inspire the Broncos to whip the Gaels.

One discovers a great deal about oneself playing football. One's strength, courage, durability and unselfishness are tested, often in practice as well as in games. One's race, ethnicity, popularity, economic and social status are irrelevant. What counts is one's innate ability, heart and toughness. In the '20s and '30s the Little Big Game was a showcase for these invaluable traits of the human spirit.

Over 55,000 enthusiastic fans turned out on November 1, 1931, to watch the Little Big Game—a record-breaking crowd for a Kezar Stadium event. Fans witnessed another St. Mary's–Santa Clara nail-biter. Although a fog crept into the stadium shortly after the opening kick-off, making it cold and uncomfortable, not a single fan exited the arena before the game's end. Each team threw a touchdown pass making the halftime score 7–7.

The man the press now called "Diamond" Joe Paglia was playing in agony, grimacing both when tackling and being tackled. In the third quarter Paglia recovered a fumble on St. Mary's 14-yard line. Two plays later Diamond Joe carried the ball into the end zone and kicked his second extra-point, giving the Broncos a 14–7 lead. After tackling a Gael runner on St. Mary's next possession, Paglia didn't get up. Knocked cold, Paglia, at least momentarily, felt neither his blistered back nor the two broken ribs he sustained on the play. Carried from the field on a stretcher, Paglia was taken by ambulance to the hospital. At that point coaches Smith and Shaw were more concerned about Paglia's welfare than the contest's outcome. Soon after, the Gaels' Bud Toscani ran 48 yards for a touchdown, and Herc Fletcher's extra-point kick tied the score at 14. The first 10 minutes of the fourth quarter became a punting duel. However, Santa Clara's replacement punter, "Lefty" Powers, couldn't kick as far as the injured Paglia. With each exchange of punts, the Broncos lost ground. With five minutes remaining St. Mary's took possession at Santa Clara's 33-yard line and began a time-killing drive, culminating with Charley Baird bulling two yards to paydirt. The final score: St. Mary's 21, Santa Clara 14.

In the post-game locker room, an effusive Clipper Smith gushed, "That's the greatest St. Mary's team I have seen! We had the jump on them, we might have won from a team with less power and courage. But they came rolling back, overcame our leads and won. It's a great team, and one that too much cannot be said about. We gave everything we had.... Theirs is a really great eleven."[24]

Without "Diamond Joe" Paglia the following week, Santa Clara blanked Coach Tom Lieb's undefeated Loyola squad 6–0 under the lights at Los Angeles' Wrigley Field. Returning to Kezar Stadium the next Sunday, the Broncos faced the University of San Francisco in a charity game. Behind Bob Kleckner's 120 rushing yards, the Grey Fog earned a 7–0 upset win over the heavily favored Broncos —its first-ever win over Santa Clara. After expenses, the schools' split the gate profits with St. Patrick's shelter for destitute men; with thousands riding the rails during the Depression seeking work, there were plenty of down-and-out men sleeping on Bay Area park benches.

On Friday morning, November 21, Clipper's crew departed by train for the first leg of an intersectional trip to Cheyenne to play the University of Wyoming Cowboys. Unbeknownst to coaches Smith and Shaw, the Wild West was still alive and kicking in Wyoming. Only a month earlier at the university campus in Laramie, three masked men overpowered a campus security guard at three o'clock in the morning, gagged him and bound him to a chair, and blew the business office's safe with explosives. The desperadoes made off with $2,600, the receipts from both the Homecoming dance and football game against Utah State. Earlier that spring Bay Area sportswriters had questioned the sagacity of Santa Clara scheduling a late season game in windswept Wyoming. The scribes' words were prescient. The temperature was 0 degrees and the Warren Bowl field was snow-covered when the Broncos stepped off the train from sunny California hours before kickoff. For many Santa Clara players, it was the first time they had seen snow. Few spectators braved the bitter cold to witness the contest, and those who did spent most of the game huddled around large cans with kindling fires in them to keep warm. Donning gloves, the Broncos seemed undaunted by the numbing cold and controlled the action from start to finish. The game's only score came when Santa Clara's Johnny Beckrich skirted around end for a five-yard touchdown.

Leaving the Equality State with a 6–0 win, the Broncos headed south to New Orleans to thaw out. There they would play still another Wolf Pack team, Loyola of New Orleans, on Thanksgiving. Clark Shaughnessy, who would gain national acclaim in eight years for reviving the T formation, coached the Jesuit school. With the Crescent City's weather more accommodating than frigid Wyoming, Santa Clara prevailed in a nip and tuck contest 13–7. Johnny Beckrich scored both Bronco touchdowns. It was quite a week for the sophomore, who accounted for all three Santa Clara touchdowns during the two-game road trip. The win gave Santa Clara a final record of five wins, four losses and a tie for the '31 season.

* * *

Under Smith and Shaw Santa Clara's football program continued to improve. Proof came in the 1932 season opener at California. "Sailor" Bill Ingram's statement after Cal eked out a 6–2 win over the Broncos the year before—"that a team like that [Santa Clara] should not be serious for California" —rang hollow as Clipper's club blanked "Navy" Bill's boys 12–0 before 50,000 stunned fans. Anton Judnich's nine-yard touchdown jump pass to Johnny Beckrich followed by Frank Sobrero's five-yard scoring pass to Frank "Hands" Slavich, provided the kill shots. In the post-game handshake, Ingram, forgetting his previous year's declaration regarding Santa Clara's athletic prowess, told Smith, "You had the best team today and if we are going to lose, I'm glad it was to Santa Clara."

Humble in victory and perhaps hoping to apply salve to Ingram's wounded ego, Smith replied, "I'm glad we played you today and not two weeks hence."[25]

In the victor's locker room the Broncos were elated, yet restrained. Among the congratulatory back-slapping was a sense of relief and satisfaction at their accomplishment. After all, the Broncos had previously dropped nine straight games to Cal. Santa Clara seemed to be on the verge of earning its place among the Pacific Coast football powers. Clipper Smith certainly hoped so. However, as the adage says, "if wishes were horses beggars would ride." Events over the next two weeks demonstrated that the Broncos hadn't yet scaled that mountain.

On October 1, Santa Clara visited Eugene to face an up-and-coming Oregon team in their inaugural gridiron meeting. Looking lethargic early, the visitors failed to gain a first down in the game's first 30 minutes, while Oregon rang up seven points. In the second half, Santa Clara outplayed the hosts but failed to score in a disappointing 7–0 loss. Calamity struck the Broncos early the following week at Stanford. On Santa Clara's first possession the Cardinals' Bill Bates blocked Joe Paglia's punt and recovered it on the two-yard line. From there Harry Hillman plunged into the end zone giving Stanford an early 7–0 lead. Santa Clara never overcame that initial blow. Stanford added a fourth-quarter touchdown for a 14–0 win. Santa Clara rebounded the next week by blanking the San Diego Marines 32–0. The Little Big Game was next.

Stories heralding the upcoming battle and advertisements as to where to purchase game tickets filled the sports pages the week of the contest. On Wednesday before kick-off, Clipper Smith predicted, "If we can muster the same heads up spirit on the field that we had against California, we should have practically an even chance."[26] At Thursday night's media meeting the psychological gamesmanship was in earnest. St. Mary's assistant coach Red Strader predicted that Santa Clara would win because several Gael starters were battling the flu. During his turn at the microphone, Bronco assistant Al Ruffo claimed St. Mary's would prevail because of their superior depth, size and experience. The so-called experts had St. Mary's as a 2 to 1 favorite.

Such prominent coaching dignitaries as UCLA's Bill Spaulding, USC's Howard Jones and Stanford's Pop Warner sat among the 59,000 fans at Kezar Stadium. It appeared as if Clipper Smith's desire to see Santa Clara regain the "heads up" spirit that it had demonstrated against Cal was materializing as the Broncos surged to a 13–0 halftime lead.

The Gaels returned for the second half with a look of sheer determination and fire in their bellies. Always the ultimate showman, Slip Madigan dramatically read a Walt Whitman poem to his squad in the halftime locker room, "There will never be any more perfection than there is now."[27] Taking a page from his mentor Knute Rockne, the fiery Madigan besought his squad to win the game for Harry Lawler, an 18-year-old St. Mary's student with aspirations of becoming a varsity football player who suffered a fatal injury playing intramural tackle football a week earlier.[28] Theatrics aside, the Gaels needed a break and they got a big one early in the third quarter when Carl Jorgenson recovered a Bronco fumble at Santa Clara's five-yard line. Three plays later Angel Brovelli bulled into the end zone. Jorgenson's extra-point kick narrowed the score to 13–7. St. Mary's later caught Santa Clara's defense off guard when Jack Baat connected on a 42-yard pass to Fred Canrinus for a first down at the Bronco three-yard line. Gael Al Nichelini then hurdled into the end zone to tie the score at 13. The Danish-born Jorgensen calmly kicked the extra-point to give the Gaels a 14–13 lead.

On the St. Mary's sideline an ecstatic Slip Madigan danced and gestured wildly as throngs of fans yelled in unison, "Sit Down Slip!" Fans had repeatedly yelled the chant throughout the Gaels' '32 season. The inspired Gaels had the momentum and were determined to keep it. The nail-biting fourth quarter was scoreless, and St. Mary's prevailed for the ninth consecutive year of the spirited rivalry, 14–13.

In his October 31 column for the *San Francisco Examiner* Pacific Coast football official Herb Dana lauded, "Down there on the field we saw plenty of that old football fight—vicious blocking and tackling—all of it clean." He then added, "It was a great football game in every way—real competition, hard and clean—one of the great reasons this game is the classic that it is."

In the same paper sportswriter Curley Grieve wrote of the epic battle, "If I heard one I heard a hundred say, on the way out, 'The greatest game yet.' Maybe so. Last year's Little Big Game was the very same sort of lung-spoiler. Little Big Games are that way. At least here's one football game that doesn't disappoint the crowds."

During his team's post-game locker room celebration Slip Madigan exclaimed, "Our men played the greatest game of their lives in the second half, realizing the pitch I have been expecting all season," then added, "Santa Clara had us on the run in the first half. It was a tough game for them to lose."[29]

Madigan's last remark was a colossal understatement. The loss devastated Santa Clara. Sniffles stifling tears intermittently escaped from the bowed heads of the vanquished but gallant Bronco players. From the miasma of heartbreak permeating the loser's locker room a solemn, but gracious Clipper Smith stepped outside to tell reporters, "That deceptive pass to the right [Baat to Canrinus] caught us off stride. The Gaels are a great team to come back like that. You never know if you have them beaten or not."[30]

For Smith and assistants Shaw and Ruffo, enduring the heartbreaking loss over the next 24 hours almost equated to losing a beloved family member. Yet, life goes on. The grieving persisted until Clipper blew the whistle for Monday's practice. The season still had four games to play. To the coaching staff's credit and attesting to the team's overall resilience, Santa Clara won them all. They blanked the College of the Pacific, 27–0; the University of San Francisco, 7–0; and the Olympic Club 12–0. In the 1932 season's finale at Los Angeles they defeated Loyola 18–6, for a record of six wins and three losses.

* * *

Although Santa Clara experienced considerable controversy in 1933, the season kicked off on a high note by again defeating Bill Ingram's California Golden Bears before 60,000 fans at Berkeley's Memorial Stadium. Played on a stifling hot day in late September, the Broncos took a 7–0 lead into the locker room at halftime. Joe Paglia's "coffin corner" punts kept the Bears pinned deep in their own territory for the entire half. During intermission a concerned Smith wondered if his starting 11 could hold on for another 30 minutes in the afternoon's draining heat. Turning to Buck Shaw he asked for his assistant's thoughts on the second half. Shaw calmly answered, "Start the second string this half."

Stunned, Smith asked in disbelief, "But you have said repeatedly that they're not ready!"

A smiling Shaw replied, "Start them."

The dubious head coach acquiesced. To Smith's astonishment the second team played lights out, holding Sailor Bill's Bears scoreless in the third quarter. Repeatedly dropping Cal's ball carriers for losses was a 148-pound second-string phenom named Jack Idiart. Re-entering the game at the start of the fourth quarter, the revived first-stringers picked up where the second-string left off in blanking the Bears to give Santa Clara a 7–0 win. In a post-game interview Clipper heralded both the second-stringers and Buck Shaw for the victory.[31]

On September 27 *San Francisco Examiner* sports columnist Curley Grieve wrote: "Santa Clara has arrived—latest big league threat for any team on the Pacific Coast. For the first time in its history, Santa Clara will enter the Stanford conflict no worse than an even bet to win." Perhaps, but a strong Stanford team now coached by Tiny Thornhill (Pop Warner left to become head coach at Temple) and bad luck awaited Santa Clara at Palo Alto. Trailing the Cardinals 7–0, a controversial call negated what appeared to be a 70-yard scoring pass from Santa Clara's Frank Sobrero to Wes McCoy. Officials ruled that the pass clipped Bronco Ike Britschgi's helmet before McCoy caught it, making it illegal. Any luck the Broncos had that day was all bad, for later in the game Sobrero tossed a beautiful pass to Jim Arnerich in the end zone. Arnerich grasped it momentarily before teammate Al Dowd inadvertently plowed into him knocking the ball to the turf. Officials ruled it an incomplete pass and Stanford held on to win 7–0.

Shaking with anger and ashen-looking, Clipper Smith railed to reporters in a post-game interview: "I thought we were entitled to two touchdowns: the first when McCoy caught that forward pass and ran to a touchdown only to have the officials rule that a Santa Clara man had touched the ball before McCoy. I thought that a Stanford man touched the ball before McCoy got his hands on it. The second was when Arnerich caught a pass in the end zone. I thought that should have been ruled a touchdown."[32]

When a reporter tried to console the distraught coach by offering that one game doesn't make a season Smith barked, "I don't care what becomes of me. That is just the way I feel for I don't concede Stanford anything." Another reporter attempting to get the crazed coach's mind off the loss asked Smith what he thought of California upsetting St. Mary's that very afternoon, 14–13. Taking a moment to absorb the news Smith lamented, "I just can't believe it … but I'm too sick to fully realize it because I still think we should have won today's game."[33]

The only elixir for renewing Smith's spirits was winning the next game. That didn't happen. Santa Clara traveled south where they lost to a superbly talented and determined San Diego Marine squad 14–7. Returning to Kezar Stadium, Santa Clara got off the schneid by blanking the Olympic Club's Flying-O's 19–0, and Rice University 13–0, on successive weekends. The stage was now set for the Little Big Game on Sunday, November 19.

Fresh from a cross-country train trip resulting in a 13–6 victory over Fordham, the Galloping Gaels entered the fray with a record of four wins and two losses. Santa Clara had won three and lost two. With its nine-game winning streak over Santa Clara, St. Mary's was a 10 to 7 favorite to make it 10 in a row. The game was played before 59,000 fans at Kezar Stadium with part of the gate receipts going to the *San Francisco Examiner's* Christmas Fund to aid struggling families in the area. Fireworks came on the first play from scrimmage when Gael halfback Al Nichelini bolted 66 yards for a touchdown. When Carl Jorgensen missed the extra-point, the score remained 6–0. Answering immediately, Bronco Frank Sobrero hit Joe "Salty" Solatino on a nine-yard scoring pass. Like Jorgensen, "Diamond" Joe Paglia's missed extra-point kept the game tied at 6. Before being carried off the field at the end of the third quarter with what was later diagnosed as a small fracture of a vertebra, Paglia's coffin corner punts kept St. Mary's in a hole. In the game's waning minutes, hundreds of fans left the stands and swarmed along the sidelines. On what turned out to be the game's last play, Santa Clara's Bob Bosshart intercepted George Wilson's pass and returned it to Saint Mary's 27-yard line. After being tackled, Bosshart immediately called time out. Time had actually expired during Bosshart's interception return, and field judge Rufus Klawans intended to fire the gun as soon as the ball was downed. However, Klawans couldn't extricate the pistol from his pocket before Bosshart called time out.[34] The game ended in a 6–6 tie. Bronco fans, angry that Santa Clara wouldn't get one more play, interspersed with Gael rooters milling along the sidelines. Opposing fans who had been chirping at one another now resorted to fisticuffs. A full-blown riot erupted on the sidelines. It took the undermanned police swinging billy clubs 15 minutes to restore order.

During the brawl both teams retreated to their respective locker rooms. In Santa Clara's, concerned teammates watched Joe Paglia being placed on a gurney for the trip to St. Mary's Hospital. For the second time in three Santa Clara–St. Mary's contests Paglia left the game on a stretcher. Before being wheeled out, the selfless Paglia apologized to teammates and coaches alike for missing the extra point that would have won the game. (At St. Mary's Hospital "Diamond" Joe was fitted in a plaster brace and hospitalized for three weeks with a fractured vertebra.)

After their injured teammate's departure, when the realization set in that the tie had snapped their nine-game losing streak to St. Mary's, congratulatory back-slapping and boisterous cheering permeated the Bronco locker room. In the midst of the bedlam, an emotionally drained Coach Smith, demonstrably concerned over the injured Paglia, fielded questions from the press. The next day, Monday, November 20, the *San Francisco Chronicle*

Joe Paglia, Santa Clara's fullback and "coffin corner" punting specialist, was carried off the field on a stretcher in two of three brutal contests with St. Mary's College in the early '30s (courtesy Archives and Special Collections, Santa Clara University).

printed a comment Clipper Smith allegedly made during his post-game remarks: "What gets me down is that St. Mary's lays for these kids every year and they get away with murder. The officials don't seem to see it."

Indignant at the alleged statement, St. Mary's Board of Athletics convened that very evening and sent Father Lyons, Santa Clara's president, a telegram asking for an apology from Coach Smith. As Father Lyons was out of town, the telegram was not immediately read. With no reply by 2 p.m. the next day, St. Mary's athletic director Louis LeFevre telephoned Santa Clara and learned of Father Lyon's absence. That evening St. Mary's officials contacted Father Crowley, Santa Clara's vice president, asking him to open the telegram addressed to Father Lyons. Crowley did and responded that the matter would be addressed upon Father Lyon's return. Still dissatisfied, St. Mary's officials met again Wednesday evening and sent another telegram asking that the first telegram be shown to Coach Smith.

On Thursday morning, November 24, Coach Smith sent St. Mary's the following telegram:

L.F. LeFevre
St. Mary's College

A story appeared in the *San Francisco Chronicle* of Monday, November 20, quoting me as saying "St. Mary's football team used unfair tactics in our game of November 19." I wish to emphatically deny making any such statement to any representative of any publication.

In the five St. Mary's games in which Santa Clara teams I have coached have participated, every St. Mary's team has played a clean game, although each game has been bitterly contested and rivalry has been at a high pitch.

I sincerely regret the unauthorized, unjustified and unfavorable publicity this has reflected

on Edward "Slip" Madigan, St. Mary's, College and your varsity squad. Kindly have your publicity department release this statement in order that these charges may be refuted.
  M.J. "Clipper" Smith[35]

While willingly complying with St. Mary's original request, Smith's apology did not satisfy the Moraga school's officials. Before departing for Los Angeles Louis LeFevre declared, "I have been instructed to announce that St. Mary's Board of Athletic Control will further consider the charges of 'Clipper' Smith next week, and that the Board of Trustees will take up the matter later. As far as St. Mary's is concerned, the 'Little Big Game' is still a very uncertain matter for 1934."[36]

In the controversy's wake, Santa Clara played its last home game of the season against the University of San Francisco before a sparse crowd of 5,000 at Kezar Stadium. Distracted by the "Clipper quote" furor and the emotional letdown from tying St. Mary's, the Broncos played lethargically. However, with just two minutes remaining in the contest Frank Sobrero connected with Ike Britschgi on a 30-yard touchdown pass to give Santa Clara a 6–0 win. With a record of four wins, two losses and a tie, the Broncos were scheduled to depart for Hawaii in mid–December to play the final two games of the season. The first was against a Kamehameha High School alumni team billed as the "Townies" on Christmas Day. The second was on New Year's Day against the University of Hawaii.

On December 4, the "Clipper quote" controversy reached a head when Santa Clara president Father Lyons, S.J., sent the following telegram to Brother Jasper, president of St. Mary's:

Please be advised that according to the tenor of my letter to you under the date of December 1, the Board of Athletic Control of the University of Santa Clara has unanimously decided to terminate all athletic relations between our schools.[37]

Feeling his school had been beaten to the punch, the irascible Slip Madigan responded, "the St. Mary's Board of Control had taken a similar action on November 21, and would have announced it after the meeting of the board of trustees on December 16."[38]

With the announced termination of the Catholic school rivalry, Clipper Smith's squad steamed out of San Francisco Harbor for Hawaii on December 15. More important for the future of Santa Clara football than its sweep of their island hosts—the "Townies" 16–6, and Otto Klum's University of Hawaii 26–7—was a meeting that convened in Honolulu on January 3, 1934.

On the day that Santa Clara was scheduled to depart on the SS *President Pierce*, Slip Madigan arrived for a family vacation aboard the SS *President Coolidge*. In the 90 minutes between Madigan's arrival and Santa Clara's departure, the St. Mary's coach met with Clipper Smith, Buck Shaw and Hawaii coach Otto Klum. All involved wanted to see the rivalry renewed in 1934 but agreed that it would take more than a coaches' conference to settle the dispute. Before leaving Hawaii, Clipper Smith told reporters: "Big interest will demand the return of the Little Big Game to the Pacific Coast. When 60,000 persons pay good money to support such an event, it shows that it has a place on the football calendar. To deprive them of that game, to me, isn't altogether right."[39]

Despite media pressure asking the schools to find a solution for salvaging the rivalry, neither the St. Mary's Christian Brothers nor Santa Clara's Jesuits would budge. The clerics may have felt that the gridiron rivalry had become too intense if it resulted in over-zealous fans rioting after games. St. Mary's officials adamantly rejected both Clipper

Smith's explanation and apology. Whatever the reasoning, the ecclesiastical in-fighting continued for months. During that time both schools shopped around for intersectional opponents to replace their traditional rival. However, public pressure and the financial realities of canceling the rivalry came to bear. In late July a crack appeared in the impasse when coaches Madigan and Smith emerged from a meeting revealing they had made "mutual" recommendations to their respective presidents as to an agreement on which relations might be resumed.[40] Finally, on August 9, after a two-day meeting between the schools' presidents and football coaches in the William Taylor Hotel, the institutions jointly announced that a three-year contract had been signed to resume the "Little Big Game" in 1934. Following a hectic eleventh-hour scramble to readjust their respective schedules, the schools set November 17 as game day.

* * *

In a collaborative off-season effort Clipper Smith and Buck Shaw devised what Smith later tabbed as the "Double Distractor." It basically aimed to consistently employ one or two flankers to "open up" the offense while retaining deception. The *Oakland Tribune*'s Don Glendon vividly personified Santa Clara's new strategy as follows: "The Smith-Shaw creation is an adroit fencer, feinting at the opposition, sending the touch-down foil home, then parrying and waiting patiently until another opening presents itself, but always being on the alert; always being the essence of grace, skill and perfection; always probing the opposition to determine where the *coup de grace* can be executed with the minimum of physical exertion."[41] Clipper accurately predicted, "It will take us at least five weeks to get our combinations functioning. In the meantime, Stanford should beat us but we'll be all set for California."[42]

With more depth than previous Santa Clara teams and a wider open offense, the Broncos crushed Coach Brick Mitchell's Nevada Wolf Pack 40–0 in a game where Smith used a dozen different running backs. When Santa Clara tied Stanford the next week 7–7, Bay Area reporters began touting Santa Clara as the school's best team ever. The Broncos then reeled off five consecutive wins over the University of San Francisco 6–0; undefeated Loyola, 9–0; the Olympic Club's Flying-O's, 13–6; Fresno State, 19–0; and California, 20–0. Elated with the win over Cal, Smith considered it the best game his team had played all year, and a great prelude to the much-anticipated renewal of the St. Mary's rivalry the following week.

Nearly 60,000 tickets were sold for the Little Big Game at Kezar Stadium. Unfortunately, a downpour engulfed the Bay Area hours before kick-off and only 45,000 brave souls actually attended. With the rain continuing throughout the game and the field a quagmire, passing the ball became impossible. Both squads spent most of the second half jockeying for field position by exchanging punts, often on first down. The game's only score came when Santa Clara punter Frank Sobrero fielded an errant snap in his own end zone. Tackled as he began to punt, Sobrero fumbled the slippery ball and Gael Felix Pennino fell on it in the end zone for a touchdown. Only 25,000 stouthearted fans remained when the final gun sounded signaling St. Mary's 7–0 win. The St. Mary's jinx was back.

Thirty-three Bronco players junketed north to Portland to battle Columbia College where Clipper Smith got his first college coaching job. Santa Clara prevailed over an upset-minded Columbia squad 12–6. The Broncos then returned to Kezar Stadium for an intersectional clash with the TCU Horned Frogs in the season's finale. With his pin-point passing, excellent punting and overall defensive play, TCU's Sammy Baugh was the game's standout player. Leading at one point 7–0, the Broncos lost a heartbreaker when TCU's Taldon Mandon kicked a last-minute 17-yard field goal to give the Horned Frogs a 9–7 victory. Despite the loss, Santa Clara finished the 1934 season with seven wins, two losses and a tie, earning the respect of the press and opposing coaches alike as a legitimate West Coast power.

Six

Buck Takes the Broncos' Reins

Because of his premature gray hair and vast football knowledge, sportswriters began referring to Buck Shaw as the "Silver Fox" in their columns. Neither his wavy hair turning gray nor the nickname perturbed the amiable Shaw. Smiling and soft-spoken in demeanor, Shaw had an optimistic outlook on coaching and life in general. Buck saw the glass as half-full, while his boss Clipper Smith often saw it as half-empty. The two complemented each other and enjoyed both their professional and personal relationship. As an added bonus their wives were also good friends. Louise Smith and Marge Shaw sat together at Santa Clara games cheering heartily for the Broncos—win, lose or tie. During these years Marge adopted a tactic that she'd use throughout her husband's coaching years. She learned that introducing herself to spectators sitting around her usually, but not always, resulted in less vocal criticism and abuse directed at her husband and his teams.[1] Unfortunately, in 1935 they would see their husbands' Santa Clara team experience their first losing season at the school.

The season started fairly well with the Broncos sandwiching two shut out wins over the University of San Francisco (12–0) and Fresno State (24–0) around a lethargic 13–6 loss to the University of Washington. With the exception of Ray "Frisky" Kaliski's 83-yard kick-off return for a touchdown, Santa Clara's play was as dismal as Seattle's overcast sky. Coach Jimmy Phelan's Huskies kept the Bronco offense bottled up all afternoon. Part of it could be attributed to Santa Clara's fastest back, Henry Thomas, sustaining a broken leg three minutes into the contest.

In their fourth game before 50,000 fans at Berkeley the Broncos ran into the best California team they had encountered during Smith and Shaw's seven years at Santa Clara. The Bears shut down Santa Clara's running game and eliminated the Broncos' passing attack when they knocked Don DeRosa out of the contest early with a separated shoulder. The football gods caused havoc when Bronco Joe Kelly sliced a punt off his foot that landed two yards beyond the line of scrimmage and then rolled backwards before the panicked Kelly recovered it for a 25-yard loss. The mishap set the stage for Floyd Blower's 33-yard touchdown pass to Henry Sparks for the only score of the day in Cal's 6–0 win.

After defeating Portland University 20–7, the Broncos went into a tailspin losing their last four games to Stanford (9–6), St. Mary's (10–0), Loyola (7–0) and TCU (10–6). The loss to archrival St. Mary's was ugly. The Gaels held Santa Clara to two first downs the entire game and ran 52 plays from scrimmage to the Broncos' 21 before a Kezar Stadium crowd of 59,967. In the season finale against TCU, the Broncos were treated to heavy dollops of one "Slinging" Sammy Baugh. Baugh's surprise 76-yard quick-kick over the head of Bronco safety Hal Seramin set up TCU's lone touchdown. When Seramin finally scooped up the rolling pigskin, he fumbled when tackled by Drew Ellis, who recovered the ball inside Santa Clara's 10-yard line. Two plays later Baugh flipped a six-yard scoring pass to George McClean. In an era when a team throwing a dozen passes a game was considered an aerial bombardment, Baugh completed 14 passes in 28 attempts for 120 yards, and a touchdown pass. Defensively, Baugh made tackles all over the field, and his interception on TCU's three-yard line killed a Bronco scoring drive.

Throughout the season, local sportswriters grew more critical of Smith's coaching and personality. They questioned Smith's heavy reliance on the ground game and reluctance to call passing plays, especially in the California, Stanford, St. Mary's and TCU contests. Sportswriters often referred to Clipper as "Sad Eye" Smith or "Maurice the Morose," describing him as "mortician-like" and often inconsolable after a loss. They poked fun, not always jokingly, at Smith's awkward utterances such as "too much unsuccess." In his seven years at Santa Clara's helm Smith had achieved an impressive record of 37 wins, 23 losses and four ties. During that time he had received coaching feelers from Kentucky and Alabama Poly (Auburn). In 1931, his name emerged as a possible successor to the late Knute Rockne at Notre Dame. As recently as January 1935 he had turned down an offer to become head coach at the University of Idaho.

In early June 1936, Clipper traveled to Illinois to visit to his parents. He also wanted to explore the possibility of scheduling an intersectional game. The Bay Area Jesuits had a so-called "Four Day" rule, which prohibited any athletic team from taking a trip requiring it to miss more than four days of classes. Smith wanted to investigate a new train line running directly from Chicago to San Francisco. If the coach could work it out, his Broncos could leave on a Thursday evening for a Midwest contest and be back in time to attend 8 a.m. Monday classes in Santa Clara. A good son, Smith spent several days with his parents before driving to Detroit, where he intended to buy a car for a friend and drive it back to California. As Clipper was checking out of a Detroit hotel, he supposedly received a phone call from Villanova. Several weeks earlier, Harry Stuhldreher, one of Notre Dame's famed "Four Horsemen," left Villanova to become head coach at Wisconsin.

"I didn't think they had ever heard of me and I certainly had no reason to believe they wanted me as a coach," said Smith. He then related what transpired: "They offered me the job. I told 'em I had a job and wasn't looking for any additional work. But they wanted to see me.... I drove toward Philadelphia, headed up the Lancaster Pike and rolled to a stop about a mile from Valley Forge. That was Villanova. Two hours later I signed on the dotted line."[2]

Returning to California, Smith resigned as Santa Clara's head football coach on June 19. The next day Villanova announced its hiring of Smith as head coach and athletic director. While no one at Santa Clara wanted to see Smith depart, Clipper explained the reasons for his decision: "Santa Clara is the only Bay Area school which can't travel (actually, the Jesuit University of San Francisco couldn't either) and the competition for material is too keen to allow us to get many good gridders when our boys can't go anywhere." Citing Santa Clara's scholastic strictness as another factor, Smith added, "Villanova has been around since 1842 and isn't particularly afraid of over-emphasis of athletics. As for salary, I'll have about the same arrangement as at Santa Clara."[3]

Acting swiftly, Santa Clara appointed Shaw to succeed Smith as head football coach on June 20. Buck was thrilled with a coaching opportunity that allowed his family to remain in the Bay Area. His first act as head coach was to make Al Ruffo his first assistant. A week later he hired Santa Clara alumnus Len Casanova to succeed Ruffo as freshman coach. Buck vividly remembered Casanova's key role in defeating his 1926 Nevada team. That same year against St. Mary's, Casanova's 97-yard punt set a college record that stood until 1950, when Nevada's Pat Brady's 99-yard punt broke it.

After seven years at Santa Clara, Buck was well aware of the challenges confronting him now as head coach. With an all-male enrollment of only 500 students, team depth posed a persistent problem. As his departed predecessor explained, the school's heavy academic demands often made it difficult to retain good players. That spring alone Santa Clara expelled three football players for subpar academic performance. Strict disciplinarians who demanded gentlemanly behavior, the Jesuits brooked no sophomoric shenanigans. The case of one Henry "Patches" Thomas illustrates the point. Thomas was a speedy Bronco halfback who sustained a broken leg in the '35 Washington game. Fortunately for Patches, his leg healed in time for Santa Clara's '36 baseball season. That March the team was staying at Los Angeles' posh Jonathan Club when the mischievous Thomas dropped a water-filled brown bag out his room's window. The water bomb nearly skulled Father William Gianera, S.J., Santa Clara's former athletic moderator and future university president, standing on the sidewalk several stories below. The good father recognized it was not a sign from heaven and stormed into the hotel to apprehend the culprit. The Jesuits rendered swift justice by immediately expelling Thomas from school. A student with above average grades, Thomas hoped to re-join his Bronco teammates on the gridiron that fall. Truly repentant, Patches applied for re-admission in August. Despite the support of several distinguished alumni, the Jesuit "powers that be" deemed that re-admitting Thomas would set a poor example for others. His application was denied.[4]

Buck Shaw became head coach of Santa Clara in 1936. During the '20s and '30s coaches often used megaphones at practice to be heard (courtesy Archives and Special Collections, Santa Clara University).

An interesting opportunity momentarily distracted the new head coach a month before the season opener. On August 22, John McGuire, a former Santa Clara quarterback, dropped in to pay Buck a visit. Now a featured actor for Fox Studios, McGuire introduced his old coach to Irving Cummings, a movie director for Fox. As McGuire and Shaw reminisced over gridiron "war stories," Mr. Cummings repeatedly walked around the office looking at Buck from all angles. Shaw finally asked the director if there was anything wrong. Cummings replied: "No, everything's all right. You'll pardon me for gaping, but I was just looking at you from camera angles and what I see pleases me so much I'd like to talk to you about a movie contract. You know,

Buck, you are just wasting your time coaching football. You'd be a sensation in pictures with your looks and poise, and you wouldn't have to worry whether or not 11 kids were going to do what you had told them on Saturday afternoon."

Blushing at the compliment, the man his Notre Dame teammates nicknamed "Adonis" listened to Cummings' sales pitch for 10 minutes. Then Buck replied, "I appreciate your kind offer, Mr. Cummings, but I'll struggle along trying to coach football. I know my limitations and I'd be as much use to you as a movie actor as the Marx brothers would be to me as a backfield."[5]

The persistent director continued his pitch until it was time for him and McGuire to leave for the airport. Although Shaw never went into acting, it was rumored that he later visited Hollywood for a screen test. In any case, the incident prompted Bay Area writers to often refer to Shaw as "Buck the Beautiful" or "Lawrence the Handsome."

Entering the 1936 season, Shaw knew he had several quality players returning and was optimistic about the upcoming sophomores. While Shaw enjoyed passing the ball and razzle-dazzle plays as much as anyone, he believed the Broncos offense had become too intricate over the last few years, with an over-emphasis on "spinner" plays and ball handling. He intended to employ the more simplified Rockne or Notre Dame system.[6] While the quarterback called the signals in those days, he was primarily a blocker. Regarding fullback Nello Falaschi as the team's best blocker, Shaw moved him to quarterback—a decision that paid tremendous dividends.

Sportswriters noticed that Santa Clara's September practices were unusually spirited and lively. Players would jog the length of the field under assistant coach Al Ruffo yelling "ee-yah" and often beat their chests like Tarzan. When asked about his players' exuberance, the soft-spoken Shaw, who enjoyed lighthearted banter with reporters replied: "You allude I suppose, to the yelling. Well, let me say that my men yell in the sheer joy of living. They are merely showing how happy they are."[7] The Silver Fox then elaborated that yelling denoted spirit and that it forestalled brooding. A guy busy yelling wasn't likely to be concerned about his aching shins or the rigors of practice. As the season progressed, the local media also came to appreciate Shaw's candor when it came to reporting injuries. Other area coaches often refused to address the issue or claimed injuries to project their squads as underdogs or to use as alibis.[8]

Shaw was quietly confident about his charges as the season's opener against Stanford approached. The Broncos hadn't beaten Stanford in seven years. Because of his team's lack of depth, Buck secretly hoped September 26 would be a cool day at Stanford Stadium. Believing that Santa Clara's traditional red and white uniforms too closely resembled Stanford's cardinal and white, possibly causing confusion, Shaw attired his Broncos in Old Gold jerseys with silver numerals. His lads performed well in their flashy new duds. The Broncos drew first blood when quarterback Nello Falaschi, playing with a taped bruised left shoulder and his abscessed left elbow heavily bandaged, flipped a seven-yard touchdown pass to scatback Manny Gomez. The Broncos' Jules Perrin, subbing for Falaschi, scored the game's last touchdown on an eight-yard run in the fourth quarter for a 13–0 win.

In the victor's post-game locker room, Shaw made the rounds congratulating every player on the squad. When asked to name his team's standout player Buck stated, "I wouldn't like to do that. They all played a good game."[9]

Later that evening, in a display of sportsmanship that is rare in today's world, Mrs. Thornhill, wife of Stanford coach "Tiny" Thornhill, telephoned the Shaw residence. "It surely was nice of her," Shaw told reporters. "She said she didn't relish seeing 'Tiny's' team lose, but since it had to lose, she was glad it was to Santa Clara. Tiny himself congratulated me after the game and said much the same thing."[10]

The following week, Santa Clara played a game at its home Ryan Field for the first time in 10 years. To accommodate the event, temporary stands were added to expand the seating to 4,500. On a blistering hot afternoon over 5,500 fans shoe-horned into the venue to watch Shaw play 41 of his 47 players en route to a 26–0 win over the University of Portland. After the game, Pilot coach Eugene Murphy praised Shaw's squad, "They did everything right."[11]

Returning to Kezar Stadium on October 11, the Broncos blocked four San Francisco Don punts, three of which led to scores as Santa Clara edged their local Jesuit rivals 15–7. A visit to San Jose State was next on the docket. After a scoreless first quarter, the Broncos came to life when Nello Falaschi entered the contest. His devastating lead blocking consistently opened running lanes for halfback Don DeRosa. Santa Clara's first score came on a 16-yard pass from Manny Gomez to DeRosa. Falaschi kicked the extra-point to make it 7–0. On yet another sweltering afternoon, the Broncos' superior depth wore down the Spartans to earn a 20–0 victory.

After a bye week, Santa Clara hosted Alabama Poly—a school known as Auburn today. The intersectional rivalry was scheduled over two years earlier when Shaw's old Notre Dame teammate and "Carlinville Eight" cohort, Chet Wynne, coached the Tigers. After the '33 season, Wynne left Auburn to assume the coaching reins at Kentucky. Jack Meagher, another Golden Domer, succeeded Wynne and was now bringing his undefeated 55-man Auburn squad to Kezar Stadium. The only blemish on the visitors' record was an early season scoreless tie with Tulane. Since then they had defeated Detroit, Tennessee and Georgia. The club featured speedy fullback Wilton Kilgore, who the week before rushed for more yardage than Georgia's Bulldogs had in total offense. Future All-American Jimmy Hitchcock manned the left halfback position.

The visitors enjoyed a special sight-seeing tour the day before the game. Although the newly finished San Francisco-Oakland Bay Bridge was not to scheduled to open until Monday, November 2, Auburn became the first party to officially cross the bridge on October 30. California's chief state engineer Col. Jack Skaggs, an Auburn alumnus, arranged the walk-across for the wide-eyed Tigers.[12]

The visitors weren't treated so hospitably at 2 p.m. on Halloween. Playing inspired defense, the Broncos totally stymied Auburn's heralded running game. Wilton Kilgore, who ran roughshod over Georgia a week earlier, injured his knee on the game's second play. Hobbling for six total yards on seven carries, the fullback left the game for good at the start of the second quarter. Halfback Jimmy Hitchcock hardly fared better, managing 11 yards on four carries. With its ground game ineffective, Auburn took to the air only to have five passes intercepted. Santa Clara scored in the first quarter when Norman Finney took a hand-off from Jim Barlow on a 25-yard end around. The Broncos added the day's final score when Don DeRosa lobbed a 19 pass to a wide-open Manny Gomez in the end zone for a 12–0 win.

Asked what he thought of quarterback Nello Falaschi's performance, losing coach Jack Meagher replied, "I liked him at everything, his blocking, his hitting, absolutely everything." He then added, "Buck has a wonderful club. It will be hard to beat."[13]

The win garnered national acclaim for Buck's undefeated squad. Several football savants even hinted that Santa Clara was in line for a Sugar Bowl invitation. While the Broncos weren't flawless, Buck felt his team had played its best game to date against Auburn. Although elated with his team's latest performance, a jittery Shaw told reporters days later that he hoped his charges hadn't peaked too soon. Shaw had reason for concern, for up next came The Little Big Game with Slip Madigan's St. Mary's Gaels, whom Santa Clara hadn't whipped in 12 straight tries since 1923.

Despite entering the contest with recent losses to Fordham and Marquette, the supposed "smart" money was on St. Mary's to continue its hex over the Broncos. After her husband's season-opening win at Stanford, Marge Shaw made the following prediction: "We'll win from St. Mary's this year. They can't make it 13 victories over us because my birthday is the 13th and so is one of my daughters'!"[14] Mrs. Shaw was prophetic. Before 60,500 raucous fans at Kezar Stadium, Santa Clara—despite being out-gained in total offensive yardage 121 to 72—broke the Gael jinx by blanking St. Mary's 19–0. The Broncos' Manny Gomez caught a six-yard scoring pass and later threw a seven-yard touchdown pass to Norman Finney. Lionel Rodgers tallied the team's last touchdown when he ran 10 yards with a blocked punt.

In the winning locker room the Broncos were joyful but not boastful. "Don't kid yourself," said Santa Clara guard Lionel Rodgers, "those Gaels were tough!"[15]

A bruised and fatigued Nello "Flash" Falaschi, whose stellar defensive work was key in the shutout victory told reporters, "Boy! Am I happy, but I'm going home and go right to bed."[16]

Some, like assistant coach Al Ruffo, couldn't express their joy over snapping the jinx. "I am too darn happy to say anything. I've been here as a student, a player, and a coach, but this is one day when I can say I am really too flushed with victory to speak."[17]

Others, like Santa Clara trainer Henry Schmidt knew exactly how they were going to celebrate. "Know what I'm going to do? Smoke a big cigar tonight. No, I've never smoked in my life, not even a cigarette. But tonight I smoke my first cigar."[18]

Beaming with pride and joy as he worked his way around the locker room shaking every player's hand, all the soft-spoken Buck Shaw could say was, "The boys played very well."[19]

The losers were gracious in defeat. Gael guard Marty Kordick praised the victors, "They were all exceptional footballers. That was a team victory."[20]

Coach Slip Madigan admitted, "We haven't an alibi in the world. It wasn't any one thing they did that bothered us. It was everything."[21]

* * *

With a record of six wins and no losses, Santa Clara now stood as one of only three major undefeated and untied teams in the nation. With only two games remaining, Buck Shaw's squad had a shot at running the table. But first, Santa Clara had to get by the Lions of Loyola at the Los Angeles Coliseum on November 22. The Broncos needed no reminder that Loyola had whipped them for the first time ever the previous year, 7–0. Tom Lieb's Lions entered the fray with only one loss, which was to St. Mary's, 19–7. A general consensus among West Coast sportswriters was that Loyola was the stronger overall team and would have defeated the Gaels if the Lions had not made errors at two critical junctures in the game.

Desperate to prove that Loyola's 1935 win over Santa Clara was not a fluke, Coach Tom Lieb scouted every one of the Broncos' previous games. Furthermore, toppling Shaw's squad from the undefeated ranks would earn Lieb's Lions national recognition. Hoping to surprise the visitors, Lieb added a new offensive formation with a true "split" flanker to enhance the Lions' passing game. His plan did both.

Loyola football coach Tom Lieb poses with mascot lion cub 'Lil Akron in 1935. Lieb and Shaw were teammates at Notre Dame (courtesy of University Archives, Archives and Special Collections, William H. Hannon Library, Loyola Marymount University).

Meanwhile, Buck and graduate manager Sam Dunne were planning a surprise of their own. However, this surprise wasn't aimed at Loyola, but rather at Santa Clara's zealous alumni base waiting to greet the team in Los Angeles. Dunne had planned for the Broncos to take the train south on Friday evening and have the squad spend Saturday resting. However, dozens of exuberant alumni living in Los Angeles made it known that they intended to visit the team's hotel on Saturday to extend their best wishes. Buck knew such a visit would be a major distraction, disrupting the team's focus and possibly depriving it of needed rest. Thus, Shaw had Dunne publicly announce the canard that the

Opposite: In 1936, the Loyola student body built a massive bonfire structure in anticipation of defeating Santa Clara for the second year in a row. Their efforts went for naught as Shaw's Broncos eked out a 13–6 victory over the Lions (courtesy University Archives, Archives and Special Collections, William H. Hannon Library, Loyola Marymount University).

Broncos had changed plans and would now depart for Los Angeles on Saturday evening. Under this ruse Santa Clara secretly left for Los Angeles on Friday night and dodged the disruptive fanfare.[22]

On game day—Sunday, November 22—Buck Shaw awoke to both a steady rain and to learn that Santa Clara was now the lone undefeated and untied major college team in America. Buck's beloved alma mater, Notre Dame, upset previously undefeated Northwestern 26–6, while Duquense dumped Marquette 13–0. The morning-long rain resulted in only 30,000 of the anticipated 50,000 spectators attending the game. Upset-minded Loyola demonstrated that it came to play early when Lion "Race Horse" Billy Byrne intercepted Don DeRosa's pass and returned it to the Santa Clara 40-yard line. Only four minutes into the contest, the aerial thief Byrne, plowed into the Bronco end zone from the two-yard line. Santa Clara's "Mississippi" Smith blocked the extra-point attempt.

A short Lion punt later gave Santa Clara the ball in good field position. Driving to the home team's 22-yard line, "Flash" Falaschi dropped back to pass. Failing to find an open receiver and about to be buried by oncoming Lions, Falaschi scampered through a small opening on his left and raced the 22 yards to score. Pellegrini's extra-point kick put the Broncos up 7–6. There was no more scoring until the third quarter, when Santa Clara fullback Chuck Pavalko busted 12 yards off tackle for a touchdown. This time Loyola blocked the extra-point try to make the score Santa Clara 13, Loyola 6. In the game's waning moments Bronco Phil Dougherty made a great defensive play by knocking the ball out of the hands of receiver Johnny Polish in the end zone. Seconds later, the Lions' Byrne seemingly connected on a pass to a wide-open George Schneider on Santa Clara's six-yard line with a clear path to paydirt. However, the ball bounced incomplete off Schneider's chest and ended Loyola's hopes for a come back.

In the post-game locker room Buck Shaw breathed easier, "Man, that was the longest afternoon I ever spent. We weren't prepared adequately on those flanker plays," he confessed. He then added, "That boy Byrne could make anybody's team."[23]

Shaw and Santa Clara enjoyed a pleasant ride home reflecting on their 13–6 victory. As the train neared San Francisco their thoughts turned to the last obstacle in achieving an undefeated and untied regular season—the TCU Horned Frogs.

* * *

With a three-week hiatus before hosting TCU at Kezar Stadium on December 12, Shaw and the players enjoyed nearly a week off. On December 4, the Santa Clara community grew ecstatic when school officials accepted an invitation to meet the LSU Tigers in the third annual Sugar Bowl in New Orleans on New Year's Day. After breaking the news to his team, the first thing Buck Shaw told the squad was "Your first and only concern right now is getting ready for Texas Christian."[24]

In the days leading up to the TCU game, local sports scribes questioned whether the Broncos might be looking past the Horned Frogs in anticipation of the Sugar Bowl. Shaw addressed that concern head on: "I feared the boys would get so hopped up over the New Orleans date they'd forget about Texas. Nothing could be further from the truth. With the important New Year game facing them, they're more determined than ever to go south with an unblemished record."[25]

Sporting a record of seven wins, two losses and two ties, TCU arrived in the Bay Area Thursday evening, December 10. Traveling with the 33-man squad was the university's highly acclaimed 40-piece swing band as well as 200 robust supporters. The next morning the entire group was up early sight-seeing. The streets of San Francisco hadn't seen so many cowboy boots and hats since the 1849 Gold Rush. Walking along the waterfront while gawking at the city's sights, one grizzled TCU booster upon spotting a ferry named *The Santa Clara* exclaimed, "Imagine, a school owning its own steamer. It's pretty classy, I reckon."[26] Among the visitors enjoying the sights was a long, lanky fellow from Sweetwater, Texas, "Slinging" Sammy Baugh. The 6-foot, 2-inch, 180-pound tailback had played a key role in defeating Santa Clara in both 1934 and '35, and now back for a return engagement. Later that afternoon the affable Baugh demonstrated his passing grip to local reporters. Unlike most passers who placed their fingers across the football's laces, Baugh gripped the ball with his fingers across one of the football's four seams and the palm of his hand over the laces. He also placed his throwing hand near the end of the football rather than the middle. With his unorthodox grip and decades before Bill Walsh's famed "West Coast Offense," Slinging Sammy—under the tutelage of TCU coach Leo "Dutch" Meyer— was developing the sport's first short passing game offense.

The week prior to the game Buck Shaw repeatedly reminded his Broncos that stopping Baugh was

Opposite: **One of the All-Time football greats, TCU's "Slinging" Sammy Baugh was instrumental in the Horned Frogs defeating Santa Clara from 1934 through 1936. TCU spoiled Santa Clara's bid for an undefeated season in 1936 (Texas Christian University, Mary Couts Burnett Library Special Collections).**

BAUGH

the key to winning. How successful was Baugh in his third straight appearance against Santa Clara? The *San Francisco Examiner's* sports headline of December 14 most aptly described it "Baugh's Play Shatters Santa Clara's Undefeated Record."

The kid from Sweetwater, Texas, completed 13 of 26 passes for 120 yards, including a five-yard touchdown pass to Walter Roach. Moreover, he averaged 42.6 yards per punt on 17 boots, placing five coffin corner kicks inside Santa Clara's 10-yard line. Texas Christian's L.D. Meyer, the coach's nephew, added a 22-yard field goal in the Horned Frogs' 9–0 win.

Santa Clara had two scoring opportunities but couldn't cash in. On TCU's first possession Nello Falaschi intercepted Baugh's pass and returned it to the visitors' four-yard line. Hoping to fool the Horned Frogs on first-and-goal, Falaschi rolled out and overthrew a pass to Norm Finney in the end zone. TCU threw Chuck Pavalko for a four-yard loss on second down. On third down Don DeRosa's pass to Manny Gomez was way over the receiver's head and out of the end one. The rules of the day read that a second incomplete pass thrown out of the end zone on the same possession resulted in the ball going over to the opposing team. (Similar to a touch back today.) Several local sportswriters later took Shaw and Falaschi to task for that series of play-calling.

The next opportunity came in the second quarter, when Bronco Hal Semarin intercepted a Baugh pass and returned it 55 yards for an apparent touchdown. Unfortunately, the score was negated by a controversial clipping call on Manny Gomez during the run. Despite taking possession on the Horned Frogs' 29-yard line, Santa Clara didn't score. (The *San Francisco Examiner* published a series of game photos on December 16, clearly showing that on the play Gomez blocked TCU's Vic Montgomery from the front, not the back).

In Santa Clara's post-game locker room the silence was deafening. When asked about the controversial clipping call Shaw replied, "I don't know. I couldn't see it from where I was sitting."[27]

The Horned Frogs impressive win over Santa Clara earned TCU an invitation to play Marquette in the Cotton Bowl. While Baugh and company would be playing in Dallas on New Year's Day, Santa Clara would be pitted against LSU's Bayou Tigers in the Sugar Bowl.

SEVEN

Two Sugar Bowls

When Shaw's squad resumed practice on December 15 to prepare for their Sugar Bowl engagement, few, if any, Bay Area reporters gave the Broncos a chance. If Santa Clara couldn't defeat a TCU squad that had lost two and tied two, how were they going to beat an undefeated LSU team that had scored more points (281) than any other major school in the country? After a 6–6 tie with Jack Chevigny's Texas Longhorns in the second game of the season, the Tigers won eight straight to finish undefeated with nine wins and a tie. The eight-game winning streak included shutouts over Mississippi, Vanderbilt, Mississippi State and Tulane, as well as a 93–0 massacre of Louisiana-Lafayette. LSU featured end Gaynell Tinsley, a two-time consensus All-American, who had eight touchdown catches on the year. Furthermore, playing in New Orleans would be like a home game for LSU while Santa Clara faced an arduous four-day train trip. Nevertheless, many in the Louisiana press corps felt that the Rose Bowl committee had snubbed the Tigers by not extending them an invitation to meet the Washington Huskies.

Two days after his Horned Frogs defeated Santa Clara, TCU coach "Dutch" Meyer predicted that LSU would win the Sugar Bowl.[1] Most Bay Area reporters agreed with Meyer's assessment. The Alabama *Selma Times* bolstered Meyer's prediction when it polled the two schools' only common opponent, Auburn, as to who would prevail. Coach Jack Meagher and all but one Auburn starter believed LSU would handle Santa Clara.[2]

However, the pundits were overlooking just how good TCU and Sammy Baugh were. On December 12, 1937, exactly one calendar year after Baugh led TCU to its 9–0 victory over Santa Clara, "Slinging Sammy" led the Washington Redskins to a 28–21 victory over the Chicago Bears for the National Football League (NFL) championship. Both Earl "Dutch" Clark, coach of the Detroit Lions, and Redskins coach Ray Flaherty agreed that Baugh's performance in the championship game, "was the greatest one-man show ever put on by professional football."[3] Quite a climb for a teenager who, wanting to improve his passing before his sophomore season at TCU, spent hours throwing footballs through a tire hanging from a backyard tree in Sweetwater, Texas. J.B. Whitworth, who scouted the Santa Clara–TCU game for LSU, remarked, "I never saw a ball club get more tough breaks than did Santa Clara in that TCU game." After questioning the contest's officiating, Whitworth opined, "Santa Clara showed me the best downfield blocking I've seen in years. I figure we have too much power for Santa Clara, but I know they're a better club than they showed Saturday."[4]

On Christmas Eve, Buck sat in a tiny dressing room next to Santa Clara's Ryan Field answering questions from local sportswriters. Painted on the locker room wall was a jungle scene with a huge tiger, bound by ropes. Underneath in huge letters was the caption "Bring 'Em Back, Alive, Buck!" It was the team's last practice before departing for New

Orleans on December 26. The soft-spoken Shaw replied to one question: "I've heard a lot about those Louisiana State players. I've heard about their being three deep in every position, about their power on the ground and in the air. But we look at it from one angle. That is, LSU can only put 11 of those men on the field at the same time. And I think I have eleven who will be the equal of any combination they can muster."[5] The comment characterized Shaw's coaching style: no braggadocio, just simple, cogent statements meant to instill confidence in his players.

An attribute his players adored about Buck was his modesty. Shaw often concluded interviews with sportswriters by asking them to write about his players, not about him. While most of the media gave Santa Clara as much chance of defeating LSU as a one-legged man had of winning a butt-kicking contest, Shaw's exceptional work in bringing the Broncos to a seven-win and one-loss record garnered him national recognition. When reminded of it Buck responded, "Heck, I win a couple of games and then they think I'm a miracle man. I have a grand bunch of boys here. They like to play football and I like to teach them. That's the answer to it."[6]

A special 14-car train departed San Francisco the day after Christmas carrying coaches, 35 players and an entourage of 100 undergraduates bound for New Orleans. On the night of December 27, the train stopped at Phoenix, Arizona, where a jubilant group of 500 alumni awaited. Shaking hands and visiting with the well-wishers buoyed the spirits of players and coaches alike, so much so that Shaw opted to forgo the limbering-up session he hoped to have for his players during the two-hour layover. Shaw compensated for it by holding two practices daily during a two-day stay in Houston on December 29 and 30. Fearing the possibility of injury, Buck canceled a scrimmage originally scheduled with a group of Houston All-Stars. The team arrived in New Orleans on New Year's Eve, where Shaw told waiting reporters, "I understand we are not given much of a chance to win because of the numerical strength of the LSU team. But we'll be in there doing our best from the first whistle."[7]

The Broncos then shuttled 60 miles to Bay St. Louis, Mississippi, to catch a light workout at St. Stanislaus College and spend New Year's Eve away from Bourbon Street's boisterous levity. On that same day *New York Times* sports columnist Arthur Dailey wrote that since TCU had defeated Santa Clara in the regular season finale, the Sugar Bowl had become just another football game. Dailey may have viewed it that way, but to Shaw and Santa Clara it was a shot at redemption. They came to win.

Marge Shaw had traveled separately to the Crescent City with a close friend, Mrs. Dorothy McMahon, to watch her husband's team play. Unfortunately, both women came down with influenza and were confined to their New Orleans hotel room at game time. Buck Shaw never mentioned his wife's illness to the team, but somehow quarterback Nello Falaschi learned of it. As the team huddled on the sideline just before kickoff Falaschi informed his teammates, "I just found out that Buck Shaw's wife is not here today. She came 2,500 miles and cannot see the game. She had an attack of the flu and her temperature was 103 degrees this morning. Buck is worried sick about it, but he didn't tell us a thing. Let's dedicate this game to Mrs. Shaw … and let's go out there and win it for her and Buck."[8]

Bedridden and deathly ill, both Mrs. Shaw and Mrs. McMahon struggled futilely to stay awake during the game's radio broadcast.

As the teams prepared to kick-off at 1:30 p.m. on Friday, January 1, the field at Tulane Stadium was still muddy from a heavy rain on Wednesday night. While the rain broke

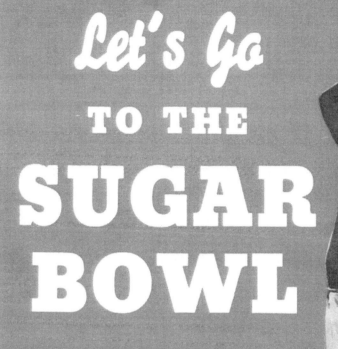

Santa Clara quarterback Nello Falaschi is pictured on a 1937 Sugar Bowl advertisement. Years later, Buck Shaw called Falaschi one of the two best football players he ever coached (courtesy Archives and Special Collections, Santa Clara University).

the city's sweltering week-long heat wave, the afternoon was still warm and extremely humid. There were only about 1,000 Santa Clara fans among the sell-out crowd of 41,000. That didn't seem to bother the Broncos. Ten minutes into the contest Santa Clara's Nello Falaschi heaved a 27-yard touchdown pass to the speedy Manny Gomez for the game's first score. Bruno Pellegrini's kick made it 7–0. Minutes later the Broncos scored again when Chuck Pavelko's punt rolled out of bounds on LSU's 6-inch line. Punting on first down, the Tigers' Bill Crass kicked it out of bounds on LSU's 28-yard line. Pellegrini connected on a 25-yard scoring pass to Norm Finney three plays later. Pellegrini's second extra point gave the Broncos a 14–0 first-quarter lead, silencing all but the 1,000 delirious Bronco fans in the stands. With a minute left in the half, All-American Gay Tinsley, finally getting traction on the muddy field, got behind Santa Clara's secondary to haul in a 50-yard touchdown pass from Crass. Crass' extra-point kick made the halftime score Santa Clara 14, LSU 7.

It began spitting rain when the teams returned for the second half. Anticipating a humid day and wet field, Shaw arranged with nearby Loyola University to provide his boys dry football cleats and socks during intermission, which made the Broncos feel lighter and faster upon entering the second half. "When we got to the dressing room," tackle Al Wolff recalled, "there were dozens of shoes sent over by Loyola, just scattered around the floor. The coaches said, 'Find a pair that fits and put 'em on.' Then we changed into our practice uniforms for the second half, and we were ready to play again."[9]

The Bayou Tigers lumbered back to the fray in their water-logged football shoes and mud-laden white with purple striped jerseys. The fast-paced game saw six interceptions, 10 total fumbles and 24 punts, which thrilled the crowd, but gave the coaches heart palpitations. In the third quarter the Broncos' Manny Gomez intercepted a Tiger aerial and returned it 23 yards to LSU's 15-yard line. On third-and-goal from the four-yard line, Santa Clara's Frank "Mississippi" Smith carried the ball on an end around. Just as two Tiger tacklers belted Smith at the two-yard line, he pitched the ball back to Falaschi, yelling, "Catch it!" Falaschi did before plunging into the end zone. Manny Gomez bobbled the extra-point snap, but quickly recovered it and rolled out to his left passing to "Mississippi" Smith in the end zone to make the score Santa Clara 21, LSU 7.

At the start of the fourth quarter Shaw sent in a whole new team to allow his starters a breather. Tempers flared when Santa Clara end Pete Foley threw a roundhouse punch at Tiger Clarence Strange and was subsequently ejected. The penalty helped set up LSU's last touchdown, a 17-yard scoring toss from Crass to Rock Reed. Cotton Milner's extra-point kick made the final score Santa Clara 21, LSU 14.

When the final gun sounded the crazed contingent of Santa Clara fans exuberantly rushed the field and tore down the goal posts. It was an amazing upset. LSU entered the fray a 5 to 1 favorite. The Broncos had scored a season-high 21 points against LSU while limiting them to only 44 yards rushing. Buck Shaw devised six different defenses for the game, and nose tackle Phil Dougherty, who called the defensive signals, did a great job mixing them up and keeping the Tigers confused.

In the post-game locker room an elated Shaw was effusive in praising his players. "Nello Falaschi played the greatest game of his career," Buck said of his team captain. He then added, "I think Falaschi is the greatest blocking back I ever saw."

Frank Thomas, the head coach at Alabama, was visiting the locker room to congratulate his old Notre Dame teammate. Upon hearing Shaw's assessment of Falaschi, Thomas offered, "I wish I had 11 like him."

Two-time All-American Gaynell Tinsley led the Tigers into the 1937 Sugar Bowl. LSU coach Bernie Moore declared, "Tinsley could have been an All-American at any position. He's the greatest lineman I ever saw." Tinsley later served as LSU's head football coach from 1948 to 1954 (LSU photographic collection, Louisiana State University Archives, LSU Libraries, Baton Rouge, LA).

To which Buck replied, "Two like him would be all you would need."[10]

Buck then lauded his shifty halfback from Mexico City, who not only scored his team's first touchdown, but intercepted two LSU passes on the afternoon: "Little Manny Gomez is as sensational a 'money' player as I have ever seen."[11]

"Do I think Santa Clara is the national champion?" Buck repeated an interviewer's question. "Well, I am making no claims. I would rather have others do that. But I will say this: I think the Broncos have as legitimate a claim on the national title as any other team in the country. Certainly on the basis of results, no team can logically be rated over the Broncos."[12]

Here's how columnist Joe Carter of the *Shreveport Times* described Santa Clara's performance:

> Approximately 41,000 persons were in Tulane stadium to see the Bengals wage their losing battle, and they watched a well coached machine from Santa Clara outplay the representatives of the South in all branches of the game and give as fine an exhibition of defensive and offensive play, coupled with quick thinking, as probably ever displayed in this section.

Losing coach Bernie Moore succinctly summarized the afternoon, "We just met a better club than ours, that's all."[13]

After expenses, each university cleared about $38,000 from gate receipts. However, it was a million-dollar victory for Santa Clara's football program in terms of national recognition and prestige. The Broncos' train trip home was joyous and relaxing. When the special 14-car train carrying the victors pulled into the Southern Pacific station the scene was a madhouse. Blaring bands, shrieking sirens, exploding fireworks and ecstatic, yelling fans greeted the train at its 8:50 a.m. arrival on January 6. Santa Clara Mayor Patrick Concannon and university president Father Louis Rudolph had a planned reception for the team and hoped to greet Shaw as soon as he stepped onto the railroad platform. However, their plans went awry when over a thousand fans rushed the train. It took both dignitaries over an hour to plow through the throng of celebrants to finally shake the victorious coach's hand. Shaw, who had lost 12 pounds since the start of the season, told the crowd that his immediate plans were to return to his home in Burlingame and rest for at least three days. Shaw and assistant coach Al Ruffo were then whisked away in a waiting car.

Because Buck's coaching contract with Santa Clara had expired, it was only days before rumors swirled regarding Buck's future. On Friday, January 8, the *Des Moines Tribune* reported that both the universities of Iowa and Texas were wooing Shaw to become their next coach. Shaw denied that either school had made any overtures, but that as a businessman he would entertain "any offers which might mean an advancement or increase in salary."[14] Since coming to Santa Clara in 1929, Buck spent the off-seasons working for Standard Oil. Now, the company dangled before the popular coach the prospect of securing an administrative position with the oil giant if he came to work for them full-time. Knowing the precarious nature of the coaching profession, Shaw seriously contemplated the company's offer. Perhaps now was the time to exit coaching, going out on top. Yet coaching was in his blood, and he was helping build something special at Santa Clara.

When Santa Clara officials learned that Buck had not only received overtures from Iowa but had actually been offered the job, they offered the "Silver Fox" a new five-year contract. The terms called for a base salary of $7,500 plus a guaranteed percentage of the gate that could earn Buck an additional $2,500 annually. After weighing the offer for a week, Buck signed the deal on February 3.

Buck's signing thrilled his wife Marge who exclaimed, "I think its grand! I don't know what on earth could have possessed Buck thinking about going to Iowa even for a second."[15]

Perhaps no one was more appreciative of Buck's signing than *San Francisco Chronicle* columnist Bill Leiser who wrote, "To my mind, there isn't a finer coach, nor a finer influence on boys, in any American university than Buck Shaw. The whole San Francisco sports community rejoiced in Santa Clara's ability to announce that Buck will keep command for at least another five years."[16]

* * *

Buck opened Santa Clara's 1937 season without his best "money" player. After returning from the Sugar Bowl, junior halfback Manny Gomez caught a cold. While working on a San Francisco weekend construction job, he rode in the back of an open truck, exposed to a heavy rain, from Santa Clara to San Francisco. By early February his cold had developed into pneumonia, a blood infection and meningitis. Shaw visited him often at St. Mary's Hospital, where he was at death's door. Showing slow but steady signs of improvement, the gutsy Gomez was eventually transferred to a sanitarium to recuperate. His return to the gridiron was out of the question. When doctors refused to allow Gomez to attend Santa Clara's season-opener at Stanford as a spectator, his teammates decided to dedicate the game to him. In tribute to their beloved and missing halfback, the team displayed Gomez's worn and weathered football cleats in front of the Bronco bench.

On a broiling afternoon, Shaw's repeated substitutions of 11 men at a time, as well as Jess Coffer's block of a Cardinal punt, resulted in a touchdown, and Santa Clara's 13–7 upset win of Stanford. All of the scoring came in the game's last 10 minutes. Shaw's decision to rotate 11-man units may have aided Santa Clara's late game-winning surge. Upsetting Stanford for the second year in a row bolstered the team's confidence and immediately started Bronco players talking about earning another Bowl game invitation.

Confidence is great, but not if it leads to complacency. After a bye week the Broncos looked lethargic in winning their next three games over the University of San Francisco (13–0), University of Portland (27–0) and Loyola (7–0). In a nerve-racking contest at the Los Angeles Coliseum, Tom Lieb's Loyola Lions gave Buck Shaw more gray hairs before Bill Gunther's heroic fourth quarter 56-yard "pick six" saved the day for Santa Clara.

Shaw declared, "Manny Gomez is as sensational a money player as I've ever seen." A near-fatal disease ended the football career of one of the 1937 Sugar Bowl heroes (courtesy Archives and Special Collections, Santa Clara University).

Concerned that his kids weren't playing to their potential, an apprehensive Shaw wondered how they'd handle the upcoming trip to Chicago to meet Marquette at Soldier Field on October 30. Perhaps the accompanying coaches' wives, Marge Shaw and Mrs. Al Ruffo, brought the team good luck, or maybe the players rose to the occasion sensing their coach's anxiety, but Santa Clara played its best game in over a month. Buck played all 35 players who made the trip in thumping the Golden Avalanche 38–0. After the game Marquette coach Paddy Driscoll admitted, "We were completely outclassed in all departments by a great team. Any coach who can substitute 11 men as a unit and have second-and third-stringers of the class of Santa Clara is going places. I mean to the top."[17]

Like steam rising from a boiling pot, rumors often emerge about coaches during the course of a season. In early November rumors percolated throughout California that Buck was in line to replace USC's venerable coach Howard Jones, who was said to be soon retiring—voluntarily or otherwise. When queried by local reporters on the story Shaw replied, "Until actual negotiations are begun by responsible persons, I have nothing to say. It isn't fair to Jones or me to have these so-called 'reliable source reports' circulated."[18] Despite the media's claims to the contrary, Howard Jones continued to coach the "Men of Troy" through 1940. Nevertheless, the frivolous reports were a major distraction for Buck and his squad.

Shaw, however, continued gaining national notoriety and ranked among a coterie of coaches that trained observers and pundits now approached seeking their opinion on ways to improve the game of football. Shaw argued for the following rule change: "If rules demand that at least seven men be on the offensive line, why is it not reasonable to limit the maximum number of men on the defensive line?" Buck proposed that the defensive line be limited to six men, with linebackers limited to two and aligned no closer than two yards to the line of scrimmage until the ball was snapped. Buck felt that most defenses at the time played seven-man lines with two linebackers on their heels ready to plug a gap, making it a nine-man line. He predicted that if defenses were allowed to go unbridled, in a few years football would become very dull and drive fans away. "I myself like to see a 21–14 game better than a 7–0 one in which the defense nullifies every effort of the offense. And I believe that fans like high-scoring games."[19] What's curious about Buck's recommendation is that his use of multiple defenses helped Santa Clara defeat LSU in the Sugar Bowl, and his continued use of numerous defenses would benefit his future college and pro teams. It would indeed be interesting to get Buck's take on the pass-run-option offenses employed by college teams today that have defensive coordinators pulling their hair out devising ways to stop them.

In 21st century sports parlance Santa Clara regained its "swagger" in Chicago. However, they'd need more than swagger the following Saturday at undefeated San Jose State. Due to the schools' geographic proximity, both coaches worried about spies eye-balling their practices during game week. To prevent such espionage, Shaw announced that the only onlookers allowed at Ryan Field that week would be accredited alumni and members of the press. Meanwhile, coach Dud DeGroot attached a six-foot-high canvas covering to the fence surrounding the Spartan practice field to deter "Bronco spies." San Jose officials managed to cram 13,000 fannies into its 10,000-seat stadium to witness the spirited neighborhood showdown. Despite sustaining numerous injuries, Santa Clara emerged undefeated with a 25–0 win.

The annual Little Big Game loomed next for Santa Clara. In the minds of the Bay Area press, the Broncos had now surpassed St. Mary's as the Pacific Coast's top football independent. In nearby Moraga, coach Slip Madigan was determined to change that mode of thinking. Madigan and his assistants, Red Strader and Eddie Erdelatz, had reached a consensus after scouting the Santa Clara-San Jose tilt—that Santa Clara was good but beatable. Madigan, for the first time since the rivalry's renewal in 1922, boldly predicted a Gaels' victory, citing four reasons. One, punter Jerry Dowd and place-kicker Lou Ferry gave St. Mary's an edge in the kicking game; two, Santa Clara was due to be upset; three, injuries Santa Clara sustained against San Jose left the Gaels in better shape; and four, the "bad luck" St. Mary's had suffered throughout the season was destined to change. Visions of victory may have danced in Madigan's head, or perhaps the master motivator's statements were an attempt to bolster his squad's confidence.

Many Gael backers believed that spiraling talk of another post-season Bowl invitation for undefeated Santa Clara made them a ripe apple ready to fall. St. Mary's hyperbolic publicity man "Tom Tom" Foudy proclaimed, "Santa Clara has one foot in the Sugar Bowl and one foot in the clouds—and that should make them easy to block."[20]

On the eve of the Little Big Game, Slip Madigan doubled down on his prediction telling *Oakland Tribune* columnist Alan Ward: "The Gaels now are more full of fight than at any time of the season. This is going to be their 'Big Game.' Once a season, my team, any team, outdoes itself."[21]

On a cool, cloudy day before 50,000 animated fans it looked like Slip's predic-

Buck Shaw focuses on game action during a 1937 contest, while Bronco trainer Henry Schmidt jumps for joy at an on-field occurrence (courtesy Archives and Special Collections, Santa Clara University).

tion might materialize in the second quarter, before Gael kicker Lou Ferry's 37-yard field goal attempt barely missed. Minutes later, St. Mary's had the ball first-and-goal at the Bronco nine-yard line when Gael fullback "Whitey" Smith fumbled the pigskin away to Santa Clara's Jess Coffer.

The Gaels wouldn't muster another scoring threat until the third quarter. As with any Little Big Game, fierce blocking and tackling characterized the contest. With 48 seconds remaining in the third quarter, Santa Clara's Jim Barlow took a hand-off on a reverse and running to his left, rifled a 10-yard touchdown pass to Everett "King" Fisher. An overwhelming Gael rush blocked Bruno Pellegrini's extra-point attempt. But the Gaels were caught napping. The rules of the day allowed for the kicking team to advance a blocked extra-point kick. While the Gaels were celebrating their valiant defensive effort, alert Bronco tackle Al Wolff picked up the rolling spheroid and ran for the extra-point. With that, an irate Slip Madigan drop-kicked his imported Borsalino hat ten yards onto the field. The touchdown sealed the deal for Santa Clara in Shaw's second victory over archrival St. Mary's in as many tries.

In the post-game locker room, Shaw—visibly relieved with his team's 7–0 win— lauded Gael Jerry Dowd's punting as well as guard Ernie Jorge's defensive line play in stifling the Broncos' inside running game.

Before ushering his team off to catch a train bound for New York to play Fordham, Slip Madigan managed a smile while chalking up Santa Clara's winning touchdown to a blown assignment in the secondary.

* * *

Santa Clara had two weeks to prepare for the regular season finale against Gonzaga on November 28. The undefeated and untied Broncos were virtually assured a return engagement to the Sugar Bowl with a convincing win over the Zags. Shaw and his squad now found themselves in a situation nearly identical to where they were one year earlier. In 1936, they were undefeated and untied, with seven wins and a ticket to the Sugar Bowl in hand, and a three-week wait before the season's finale against TCU. Now, they were again undefeated and untied, with seven wins, and a two-week wait before the finale against Gonzaga. Unlike in 1936, however, Santa Clara had not yet received a Sugar Bowl invitation. An invite depended on earning a convincing win over Gonzaga. While the Bulldogs didn't have a phenom like Sammy Baugh pitching the pigskin, they did have a legitimate triple threat halfback in George "Automatic" Karamatic, one of the best all-around players on the Pacific Coast. No pushover, the Zags had played St. Mary's to a scoreless tie earlier in the season. A loss or even a tie for Santa Clara meant Shaw's boys would be staying home for New Year's.

In a strange twist, the contest was played at Sacramento's Municipal Sports Stadium as a "charity" game to benefit both the San Jose and Sacramento Elks Clubs' Christmas Fund. Bay Area sportswriters speculated as to whether the Broncos had the focus to finish undefeated, or by "counting their chickens before they were hatched" might lose the finale like they did against TCU in '36. Speculation heightened when Buck Shaw became bedridden with the flu as Santa Clara resumed practice several days later. Weak and gaunt, Shaw attended practice on November 22 and 23 before suffering a relapse. Ordered to remain in bed, Buck did not travel with the team when they departed for Sacramento on Saturday, November 28. Upon arriving at the Hotel Senator that night, the team found a telegram waiting for them, addressed to Captain Everett Fisher and the Santa Clara football squad, c/o Coach Al Ruffo.

It read:

> Sincerely sorry cannot be with you today in our last scheduled engagement, but orders make my confinement imperative. Try to realize just a little more effort on the part of every man on every play represents the difference between the champion and the second rate.
>
> Remember, you cannot only be Santa Clara's first undefeated football team but by a decisive

victory be virtually assured of a Sugar Bowl invitation. Am sure radio will confirm confidence I have in you. Give Al [Ruffo] your best. Regards and good luck, Buck.[22]

The telegram had its desired psychological effect on his kids. But just to make sure, Shaw had arranged for a special telephone bedside connection from his Burlingame home to the Santa Clara bench on game day. While he couldn't be there in the flesh, he would be there in both voice and spirit as he communicated directly with coach Al Ruffo during the game. The Broncos' defense bottled up Gonzaga's "Automatic" Karamatic throughout the contest. Playing "lights out," Santa Clara gained 392 yards in total offense while limiting coach Mike Pecaravich's Bulldogs to a mere 87 yards in the Broncos' 27–0 win. Scoring in every quarter, Santa Clara probably might have doubled the score had not coach Al Ruffo, thinking of the players more than a second invitation to the Sugar Bowl, played nearly every man on the squad.

At the game's conclusion Buck told Ruffo over the phone, "Tell the kids thanks for me." His loyal assistant did just that, shaking each individual player's hand in the post-game locker room while telling him, "Buck says thanks!"[23]

Watching the one-sided event on the Bulldog sideline was Gonzaga's most famous alumnus, Bing Crosby. An ardent supporter of his alma mater, the crooner could only sing the blues that afternoon.

* * *

On December 1, the Sugar Bowl Committee sent Santa Clara officials a formal invitation to play in the 1938 Sugar Bowl on New Year's Day. The game would be a rematch of their 1937 encounter with LSU. Buck first heard the news in a San Francisco hotel while visiting his good friend and former boss, Clipper Smith. Smith's undefeated Villanova squad was enjoying a stop over in the City by the Bay en route back home after blanking Loyola in Los Angeles 25–0. Smith was holding "open house" in his hotel room, hosting old friends and colleagues. Spending his first day out of bed in nearly two weeks, Shaw wasn't on his feet long. The coach suffered a relapse during the visit and sent to bed at the Hotel Whitcomb. Before retiring to convalesce, Shaw spoke of his squad's delight at returning to New Orleans, but added the caveat, "The only trouble is I know little of what Louisiana State has been using this season. I hope they aren't as tough as Bernie Moore had them last time."[24]

In Baton Rouge, coach Bernie Moore's remarks about the rematch sounded like a pledge to defend the "Honor of the South." Moore stated: "We hope that we can play well enough so that the game will be a source of pleasure to football lovers in Louisiana and the remainder of the South. I believe that this present LSU team will make a tremendous effort to uphold the prestige of the Southeast Conference and Southern football."[25]

The Bayou Tigers entered the contest with a record of nine wins and one loss. They suffered a one-point loss to Vanderbilt while shutting out Florida, Texas, Rice, Mississippi, Mississippi State and Northwest Louisiana. Sophomores Young Bussey and Ken Kavanaugh were hailed as the squad's stars. Bussey led the team in both rushing and passing, while Kavanaugh led it in receiving. On strength of schedule, LSU was rated a slight favorite. On the flip side, Buck's undefeated and untied Broncos surrendered a meager nine points all season, with only Stanford crossing its goal line.

A healthy Buck Shaw greeted the Santa Clara squad upon their return to practice a week later.

1937
GEORGE KARAMATIC
ALL COAST HALF BACK
LITTLE ALL AMERICAN

Gonzaga University's George Karamatic earned the nickname "Automatic" Karamatic for his consistent place-kicking and long-range punting. Santa Clara bottled up the 190-pound fullback in the Broncos' 1937 win to secure an invitation to the 1938 Sugar Bowl (courtesy Gonzaga University Archives and Special Collections Department, Rg_1936_1937_1940).

The team's itinerary for the trip to New Orleans paralleled the previous year's. After a two-and-a-half-hour practice the day after Christmas, 36 players, coaches, school officials and 250 fans entrained for New Orleans. Among the passengers were Hollywood movie personalities and Santa Clara alumni Edmund Lowe and Andy Devine. (The latter had actually played football for the Broncos.) En route, the squad again spent two days in Houston practicing twice daily at Rice University. The team then sequestered to Bay St. Louis, Mississippi, where it spent its second consecutive New Year's Eve.

A morning rain left Tulane stadium's field sloppy when the Tigers kicked off to Santa

Clara's Jack Roche to start the game. On the return halfback Tommy Gilbert, blocking for Roche, was knocked unconscious and carried off on a stretcher. The inauspicious start worried Buck. Injuries had already taken their toll on the Broncos. A doctor's 11th-hour decision kept halfback "King" Fisher from playing. Fisher, the hero of the St. Mary's game, sustained a fractured tibia in that contest. Although the fracture had healed, Fisher still suffered from complications. Furthermore, end Bryce Brown was playing with a special pad protecting two broken ribs, while halfback Jack Roche was nursing a sprained shoulder. How long either could play was unclear.

When LSU recovered Orville Hanners' fumble on the Bronco 29-yard line on Santa Clara's first possession Shaw's anxiety exacerbated. Several plays later the Tigers had first-and-goal on Santa Clara's seven-yard line. However, the Broncos cowboyed up behind the stellar defensive play of linebacker Phil Dougherty and tackle Al Wolff to take over on downs at their own one-yard line.

One of Buck Shaw's aims during spring football was to develop two separate 11-man units that could be effectively interchanged throughout a ball game. With the aid of assistants Al Ruffo and Nello Falaschi, the Broncos developed enough skilled players to field two quality teams, a luxury many schools lacked. The first 11, or "A" team, was tagged "Dougherty's Dragoons," because when the Dragoons were in action Phil Dougherty snapped the football and called the defensive formations. The second 11, or "B" team was nicknamed "Schiechl's Snipers," because Johnny Schiechl assumed those same tasks for the B team.

Early in the second quarter the "Snipers" threatened on Jim Barlow's 21-yard completion to Raymond McCarthy, putting the ball on LSU's 10-yard line. Three plays later Bruno Pellegrini lofted a scoring pass to James Coughlan. Pellegrini missed the extra point, and the score remained 6–0. Later that quarter, Pellegrini missed a 23-yard field goal that would have given the Broncos some breathing room.

To the delight of LSU's 200-piece marching band the rain stopped at halftime. But the sun came out, subjecting both teams as well as the 41,000 spectators to insufferable heat and humidity. The sloppy field conditions had stifled each club's running game, forcing both squads to go to the air early and often. Despite having the edge in offensive statistics, LSU never threatened to score again until late in the fourth quarter when Cotton Milner ran 21 yards on a reverse before being knocked out of bounds by Jim Barlow's touchdown-saving tackle. With only minutes remaining in the contest, and the game on the line, LSU had the ball first-and goal on the Broncos' four-yard line. "Dougherty's Dragoons" came through heroically. Not only did they keep LSU from scoring in four tries, they pushed the line of scrimmage back to the 10-yard line when Santa Clara took over on downs.

LSU's last crack at scoring came on its next possession when Bussey completed a long pass to Ken Kavanaugh, who was tackled at the Bronco 25-yard line as the game ended. With their 6–0 victory, Santa Clara had again shocked the football world in back-to-back years by twice upsetting Sugar Bowl favorite LSU.

In the winner's locker room an elated, but relieved Buck Shaw told reporters, "I spent a great many uneasy moments on the bench today ..., I never knew when Young Bussey might throw a touchdown pass to Ken Kavanaugh."[26]

While in the LSU dressing room a somber Bernie Moore could only mutter, "It was a tough loss. There's nothing else to say."[27]

The victors enjoyed New Year's night and the next day seeing the Crescent City's sights before departing on January 3. On a northern route home, the train pulled into Bolivar, Missouri, the hometown of Bronco George Locke. The muscular tackle had contributed to the New Year's Day victory by blocking an LSU punt. Locke left New Orleans alone immediately after the game to visit his family. Hailed as a celebrity upon his return home, Bolivar officials arranged for the town's residents to turn out *en masse* behind a 25-piece band to salute Locke's Sugar Bowl winning teammates during their brief stopover.

While the victors' train whistled across Nebraska's flatlands, *San Francisco Examiner* sports columnist Curley Grieve was writing an apology. In his New Year's Day column Grieve opined that LSU's overall talent and depth would prevail over Santa Clara. He wrote, "If Santa Clara wins, it could only be attributed to the miracle coaching of 'Buck' Shaw." On January 4, Grieve wrote of Santa Clara's Sugar Bowl victory, "I can only attribute it to the miracle coaching of 'Buck' Shaw."[28]

Over 3,000 fans greeted the victors' train when it arrived home. The Santa Clara Fire Department, city officials, alumni and fans accompanied the team as it paraded to the university campus surrounded by blaring sirens, honking car horns, flying confetti and exploding fireworks—an impressive tribute for the Jesuit school with a student body of 500.

EIGHT

Santa Clara

A Football School

In his column on September 5, 1936, *San Francisco Examiner* sportswriter Prescott Sullivan expressed his opinion that Santa Clara feared being branded as a "football school." He wrote: "That is an appellation which the good Jesuits despise. Santa Clara is not a football school and never has been." Sullivan's piece was written three weeks before Buck Shaw's first game as Santa Clara's head coach. In just two years since taking the helm of the school's football program, Shaw proved that statement wrong by not only making Santa Clara a football school but making it a national football power. In his two seasons as boss, Santa Clara won 17 of its 18 games, including two Sugar Bowls. In 1936 and 1937 the Broncos were respectively ranked sixth and ninth nationally. During both years, the Broncos were also ranked first among the nation's major independents. Interestingly, men who had played for Knute Rockne coached four of the nation's top five independents in 1937. Besides Buck Shaw at top-ranked Santa Clara, the list included Clipper Smith at Villanova, Jim Crowley at Fordham, and Eddie Anderson at Holy Cross, whose schools were ranked third through fifth, respectively. "Jock" Sutherland coached number two-ranked Pittsburgh.

Taking note of Santa Clara's gridiron success, schools nationwide approached Santa Clara about scheduling games in hopes of attracting larger crowds and collecting bigger gate receipts. Beginning in 1938 Santa Clara's football schedule took on more of an intersectional flavor. Customary games with the University of Portland, Gonzaga and Loyola were replaced by the likes of Texas A&M, Arkansas and Michigan State. This football transformation occurred without the university reducing its classroom demands on student-athletes, as evidenced by the academic dismissal of key football players Chuck Pavelko and Orville Hanners in January of 1938.[1]

Shaw had experienced only mediocre success in earlier head coaching gigs at North Carolina State and Nevada. What accounted for the turn around at Santa Clara? One explanation is that Buck had more talented players than he had at either Raleigh or Reno. Yet many coaches with talented teams can't crank out winners. Buck not only spotted talent, but he knew how to best employ it. The "Silver Fox" had a knack for positioning players where they excelled, contributing more to the team's overall success. For example, in an era when the quarterback was primarily a signal caller and blocker, Shaw moved Nello Falaschi from fullback to quarterback to capitalize on his tremendous blocking ability. He later successfully switched guard Chuck Pavelko to quarterback for the same reason. Both moves enhanced the Bronco offense.

Like other winning coaches, Buck allocated hours to both teaching fundamentals

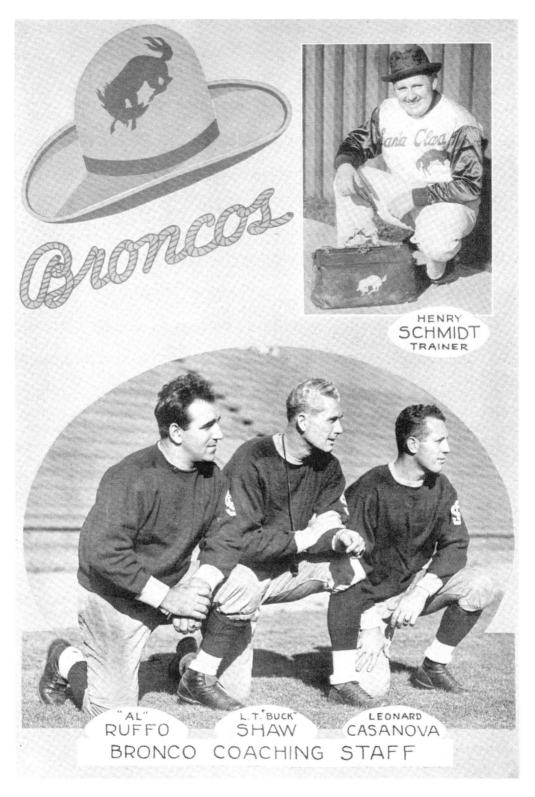

BRONCOS

HENRY
SCHMIDT
TRAINER

"AL"
RUFFO

L.T. "BUCK"
SHAW

LEONARD
CASANOVA

BRONCO COACHING STAFF

The 1938 Santa Clara University coaching staff as pictured in that year's Texas A&M game program. Left to right: Al Ruffo, Buck Shaw and Len Casanova (courtesy Archives and Special Collections, Santa Clara University).

and having his teams practice them. "He drilled us in 'moving your feet, keeping your balance,' things like that," recalled center Phil Dougherty.[2] Committed to making his players students of the game, Shaw held half-hour chalk talks daily, often having players diagram plays in which they not only had to draw their own position's assignment, but the assignments of the other 10 players as well. Hoping to eliminate mental mistakes, he gave his squads weekly examinations, graded them himself and then posted the grades on the team bulletin board. As a result, many of Buck's former players professed to have a deeper understanding of the game than the teams they played against.[3] While such practices are common today, they were cutting-edge in the 1930s.

Shaw had honed his analytical skills and meticulous attention to detail during his apprenticeship under his predecessor Clipper Smith. Buck's well-organized practices kept players hopping and engaged from start to finish. (Nothing loses player interest in practice faster than periods of idle standing.) Players appreciated their coach planning training table menus and repeatedly checking their equipment to insure it was of the best quality. (Having no say over such matters irked Shaw while coaching at Nevada.)

Shaw retained Clipper Smith's practice of selecting individual game captains. Believing it bolstered team morale, Buck appointed a different senior as captain before each game. If Santa Clara won, the captain received the game ball as a memento. In 1937, the coach faced a dilemma in having 13 seniors but only eight games. Improvising, Buck opted to name a captain—and a new ball—for each half. As a result, all 13 seniors received a game ball. In 1938, Buck resumed the two-unit system he had implemented in 1937. He tabbed the first eleven the "Buckaroos" and the second unit the "Shawnees."

Buck Shaw's greatest coaching asset may have been his personality and the way he treated young men. Unlike many coaches who shouted themselves hoarse, Buck neither used profanity nor yelled on the practice field. Eschewing humiliating a player with a public scolding, Shaw preferred to modify subpar performance by whispering an appropriate observation or suggestion in one's ear. On the eve of home games Buck showed his team a full-length movie on campus, followed by serving sherbet and wafers, and then led the squad on a relaxing walk around campus before the 10 p.m. curfew. Swagged out in the latest headphones, today's college player might guffaw at being served sherbet and wafers, but it was one of the many reasons why his teams loved Buck.

Santa Clara opened the 1938 campaign with an impressive 22–0 win over Stanford before 50,000 fans at Palo Alto. From the opening kickoff to the final gun, when the Bronco fourth string was threatening to score, Santa Clara controlled the action. It was Shaw's third successive win over Stanford. Late in the game a bunch of rowdies sitting behind the Santa Clara bench began taunting Stanford coach Tiny Thornhill. Hearing the ruckus, Shaw rose from his team bench, approached the group and told them to stop.[4] They did. The act was typical of Shaw's gentlemanly behavior.

Shaw was apprehensive about hosting Texas A&M at Kezar stadium the following week. In the days before film exchanges and software programs such as Hudl, coaches scouted upcoming opponents in person. When conflicts or distance prevented that, coaches often contracted to have college or high school coaches in the opponent's locale scout for them. In this case, the College Station coach Buck hired to scout the Aggies failed to diagram or even mention the "double shift" in the scouting report he sent Santa Clara. Hearing through the coaching grapevine that A&M coach Homer Norton had employed a deceptive "double shift" in previous wins over Texas A&I and Tulsa had Shaw worried. It took Shaw and assistant coach Al Ruffo most of the first half to get a bead on A&M's shift. Although the "double shift" troubled Santa Clara early, the game remained scoreless after 30 minutes. At halftime Shaw made several defensive adjustments, one of which was his decision to play only his first unit "Buckaroos" in the second half. The move paid off as the Buckaroos stymied heralded A&M halfback Dick Todd, while managing to score on Ray McCarthy's four-yard run. Santa Clara's 7–0 win sent 35,000 Bronco fans home happy.

On the afternoon of October 13, the Santa Clara Special departed the Third and Townsend station carrying the team and over 100 alumni and fans to Phoenix, where two nights later the Broncos would meet coach Orian "Toad" Landreth's Arizona Wildcats, who junketed up from Tucson. Playing their first night game since 1933, Santa Clara rolled to a 27–0 victory while using three separate units. It was Santa Clara's 13th consecutive victory.

Santa Clara hosted the University of Arkansas at Kezar the following week. The Razorbacks billed themselves as the "passingest team what am," a claim confirmed by throwing the ball an unheard of 103 times in its previous three games.[5] Treating the contest as a junior Rose Bowl, Arkansas Governor Carl E. Bailey and the Razorback band accompanied the team. To enhance his team's passing attack, coach Fred Thomsen recruited several basketball players including 6-foot, 8-inch "Treetop" Freiberger as pass-catching ends. Thomsen believed that a basketball player's jumping and ball handling ability made him a natural pass catcher. Asked how he thought his Razorbacks would fare against Santa Clara, Thomsen replied, "Buck Shaw has taken all the good points of the Notre Dame System, added to it and modernized it. They'll be tough."[6]

Over 30,000 fans enjoyed one of the most exciting, wide-open games to hit the Bay Area in years. Combined, the teams passed 45 times for over 240 yards. Ironically, while only completing four of 22 passes, Santa Clara gained 164 yards through the air compared to Arkansas' 78 yards on seven completions in 23 attempts. Santa Clara's ball-hawking defense created excitement by intercepting six Razorback passes that netted 133 yards in return yardage. Perhaps the contest's most thrilling play came with the ball on Arkansas' 46-yard line. Bronco Dick Clark tossed a short pass to his Hawaiian end Bill Anahu. Hit immediately by a Razorback defender, Anahu alertly lateraled the ball back to 220-pound center Johnny Schiechl, who barreled the last 35 yards for Santa Clara's first score of the game. Santa Clara rang up two more touchdowns in downing the Razorbacks 21–6. The win not only earned Buck Shaw the United Press' "Coach of the Week" Award, it also sparked rumors that UCLA officials were courting Shaw to succeed Bill Spaulding as coach. Spaulding, who was finishing his 32nd year in the profession and his 14th at the Bruin helm, had already announced his retirement at season's end.

* * *

Winning on the road is always a challenge because so many travel variables are beyond the coaches' and team's control. Despite scrupulous attention to detail, things can and often do go awry—as when Santa Clara traveled east to meet former Golden Domer Charley Bachman's Michigan State Spartans. Believing the college town of East Lansing wouldn't afford his squad a tranquil night's sleep, Shaw opted to spend the eve of the game in nearby Battle Creek. However, the "Silver Fox" never imagined how excruciating the next day's 45-mile trip to State's Macklin Field would be. Upon leaving Battle Creek, Shaw noticed the driver of the team bus traversing the countryside at a leisurely pace. Looking out the window it seemed like young boys peddling bicycles were keeping pace with the Bronco bus. Between worried glances at his watch, Shaw repeatedly dropped gentle reminders to the driver that the team had a two o'clock kickoff. As the bus trundled slowly by each mile marker, Shaw grew increasingly apprehensive about being late for the kickoff. His gentle reminders to the seemingly comatose driver to step on it turned to urgent pleas. But Buck's desperate entreaties fell on deaf ears. After covering 45 miles in an agonizing hour and 50 minutes, the bus, belching black exhaust fumes, mercifully arrived at Macklin Field 20 minutes before the scheduled kickoff. The sell-out crowd of 21,000 began to wonder if there was going to be a game at all.

The Broncos barely had time to unload the bus and change into their uniforms, let alone warm up. It showed, as the Spartans totally dominated the first quarter, taking a 6–0 lead on Johnny Pingel's four-yard scoring run. The game's momentum changed minutes later when substitute Bronco tackle Nick Stubler blocked Casimir Klewicki's punt, which ricocheted 20 feet in the air before descending into the waiting arms of Santa Clara's Walter Smith, who lugged the pigskin 30 yards into State's end zone. Tom Gilbert's extra-point kick gave Santa Clara a 7–6 lead. Neither team scored in a physically brutal second half. Santa Clara's 7–6 win was costly, as halfback Ray McCarthy sustained a concussion, fullback Bill Gunther left the stadium on crutches, Jim Barlow suffered a broken nose, and tackle George Locke and halfback Jack Roche sustained shoulder injuries.

Several days after the Michigan State game, the *Oakland Tribune* reported on a Washington, D.C., sports editor who compiled a consensus by national coaches opposed to the point-after-touchdown. He quoted Buck Shaw's opinion on the matter as follows: "The point-after-touchdown is grossly unfair. It should not decide a football game because it is not an integral part of the game."[7] The *Tribune* then asked Buck the following: So how does it sound after the Broncos' 7–6 victory over Michigan State last week?[8] Little did anyone know what an omen the extra point discussion would turn out to be for Shaw and Santa Clara.

* * *

On November 2, the team's first day back from its six-day trip to East Lansing, Buck Shaw put his squad through a rugged intra-squad scrimmage. Believing the quality of his kids' overall play had been gradually slipping since the season-opening shutout of Stanford, Shaw hoped scrimmaging might help them regain their early season form for the upcoming game against the University of San Francisco. Ignoring the pundits rating them a 2 to 1 underdog, San Francisco coach George Malley's Dons were fired up to meet their Jesuit rival. Acknowledging Santa Clara's superior depth, Malley confidently predicted that his starting eleven would more than hold their own. The Dons did for much of the afternoon. The first half ended scoreless. Despite controlling the game's tempo, the Broncos seemed lethargic until early in the third quarter when sophomore Jimmy Johnson, behind great blocking, bolted 27 yards for the game's only score. While glad his team had won, a concerned Shaw told reporters after the game, "We weren't primed today. We looked like we did against Michigan State. We looked tired."[9] Santa Clara's 7–0 defeat of the Dons was its 16th consecutive victory, and Buck Shaw's 23rd win in 24 games since taking the school's football helm in 1936.

Since the Dons had lost a close one to St. Mary's earlier in the season, sportswriters queried San Francisco coach Malley for his take on the upcoming Little Big Game. "They [Santa Clara] won't find St. Mary's as easy to wear down as we were," replied Malley. "St. Mary's can replace man for man and not weaken its line-up at all."[10]

Scouting Santa Clara that afternoon was St. Mary's assistant coach Red Strader. Strader had been on the sidelines of New York's Polo Grounds the day before when Fordham eked out a 3–0 win over his Gaels. He then boarded a plane to San Francisco and caught the Bronco-Don contest at Kezar Stadium. Days before the Little Big Game he told the *San Francisco Examiner,* "Our line looked better against Fordham than Santa Clara's line looked against U.S.F.—and you know what they say—football games are won and lost in the line."[11]

When asked if he thought Saint Mary's transcontinental train trip might hinder the Gaels' performance in the Little Big Game, Shaw responded, "Back in 1935, they arrived home on Wednesday to play us on Sunday and they had more punch than they did all season. We were licked 10–0 and outplayed 40–0. And as I recall, St. Mary's had dropped a close game to Fordham that year too."[12] Shaw also conceded that the Gaels had steadily improved during the season while his Broncos' play had tapered off.

* * *

John Bridgers was the head football coach at Baylor University from 1959 through 1968. He later became athletic director at Florida State University, where he hired Bobby Bowden to lead the Seminole football program. During his 34-year tenure at Tallahassee, Bowden consistently led Florida State to national prominence. Bridgers told this author that Bowden's greatest attribute as a coach was how quickly he shook off a loss to totally focus on the next opponent. From all accounts, St. Mary's coach Slip Madigan possessed that same unique quality. His 1938 loss to Fordham only seemed to energize the "Moraga Maestro" in preparing for undefeated Santa Clara, which the pundits rated as a 2 to 1 favorite entering the Little Big Game.

Before 59,852 anticipatory fans jammed into Kezar stadium, the two former Notre Dame teammates, Buck and Slip, matched coaching wits again. Vicious blocking, tackling and the usual bloodletting resulted in a scoreless first half. In the third quarter Bronco Tom Gilbert intercepted Ed Heffernan's pass only to fumble while being tackled, which sparked a mad scramble in pursuit of the bouncing pigskin. The loose ball eluded the clutches of a half-dozen outstretched arms before Gael tackle George Cantwell, assuming the perfect fetal position, corralled the slippery spheroid at the Santa Clara 29-yard line. Three straight pass completions gave the Gaels first-and-goal at the Bronco four-yard line. On fourth-and-goal with 90 seconds remaining in the third quarter, St. Mary's "Whitey" Smith plowed into the end zone from a yard out. An elated Slip Madigan danced a jig and wildly waved his hat on the sideline as Mike Perrie booted the extra point giving St. Mary's a 7–0 lead.

Enraged at the prospect of their 16-game winning streak ending, Santa Clara shifted into high gear in the fourth quarter. Despite driving inside the Gael red zone on their next three possessions, Madigan's men kept the Broncos from scoring and St. Mary's earned a 7–0 upset win.

As the two head coaches shook hands at midfield a grinning Madigan told Shaw, "Your team played great!"

To which Shaw replied, "Your team played great!"[13]

In the victor's locker room jubilant players danced on benches and tables as St. Mary's president Brother Albert, ecstatic in the wake of his school's triumph, excitedly announced, "Jimmy Roosevelt was sitting with me as my guest. We both nearly went crazy. I think Jimmy was as excited as I was. We both acted like maniacs."[14] Jimmy, of course, was President Franklin Roosevelt's son, who was in California convalescing from an illness. Seeing an opportunity to cash in on Brother Albert's elation, Gael players began chanting, "No school tomorrow!"[15] Their chants, however, bounced off Brother Albert's ears like torrential rain splashing off a flat rock. Classes were held as usual the next day in Moraga.

When Santa Clara coaches Shaw, Ruffo and Casanova entered the sullen Bronco locker room many players were in tears. Suddenly, the gloom lifted as players rose in unison to give their coaches a rousing three cheers of "Hip, hip, hooray!"[16] The respectful gesture brought a smile to Buck's face. When asked his thoughts on the end of his team's winning streak, Buck confessed, "The kids feel the same way about it that I do. We're glad the pressure is off. Those 16 straight wins were mighty heavy to carry."[17]

Al Ruffo, Buck's right-hand assistant, echoed his boss' sentiments: "That streak created a tension in the last three weeks that was felt by every man on the squad. The strain was terrific. It always is when teams are trying to protect long winning streaks."[18]

* * *

That evening Buck Shaw met with UCLA graduate manager Bill Ackerman at the Palace Hotel. Ackerman had attended the Little Big Game that afternoon. Since Bill Spaulding had recently announced his retirement as the Bruins' football coach to devote all of his attention to the being athletic director, the two undoubtedly discussed Shaw going to UCLA. When reporters queried Buck on reports that he might be heading to Los Angeles, Shaw replied, "They haven't made any decision down there. And I haven't made any here."[19]

* * *

Despite losing to St. Mary's, Santa Clara could still go "Bowling" with a win over the University of Detroit in its season finale. Like the previous year against Gonzaga, the finale would be a charity game played in Sacramento. Winners of three straight, the Titans came west sporting a record of five wins and four losses. Gus Dorais, whose brilliant 1913 passing performance on the plains of West Point put Notre Dame on the football map, now coached Detroit. As an assistant to Knute Rockne he had coached Buck Shaw at Notre Dame in 1919 before leaving to become head coach at Columbia College, which later became the University of Portland. In 1925, Dorais became head coach and athletic director at Detroit.

Knowing that Buck Shaw favored outlawing football's extra-point as much as he did, Dorais contacted Shaw weeks earlier suggesting that they play their game as a trial case for jettisoning extra-point attempts. Dorais recommended that should the game end with the score tied, the team with the most first downs be given an extra point and declared the winner. If both teams had an equal number of first downs, the team with the most offensive yardage gained would win. Shaw eagerly agreed. For whatever reason, the two men never formalized the agreement and played the game by the rule book. Captious sportswriters later lambasted Shaw for his forgetfulness in failing to finalize the deal. However, Dorais later claimed that Buck sent him a telegram while Detroit was en route to Sacramento stating that he had changed his mind.[20]

Clipper Smith, now coaching at Villanova, wrote Buck a week before the Sacramento contest warning, "Dorais has a good team, despite its four defeats this year, and you cannot afford to hold it lightly."[21] The message resonated with Buck that very afternoon while witnessing the freshman squad knock his varsity around in a scrimmage. Shaw warned his charges that unless they snapped out of their "funk" from the St. Mary's loss, they'd be a pushover for Detroit.

Played before 18,000 fans at Sacramento's Municipal stadium, Santa Clara scored first on Ray McCarthy's beautiful fingertip catch of Bruno Pellegrini's 24-yard pass. Tom Gilbert's extra-point kick missed wide right. In the third quarter, Detroit's Ed Palumbo heaved a pass intended for Bill Schauer. In good position, Santa Clara defender Tom Gilbert intended to bat the pass down. Unfortunately, he accidentally deflected it into Schauer's arms, who raced 69 yards to score. Nicholas Pagen then successfully kicked what would become a most debated extra point. The Titan's quirky touchdown came immediately after a 15-yard unnecessary roughness penalty on Bronco Jim Coughlan, which gave Detroit a first down. The officials later negated an 80-yard Santa Clara touchdown when they ruled it an illegal forward pass. With only three minutes left in the contest the Broncos took possession on their own 33-yard line and drove to Detroit's 10-yard line. With just 10 seconds remaining in the game, the snake-bit Tom Gilbert attempted a field goal. However, the Titans' Emerson Addison blocked the kick giving Detroit a 7–6 win.

For one of the few times in his coaching career Buck was angry after a game. Santa Clara had 12 first downs to Detroit's four, and outgained them in offensive yardage 266 to 147. On three occasions Shaw's team had penetrated inside the Titans' 10-yard line and failed to score—twice when Jimmy Murphy intercepted Bronco passes in the end zone. When asked to explain the loss, Buck replied: "Explain it? How else but that it must have been the coach's fault? The kids didn't let down. They pushed Detroit all over the field. Don't blame them for losing—blame me."[22]

When *Oakland Tribune* reporter Bill Tobbit asked if he could give Detroit credit for winning, Buck replied bitterly, "Not much."[23]

In the winners' locker room a joyful Gus Dorais confirmed Buck's assessment to Tobbit: "No team of mine has ever taken a worse physical beating and come out on top. We came out here with only two fullbacks. Both were knocked cold in the first quarter, and I had to move a halfback over to play there the entire game." Dorais then added, "Santa Clara is the best team I've seen all year and that includes Purdue, which beat us 19–6 and which plays the Broncos next year."[24]

The loss killed any hopes of Santa Clara going "Bowling." The Cotton, Sun and Orange Bowls never pursued earlier feelers sent to the school. Had Shaw confirmed his initial agreement with Dorais to play the game without kicking extra points, Santa Clara would have been declared the winner by the tie-breaker rules mutually agreed upon— namely, by gaining more first downs (12) than Detroit (four). Of course, there was no guarantee that a Bowl would have invited the Broncos for winning the game under such circumstances. However, that didn't stop the Bay Area media from speculating that some Bowl would have extended the Broncos an invitation. Several writers criticized Shaw for his "forgetfulness" in letting the extra-point matter drop or change of heart, that could have cost the University as much as $50,000 from Bowl revenue. There's no record of Buck ever addressing these accusations either privately or publicly. Another outcome of the Broncos' loss to Detroit was that UCLA lost interest in wooing Shaw to become its next football coach.

Although kicking an extra point allowed his team to win, Gus Dorais remained adamant that extra-point attempts should be stricken from the rules. Immediately after the contest he argued: "It is not fair to the spectators to have the result of the game hinge on a conversion. It is not football to decide a game by the outcome of a try for goal. I am still of the opinion that the point after touchdown should be abolished."[25]

Dorais then elaborated: "Today's game illustrates just exactly what I have been driving at. The best team did not win. Santa Clara outplayed us and just because we had a placekicker on the squad we get the victory. It isn't right although I'm tickled to death right now."

NINE

"Slip" Departs
and the T Formation Arrives

Buck Shaw used spring practice to evaluate personnel, and experiment with new defenses and offensive wrinkles. Once he decided on what, if any, changes to implement, he honed them in the fall. He'd make personnel changes when warranted and add plays from previous years as the season progressed, but he never tinkered with totally new concepts during the season. Seeking ways to reduce player injuries, Shaw purchased padded blocking aprons for his defensive players to wear during drills and scrimmages before the '39 season. Although cumbersome, the aprons shielded players from absorbing the full impact of blocks while still enabling defenders to run. Shaw would have marveled at the lightweight, padded compression shorts and undershirts protecting today's players.

Having lost over a dozen key players from the '38 squad to graduation, his team's overall lack of experience concerned Buck, especially in the face of another formidable intersectional schedule. Although the '38 freshman squad went undefeated, spring practice convinced Buck that few of the soon-to-be sophomores were ready for yeoman's duty with the varsity. The season opener confirmed Shaw's assessment.

Santa Clara opened the '39 campaign at the University of Utah. The Utes were no pushover. Yet oddsmakers had the Broncos a two-touchdown favorite. The team may have encountered a bad omen en route to Salt Lake City when their Southern Pacific special crashed into a railroad handcar. Fortunately, the mishap caused no injuries and resulted in only a 10-minute delay.[1] To the visitors' surprise, the University of Utah band and school officials gave them a warm welcome at the train station.

Santa Clara's inexperience quickly became evident to both Buck and 17,000 fans at Utah's sun-splashed stadium. While Shaw's first unit "Buckaroos" jumped to an early 7–0 lead, the play of his second unit "Shawnees" was shaky. Their inevitable collapse came in the fourth quarter when Shawnee Dick Clark fumbled future NFL Hall-of-Famer Mac Speedie's punt and Utah recovered on the Bronco 20-yard line. Before Shaw could send his first unit back into the game the Utes had tied the score at 7. The Broncos' first unit played the rest of the way but couldn't score, and the game ended in a 7–7 tie. His team's lack of experience compelled Shaw to temporarily abandon his coveted two-unit system.

The Broncos returned home to meet the rugged Texas A&M Aggies under the lights at Seal Stadium. Halfback Johnny Kimbrough, who would finish second in the 1940 Heisman balloting, led the Aggies into San Francisco. Abandoning the two-unit system, Santa Clara led 3–0 midway through the fourth quarter when A&M's Marion Pugh connected on an 18-yard touchdown pass to Jim Thomasen to give the Aggies a 7–3 win.

Coach Homer Norton's Aggies would finish the season undefeated and beat Tulane in the Sugar Bowl.

Santa Clara hoped to break into the win column the following week against the University of San Francisco. However, George Malley's Dons came to play and led 13–7 with only 72 seconds remaining in the contest. That's when Bronco sophomore Ken Casanega heaved a pass into the end zone where Jack Roche out-jumped two Dons to make the scoring catch. However, the Dons' Grant Hill blocked the extra-point attempt and the game ended tied at 13.

> After three games the Broncos were still looking for that elusive first win. Since becoming head coach in 1936, Buck's teams had achieved the enviable record of 23 wins, four losses and two ties, with two Sugar Bowl victories. His teams' worst defeat was a 9–0 loss to TCU. Including the last two contests of the '38 season—losses to St. Mary's and Detroit—Shaw had coached five straight games without a win. Despite his impressive overall record at Santa Clara, some Bay Area writers now wielded their pens like rapiers in slicing up the "Silver Fox." Art Cohn, the *Oakland Tribune's* sports editor wrote: Handsome Lawrence built himself a $15,000 manse down on the peninsula. Obviously, he figured he was set for life at Santa Clara. A dangerous hunk of wishful thinking, there. Already he has played three games this season … without one win to show for it. The Broncos couldn't beat Utah, Texas A&M, or even little U.S.F. yesterday. How then, are they gonna take St. Mary's this Sunday? … or, one week later, the Purdue team that has already held Notre Dame to a lucky 3 to 0 nod, and that tied Minnesota Saturday, 13 to 13 … or Stanford, Michigan State, U.C.L.A. and Loyola the following weekends?
>
> Handsome Lawrence better hurry up and win a game … or get an FHA 20-year contract at Santa Clara, to go with his house.[2]

If such flapdoodle ever bothered the Silver Fox, he never let on. Shaw and his assistants merely set about preparing their squad for the Little Big Game. They didn't browbeat the troops, but they did emphasize open field tackling. Cutting a practice short, Shaw showed his team the game film of their previous year's loss to St. Mary's. To further fan their competitive fire, he showed various movie clips of the previous Sunday's USF game. Sitting silently in the dark as the projector whirred, Buck offered no commentary. He merely let his audience absorb the mediocrity flickering on the screen before them, hoping it would get their competitive juices simmering.

On game day an undefeated St. Mary's team jogged jauntily onto the Kezar gridiron. Local media pundits predicted that only Santa Clara and Fordham stood between the Gaels and a Sugar Bowl invitation. Most picked St. Mary's to win by a touchdown. Fiercely determined to beat the Gaels, Bronco All-American candidate Johnny Schiechl emphatically promised days before the game, "We'll beat them or they'll carry me off dead. We'll beat 'em or they'll back up an ambulance for me." He then unabashedly declared, "We've got to win one for Buck Shaw. Never mind me…. Buck Shaw hasn't smiled this season. It's about time we put a smile on his face. He's a great guy. We've got to win this one for Buck!"[3]

Under a blazing autumn sun, a smaller than usual Kezar crowd of 45,000 sat in shirtsleeves awaiting the kick-off of the 23rd annual Little Big Game. Fans witnessed a contest they didn't expect. The Gaels' most explosive play of the afternoon came on Whitey Smith's 34-yard run in the second quarter. Little did Gael fans know that Smith's run would comprise nearly half of St. Mary's total offense for the day. Anticipating the Broncos would run wide sweeps and throw into the flats, St. Mary's aligned their defensive guards wider than normal—on the outside shoulders of Santa Clara's guards. Spying the opening in the middle, Bronco Jack Roche called numerous inside running plays that shredded the Gael defensive line while chewing up the clock. After a scoreless first half, the Broncos launched an 80-yard scoring drive that culminated on Jack Roche's seven-yard touchdown pass to Joe Lacey. Jimmy Johnson booted the extra-point. Santa Clara's 7–0 win didn't accurately portray the Bronco's dominant performance. Santa Clara made 11 first downs to the Gaels' two, while gaining 253 yards of total offense to 73 for St. Mary's. The Gaels completed only one of eight passes while throwing three interceptions.

In the victors' locker room exuberant captain Johnny Schiechl wildly waved the game ball for all to see. "The first one, you mugs!" The excited Schiechl repeatedly yelled. "The first one. We got a football at last."[4] Since Buck's Santa Clara teams had earned victories over St. Mary's in 1936 and '37, Schiechl's claim wasn't accurate, but he was spot-on with his promise to win the game for his well-respected coach. Looking like the cat that swallowed the canary, Shaw walked through the dressing room shaking hands with each player.

Smiling, but emotionally drained, Shaw told reporters, "It's hard to single out individuals. This victory was the result of unit play. They were all great."[5]

With St. Mary's dreams of a Sugar Bowl invitation crushed, Slip Madigan graciously declared, "I have nothing but praise for Santa Clara. They played their best game since they trounced Stanford at the start of last season."[6] As a point of emphasis Madigan added, "I do know we were up against the real goods today. Santa Clara outplayed us and that's all there is to it."[7]

Upsetting St. Mary's proved to be the turning point of the Broncos' season. The following week they dispatched Purdue 13–6 at Kezar. Purdue coach A.H. "Mal" Elward, another former Notre Damer, Class of '15, opined after the loss, "The Santa Clara football team can be compared favorably with the outstanding eleven's in the country."[8] On November 4, Santa Clara rode roughshod over Stanford 27–7 at Palo Alto for their fourth consecutive win over the Cardinals since Shaw took the team's coaching reins in '36. In the wake of the visitor's impressive showing, Cardinal coach Tiny Thornhill professed, "That's the smoothest Santa Clara team I have ever seen. In fact, it's the best club we've met this season."[9] Leaving the press box after the game Spud Lewis, the former University of San Francisco head football coach turned sportswriter, remarked, "That Santa Clara team has more tricks than Houdini. It is such a confident outfit that it will take a great team to stop it."[10]

At Kezar Stadium the following week a good Michigan State team gave Santa Clara all it could handle. State coach Charley Bachman directed his Spartans to play conservatively in the first half, punting frequently to gain field position and waiting for a break. The only break, however, came when Bronco Dick Clark tossed a 25-yard touchdown pass to Bill Anahu to give Santa Clara a 6–0 halftime lead. Taking the gloves off in the third quarter, Bachman's Spartans unleashed a variety of trick plays and passes that took them to the Broncos' two-and-a-half yard-line. The scoring threat ended, however, when Spartan Lewis Smiley dropped Ed Pierce's fourth-down pass in the end zone. Santa Clara held on to win 6–0. Winners of four straight, the revitalized Broncos now headed south to meet UCLA.

After losing interest in hiring Shaw as its head coach in 1938, UCLA hired former California All-American Edwin "Babe" Horrell to run its team. Horrell was one of several starters California coach Andy Smith took with him to scout Stanford in 1923, and whose absence contributed to Nevada's Wolf Pack holding the undefeated "Wow Boys" to a scoreless tie. Since then Horrell witnessed Buck Shaw's Broncos defeat LSU in two Sugar Bowls, while working as an assistant coach for the Tigers. Horrell inherited exceptional

Bronco center Johnny Schiechl was determined to win the 1939 St. Mary's game for Buck Shaw. Schiechl's efforts paid off as Santa Clara won 7–0. Schiechl and Santa Clara tackle Al Wolff were consensus All-Americans that year (courtesy Archives and Special Collections, Santa Clara University).

athletic talent when he took the UCLA job, much of it in the form of three African American players: halfbacks Jackie Robinson and Kenny Washington, and end Woody Strode. Fortunately for Santa Clara, the speedy Robinson, who would later break major league baseball's color line, was injured and wouldn't play.

The game was a defensive masterpiece characterized by crisp tackling. With only three seconds left in a scoreless contest, the game came down to UCLA's Jack Sommers' 27-yard field goal attempt. The crowd of 50,000 held its collective breath as Sommers' kick fell short of the goalposts. The exciting contest ended in a scoreless tie.

Navy coach Eddie Erdaletz once quipped, "A tie is like kissing your sister." In this case the sister looked like Marilyn Monroe. Neither team deserved to lose. The brutal battle saw only two injuries. The first, when Santa Clara's Henry Sanders suffered a separated shoulder. The second occurred on the Bruins' sideline. Hollywood comedian Joe E. Brown, a guest on the UCLA bench, became so excited in the game's final seconds that he threw his trick knee out of place and needed medical attention from the Bruins' trainer.[11]

Afterwards UCLA's Woody Strode, the game's defensive standout, told reporters, "They [Santa Clara] are a clean bunch and fun to play against." He then added, "That Santa Clara offense is so tricky you can't do any hard charging against the Broncos. All you can do is walk in about three steps and start looking to see what's happening."[12]

Strode and teammate Kenny Washington would be two of four African Americans to integrate professional football in 1946. Strode and Washington both signed with the NFL's Los Angeles Rams while Marion Motley and Bill Willis played for the Cleveland Browns in the All-America Conference. After his playing days Strode enjoyed a lengthy and successful Hollywood movie career.

The Broncos returned to Los Angeles again the following week for the season's finale against Loyola's Lions. It had been a trying year for Loyola. Winning coach Tom Lieb had resigned as head coach after nine seasons to care for his terminally ill wife. Relishing his time at Loyola, Lieb had especially enjoyed posing with lion cubs for publicity photos. After his wife's passing, Lieb became the head coach at the University of Florida in 1940.

Mike Pecarovich succeeded Lieb at Loyola. Unfortunately, Pecarovich's squad suffered a near disaster early in the season when infantile paralysis afflicted Lion starters Burch Donahue and Bob Link. It quarantined the team for several days and games with St. Mary's and the University of Arizona were postponed until December. Luckily, the illness was limited to those two players, enabling Loyola to play out its schedule. Sporting a record of two wins, three losses and a tie, the Lions aligned to receive the opening kickoff at Gilmore Stadium before 10,000 fans. One of the spectators was Burch Donahue, who—for the first time since contracting the illness a month earlier—was released from the hospital to watch the game from the back of an ambulance. If ever the stage was set for an inspirational upset, this was it. Even so, the Broncos steamrolled over the outclassed Lions 41–0. Shaw may have had a grudge against either Pecarovich or Loyola, for one of the few times in his career he reinserted the first team after the game was well in hand. In any case, after a shaky start, Santa Clara rallied to finish the season with a record of five wins, one loss and three ties.

* * *

Rumors abounded about Buck Shaw's coaching future on New Year's Day of 1940. After winning only one game in 1939, Stanford fired football coach Tiny Thornhill. As weeks passed without the university's board of athletic control (BAC) announcing a successor, speculation grew rampant about who would be the school's next coach. By early January the media's list of possible candidates ballooned to nearly two dozen. In a December campus survey, Stanford students cast 288 out of 735 votes for Buck Shaw to become the school's new coach. San Jose State's Dudley DeGroot finished second with 237.[13] The remaining ballots were scattered among a half-dozen candidates including Missouri's Don Faurot, Oregon's "Tex" Oliver, Wisconsin's Harry Stuhldreher, Columbia's Lou Little and the University of Chicago's Clark Shaughnessy. While the student body preferred Shaw, the alumni overwhelmingly supported fellow alumnus Dud DeGroot.

However, their influence was minimal as the university's BAC would make the final recommendation to university president Ray Wilbur. Meeting on January 7, to select a new coach, the board adjourned without announcing a successor. However, it promised to do so by January 12. Frustrated alumni and media now believed that the "chosen one" would come from another geographical area. If either Shaw or DeGroot, who both lived a stone's throw from Stanford, had been selected, the hiring process would have wrapped up sooner.

On January 11, President Wilbur named Clark Shaughnessy as the Cardinal's new coach. Shaugnessy's hiring precipitated a maelstrom among Stanford's alumni. Most were baffled that Shaughnessy, whose 1939 University of Chicago team had given up more points than any major college team in the country, got the nod over Cardinal alumnus Dud DeGroot, whose San Jose State Spartans led the nation in scoring. Furthermore, because the University of Chicago and Loyola of New Orleans had both dropped football—two schools where Shaughnessy had previously coached—many wondered if Shaughnessy's hiring signaled the death knell for Stanford football. University of Chicago president Robert Hutchins dropped football after Chicago's disastrous 1939 season that saw Shaughnessy's Maroons lose to Harvard and Ohio State by matching 61–0 scores and suffer shutouts at the hands of Michigan (85–0) and Illinois (46–0). Even tiny Beloit College blanked hapless Chicago 6–0. Nevertheless, the professorial Shaughnessy had developed a reputation as an offensive genius whose severe lack of talent at Chicago had prevented his teams from winning.

However, would Shaughnessy ever prove the skeptics wrong! While serving as an advisor to the NFL's Chicago Bears during his time in the Windy City, he began tinkering with the T formation. Used early in the 20th century, the T was eventually jettisoned by most schools in favor of the single-wing and double-wing formations. Shaughnessy had played the T under coach Doc Williams at Minnesota in 1911. Shaughnessy's T emphasized quickness and deception instead of brute power. It also put the quarterback directly under center, a tactic few college teams had ever seen in 1940. That spring Shaughnessy brought Chicago Bears quarterback Ben Masterson to Palo Alto to help teach the T formation to the Cardinals. Shaughnessy's 1940 Stanford squad silenced his hordes of critics and disgruntled alumni by going undefeated and beating Nebraska in the Rose Bowl.

Numerous changes came to the Pacific Coast's coaching scene in 1940. In Los Angeles, Loyola refused to renew the contract of the snake-bitten Mike Pecarovich. In a stunner, Loyola hired none other than Shaw's old boss and predecessor at Santa Clara, Maurice "Clipper" Smith. Having won 29 games in four seasons at Villanova, Smith believed he had taken the program as far as he could. The Clipper intended to take assistant coach Vince McNally with him. (McNally would later play a key role in Shaw's career.) However, football coaches can be as fickle as a bouncing pigskin and to the chagrin of Loyola University officials, both men changed their mind two weeks later.

Loyola initially declared its intention to hold Smith to the agreement he expressed in letters and telegrams. But when Smith recommended LaSalle's Marty Brill as his coaching replacement, the California school let the matter drop and signed Brill to a three-year contract. Brill had been a devastating blocking back on Knute Rockne's 1930 national championship Notre Dame team.

California's college coaching carousel delivered one more shocker in early 1940, when the St. Mary's athletic board relieved the flamboyant and highly successful Edward "Slip" Madigan of his coaching duties after a 19-year tenure at the school. No individual played a greater role in St. Mary's moving its campus from the brick pile site on Broadway Street in Oakland to a beautiful, rustic setting in Moraga. Funds used to purchase the Moraga site came from the school's enhanced football gate receipts, and Slip Madigan was responsible for that. The year before Madigan took the reins at St. Mary's, California massacred the Gaels on the gridiron 127–0. Madigan's leadership, marketing zeal, and coaching skills transformed St. Mary's football from a laughing stock into a national power. His winning teams and colorful personality made him a favorite of numerous Hollywood celebrities and politicians. Babe Ruth attended St. Mary's games. As Dave Newhouse writes in *The Incredible Slip Madigan*, "By 1939, though, St. Mary's College officials had grown tired of hearing that the 'SMC' on the hill overlooking the campus stood for 'Slip Madigan College.'" St. Mary's hired Red Strader, the school's first All-American and Madigan's long-time assistant, as its new head coach.

* * *

That summer football fans living in the Far West voted Buck Shaw as one of the men to coach the College All-Stars. The brainchild of *Chicago Tribune* sports editor Arch Ward, the late summer clash between the College All-Stars and the National Football League champions had gained wide acceptance since its inception in 1934. In the '30s college football was immensely more popular than the professional game. When Ward first proposed the game to benefit the *Chicago Tribune* Charities, Inc., NFL team owners—seeing it as a chance to gain national exposure—enthusiastically embraced the proposal. Often played before crowds of 90,000, the game was an unqualified success that heralded the start of the football season for over 40 years.[14] For various reasons the NFL opted to end the traditional contest in 1976.

Iowa's Dr. Eddie Anderson, Buck's blocking partner at Notre Dame, served as the All-Stars' head coach. In 1939, Anderson coached Heisman Trophy winner Nile Kinnick and Iowa's famed "Iron Men" to a six-win, one-loss and one-tie record. The good doctor earned the honor by receiving over four million votes in a national poll, a million more than runner-up Don Faurot of Missouri. Voting by region, fans elected Faurot from the Midwest, Princeton's Tad Wieman from the East, Tulane's Lowell (Red) Dawson from the South, and Shaw from the Far West. Anderson's Iowa assistants, Frank Carideo and Jim Harris, rounded out the All-Star staff.

On August 11, 1940, 67 players reported to the All-Star camp at Evanston, Illinois, for three weeks of practice to meet the NFL champion Green Bay Packers. Shaw would coach two of his own Santa Clara players, Johnny Schiechl and Bill Anahu, as well several kids who had previously squared off against his Bronco squads. That list included Kenny Washington (UCLA), Ken Kavanaugh (LSU), Stan Andersen (Stanford), Jack McDermott (Detroit); as well as Purdue's Felix Mackiewicz, Lou Brock, Frank Bykowski and Ted Hennis. Shaw enjoyed meeting and working with the All-Stars. The feeling was mutual as players soon referred to the 41-year-old coach as "The Great White Father" because of his premature gray hair and calm demeanor.[15]

The All-Star camp certainly had its humorous moments. Before one practice a local cub reporter spied Shaw walking through the locker room.

"Coach Shaw," the reporter asked. "How does it feel to be reunited with your old Notre Dame teammate, Eddie Anderson?"

"Hell," replied Shaw. "I had to carry that guy for three years at Notre Dame. Now, look at him!" With that Shaw smiled, waved and exited the room. No sooner had Shaw departed than Anderson entered through another doorway.

Still looking for a human-interest angle, the rookie reporter asked, "Dr. Anderson, how does it feel to be working with Buck Shaw again after all of these years?"

Cracking a crooked smile Anderson explained, "Do you know that I carried that guy for three years at Notre Dame? I guess I can carry him for a few more weeks."[16]

The All-Star game saw Anderson matching coaching wits with another of his former Notre Dame teammates, Curley Lambeau. Both had lettered during Anderson's freshman year at South Bend in 1918, before Lambeau left school to play professional ball. Lambeau was now Green Bay's head coach and still seething from his Packers' loss to coach Gus Dorais' All-Stars in 1937. On August 29, the afternoon's clouds dissipated, leaving a star-filled sky for the spotlights of Chicago's Soldier Field to illuminate during player introductions. Sparked by Don Hutson's three touchdown receptions, Green Bay prevailed 45-28 in a wide-open contest before 84,567 fans. USC's Albert Schindler, whose interception set up one of his two touchdowns, was named the All-Stars' Most Valuable Player.

Buck Shaw's only post-game comment to reporters was "That Hutson sure was bad news, wasn't he!"[17]

* * *

Santa Clara hosted the University of Utah in the first game of a college double-header at Kezar stadium to open the 1940 season. In the nightcap, coach Clark Shaughnessy unveiled Stanford's new T formation against the University of San Francisco. The Broncos looked impressive in a 34-13 win over coach Ike Armstrong's Utes, who went on to win seven games that year. After the opener, Utah's Mac Speedie returned to the field to watch the nightcap. Taking one look at Stanford's offense, Speedie ran back to his locker room shouting, "Hey, you guys, come out here. There's this crazy formation and these guys are running all over the place. I can't find the football."[18]

The following Friday night Santa Clara eked out a 9-6 win over UCLA before 50,000 fans. Having scouted Stanford against USF, Shaw and assistant Al Ruffo knew they'd be in for a rough contest at Palo Alto on October 12. With savvy southpaw Frankie Albert at quarterback, Hugh Gallarneau and Pete Kmetovic at halfbacks, and 225-pound Norm "Big Chief" Standlee at fullback, Shaughnessy's T formation backfield was more than for midable. The Cardinals drew first blood on Standlee's 11-yard scoring run against Shaw's second unit Buckaroos. (That year Buck tagged the first unit as the Shawnees and the second as the Buckaroos.) Albert kicked the extra-point to give Stanford a 7-0 lead. In the third quarter Bronco Ken Casanega connected on a beautiful 43-yard touchdown pass to Johnny Thom. Unfortunately, Jimmy Johnson missed the all-important extra-point. In a tight defensive struggle, punctuated by brutal hitting, Stanford's starters began to wear down in the fourth quarter, but Norm Standlee's punting continually kept the Broncos pinned deep in their own territory. Albert's extra point proved to be the difference in Stanford's 7-6 win. The win snapped the Cardinals' four-game losing streak to Buck's Broncos.

During their post-game handshake Shaw told Shaughnessy, "We didn't deserve to win today, Clark. Had we won I think I would have given the game back to you. Your gang was certainly in there fighting, mine seemed lethargic, just didn't have the old pep."[19]

Later in the locker room Buck confessed to reporters that he felt he spent too much

In 1940, Buck Shaw claimed Santa Clara halfback Jimmy Johnson was a better punter, quick-kicker and passer than 1939 Heisman Trophy winner Nile Kinnick of Iowa. Johnson received All-American recognition in 1940 (courtesy Archives and Special Collections, Santa Clara University).

time on defense preparing for the T formation. "It hurt us," said Shaw. "The boys just didn't know what to do on offense. I'm to blame on that one."[20]

After a bye week to lick their wounds, Santa Clara rode east to be the Homecoming guest of Michigan State. Hoping to avoid a repeat of the seemingly interminable game-day bus ride his team endured from Battle Creek to East Lansing in 1938, Shaw's boys bivouacked the night before in Jackson, Michigan, only 30 miles from Macklin Field.

With no score and only four minutes remaining in the game, the Spartans were in the midst of what appeared to be a game winning drive. However, one determined Bronco had other ideas, and for the next three-and-one-half minutes the game became the Jimmy Johnson show. Johnson intercepted a Spartan pass on his own five-yard line and returned it to the Santa Clara 27. Switching to offense, Johnson proceeded to complete six of eight consecutive passes giving the Broncos a first-and-goal on State's eight-yard line with only 30 seconds remaining. Rather than attempt a pass or two into the end zone, Johnson aligned for a 16-yard field goal try. However, as Johnson's kick sailed wide right of the upright, grateful green-clad State rooters clapped joyously. The game ended a scoreless tie.

Buck and company returned to Kezar the following Sunday to meet the University of San Francisco. The Dons would be without head coach George Malley, who was still recovering from the shock of his wife dying from a fall in their home shortly before the start of the season. Believing he was on the verge of a nervous breakdown, doctors ordered Malley to take a few weeks away from coaching to convalesce in Lake Tahoe. Determined to present their despondent coach with the winning game ball over their Jesuit rival, USF played lights out for the game's first 27 minutes. But then Ken Casanega, whose last-minute touchdown pass enabled Santa Clara to tie the Dons in '39, hurled a 55-yard scoring bomb to Tom Matula. The play disheartened the Dons, and the Broncos rolled to a 27–0 win. However, as is sometimes the case, a coach can prevail on the gridiron one day, but still get roasted in the papers the next. On Monday, Prescott Sullivan of the *San Francisco Examiner* shamed Shaw for supposedly "running up" the score on a team missing its ailing coach. Sullivan's accusation failed to mention that Don fumbles and penalties deep in their own territory led to a couple of Bronco second-half scores. Buck Shaw had no control over that.

The game, however, did give Santa Clara a scare when Dr. Eddie Amaral and trainer Henry Schmidt led a teary, confused and concussed Jimmy Johnson to the locker room. Afterwards Buck spoke highly of the talented halfback, a key player. "Jimmy Johnson," declared Shaw, "is a better punter, superior quick kicker, more effective passer, and as good a runner as Nile Kinnick."[21] Shaw, who coached the Heisman Trophy winner Kinnick in that summer's College All-Star game, was qualified to offer such an assessment.

After defeating USF Buck shared some of his coaching beliefs with sportswriter Harry Grayson. "Enthusiasm," said Shaw, "is the most important thing in football ... 75 percent of the game is enthusiasm where blocking and tackling are concerned. The other 25 percent is technique. You can do no more than teach a player how to block and tackle. If he hasn't the enthusiasm for it on any one day he won't be of much use.... I am convinced that one's enthusiasm for the game spells the difference between victory and defeat."[22]

* * *

In the absence of Slip Madigan, the 1940 Little Big Game took on a different tenor. Fans missed the demonstrative sideline antics of the architect responsible for St. Mary's emergence as a gridiron power. Sportswriters grew nostalgic for the colorful copy Madigan's words produced, and Buck Shaw missed the booming voice of his former coaching adversary echoing across the gridiron. When their squads battled at Kezar, only a thin wall separated the teams' locker rooms at halftime. In one anecdote, Madigan's voice was so loud that Buck supposedly told his players during the intermission, "I'm not going to say anything. Just listen to what Slip is saying, and that's what you're going to be facing in the second half."[23]

Shaw had two weeks to prepare for St. Mary's new coach, Red Strader. Returning from a successful transcontinental trip in which the Gaels upset previously undefeated Fordham 9–6, St. Mary's eagerly anticipated doing the same to Santa Clara. Days before the game Strader told reporters, "We haven't the record or experience of Santa Clara, but we'll give Buck Shaw a busy afternoon next Sunday."[24]

With the threat of rain imminent, only 40,000 of the expected crowd of 60,000 braved the weather to witness the Little Big Game. Strader quickly made good on his earlier promise by unveiling a trick spread formation that caught the Broncos flat-footed, allowing Ed Heffernan to toss a 50-yard touchdown pass to Roy Ruskusky. Joe Aguirre's extra-point kick gave the Gaels a 7–0 lead. St. Mary's led until two minutes remained in the first half when Buckaroo Ken Casanega toted the football from his own 48-yard line to the Gael 15. While being tackled the quick-thinking halfback lateraled to Harry Sanders, who raced into the end zone. Bill Collier's conversion kick tied the game at 7. The Broncos scored twice more for a 19–7 win.

Sporting a record of four wins, one loss and a tie, Santa Clara hosted Loyola University next. The contest was originally scheduled to be played in Los Angeles, but with no games scheduled in San Francisco the weekend of November 23–24, school officials switched the game to Kezar in hopes of drawing a larger gate. Having hosted dozens of college and high school games the grass at Kezar was now threadbare, and the day's steady drizzle quickly turned the field into a soupy mess.

The weather and Loyola's poor record kept the game's paid attendance to a meager 2,500 fans. Fortunately, Santa Clara's graduate manager Sam Dunne had purchased rain insurance for $1,000. His foresight earned the university an additional $7,000 which prevented the game from being a financial loss.[25] Despite enduring an abysmal season, first-year Loyola coach Marty Brill remained upbeat, optimistically declaring, "We're going to throw the ball all over the lot."[26] Brill's boast was easier said than done, especially since the Lions had lost Jack Peck, the team's best passer, to injury during the previous week's loss to Arizona—a game in which Loyola attempted an unheard of 42 passes. Gentleman Shaw started his second unit and played the first-team Shawnees only long enough to score two second-quarter touchdowns. Buck played his third-and fourth-string teams the entire second half, attempting to keep the score down. Santa Clara still breezed to a 26–0 win. Despite Brill's promise to "throw the ball all over the lot," Loyola completed only one pass in 11 attempts.

In the post-game locker room a sympathetic alumnus suggested that Loyola might have done better if it had a better passing attack, to which the offended Brill responded, "What do you mean, no passing attack? Why, every time we threw we were dangerous!" Then he added in a whisper, "Dangerous for us."[27] Brill then praised Shaw for reining in his Broncos and keeping the score down. In a letter to a friend in Des Moines, Brill again reaffirmed Shaw's sportsmanship writing: "He [Shaw] could have beaten us by 100 points."[28]

The Broncos hosted the Oklahoma Sooners in their season's finale at Kezar before 20,000 fans. Sporting a record of six wins and two losses, the Okies struck with tornado-like speed when Orey Matthews returned the opening kickoff 91 yards for a touchdown. Minutes later the speedy Matthews scored again on a 25-yard pass from Huel Hamm. Stunned, the Broncos rebounded to tie the score at halftime, 13–13. Taking control of the contest in the second half, Jimmy Johnson and Ken Casanega both hurled touchdown passes giving the Broncos a convincing 33–13 win over the formidable Sooners. In the process the Broncos rolled up 437 yards in total offense, most of it on Casanega's passing. Casanega's performance caused Oklahoma coach Tom Stidham to exclaim, "Casanega is the greatest passer I ever saw. Before the game I heard that Casanega could pass on the dead run and thread a needle at 50 yards, but I didn't believe it. I do now!"[29]

Ken Casanega carries in Santa Clara's 13–6 win over Purdue in 1939. Casanega would serve as a Naval aviator in World War II before becoming one of the original San Francisco 49ers in 1946 (courtesy Archives and Special Collections, Santa Clara University).

* * *

In today's college football world, finishing a Division I season with a record of six wins, one loss and a tie (granted, overtime play has eliminated ties), would certainly merit a school a Bowl invitation. But in an era when there were only a half-dozen Bowls, Santa Clara's record didn't cut it. Buck's solid coaching, however, once again started rumors swirling about his moving to a larger school for a fatter contract. The major impetus this time was Francis Schmidt's retirement from Ohio State. Although Shaw was contracted through the 1941 season, Santa Clara officials acted quickly to quash any Buckeye overtures by signing Buck to a three-year extension. Ohio State eventually signed a highly successful high school coach from Massillon, Ohio, named Paul Brown. Brown and Buck would cross coaching paths numerous times in the future.

TEN

Rumors and the War Years

Despite signing a contract extension at Santa Clara three months earlier, Buck Shaw's name surfaced again as a leading coaching candidate at another prominent university. On February 3, Elmer Layden resigned as Notre Dame's football coach to accept a lucrative five-year deal to become the commissioner of the National Football League. Notre Dame's president, the Rev. Hugh O'Donnell, announced his intention to have Layden's successor in place by the start of spring football on March 1. He hoped to hire an alumnus, and the initial list of successful Rockne-tutored candidates appeared endless: Joe Boland, Layden's assistant; Jim Crowley of Fordham, one of the school's famed "Four Horsemen"; Harry Mehre, Mississippi; Frank Thomas, Alabama; Jack Meagher, Auburn; Jimmy Phelan, Washington; "Clipper" Smith, Villanova; Frank Leahy, Boston College; and a half-dozen others. However, with his five-year Santa Clara record of 34 wins, five losses and four ties, Buck Shaw quickly emerged as a top candidate.

As rumors swirled regarding Layden's successor, the Rev. John Cavanaugh, vice president of Notre Dame and former classmate of Buck's, was in Los Angeles to establish a new high school. He phoned Shaw and offered him the job over the phone. He then asked to meet with him the following evening to work out the details. Before that rendezvous occurred, however, Shaw phoned Santa Clara athletic director, Sam Dunne, and invited him to his Atherton home for a talk, where Buck informed him of Notre Dame's offer. "We talked for some time about everything involved, and I tried to be objective," recalled Dunne. "However, I wanted to be honest about it, also, because I did not want to lose Buck. I thought he was the best football coach in the country, and his record over a five-year period supported this. It wasn't going to be an easy decision for Buck to make, attractive as the job of head coach at Notre Dame might be. Buck was very happy at Santa Clara because we had a good setup there. A beautiful setup, in fact."[1]

Sitting in Shaw's car on a rainy evening in the Bay Area, Cavanaugh offered Shaw the dual post of head football coach and athletic director. Shaw then pitched the priest his counter terms for accepting. Cavanaugh, saying he had to run Shaw's conditions by Father O'Donnell, returned to South Bend. Whether Shaw's counter proposal was ever accepted is unknown, for on February 10, Shaw wired Cavanaugh: "I am highly honored that the Notre Dame authorities have seen fit to consider me for the position. After careful deliberation, however, I feel that in justice to my family and to the University of Santa Clara authorities, who have been most cooperative and eminently fair since I became head coach, I should remain in my present position."[2]

Shaw's decision thrilled his wife Marge and daughters Joan and Patricia, who loved their new home and schools in Atherton. Upon learning of Buck's decision to remain at Santa Clara, a delighted Marge Shaw remarked, "I'd rather live in a tent in California than a castle in Indiana."[3] Unfortunately, the statement appeared in the papers, which didn't play well with many Hoosiers.

Fifteen years later, the venerable Al Masters, who served as Stanford's athletic director for 38 years, revealed how he may have had something to do with Shaw turning down the Irish job. "When the offer came," Masters related, "Mrs. Shaw phoned me. There was a note of desperation in her voice when she said, 'Buck is thinking of going to Notre Dame. Can't you do something to stop him?' So the next day I got in touch with Buck and did my best to talk him out of it. Soon afterward I heard again from Mrs. Shaw. All she said was 'Thanks—thanks a lot.'"[4]

On February 13, Notre Dame hired Frank Leahy as football coach. Leahy, of course, would lead the Irish to four national championships during his tenure at South Bend.

* * *

Santa Clara defeated the University of San Francisco in the 1941 season-opener 32–7. One of the 25,000 fans in attendance was Lt. Jimmy Johnson, the previous season's standout Bronco performer that Buck Shaw once rated over 1939 Heisman Trophy winner Nile Kinnick. After the game Johnson stopped by the Bronco locker room to congratulate his former teammates. Wearing his Army uniform—a uniform millions of Americans would don within a year—Johnson was on leave from Fort Sam Houston. Upon entering the victors' locker room, he declared, "Well, boys, it's back to the Sugar Bowl for you!"

"No, it'll be back to fundamentals for them, Jimmy," replied Buck. The taskmaster Shaw then added, "We need physical conditioning. Our first string particularly, was a tired group at the end of the first quarter and the boys must block and tackle better than they did today."[5]

The following week Santa Clara knocked off Marty Brill's Loyola squad 20–6 in a prelude to a much anticipated matchup with the University of California. The two schools hadn't rendezvoused on the gridiron since 1935.

Coaches often engage in psychological warfare. A common practice in the coaching ranks is exaggerating to the media a supposed weakness of one's own team in the hopes that the opposition will swallow it and devote extra practice time trying to exploit it. Some refer to it as "sand-bagging." While usually candid about his teams' strengths and weaknesses, Buck occasionally enjoyed heaving a sandbag. Weeks before meeting Cal, Shaw repeatedly lamented his squad's lack of a competent punter, despite the fact that he had discovered a darn good one in Al Santucci. By publicizing the canard, he hoped Cal's punt returners would align shallower than usual.

Despite a scoreless first half, 65,000 fans at Berkeley saw Shaw's Broncos dominate the action from start to finish. Ken Casanega broke the scoring ice in the third quarter by returning Bob Reinhard's punt 67 yards for a touchdown, before Al Santucci returned an interception 29 yards to paydirt, making the final score Santa Clara 13, California 0. A highlight for the victors was Santucci's punting. His 43.4-yard average on 11 punts surpassed the 41.2 average of Cal's All-American Bob Reinhard. Part of the reason Santucci out-punted Reinhard stemmed from Cal's return men—who believing the Broncos lacked an efficient punter—initially aligned shallower than usual. They then had to chase down punts that Santucci sent sailing over their heads.

California coach Stub Allison denied being sand-bagged after the game, "They weren't fooling me about that Santa Clara kicking," he said. "When it came out in the papers they were worried about kicking I wasn't concerned. But when 'Buck' Shaw started talking, then I knew something was up."[6]

The atmosphere in the winner's locker room was happy but restrained. When the *Oakland Tribune's* Bill Tobitt asked about the lack of excitement Shaw replied: "It's a let down, Bill. The boys were so worked up for this game it'll take them two days to get back down again to realize what they've done. In fact, they were almost too high."[7]

Buck Shaw taught clean play and good sportsmanship and respected and appreciated opponents who practiced the same. In his post-game remarks he added: "Our kids thought California was the cleanest team they have played. Not that we mean to infer that we have met any dirty playing teams. But occasionally an opponent gets over enthusiastic."[8]

Charley Bachman brought his Michigan State Spartans to Kezar Stadium the following week. Heading west, his team endured a 17-hour train delay in Grand Junction, Colorado, due to a train wreck. Arriving in San Francisco at seven o'clock the night before the Saturday afternoon kickoff, and intent on beating Santa Clara for the first time in four attempts, Bachman scoured the city to find a lighted park in which to practice his squad. After practicing for two hours under dimly lit lampposts, the travel-weary Spartans finally checked into the Claremont Hotel after 11 p.m.

Bachman's nocturnal practice helped as the Spartans played stellar defense the next afternoon and out-performed the Broncos in every category but one: the scoreboard. Santa Clara's Ken Casanega hit a wide-open Alyn Beals on a 20-yard out-and-up pattern for the game's only scoring play. The Spartans later drove inside the Broncos' 10-yard line on three separate occasions but never scored. Santa Clara prevailed 7–0.

After the game, State's frustrated Coach Bachman moaned, "I'll trade all the statistics in the world for a lucky ball club. We should have won this game. We had the best team, and we showed it every place but on the scoreboard."[9]

The following Tuesday evening Santa Clara departed for Norman, Oklahoma, to take on the Sooners. The game held special significance for Buck. His father and three brothers were coming from Des Moines for an informal mid-season reunion. Unfortunately, neither the weather nor the Sooners cooperated. Playing in a downpour that turned Owen Field into a quagmire before 25,000 die-hard Okie fans, Coach "Snorter" Luster's Sooners proved to be better "mudders" than Shaw's Broncos. Oklahoma's Jack Jacobs, a full-blooded Creek Indian, starred for the home team. On that day, Jacobs threw a seven-yard touchdown pass to Orey Matthews, ran four yards for a score, intercepted a pass and punted a water-logged football 73 yards before it plopped to a stop in the mud. Santa Clara's only score in the 16–6 loss came on the same Casanega-to-Beals' touchdown pass that scored the previous week against Michigan State.

In an era of colorful nicknames the monikers of Oklahoma head coach Dewey "Snorter" Luster and his assistant, Lawrence "Jap" Haskell, stood out. How the 5-foot, 4-inch, 135-pound Luster came by the cognomen "Snorter" is a mystery for the ages. Though it may sound politically incorrect to the modern ear, Haskell's moniker has a pedestrian origin. It seems that Haskell was quite a ladies' man during his teenage years in Anadarko, Oklahoma. He often took dates on rides in his rubber-tired, maple-wheeled buggy pulled by a horse named "Jasper." Residents saw Haskell and Jasper conveying young ladies so often through the streets of Caddo County that they began calling Haskell "Jasper," and eventually shortened it to "Jap." The name stuck and for the remainder of his life he was called "Jap" Haskell.[10]

In the visitors' post-game dressing room a sopping wet Buck Shaw told journalists, "A lot of people didn't believe me when I told them we didn't have a real good ball club. I guess they will believe me now."[11]

Program cover of 1940 Santa Clara–St. Mary's football game. Santa Clara won 35–13 (courtesy Archives and Special Collections, Santa Clara University).

Over the next two weeks more people came to believe Shaw, for the Oklahoma contest was the first in a three-game losing skid. Behind quarterback Frankie Albert's generalship and long scoring runs by Pete Kmetovic and Buck Fawcett, Stanford dropped the Broncos 27–7 at Palo Alto on November 1. Then, in Portland's Multnomah Stadium for an Armistice Day clash with "Tex" Oliver's Oregon Ducks, Santa Clara rallied from a

21-point second-half deficit only to come up on the short end of a 21–19 loss. Having two of their extra-point attempts blocked kept the Broncos from earning a tie. By all accounts the game's officiating was highly questionable at best, and at worst, myopic. Both Bay Area and Oregon sportswriters decried the "no-call" on Dick Ashcom's blatant clip on Ken Casanega as he was about to tackle Oregon's Tom Roblin. The "no-call" resulted in Roblin racing 71 yards for a touchdown. For the first time in his coaching career, the officiating caused Buck Shaw to visit the officials' locker room after a contest.

It was an angry and determined Santa Clara team that aligned for the opening kick-off of the 1941 edition of the Little Big Game. The 35,000 folks in attendance witnessed the most one-sided contest since the rivalry's renewal in 1922. Red Strader's Gaels jumped to an early 7–0 lead. The lead was short-lived, however, as Bronco Alyn Beals intercepted Johnny Podesto's lateral to Ray Ruskusky and returned it 34 yards to score. Bill Braun's conversion kick tied the score at 7. The game-breaker occurred with five minutes remaining in the half and the ball on St. Mary's nine-yard line. Casanega dropped back to pass before a seemingly overwhelming pass rush chased him back to the 30, where he tucked the ball and raced through the entire Gael team to score. Braun's kick gave Santa Clara a 14–7 halftime lead that broke the Gaels' spirit. The second half was all Santa Clara as they rolled to a 35–13 win.

The season's finale came against UCLA before 28,000 spectators at Los Angeles' Coliseum. The stout Bronco defense held heralded Bruin quarterback Bob Waterfield to only three completions in 18 attempts for 84 yards. Bronco Alyn Beals, playing exceptional football, was Johnny-on-the-spot, catching a Rupert Thornton-blocked punt in the end zone for a touchdown. Beals also intercepted a pass and snagged a 24-yard touchdown pass from Jesse Freitas. Ken Casanega scored on a 27-yard run and tossed touchdown passes of 45 and nine yards to Ward Heiser and Tom Matula, respectively. Matula's touchdown came with only one second left in the contest and irked Shaw considerably. Always the gentleman, Buck didn't let the matter slide. Meeting privately with out-going senior Ken Casanega, who was calling his own plays, Buck enlightened him on the importance of good sportsmanship and "winning with class."

The Broncos finished the '41 season with a record of six wins and three losses.

* * *

The bombs dropping on Pearl Harbor on December 7, 1941, changed the United States forever. No longer would the country remain ensconced between two oceans taking little interest in worldwide affairs. George Washington's "Farewell Address"—the keystone of American foreign policy since the nation's birth—advising against permanent foreign alliances and entanglements, would be jettisoned in the post-war years to confront the growing global threat of communism. The formerly isolationist United States would become the home of the United Nations, the cornerstone of the NATO alliance and the architect of the Marshall Plan to rebuild war-torn Europe. But first the nation had to help her Allies defeat the deadly menace of Nazi Germany and Imperial Japan. To do so meant fighting a "total war" that required sacrifices in all aspects of American life and society. This included college football, which now took a distant back seat to supporting the nation's war effort.

With the advent of war the game of football came under attack at many levels. On August 27, 1942, Major General Walter Reed Weaver ordered the cancellation of all competitive football schedules of schools at Air Corps Technical training commands—schools that trained mechanics and technical specialists. Weaver's order came on the heels of Under Secretary of War Robert Patterson's warning that he was giving serious consideration to reducing spectator sports that drew upon athletes' military training. A statement that garnered greater national attention came from Commodore Gene Tunney, the U.S. Navy's Director of Physical Training and former heavyweight boxing champion of the world, who declared, "You can't train a man to be a fighter by having him play football and baseball."[12]

In September, Pennsylvania Public Utility Commissioner Richard J. Beamish announced that school boards and college authorities "are derelict in their duty when they permit the silly business of football to prevent basic wartime training which should be a 'must' in every high school and college." Beamish then added, "Football coaches should be fired for the duration of this emergency and their places filled by marines or other military instructors who will build up a level of fitness to military standards."[13]

The need for the United States Armed Forces to fill its ranks with both volunteers and draftees was boundless. To meet this demand colleges and universities across America implemented military programs. Santa Clara, with an all-male enrollment of under 500, was one such university. At the start of the 1942–43 academic year every member of Santa Clara's football team was involved in compulsory military training and drilled daily until 4 p.m. This meant that on most days football practice didn't begin until 4:30. At five o'clock the entire squad left practice for ten minutes to attend a patriotic flag ceremony at an adjacent area. Santa Clara, being predominantly a boarding school, required Shaw to end practice at 5:45 p.m. so his players could attend the only evening meal served in the dining hall. (Due to an extreme labor shortage, the university offered only one evening meal.) As a result, Buck usually had only an hour and 15 minutes to practice his squad. Exacerbating things, Shaw lost an experienced and dedicated assistant when Len Casanova joined the Navy just prior to the start of fall practice.

As a cost-cutting measure that spring, Pacific Coast Conference schools agreed not to field freshman football teams or play freshmen on the varsity. It also voted to play only non-conference schools that adhered to this policy. Since Santa Clara dare not risk losing lucrative money games already scheduled with conference members Stanford, Cal, Oregon State and UCLA, it too adopted the freshman policy. This decision later proved awkward for Shaw when his Broncos visited Salt Lake City for the season opener against Utah. At a dinner on the eve of the game Buck learned that Utah planned to start a speedy freshman in their backfield named Walter "Kangaroo" Kelly. Further inquiry revealed that numerous freshmen were listed on Utah's varsity roster.

Cognizant of his own school's adherence to the Pacific Coast Conference rule prohibiting playing teams that used freshmen, Buck informed Ute coach Ike Armstrong that his Broncos could not play them the next day. An alarmed Armstrong argued that Utah officials had fully apprised Santa Clara of the Mountain Conference rule allowing freshmen eligibility. As proof, he presented the game contract Santa Clara officials signed which expressly stated so. Being news to Shaw, he still refused to play until Father William Gianera, Santa Clara's chairman of the board of athletics, telephoned late that evening granting Buck permission to do so.[14] Unfortunately, another misunderstanding the next afternoon exacerbated tensions between the schools.

By September of '42 wartime travel restrictions included gas rationing and a mandated national speed limit of 35 mph. Furthermore, with Uncle Sam's urgent need to transport troops across the country, it became extremely difficult—if not impossible—for civilian groups to book passage on trains and charter buses. When Santa Clara arrived in Salt Lake, there were no buses available for charter, which meant privately owned vehicles had to transport the team and their luggage. When Bronco players and staff arrived sporadically at the designated stadium gate hours before Saturday's kickoff, a conscientious gatekeeper denied them entrance without tickets. Despite observing numerous young men wearing monogrammed "SC" sweaters and lugging gridiron paraphernalia queuing at the gate, the sentry repeatedly refused the visitors entrance. Not until Buck Shaw arrived with tickets in hand were the frustrated players and coaches admitted.[15]

The game kicked-off before a disappointing crowd of 12,694—only three-fourths of what Utah officials expected, an attendance trend that afflicted many colleges throughout the war years. Santa Clara's 12–0 win was a ragged affair. The only scoring coming on Bronco Jesse Freitas' two touchdown passes—one to Paul Vinolla and the second to sophomore Tom Fears, who made an acrobatic end-zone catch between two Ute defenders.

An exceptional receiver and defensive back, Fears only played one season for the Broncos. Like millions of Americans, he was drafted in early '43 and served in the Army Air Corps. Fears was especially motivated to serve in the Pacific, where the Japanese had imprisoned his father, Charles, who had been working as a civilian miner in the Philippines. Fears never served overseas, however, spending most of his military service as a flight instructor in Colorado Springs. (Fortunately, the Japanese released his father in 1944.)[16] After the war, Fears resumed his collegiate career at UCLA before signing with the Los Angeles Rams in 1947. In nine NFL seasons Fears caught 400 passes for over 5,000 yards and 38 touchdowns, and later served as an assistant coach with the Rams and Green Bay Packers before becoming the first head coach of the expansion New Orleans Saints in 1967. In 1970, he was inducted into Pro Football's Hall of Fame in Canton, Ohio.

With three sophomores starting in the backfield and his squad's limited practice time, Buck suspected his Broncos would give a spotty performance in the season opener. The team's slow start was partially attributed to Shaw's decision to run more single- and double-wing formation plays than plays from the traditional Notre Dame Box formation—a decision many Rockne disciples regarded as sacrilegious.

Up next for Santa Clara were the Stanford Cardinals, who had endured three head coaching changes in 1942. Early in the year Clark Shaughnessy, the man who popularized the T formation with his undefeated 1940 Stanford squad, departed Palo Alto to become head football coach and athletic director at Maryland. His successor, Jim Lawson, was on the job only a few months before accepting a position as a Navy lieutenant in Annapolis. Reaching deeper into its coaching staff, Stanford appointed Marchmont "Marchie" Schwartz as head coach for the war's duration. After starting his college career at Loyola of New Orleans, Schwartz transferred to Notre Dame, where he played halfback on the national champion Irish squads of 1929 and 1930 and was selected as a unanimous All-American in 1931. He later coached with Clark Shaughnessy at the University of Chicago and accompanied him to Stanford in 1940. The week of the Bronco game Schwartz told a reporter, "What do I think about Santa Clara? Any team that is coached by Buck Shaw is bound to be a tough, well-drilled outfit. But not unbeatable."[17]

Schwartz retained Shaughnessy's T formation, which showed little punch against Santa Clara. Meanwhile, Jesse Freitas connected on touchdown passes of 50 and 28 yards to Alyn Beals to give Santa Clara a 14–6 win. During the game spectators failed to notice the tug o war transpiring between holders of the sideline down-markers. Former Bronco end Tom Matula held one stick and an unidentified Stanford graduate student the other.

Although Shaw never pursued an acting career, he knew many Hollywood celebrities. Left to right: Bing Crosby, Stanford head coach Marchie Schwartz, Shaw and Bob Hope. This photograph is believed to be from a Hollywood set in 1942. Crosby and Hope would later become minority owners of the Los Angeles Dons (courtesy Greg Piers).

Each did his best whenever possible to push or pull the down-markers to aid their respective alma maters. Head linesman George Varnell complained publicly after the game that both guys drove him "crazy" and never did anything he asked.[18] Fortunately, their antics had no direct bearing on the game's outcome.

The following week Santa Clara met the University of California at Berkeley. Despite

All-American tackle Bob Reinhard and star halfback Jim Jurkovich sidelined with injuries, Stub Allison's Golden Bears gave Santa Clara a real tussle. Tom Fears saved the day for the Broncos by blocking Joe Menlo's extra-point attempt in Santa Clara's 7–6 win. After the game a relieved "Silver Fox" declared, "The last black hair I had on top is now gray."[19] Shaw's boys won another squeaker the following week over Oregon State 7–0, before heading south to meet coach Babe Horrell's UCLA Bruins.

Over 45,000 fans passed through the L.A. Coliseum's turnstiles to witness the 14th-ranked Bruins knock off eighth-ranked and previously undefeated Santa Clara. An interesting sidelight to the game pitted UCLA captain Charley Fears against Santa Clara end Tom Fears, his younger brother. Despite out-gaining UCLA in every category, the Broncos trailed 7–6 with only two minutes remaining when Jesse Freitas' desperation pass fell into the hands of Bruin Eve Riddell, whose 30-yard "pick-six" made the final score UCLA 14, Santa Clara 6. Amidst teary-eyed players in the Broncos' post-game locker room Buck Shaw praised UCLA: "The Bruins have an even better line than I suspected and they capitalized on all their opportunities, while we were backward in cashing in on ours."[20] Returning to Kezar the following week, Santa Clara eked out an 8–6 win over the University of San Francisco, before blanking Loyola 21–0 in Los Angeles on November 9. St. Mary's was up next for the Broncos.

The Little Big Game unveiled another new look on November 15, 1942. During the off-season Gael coach Red Strader joined the Navy and St. Mary's officials hired long-time Washington Husky coach Jimmy Phelan to mentor the Gaels for the war's duration. Phelan, another ex-Golden Domer, played quarterback for Notre Dame's Jesse Harper between 1915 and 1917. After successful coaching stints at both Missouri and Purdue, he began a 12-year coaching reign at Washington, winning 65, losing 37 and tying eight. A gifted bench coach and impulsive individual, Phelan freely spoke his mind, often with all the subtlety of a king cobra's bite. During his tenure at Seattle, his teams defeated USC in five consecutive years. After upsetting the Trojans 14–13 in the '41 season finale, Phelan was called into the office of Washington athletic director Ray Eckman. Believing he'd be receiving considerable kudos for his squad's latest achievement, Phelan's jaw hit the floor when Eckman fired him for drinking beer with his players at the city's Blue Moon Tavern.[21]

Hired as the Gaels' head coach on June 20, Phelan did an incredible job preparing his squad under dire circumstances. On February 27, 1942, Navy Secretary Frank Knox sent a telegram to St. Mary's officials stating that their college had been selected as a Navy training pilot site for the duration. Known as St. Mary's Pre-Flight, the program officially opened on June 12, 1942, with 500 cadets. It eventually hosted up to 200 officers and 1,900 cadets at any one time before being decommissioned on June 30, 1946. The Navy operated most of the buildings and facilities on site, and made significant improvements to the Moraga campus, including building six beautiful athletic fields. It also persuaded the East Bay Municipal Utility District to pipe water into the campus. Despite Commodore Tunney's opinion, competitive sports became a major component of pilot training. St. Mary's Pre-Flight fielded a football team, nicknamed the "Air Devils," that played major colleges and other military installations throughout the war years.

The remaining students on campus, not part of the Pre-Flight program, but under the tutelage of the Christian Brothers, now numbered just over 100. The prospect of St. Mary's continuing to field a football team appeared slim until the school hired Phelan.

After watching hours upon hours of game film, Phelan rolled up his sleeves and crafted a competitive squad. With the Gaels sporting three wins, two losses and a tie entering the Little Big Game, a confident Phelan publicly predicted, "We'll win!"[22]

Over 45,000 fans poured into Kezar Stadium to watch the traditional Catholic rivals do battle. With each squad scoring on a long run (86 yards by Santa Clara's Bill Prentice and 68 yards by St. Mary's Jack Venutti), the game was tied at 7 after three quarters. In the fourth, Bronco Jesse Freitas threw a 17-yard touchdown pass to Max Sailor and later ran four yards to paydirt to give Santa Clara a 20–7 win. For 12 straight years Saint Mary's dominated Santa Clara in the Little Big Game until Buck Shaw took the Broncos' coaching reins in 1936. Since then, Santa Clara had not only broken the jinx, but won six of their seven meetings.

The '42 season finale for Buck's Broncos came against St. Mary's Pre-Flight on November 22, at Kezar. Lt. Commander "Tex" Oliver, who previously served as head coach at the University of Oregon, coached the Air Devils who came into the contest undefeated in six games. Loaded with talented officers and cadets, Pre-Flight featured former Stanford standouts Frankie Albert and Bobby Grayson, Vic Bottari of California and Santa Clara All-American, Nello Falaschi, to name a few.

Over 25,000 fans watched the Bronco–Air Devil contest in which Pre-Flight utilized three different offensive backfields. Quarterback Frankie Albert's backfield ran the T Formation, Nello Falaschi and former Northwestern Wildcat Fred Vanzo quarterbacked two separate single-wing groups. The Air Devils scored twice on Vic Bottari's 24- and 12-yard touchdown passes to another Northwestern alumnus and former Chicago Bear, Edgar "Eggs" Manske, for a 13–6 win. The loss still left Santa Clara with a commendable record of seven wins and two losses, but Santa Clara received no Bowl game consideration.

* * *

Unbeknownst to Buck and other university officials, the St. Mary's Pre-Flight contest was the last game Shaw would coach for Santa Clara. In December 1942, Secretary of War Henry Stimson announced a national plan to make up to 350 colleges military war centers capable of training as many as 250,000 students for the armed services in addition to the 93,000 already enrolled in such programs. While military training had previously existed at Santa Clara, an Army Reserve Officer Training (ROTC) program was officially implemented on campus in the spring of 1943. Unlike Navy training programs, the Army refused to allow its ROTC cadets to participate in varsity sports. On March 18, Buck Shaw canceled spring football practice declaring, "Unless the Army changes its mind about its students taking part in competitive athletics, it's improbable that Santa Clara will field a football team this fall."[23]

The Army didn't alter its policy and Buck found himself directing the Army's calisthenics program on campus that autumn. In 1943, Santa Clara and Stanford both dropped football for the war's duration. Other major schools that dropped football in 1943, some for the duration, included: Alabama, Arizona St., Auburn, Baylor, BYU, Florida, Kentucky, Mississippi, Mississippi St., Ohio University, Oregon, Oregon St., Syracuse and Tennessee.

Buck's only direct contact with football during the '43 season was in December, when he agreed to help Washington State's "Babe" Hollingberry coach the West Team in the East-West Shrine Bowl. A game that ended in a 13–13 tie.

* * *

Buck Shaw's family was as patriotic during the Second World War as it was when he was a teen growing up in Stuart, Iowa, during the "Great War." During World War II the United States Maritime Commission authorized the building of over 2,700 cargo ships. Approximately 441 feet long and 57 feet wide, the ship had a cargo capacity of over 10,000 tons. Not aesthetically pleasing to the eye, the vessels were initially described as "ugly ducklings" by *Time* magazine. When President Franklin Roosevelt declared in September 1941 that these ships would bring liberty to Europe, the ships gradually came to be called "Liberty" ships. Any group that raised two million dollars in war bonds could suggest a name for a ship. As it turned out, a Notre Dame alumni group in Northern California did just that and suggested the name Knute Rockne. However, Rock's widow Bonnie, who was living in South Bend, said she couldn't travel to California to sponsor the ship. So Keene Fitzpatrick, Rock's former Irish teammate, and fellow alumnus Bert Dunne invited Buck Shaw's 17-year-old daughter, Joan, to sponsor the ship.[24] She joyously accepted.

On May 6, 1943, at Kaiser's Shipyard #2 in Richmond, California, Joan Shaw christened the ship's hull while her father Buck Shaw pulled the launching trigger. Other ceremony participants included Fitzpatrick, 15-year-old Patricia Shaw, Slip Madigan, Marchie Schwartz, sports columnist Bill Leiser and Father Leo Powleson, who delivered the invocation. Between May of '43 and June of '44, the SS *Knute Rockne* made 10 roundtrips to Europe. On July 19, 1946, after providing invaluable service, it joined the Maritime Commission's "Ghost Fleet" mothballed in Alabama's Mobile River. The ship was sold for scrap in 1972.

* * *

In March 1944 the Army pulled the plug on Santa Clara's ROTC program leaving the school with a small enrollment. With no cadets to train or football team to coach, Shaw had no job on campus.

Although Santa Clara was willing to honor Buck's $10,000 annual contract which had three years remaining, Shaw was a man of conscience who wouldn't accept pay for services not rendered. After compiling a record of 47 wins, 10 losses and four ties in his seven seasons at the helm, Buck resigned as Santa Clara's head football coach on July 6, 1944. In doing so he stated, "I was doing no great good for the university and certainly none for myself with no team to handle. I believe it best to tender my resignation at this time."[25]

Bay Area sportswriters had anticipated Shaw's resignation for weeks before his official announcement and freely speculated about Buck's coaching future. Rumors grew rampant when Shaw traveled to the Midwest in late April to visit family. Reports had Shaw meeting with representatives from Dartmouth about becoming the school's next coach. Others claimed that Shaw would replace Slip Madigan at Iowa. Madigan, who was pinch-hitting for Dr. Eddie Anderson as the Hawkeyes' head man while Anderson served as a major in the Army Medical Corps, was said to be pursuing a coaching gig in the East. Still others had Shaw taking the head job at Notre Dame while Frank Leahy served with the Navy in the Pacific.

Just weeks after Buck's resignation, University of Denver officials advertised that they were looking to sign a "big time" coach and offered Shaw the job. School officials began negotiating with Shaw when he was in Des Moines visiting his grievously ill 79-year-old mother, who died in late July. At the same time, Nebraska's *Lincoln Star* reported that Oklahoma Sooner publicists were exploiting the outlandish theory that Shaw might be enticed to come to Norman as an assistant to "Snorter" Lester. There the 6-foot, 175-pound Shaw would play "Mutt" to the 5-foot, 4-inch, 135-pound Luster's "Jeff."[26]

All speculation regarding Shaw's coaching future ended on September 2, 1944, with the announcement that Shaw would become head coach of the San Francisco franchise of the proposed professional All-America Football Conference (AAFC). Upon Shaw's acceptance, the franchise's major owner Tony Morabito gave Shaw a position with his lumber company as a bonus. The new league hoped to field eight to 10 teams and begin play when the war ended. When that would be was anybody's guess.

ELEVEN

California Dreaming

Buck Shaw had been off the sidelines for two years when UCLA's graduate manager Bill Ackerman approached him in January 1945 about possibly filling the Bruins' head football coaching vacancy. (Babe Horrell had recently resigned.) Ackerman had previously approached Shaw regarding the position in 1938, but when Santa Clara dropped its season finale to the University of Detroit Ackerman broke off the courtship. Yes, Shaw was committed to coaching the new pro San Francisco franchise after the war. But who knew when the conflict would end? Although Allied troops now had the *Wehrmacht* on the run after repulsing the Nazis' surprise counter-offensive at the Battle of the Bulge, no one could definitively predict when either the European or Pacific fighting would end. Shaw was antsy to coach again. But after discussing UCLA's proposal with franchise owner Tony Morabito, Buck wrote Ackerman asking to be withdrawn from consideration as he was obligated to the pro team.[1]

* * *

In the 1940s, like today, changes in the sports world were often mercurial. While Hitler's Germany was gasping its last breath in April of '45, the war still raged in the Pacific. When the All-America Conference declared it wouldn't begin play in 1945, Buck Shaw shocked the Golden State's athletic scene by signing to coach the University of California football team for an indefinite period of time. Buck's contract stipulated that he would "render services to the university until at such time it is necessary to take up the duties with the All-America Conference."[2] Shaw's coaching salary was reportedly in excess of $12,000 per year. Berkeley's proximity to San Francisco also allowed Buck to continue working part-time in Morabito's lumber business.

Christy Walsh, vice-president of the All-America Football Conference, gave Buck's signing his blessing, "Shaw's hiring was a good thing for all concerned." Walsh, who had previously served as Babe Ruth's publicity agent while organizing a nationwide group of ghostwriters for celebrity athletes added, "Buck Shaw is too valuable to remain inactive."[3]

At the time of his signing Buck's oldest daughter, Joan, was a sophomore at the university, so Buck was no stranger to the Berkeley campus. In his first act as Cal's head coach, Shaw added long-time Santa Clara assistant Al Ruffo to his staff, while retaining Golden Bear assistants Irv Uterlitz and C.M. "Nibs" Price. Price, who also served as California's basketball coach, had previously been the school's head grid coach from 1926 through 1930 before giving it up to officiate college football games. When squaring off against Buck's hapless Nevada squad in 1928, Price re-inserted the first team when leading 33–0 at the end of the third quarter to run up a final score of 60–0. Hiring Price demonstrated that Shaw was indeed a man of forgiveness.

Because the university's school term ended in late June, Shaw planned to start "spring" football in early July. When reporters asked about what offense he'd install Buck replied, "I'm going to use the T Formation with my own variations. The 'T' is good sound football and gives you a variety of offensive threats. Of course, you have to have a passer or the whole system falls apart. The way the game is played now, you're sunk without a passer. So right now, I guess I'm looking for a kid who can throw the ball."[4]

Buck oversaw a football casting call of 120 candidates, 43 of whom were veterans, for the belated start of spring football. Unfortunately, few of the candidates had any significant football experience, and fewer still exhibited exceptional athletic talent. Among the few who did was Ted Kenfield. Originally enrolled at Stanford, Kenfield transferred to Nebraska in 1943 when the Cardinals discontinued football. As a freshman that season he earned a letter as a quarterback, leading them to a win over Kansas State, one of only two Cornhusker wins that year. Why the Columbus, Nebraska, native opted to transfer to Cal is undetermined.

A spirited lad, Kenfield decided one summer's day to liven up Berkeley's mundane dormitory life by organizing a raid on the Palo Alto campus to steal the coveted "Stanford Axe." Awarded annually to the winner of the Big Game between Cal and Stanford, the Cardinals had possessed the Axe since 1942. Stanford won the Big Game that year and then dropped football for the war's duration, depriving Cal the chance of winning it back. When California's "powers that be" learned of Kenfield's sophomoric and ill-fated mission, they summarily suspended him from participating in football for the first three games of the season.[5]

At the conclusion of spring practice Buck told reporters, "I'm naturally very glad to be associated with all the grand folks at Berkeley." He then added somberly, "We didn't uncover any new talent in spring practice. Frankly, it doesn't look any too bright for the 1945 season."[6]

On August 10, the *Oakland Tribune* reported on an interview Sergeant F.X. O'Donnell, a Marine Corps Combat Correspondent, conducted with several of Buck's former Santa Clara players serving as Marine lieutenants in the Pacific. They had just learned of Buck's appointment as head coach of the Golden Bears. Collectively, they had experienced intense combat at Guam, Iwo Jima and Okinawa. When survivors of the hellish nightmares that occurred in Mount Suribachi's shadow and the Pacific jungles assess a man's character, it carries significant weight. Former lineman, Lt. Bert Gianelli declared, "Coach Shaw is blessed with a wonderful personality. He is a remarkable handler of men and knows the game inside out."

To which Lt. Mario Pera added, "Shaw is a real optimist. He refuses to make gloomy predictions. He plays to win 'em all, but never will pour it on unmercifully against a weaker foe."

Lt. Rupert Thornton, an All-Pacific Coast guard, lauded, "Shaw is a great hand for fundamentals. He is a developer of men, and everyone who plays on his team will know what it is all about."

All three also praised Cal's hiring of assistant coach Al Ruffo, whom they regarded as an excellent scout, hard-working line coach and a good man to have around.

* * *

Fall practice resumed on September 3. It became painfully apparent that California was in desperate need of a passer. Looking wistfully across the field one September afternoon, Shaw spotted Vic Bottari, one of Cal's gridiron greats from a decade earlier, standing in his Navy lieutenant's uniform watching practice. "Too bad," Buck mused. "If we had a passer like him we might get somewhere."[7]

Although World War II had ended by the time fall practice resumed, having the entire squad together for practice rarely occurred. Still active, Cal's Navy training program frequently required players to either report late to practice or miss it entirely. Naval cadets whose grades slipped were often banned from competing while other students had mandatory afternoon labs. Combined with the squad's overall dearth of talent and experience, Shaw and his staff were fighting an uphill battle. From the 65 varsity candidates remaining on September 6, Shaw assigned 30 players to the "Rambler" squad under the direction of coaches "Nibs" Pierce and former Bronco Don DeRosa. The Ramblers were the equivalent of a jayvee where the less skilled and experienced would receive more fundamental instruction. They'd also gain game experience playing a slate of contests against junior college teams while Shaw, Ruffo and Uterlitz focused on the top 35 varsity players.

Before 70,000 optimistic fans in Cal's season-opener at Berkeley, the Bears' lack of an efficient passer was woefully obvious as Jimmy Phelan's St. Mary's squad, sparked by the exciting runs of Hawaiians Herman Wedemeyer and Charles Cordeiro, upset the home team 20–13.

The day before Cal entertained USC in the first of their two meetings in 1945, Buck told reporters that his team would be vastly improved against the Men of Troy. Apparently, many Cal fans didn't believe him as attendance was only two-thirds of what it was the week before. Those who did attend saw a major improvement in Cal's overall tackling, but the offense remained abysmal. The Golden Bears failed to make a first down and never had the ball beyond their own 46-yard line. However, the Bears managed to score a safety when Cal's two "Jacks," Klinger and Lerond, tackled a Trojan ball carrier in the end zone, making the final score USC 13, Cal 2.

* * *

As more veterans were being mustered out of the service, many began enrolling at the Berkeley campus in drips and drabs throughout the semester. Billy Agnew was one such veteran who reported for football in late September. A talented high school athlete hailing from Piedmont, California, Agnew played freshman football at Stanford in 1942. When Stanford discontinued football after that season Agnew enrolled in the Army Air Corps. While serving as a bombardier-navigator on a B-24 Liberator with the 451st Bombing Group in the 727th Squadron, operating out of Fodgia, Italy, his plane was shot down over Austria on October 7, 1944. Although wounded thrice in his left leg from flak, Agnew was one of five crew members who parachuted to safety only to spend seven months as a German prisoner of war. At one stretch when the Germans were fleeing the Russians, Agnew and other prisoners were forced to march 100 miles in 20 days in heavy snow and under sporadic Soviet fire. He later spent three months at a German prison camp in Mooseburg, where 450 men were crowded into a single barracks. A dozen men lived in a space 12 feet long, six feet wide and six feet high. When Americans liberated the camp on April 29, 1945, Agnew had shed 25 pounds from his original 170-pound frame. Uncle Sam then flew Agnew to LeHavre, France, and then Stateside. He arrived in his hometown of Piedmont on June 10, and placed on inactive duty on September 13.[8]

Although Agnew was still recovering his health, Shaw knew a good passer when he saw one and started him in the backfield against the University of Washington on

October 6. Although several of his passes slithered off the fingers of intended receivers, Agnew managed to connect on a 32-yard touchdown pass to Joe Stuart in the first half. With the score tied at 14 entering the fourth quarter, Cal's Buddy Buestad zipped a nine-yard scoring pass to Stuart and Jim Gierlich's 25-yard interception return late in the game set up Bob Gray's one-yard touchdown plunge to give Cal its first win, 27–14. In the process, Cal discovered a reliable place-kicker in Eldon Mohn, who converted on three of four extra-point attempts.

On October 13, Cal made its first road trip of the season in venturing to the Los Angeles Coliseum to meet UCLA. Like USC, Shaw's Golden Bears would play UCLA twice that season. Over 40,000 turned out to see the Bruins' Calvin Rossi rush for over 100 yards and score both of the game's touchdowns in UCLA's 13–0 win. Having served his suspension for the "Stanford Axe" caper, the talented Ted Kenfield finally joined Cal's starting lineup. However, he was ineffective running behind what resembled a "Don Knotts" offensive line pitted against a "Joe Louis" defensive front. The following day an empathetic Al Wolf of the *Los Angeles Times* wrote: "Poor Buck Shaw, almost completely shy of talent, fielded a slow, unwieldy outfit that made only two mild threats and never got within 30 yards of a touchdown. Even his hodgepodge system which combines the double wing, the 'T,' the single wing and the kitchen sink failed to bother the Bruins. The Berkeley boys gave it the old college try, though, and that kept the score from mounting to proper proportions."[9]

While writers like Wolf and legitimate football people fathomed the harsh reality of the "Silver Fox's" plight, a segment of California's alumni did not. They began asking why Shaw didn't stick to just the single wing instead of fooling with the double wing and T formation. Many, who were initially thrilled at Buck's hiring, now moaned that they were glad his commitment to the All-America pro conference would take him away in '46. Buck answered his critics by stating, "I know what I'm doing and if I haven't the men to do it with, I couldn't do any better with anything else."[10]

The beleaguered coach had a strong ally in Clint Evans, the University of California's Graduate Athletic Manager, who vociferously defended Shaw in the local media. "Nobody who knows anything about football has any right to criticize Shaw," Evans declared. "Shaw's record proves what he can do when he has the right equipment."[11]

Suffering from a severe charley horse and leg cramps, symptoms from his war wounds, Billy Agnew saw limited action against UCLA. The leg problems continued throughout the bye week. While Agnew had always been a good student, he was now experiencing difficulty concentrating and focusing on his studies. On Friday, October 19, Agnew decided to dis-enroll from school with plans to spend a few months resting in Hawaii. He never played another game for Cal, but Buck made sure he received a varsity letter for the '45 season. While the term was not in use at the time, it's very likely Agnew was suffering from post dramatic stress disorder (PTSD) stemming from his war experience.

* * *

Shaw's Golden Bears returned north to tackle three days of blue book examinations before resuming practice during the bye week to prepare for Buck's old school, the University of Nevada, on October 27. The Wolf Pack was coming off a 40–0 pasting at Tulsa and looking for revenge, and for the contest's first 48 minutes played like a team determined to get it. After his long suspension, Ted Kenfield began showing the 30,000 fans what he could do. His 53-yard interception return to the Nevada two-yard line set up Cal's first touchdown—Kenfield's two-yard run on the next play. With two minutes remaining in the game Cal forged farther ahead on Joe Stuart's two-yard plunge into the end zone. In the final minute the Bears' Bob Lossie intercepted a Nevada pass and, as he was being tackled lateraled to teammate Ed Welch, who carried the pigskin 45 yards to paydirt. It made the final score Cal 19, Nevada 6, giving the Golden Bears their second win of the season.

On November 3, over 35,000 spectators turned out to see Cal host Washington State. Many in the crowd eagerly anticipated seeing and hearing World War II hero Jimmy Doolittle's halftime speech.

Doolittle, of course, helped plan and led the famous "Doolittle's Raid" in April 1942, which consisted of 16 B-25 bombers taking flight from the deck of the USS *Hornet* on the first American bombing run over mainland Japan. The bold operation was a one-way mission, for even if the planes had had enough fuel to return to the *Hornet*, which they didn't, the crews had never trained landing the bombers on a carrier deck. As a result, the surviving planes were directed to keep flying west after delivering their payloads and attempt to land in Allied China. As it turned out, Doolittle parachuted out of his aircraft and safely landed in a Chinese rice paddy near Chu Chow.

The game itself disappointed Golden Bear fans. With Billy Agnew gone for the season, Ted Kenfield picked up the slack by giving California the lead on his 12-yard touchdown run. However, the Cougars' Dean Eggers hit Bill Lippincott on a 35-yard scoring pass in the fourth quarter, and the game ended in a 7–7 tie. Regarding State's late touchdown, a frustrated Coach Shaw muttered after the game, "I warned the boys five times that a play of that sort was coming. And it did. Next week we go back to pass defense."[12]

Cal traveled to the L.A. Coliseum the following week for their rematch with USC. Although the Bears had improved since their earlier 13–2 loss to the Trojans, so had USC, who blanked Cal 14–0.

After a two-year hiatus from the gridiron, the Oregon Ducks were once again fielding a football team. Coach "Tex" Oliver, who left Oregon in 1942 for a Navy commission, had returned in August to again man the school's coaching helm. Sporting a record of two wins and five losses, the university's newspaper lambasted Oliver daily for the team's inconsistent play. Assessing Oregon's performance several days before their meeting Buck predicted: "Oregon has just about the best back in the league in Jake Leicht. He can do everything ... and does. One of these days Oregon is going to get everything together again ... like it did when it scored 26 points against Washington State in 15 minutes. Only next time it won't be for just a quarter. I hope I'm not there when it happens."[13]

Shaw's remarks proved prescient. All season Oregon had been labeled as an "up and down" team. The Ducks proved it against Cal. To get a bird's eye view of the action, Coach Oliver spent the first half in the press box communicating with his team's bench by phone. Oliver had barely assumed his perch when Cal's Joe Stuart busted loose on a 61-yard scoring run. The rest of the half was a collage of Oregon fumbles and miscues resulting in Cal's 13–0 halftime lead.

Oliver remained on the sidelines for the second half. While Oregon's play was as cold as ice in the first half, the Ducks caught fire in the last 30 minutes. Behind the brilliant passing of Jake Leicht and flashy running of Walt Donovan, who rushed for touchdowns of 17, 35 and two yards in the second half, the Ducks staged a startling comeback to earn a 20–13 win. In the locker room after the loss, a disheartened Buck Shaw reasoned that the Bears thought they had a pushover upon leaving the dressing room at halftime and thus spent the first 10 minutes of the second half counting the house.

Having predicted that Oregon would be Cal's last chance to earn another win, the Bay Area media gloomily forecast that the 1945 Bears would finish with the worst record in the school's history. In the wake of the Oregon loss, the *Oakland Tribune's* Lee Dunbar wrote: "Buck Shaw is not a miracle man. He'd be the first to admit it. He's just a darned good man who needs some cloth before he can fashion a suit of clothes."[14] The frustrating loss didn't deter Shaw from preparing his squad for the re-match with UCLA. On Wednesday of that week, Buck held the longest practice of the season, and then brought the squad out the next morning, Thanksgiving Day, for another practice. Coming off an upset win over St. Mary's, the "experts" favored the Bruins to receive a Rose Bowl bid, and UCLA coach Bert LaBrucherie intended to make that bid a reality by raining on California's Homecoming parade. When the day came, however, that wasn't necessary. Mother Nature took care of it by unleashing a steady downpour that kept 30,000 of the expected 50,000 attendees at home.

Surprisingly, Cal controlled the game's tempo after the first five minutes, but swampy field conditions and steady rain kept either team from scoring until late in the fourth quarter. In what would be one of the weirdest plays of the season, or any season for that matter, Cal lined up to punt on fourth down from their own 34-yard line. Center Bob Lossie's low snap took punter Jack Lerond an extra second to field. As a result, UCLA's Don Wahmberg got a hand on Lerond's punt, sending it skidding to the right sideline where Cal's Ed Welch scooped it out of the mud and began racing downfield. At the 50-yard line, a mud-covered Bruin defender was able to get a hand on Welch's jersey, slowing him down. A trio of other Bruins closed in to tackle Welch while he was struggling to shed the pesky defender. Just before the three flattened him into the mud, the alert Welch spotted a teammate advancing from behind and managed to lateral the muddy pigskin back to him. The teammate turned out to be the punter, Jack Lerond, who caught the desperate pitch on the dead run on UCLA's 36-yard line and seemingly hydro-planed the rest of the way to score. The bizarre turn of events stunned the drenched crowd. Even the teams' respective coaches had trouble believing what they'd just witnessed. Cal's Jack Lerond punted a 76-yard touchdown to himself! Eldon Mohn's extra-point attempt never made it out of the mud, but Cal wouldn't need it as they held on for a 6–0 win. The Golden Bears' upset victory knocked UCLA out of the Rose Bowl picture.

On the eve of Cal's December 1, football game, which would be the swansong for both Buck as the Bears' head coach as well as St. Mary's Pre-Flight (the Navy decommissioned the program in June of '46), reporters asked Shaw if he'd consider remaining at Cal. The "Silver Fox" replied, "I am definitely committed to the All-America Conference and I can't go back on that."[15] Nevertheless, Cal officials repeatedly urged Buck to stay.

Bernie Masterson, the ex-Chicago Bear quarterback who helped Clark Shaughnessy install the T Formation at UCLA in 1940, now coached the Air Devils. Pre-Flight's major offensive threat was Emil "Red" Sitko, who in 1949 would earn unanimous All-American honors playing for Frank Leahy's "Fighting Irish." The usually powerful Air Devils came into the season's finale sporting a disappointing record of two wins, three losses and a tie. The game's only score came when Ted Kenfield scooted nine yards off tackle to give California a 6–0 win, and Buck Shaw's 1945 Golden Bears a final record of four wins, five losses and a tie. It wasn't what Cal's coaches, players and fans had hoped for, but a far cry from what Bay Area sportswriters predicted would be the worst record in the school's history.

Two days later Buck addressed a group of sportswriters:

This is my last appearance as California coach. I want to tell you my relationship has been pleasant. What surprised me was that, although we had an unsuccessful season, we didn't notice that the time dragged.

Maybe that was because 75 percent of our squad was making personal sacrifices to play. Most of them were in military training and had hard courses. Desmond, Susoeff and Fong all commuted from San Francisco and didn't get home to dinners until nine o'clock.

I'm sorry we're not starting instead of being finished. We are just now getting the organization we have been striving for. I hate to leave college coaching after this kind of season.[16]

Ted Kenfield was the undisputed offensive spark plug of California's '45 squad. In 1996, nearly 50 years later, the erstwhile fullback reminisced to a reporter, "Playing for Buck was a lot of fun!"[17]

TWELVE

The Birth of the 49ers

By Christmas of 1945, San Francisco's entry into the professional new All-America Football Conference (AAFC) had a name: the 49ers. Suggested by Al Sorrel, one of three original franchise owners, the moniker heralded a significant period of the Golden State's history. Along that vein (no pun intended), the 49ers adopted gold as one of the team's colors. While most Bay Area fans approved of the cognomen, certain sportswriters complained the nickname would make for cumbersome headlines when reporting game scores and possibly confuse readers.[1] Time has shown those concerns to be unwarranted.

Busy evaluating and signing players for his new team, Buck Shaw barely noticed the contentious split developing among California alumni over who'd succeed him at Berkeley. There were two factions. The first, spearheaded by Sammy Chapman, was comprised of Cal's famed 1937 Rose Bowl team. They pushed for Frank Wickhorst's ascension to Cal's coaching throne. Wickhorst had been the Golden Bears' line coach from 1931 until 1942 before joining the Navy. Serving as a lieutenant commander, Wickhorst had coordinated the Pre-Flight athletic program before being assigned to sea duty. The second, led by former California All-American Dr. Harold "Brick" Muller, consisted of players from Andy Smith's "Wonder Teams." They advocated for Charley Erb, who had quarterbacked several Wonder Teams in the early '20s. The reader may remember that Erb succeeded Buck as Nevada's head coach in 1929, only to resign after a year. He later coached at both Idaho and Humboldt State. The Muller faction argued that as an alumnus, Erb had greater name recognition and would rally more alumni support for the program than Wickhorst, who had played his football at Navy. The Chapman group contended that Erb's overall coaching record was mediocre at best, while Wickhorst's years at Cal and his Pre-Flight leadership experience demonstrated he possessed the organizational skills to successfully direct Cal's gridiron fortunes.

With Graduate Manager Clint Evans declaring it as "a great thing for California football," school officials made the fateful decision to hire Frank Wickhorst on January 28, 1946.[2] It didn't turn out to be "a great thing for California football." That year California won only two of nine games, the worst single season record in school history. After dropping the Big Game to Stanford, irate Cal students vandalized a section of the stadium, tearing up benches and causing $1,500 in damages.[3] The following week Cal's Executive Committee held a series of meetings investigating why all but two members of the Bears' squad had petitioned for the dismissal of Wickhorst and his assistants, Irv Urterlitz and Larry Lutz. The university subsequently fired all three on December 13.

While California was hiring Wickhorst, the 49er organization was taking shape. John Blackinger had been named the team's general manager. He, in turn, hired 26-year-old Lou Spadia as his assistant. Spadia knew little about football, but could type and take shorthand, and with a pregnant wife at home, the Navy veteran desperately needed a job. In over 30 years with the organization, Spadia would serve as traveling secretary, general manager and team president before leaving the club in 1977.

While team owners Tony Morabito, Al Sorrell and Ernest Turre were taking care of front office business, Buck Shaw was assembling a first-class operation on the field. He started by hiring Jim Lawson and Al Ruffo as assistant coaches. Both were personable and well respected. Lawson played his collegiate ball at Stanford in the early '20s. Captain of Coach Pop Warner's 1924 squad that included Ernie Nevers, Lawson earned consensus All-American honors as an end. He played professional football for the Los Angeles Wildcats of the American Football League in 1926 and for the NFL's New York Yankees in '27. He later served as an assistant on the Stanford staffs of both Tiny Thornhill and Clark Shaughnessy. When Shaugnessy departed for Maryland in 1942, Lawson became Stanford's head coach for three months before joining the Navy. In 1946, Lawson joined Shaw's 49er staff, serving him loyally and efficiently throughout Buck's nine-year tenure in San Francisco.

Not many people come into the world weighing 14 pounds. Al Ruffo did. Neither could many people match Ruffo's exceptional determination and life-long achievements. Born into an Italian immigrant family in Tacoma, Washington, in 1908, young Ruffo spoke only Italian upon entering kindergarten. Despite his size at birth, he stood 4 feet, 11 inches and weighed only 95 pounds as a high school freshman. After graduating from high school, he worked in Tacoma and attended the University of Puget Sound for a year. On his cousin's advice, Ruffo earned a church scholarship enabling him to enroll at Santa Clara University in 1927. Going out for football, he became good friends with Tony Morabito. A hard-nosed guard, Ruffo earned a football scholarship for three years while a shoulder injury cut short Morabito's playing days. In 1929, Buck Shaw became Ruffo's line coach. Spending a year at Puget Sound made Ruffo ineligible to play his senior year at Santa Clara. Appreciating the guard's athletic talent and believing he'd be a good teacher, Shaw convinced head coach Clipper Smith to hire Ruffo as the Broncos' freshman coach in 1930. The industrious Ruffo graduated in 1931 with a degree in electrical engineering, and later earned degrees in both political science and literature.

Ruffo mentored the freshman squad while enrolling in Santa Clara's nascent law school in 1933. Three years later he graduated number-one in his class—a distinction that loses its luster because, as the only person in his class, he also graduated last.[4] When Shaw became head coach in 1936, he made Ruffo his top assistant, where he'd serve until Santa Clara discontinued football in 1943. During the war years Ruffo practiced law and taught classes in the university's math department. By this time Ruffo had also entered into a lumber delivery business with his old Santa Clara classmate, Tony Morabito.

A real football nut, Morabito began contemplating the idea of bringing the professional game to San Francisco.[5] Pursuing his dream, Morabito took Ruffo with him to Chicago to meet with NFL bigwigs to discuss granting San Francisco a franchise. After fielding numerous inane questions about the city's ability to support a team, Morabito was asked by NFL Commissioner Elmer Layden, "Sonny, why don't you get a football first?" Indignant, Morabito and Ruffo took their leave and walked across the street into the office of *Chicago Tribune* sports editor Arch Ward. Ward, the founder of the late-summer College All-Star game as well as Major League Baseball's All-Star game, was now advocating for a second pro football league. The imaginative Ward became the architect of the All-America Football Conference.

Although not an original investor, Ruffo performed the team's early legal work in 1944 and '45, drawing up its original papers and contracts. In 1946 and '47, Ruffo coached the 49ers' offensive line while serving as mayor for the city of San Jose. After the 1947 season Ruffo left coaching to devote more time to his mayoral and city council duties. Eventually, Ruffo bought an interest in the 49ers and held it for 24 years until he represented the Morabito family in selling the team to Ed DiBartolo.

Another key man in the original organization was trainer Bob Kleckner. In 1931, Kleckner captained the University of San Francisco football team. That year Kleckner's 120 rushing yards propelled the then-nicknamed "Grey Fog" to its first-ever win over Santa Clara. Watching Kleckner shred his defensive line that afternoon was Santa Clara assistant coach, Buck Shaw.

* * *

Talent, patriotism and a Bay Area flavor characterized the original San Francisco 49ers. Of the 34 players who graced the team's inaugural regular season roster, 30 had served in the armed forces during World War II, while 15 had played collegiate ball in Northern California. Players with Bay Area ties included Frankie Albert, Bruno Banducci, Hank Norberg and Norm "Chief" Standlee, Stanford; Gerry Conlee and John Woudenberg, St. Mary's; Pete Fanceschi, U. of San Francisco; Bob Titchenal, San Jose State; and another seven who played for Shaw at Santa Clara. Those "Magnificent Seven" included Dick Bassi, Alyn Beals, Ken Casanega, Eddie Forrest, Jesse Freitas, Viscio Grgich and Rupert Thornton. After graduating from Santa Clara's ROTC unit, Beals and Freitas both served as Army Field Artillery Commanders at the Battle of the Bulge in 1944. Beals also saw action at the Remagen Bridge, and later served on Gen. Patton's security force at the Nuremberg Trials. Three days after returning Stateside, Beals reported to the 49ers' first training camp at California's Menlo Junior College. As a Marine lieutenant, Rupert Thornton saw action throughout the Pacific, while Eddie Forrest served 18 months as an Army paratrooper in Europe. Ken Casanega was the only former Bronco to take to the skies during the war, serving as a Naval aviator.

Many players reported to camp with interesting tales to tell. End Bob Titchenal had one such story. Titchenal had captained Coach Dud DeGroot's 1939 undefeated San Jose State Spartans. His stellar play caught the attention of Preston Marshall's Washington Redskins, who signed him to a contract in 1940. During his three seasons with the team Titchenal's Hollywood looks caught the rapt attention of Marshall's wife, Corinne Griffith. Dubbed the "Orchid Lady of the Screen," Griffith had been a silent-film beauty in the '20s, who starred in over 60 productions. Also a renowned author and producer, the multi-talented Griffith composed the lyrics for the team's popular fight song, "Hail to the Redskins" (which along with the team's 87-year-old name became a victim of political correctness in July 2020). Business savvy and shrewd investments made the starlet a real estate magnate as well. Saying she would bill the blond Titchenal as "America's Handsomest Football Player," she repeatedly tried to persuade him to give the movies a shot. Wanting no part of acting, Titchenal always graciously declined.[6]

As the Redskins' 1941 season drew to a close, Titchenal began shopping for a car to drive home to California for the off-season. Answering a newspaper ad advertising a Buick for sale, Titchenal rang the doorbell of a large, gated, well-kept home on December 5. A diminutive man answered and led him to a shiny, new Buick. Stunned when the seller asked $750 for an auto that had logged only 300 miles on its odometer, Titchenal asked as to why he was selling the vehicle so cheaply. The seller replied that he had to leave town shortly and couldn't take the car with him. Having the cash in hand, Titchenal eagerly closed the deal. Before leaving, the seller asked if Titchenal needed any suits, as he wanted to sell several he'd no longer be needing. Titchenal, who at 6 feet, 2 inches and 195 pounds towered over the man, knew that even tailoring alterations by Rumpelstiltskin would never make the suits fit and passed on the offer.

Two days later, on December 7, the Redskins were hosting the Philadelphia Eagles at Washington's Griffith Stadium. The versatile Titchenal, who usually played offensive end, was snapping the ball to Sammy Baugh that day because injuries sidelined the team's first two centers. Throughout the contest the public address system repeatedly announced to the crowd of 27,000 that all military personnel should report immediately to their duty stations. It was only after Washington's 20–14 victory that Titchenal learned of the attack on Pearl Harbor. The news shocked Titchenal like it did all Americans. However, it shook Titchenal more than most when he connected the day's tragic event with the Buick he had recently purchased from a staff member at the Japanese Embassy.

Several days later he and Washington teammate Bob Seymour were driving through Arkansas when a police officer pulled over their shiny, white-walled Buick. As they had left Washington in a hurry, the car still sported Japanese diplomatic plates. Japanese pamphlets falling from the glove compartment as Titchenal retrieved the car's title heightened the cop's suspicion. Although they weren't arrested, the officer ordered the suspected Japanese agents to follow him to the local police station, where they sat on a bench outside while the lawman made numerous phone inquiries. After waiting nervously for two hours, the teammates realized that it could take days before the local authorities cleared them. Only 20 miles from Seymour's home state of Oklahoma, the two decided to make a run for it. Jumping into the Buick, the pair sped for the border. Titchenal dropped Seymour off safely at his home and experienced no further encounters with the law as he arrived in a "blacked-out" California.[7] Fearing a possible Japanese attack on the Pacific Coast in the wake of Pearl Harbor, the Golden State had ordered a mandatory blackout.

* * *

In 1946, the AAFC consisted of eight teams. The Brooklyn Dodgers, Buffalo Bisons, Miami Seahawks and New York Yankees comprised the Eastern Division, while the Chicago Rockets, Cleveland Browns, Los Angeles Dons and San Francisco 49ers comprised the Western Division. Each team would play one another twice for a regular season 14-game schedule with the winner of each division meeting for the league championship.

The 49er's made their first public appearance as a team in a 17–7 exhibition game win against the Los Angeles Dons at San Diego's Balboa Park on August 24, 1946. Only two noteworthy events sprouted from the contest. First, the actions of Los Angeles tackle Lee Artoe upset the usually mild-mannered 49er coach. Artoe had played on Buck's 1936 Santa Clara team before dropping out to get married. He later enrolled at California where his play earned him a spot on the 1940 College All-Star team that lost to the Packers. Drafted by the Chicago Bears, Artoe earned a reputation as a "hatchet man" during his four seasons with the "Monsters of the Midway." Hoping to ply those questionable skills in the new pro league, Artoe sucker-punched four separate 49ers during the afternoon. None of the acts drew a flag. The victims—Dick Bassi, Bill Fisk, John Woudenberg and Norm Standlee—never retaliated for fear of being ejected and possibly jeopardizing their chances of making the squad. Addressing Artoe's actions after the contest, an irked Shaw told reporters, "This has got to stop. The officials have got to stop him. If they don't—well, my boys will be instructed to take whatever measures they may deem necessary."[8]

The second event concerned 49er fullback Zigmond "Ziggy" Zamlynski, who incurred a season-ending knee injury early in the game. Although the rookie from Villanova couldn't play, he could still walk. Not wanting to return to Pennsylvania, but in need of a job, he approached team official Lou Spadia the following week about becoming the team's equipment manager. Spadia, thrilled at the prospect of no longer having to lug and load equipment bags himself, readily agreed.[9] A welcome addition to the organization, "Ziggy" held that position until the early '50s.

With his Chicago Rockets coming to town to play the 49ers in their second and final exhibition game on September 1, Chicago coach Dick Hanley felt compelled to answer critics who believed Buck Shaw would flop coaching the pros: "I knew Shaw would do a good job. Fact is I had to laugh out loud some weeks ago when people doubted Shaw's ability to succeed because he was a 'college coach brand new to pro football.' Any man who can turn out two winning Sugar Bowl teams as Shaw did can coach football in any league—college or pro."[10]

Having captained Washington State's 1916 Rose Bowl team, R.E. "Dick" Hanley joined the Marines in World War I and became the service's light heavyweight boxing champ. While coaching at Haskell Institute in Lawrence, Kansas, Hanley made the Indian school a formidable football power that crisscrossed the country between 1922 and '26 playing the likes of Gonzaga, Minnesota, Notre Dame, Boston College and Michigan State. He later won two Big Ten championships coaching at Northwestern from 1927 through '34. Recalled to the Marines in 1942 as a lieutenant colonel, Hanley coached the Toro Marines' football team to an eight-win, one-loss record in 1944.

While Shaw undoubtedly appreciated the vote of confidence from such an esteemed colleague, Hanley really needed to be watching his own "six" as his team's meddling owner, John Keeshin, was preparing to oust him as coach. Shaw's 49ers defeated Hanley's Rockets 34–13 before a surprisingly large crowd of 45,000 at Kezar Stadium, an encouraging sign that the Bay Area's populace might indeed be ready to support a pro team. Unfortunately, the following week the 49ers dropped their regular season opener to Coach Ray Flaherty's New York Yankees 21–7 before 35,698 paying customers. The 49er's only touchdown came when quarterback Frankie Albert threw a short pass to Len Eshmont, who quickly lateraled to Johnny "Strike" Strzykalski. Behind Alyn Beals' great block "Strike" galloped 60 yards to score.

Although San Francisco's official team colors were gold and red, many fans didn't notice that the team debuted in silver and red uniforms during its first year-and-a-half of existence. The sleight-of-hand change was attributable to Mrs. Marge Shaw. A charming lady, Marge Shaw convinced team owner Tony Morabito that the 49ers should wear silver in lieu of gold in tribute to her husband's "Silver Fox" nickname.[11]

Week two brought Coach Jack Meagher's Miami Seahawks to town. Ten years earlier, Meagher had matched coaching wits with Shaw at this same stadium when his Auburn Tigers met Santa Clara in a battle of undefeated teams. Shaw's Broncos prevailed that day 14–0, and his 49ers prevailed in 1946. The 49ers survived a late scare when facing a fourth-down-and-ten from their own 46-yard line when quarterback Frankie Albert opted to run instead of punt and lost five yards on the play. Taking possession on San Francisco's 41-yard line, the Seahawks failed to capitalize on their last-minute gift by throwing four incomplete passes before time expired, giving the 49ers a 21–14 win. Dick Renfro was the hero for the victors, scoring all three San Francisco touchdowns on runs of eight, 15, and four yards. The game was the highlight of Renfro's pro career as the Washington Sate graduate and former Army aviator suffered a career-ending knee injury the next week in his team's 32–13 home win over the Brooklyn Dodgers.

On September 25, 49er assistant coach Jim Lawson scouted a bizarre game between the hometown Chicago Rockets and the Buffalo Bisons (perhaps, that happens when a football game is played on Wednesday night). Hours before the kickoff, the Rockets lost head coach Dick Hanley. Hanley said he was fired, while Rockets owner John Keeshin claimed Hanley resigned. Keeshin supposedly complied with his team's request that a triumvirate of player-coaches take command of the team for that evening's game. The three assigned double duty were Bob Dove, "Wee" Willie Weekin and Ned Matthews. Keeshin's decision put assistant coaches Pat Boland and Ernie Nevers in

A vivacious lady, Marge Shaw customarily introduced herself to nearby fans at all of Buck's home games throughout his coaching years. She is said to have charmed 49er owner Tony Morabito into jettisoning the team's official color gold in favor of silver to coincide with her husband's nickname, the "Silver Fox," during the team's inaugural 1946 season (courtesy Pam Hammer).

limbo. Both sat on the bench during the contest but had no say in running the team. Ousted head coach Dick Hanley reportedly watched most of the game from the grandstands. As fate would have it, the Rockets won 38–35 on Steve Nemeth's 13-yard field goal with only four seconds remaining.

Professional sports has always had its share of litigation and in its brief four-year existence the All-America Conference was no exception. In late September, the Rockets' brash boss made several comments that led to some well-publicized legal squabbles. First Keeshin announced, "The football fans of Chicago may be assured that we shall do everything in our power to bring the best football brains in the country to the Rockets in order to help guide what we believe is a potentially great team."[12] Then, on September 27, he told the *Chicago Tribune*'s Ed Prell that in a secret meeting the players voted 32–1 against Hanley's retention as coach.

Following up on his promise to get the "best football brains" to guide the Rockets, Keeshin met with Chicago Bears quarterback Sid Luckman on the morning of September 30, asking him to quit the Bears and sign a multi-year contract at $25,000 annually to coach the Rockets. Pondering the lucrative proposal, Luckman visited George Halas, owner and coach of the Bears, that very afternoon and informed him of Keeshin's offer. Upon hearing the news, the volatile Halas exploded, accusing Keeshin of violating the "traditional standards of sport by making a direct offer to Sid Luckman to desert the

Chicago Bears." The NFL's founder also decried, "It is what I would call hoodlum tactics, and does not belong in sport."[13] A day later Luckman told Keeshin that he'd remain with the Bears.

Chagrined by Luckman's rejection and incensed at Halas' aspersions on his character, Keeshin—who as the former owner of the nation's largest transcontinental trucking firm and a racetrack, was no stranger to civil suits—immediately filed a $250,000 slander suit against Halas. The suit claimed that Halas distributed mimeographed handouts of a news release to reporters containing false, malicious and inflammatory matter, a reference of course, to Halas' charge of "hoodlum tactics."[14] The suit turned out to be a tempest in a teapot.

Keeshin, however, wasn't the only one initiating litigation during this tumultuous time. Deposed Rockets coach Dick Hanley filed a $100,000 slander suit against Keeshin. Although it would take until 1953, Judge Wilbert Crowley awarded Hanley a $100,000 judgment for malicious libel. Hanley's legal team based its claim for damages on the *Chicago Tribune*'s story of September 27, 1946, which quoted Keeshin as stating that 32 of 33 Rocket players had voted Hanley should be fired. Rebutting this statement, two former Rocket players, Bob Dove and Pat Leahy, testified that there was no player vote on Hanley, and that they first learned of his dismissal on September 25, 1946, when Keeshin informed them that he had fired Hanley due to a clash of personalities.[15]

* * *

Delighted that his Rockets had won their first game in three attempts, Keeshin opted to continue the triumvirate coaching arrangement for the 49ers' game on September 29. Reporting on Chicago's victory over the Bisons, scout Jim Lawson told Shaw: "I've never seen anything like it. They're trying to replace their system with the T as they go along. Don't be surprised if they run some of your plays tomorrow."[16]

Shaw was surprised all right—surprised at how magnificently the Rockets performed in the midst of their club's inner turmoil. Behind the brilliant performance of Bob "Hunchy" Hoernschemeyer, who threw two touchdown passes and had runs of 71 and 54 yards, Chicago delighted 29,000 hometown fans by coasting to a 24–7 victory. It was an inauspicious start of a five-game road swing that kept the 49ers away from Kezar Stadium during October. Before a dismal Orange Bowl crowd of 7,600, the 49ers rebounded by shellacking the Miami Seahawks 34–7. The 49ers then traveled to meet the league's other California entry, the Los Angeles Dons.

While Chicago businessman Ben Lindheimer was the Dons' major stockholder, a coterie of Hollywood celebrities were co-owners, including Bob Hope, Bing Crosby, Louie B. Mayer and Don Ameche. The team's publicist claimed that the club's nickname, the "Dons," honored actor Don Ameche, who served as president of Southern California Sports, Inc., which legally owned the team. The Dons' general manager was none other than the flamboyant showman and longtime St. Mary's coach, Slip Madigan. Madigan signed Dud DeGroot as the team's head coach and Ted Shipkey as his top assistant. However, it was rumored that the fiery Madigan and DeGroot often feuded.

Like the league's Chicago Rockets, the Los Angeles franchise had litigation issues. Only three weeks earlier the Dons won a heated court case against the NFL's Boston Yanks for the rights to quarterback Angelo Bertelli. Bertelli, the 1943 Heisman winner, had signed contracts with both clubs. The Dons hoped that Bertelli's name recognition would increase ticket sales in their nasty struggle for fans with the NFL's cross-town

Rams—a battle the Dons eventually lost. One reason was not the quality of its play, but where it played most of its home games: Gilmore Stadium. Labeling it as a "graveyard" of football, sportswriters and fans thought it a terrible venue from which to watch a game. While San Francisco—Los Angeles seemed a natural rivalry, enhanced in this case by Madigan and Shaw's historical ties to epic St. Mary's-Santa Clara battles, the Saturday night contest drew only 15,000 fans—a disappointing turnout considering the Dons were undefeated and the 49ers had won three and lost two.

Bob Seymour captained the '46 Dons, and in a pregame human interest moment, hugged former Redskins teammate and fellow suspected Japanese agent Bob Titchenal. The two cross-country travelers hadn't seen each other since the end of the '42 season, when Titchenal joined the Navy and Seymour continued playing for Washington throughout the war. All such displays of friendship vanished with the game's opening kickoff. In what 49er quarterback Frankie Albert would call "the toughest game I've ever played in—either collegiate or pro," the southpaw out-performed both Don quarterbacks, Bertelli and "Chucking" Charlie O'Rourke. Sportswriter Sid Ziff described the contest as follows: "It was a war! It was one of the toughest and most spectacular games I've ever seen."[17]

The visitors built an early 10–0 lead on Joe "The Toe" Vetrano's 25-yard field goal and Albert's six-yard touchdown toss to Alyn Beals, before the Dons' Andy Morefos scored on a one-yard run. Albert later scored on a five-yard run before throwing an interception that Los Angeles' Bob Nowaskey returned for a 40-yard "pick-six." The 49ers' Earle Parsons scored the game's last touchdown on a 65-yard run giving San Francisco a brutally-fought 23–14 win.

Despite their many bruised and hobbling players when they boarded the plane for Buffalo the next day, things were looking good for Shaw's 49ers. In disposing of their Southern California rival, they had improved their record to four wins and two losses. They had won two of three on their current road swing and now en route to play the winless Bisons. Due to two days of heavy rain, the game originally scheduled for October 18 was postponed a day. That may have partially accounted for an abysmal crowd of only 6,000. The game of football is not played on paper, however. If a team looks down its nose at an opponent, that opponent might bloody it. That happened in Buffalo. Whether the 49ers experienced a letdown after their big win over the Dons, or the game's one-day postponement or the tiny crowd affected the team, who knows? Despite playing uninspired ball, the 49ers still led 14–10 with two minutes remaining when the Bisons took possession on their own 45-yard line. Smelling blood, the Bisons drove the field's length to score on a two-yard pass from Allan Dekdebrun to Dolly King for a 17–14 win.

The loss put a crippling dent in the 49ers' chances of winning the league's Western Division title. While not mathematically eliminated, it made the final game of their road swing against the league-leading and undefeated Cleveland Browns, a crucial contest.

* * *

Coached by the team's namesake, Paul Brown, the Cleveland Browns in 1946 were the best team in all of pro football—the NFL included. Paul Brown is said to have put the "pro" in professional football. He was the first grid coach to place a major emphasis on film study and to issue his teams playbooks. Diagramming plays, studying film and absorbing their coach's football philosophy, the Browns spent as much time in the classroom as on the practice field. The innovative Brown refined face masks so they became standard equipment and was the first to install a radio device in helmets to communicate with quarterbacks. Tactically, he improved the passing game by developing "cup" or "pass-pocket" protection for quarterbacks and invented the "draw" play.[18] Recognized as a paragon of coaching organization, Brown was also regarded as a martinet who epitomized the coaching creed of "my way or the highway." An extreme example of Brown's harsh discipline was when the indignant coach traded free-spirited defensive end Doug Atkins to the Bears for reportedly "breaking wind" in a team meeting.[19] Atkins went on to earn All-Pro distinction four times during his 17-year NFL career.

Brown had played quarterback at Ohio's Miami University. After graduating he spent two years coaching high school football in Maryland before returning to his hometown of Massillon, Ohio, in 1933, where at age 24 he took the head coaching job at Washington High School. Between 1935 and 1940, Brown's teams compiled the amazing record of 58 wins, one loss and a tie. Brown's coaching achievements caught the attention of Ohio State athletic director Lyn St. John, who hired the 32-year-old to coach the Buckeyes. Brown had immediate success; his '41 Buckeye team won six of eight games and his '42 squad won the school's first national football championship with a record of nine wins and one loss. With the war depleting his team's talent, the Buckeyes won only three games in 1943, Brown's first losing season.

That year Brown joined the Navy and was assigned to coach the Great Lakes Naval Training Station team in 1944 and '45. Acting on the recommendation of local sportswriter John Diedrich, Cleveland businessman Arthur "Mickey" McBride approached Brown about coaching his Cleveland entry in the new All-America Conference.[20] Offering the former high school coach a five-year contract at $25,000 annually, five percent ownership in the team, and the promise that he'd have complete control of the team's football operation, Brown agreed. Using his time at Great Lakes to scout future prospects for Cleveland resulted in a plethora of talent reporting to the Browns' inaugural training camp at Bowling Green University. The football cornucopia included Otto Graham, Marion Motley, Dante Lavelli, Mac Speedie, Lou Rymkus, Bill Willis, Lou Groza, Frank Gatski, Lin Houston and Lou Saban.

The talented-laden Browns were undefeated and untied in seven games when Shaw's 49ers took the field against them before a Municipal Stadium crowd of 70,386. Shocked Cleveland fans watched the 49ers' Frankie Albert play his best game of the year by completing 14 of 21 passing attempts for 180 yards, while throwing three touchdown passes—two to Alyn Beals and another to Dan Durdan—in San Francisco's 34–20 upset win. After the game Browns coach Paul Brown ruefully admitted, "They outplayed us and we had it coming. And that fellow Albert is a tricky guy."[21]

Victory's afterglow is great while it lasts. Whatever winning embers still burned for Buck Shaw were quickly doused the next day upon learning that starting guard Dick Bassi missed the flight home. Losing track of time while visiting with a former NFL teammate staying at the same hotel, Bassi missed the team bus to the airport. Bassi had played for Buck at Santa Clara and later with three NFL teams over four years before joining the armed forces in '42. Having to make his own travel arrangements home, Bassi missed the team's limbering-up session on Monday. Shaw had persuaded the guard to sign with the 49ers rather than the NFL's Los Angeles Rams, and liked Bassi both personally and as a player. Considering their years together at Santa Clara and now with the 49ers, Shaw felt hurt and betrayed. With their recent win over the Browns, the 49ers had a legitimate shot at winning the league's Western Division. But everybody had to be on board and rowing in sync. Yet how important could it have been to Bassi, who so cavalierly neglected his obligation to his teammates by engaging in a "bull" session with an old friend? Pulling the delinquent guard aside before Tuesday's practice, the usually amiable and easygoing coach painfully told Bassi how disappointed he was in the player's actions. Bassi admitted he was wrong and offered to pay a fine, but Shaw told him that the consequences had to be more, and that he was through. Although uncertain how Bassi's dismissal would affect the team's esprit de corps, Shaw believed his staff and players were building something special. As head coach he couldn't let the carefree actions of one person jeopardize it.

The coach's disciplinary action didn't appear to affect the 49ers in their return to Kezar, as they avenged their earlier loss to Buffalo with a 27–14 win. As San Francisco was notching another win, the Browns were losing to the Los Angeles Dons. Should the 49ers knock off the Browns, who were coming to town on November 10, the teams would be tied for first place with identical seven and three records. Realizing the game's importance, Shaw secluded his team at the Sonoma Inn on Thursday before Sunday's kickoff to eliminate all distractions.

Over 41,000 fans turned out on a beautiful afternoon as Cleveland took the opening kickoff and with Marion Motley and Bill Lund lugging the ball most of the way, drove 67 yards to score. The Browns took a 14–0 halftime lead when Graham's 64-yard pass to Motley set up Gaylon Smith's two-yard scoring run. Norm Standlee, the 49ers' major offensive weapon on the day, carried 12 times for 89 yards. Unfortunately, Albert's play didn't match his brilliant performance at Cleveland. In critical possessions with his team in scoring distance—one just before the half and the other at the end of the game—Albert threw errant passes to wide open receivers and the 49ers came up empty. Lou Saban and

49er fullback and captain Norm Standlee carries in San Francisco's 48–7 victory over the Los Angeles Dons at Kezar Stadium on December 8, 1946 (OpenSFHistory/wnp14.2867.jpg).

Bill Willis played stellar defensively for the Browns, while Dante Lavelli made several acrobatic catches in leading the Browns to a 14–7 win.

Trailing the Browns by a full two games in the Western Division race, the 49ers lost a 10–9 heartbreaker in the drizzling rain at Yankee Stadium to New York on November 17. The 49ers finished the New York road swing with a 30–14 win over the Brooklyn Dodgers before returning to Kezar to beat the Chicago Rockets 14–0. A month earlier the Rockets had abandoned their experimental player-coach triumvirate and named Pat Boland head coach with Ernie Nevers as his assistant.

The 1946 season's finale ended on a high note for the 49ers. A newspaper report that Dick Bassi would be playing for the Los Angeles Dons against his former 49er teammates raised eyebrows in the San Francisco camp, but turned out to be false. Bassi never signed with the Dons. From his perch in Kezar's press box, general manager Slip Madigan confidently boasted to all within earshot that Dons' quarterbacks Angelo Bertelli and Charlie O'Rourke were the best passers in football. Yet it was the 49ers' Frankie Albert who threw three touchdown passes and ran for a fourth in the 49ers' 48–7 pounding of the Dons.

Addressing reporters afterwards the grinning Shaw declared, "I think we proved we have 'arrived' as a pro team. We showed 'em we had everything—passing, running, kicking and defense."[22] In thumping their in-state rivals, Shaw's 49ers finished their inaugural season with a record of nine wins and five losses.

Elsewhere, after defeating San Francisco in their re-match, Cleveland won all of their remaining games to finish the regular season with 12 wins against two losses. They then captured the AAFC's first championship on December 22 by defeating the New York Yankees 14–9.

Thirteen

The All-America Conference Years

Camaraderie is often a healthy by-product of a winning team. During Shaw's years coaching the 49ers his teams won often and shared a genuine esprit de corps. Buck's football knowledge, ability to relate to men and overall personality fostered both. Whether baby-faced college kids or hard-core World War II combat veterans, his players almost to a man loved and respected the fatherly figure dubbed the "Silver Fox." New Jersey native Joe "The Toe" Vetrano was an original 49er, who scored in 56 consecutive games. "What I remember best," Vetrano recalled in 1986, "is what a close knit group we were and that Shaw was a marvelous coach, well liked, indeed, loved, a man with supreme class and charisma. It was the best fun I ever had in my life."[1] End Alyn Beals, who became the AAFC's all-time leader in touchdown receptions with 46, agreed with Vetrano. "This closeness made the team tick," recalled Beals.[2]

A blown assignment, fumble or missed block didn't result in Shaw delivering a profanity-laced dressing down—an anomaly for pro football coaches. The Silver Fox preferred to quietly take a player aside when correcting a mistake or offering a suggestion. "When Buck got real mad, he'd say 'damn-it to hell,' and everyone knew he was really upset," recalled 49er executive Lou Spadia about the rare occasions when the coach grew angry.[3] One of those times occurred during a road trip to Chicago, when players spent most of the night passing a dead rat from one player's bed to another's.

The adage "boys will be boys" certainly applied to the 49ers. During the early years when the 49ers made eastern road swings, the team stayed in those cities between games rather than fly back to San Francisco. As a result, Shaw always chartered two buses to transport team personnel to practice sites and back to the hotel. The Silver Fox allowed players to ride the bus of their choice. They quickly became known as the "good apple" bus and the "bad apple" bus. The "good apple" bus usually arrived back at the hotel two hours earlier than the "bad apple" bus, which frequently stopped en route to pick up several cases of beer and cold cuts for sandwiches.[4] Quarterback Frankie Albert, the 5-foot-10-inch, 165-pound, ball-handling wiz, was the trigger man of the 49ers' successful T Formation. Blessed with a wonderful sense of humor and the father of three daughters, Albert always rode the "bad apple" bus.[5]

In the late '40s, concerns about flying commercially were still significant. On road trips the club flew on two planes on the theory that only one would crash. Shaw placed Frankie Albert on one plane and backup quarterback Jesse Freitas on the other. Fullback Norm Standlee flew on one and fullback Joe Perry on the other so that each plane transported a complete team.

With Albert calling the signals, San Francisco won their first three games of an opening four-game home stand at Kezar in 1947. The 49ers knocked off the Brooklyn Dodgers

Pictured here in his Santa Clara playing days for Buck Shaw, Alyn Beals saw extensive action at both the Battle of the Bulge and the Remagen Bridge in World War II. An original 49er, Beals became the AAFC's all-time touchdown reception leader with 46 (courtesy Archives and Special Collections, Santa Clara University).

(23–7) in the opener, while Joe Vetrano's 12-yard field goal was the difference in their 17–14 win over the Los Angeles Dons, and Norm Standlee scored two touchdowns as the 49ers downed the Baltimore Colts 14–7. (After the '46 season, the league relocated the debt-ridden Miami franchise—which habitually skipped town without paying its bills, and sometimes its players—to Baltimore, where they became the Colts.) In the home stand's final contest, the New York Yankees edged the 49ers 21–16 before 52,819 fans.

Ray Flaherty's Yankees had now whipped the 49ers in all three of their regular-season meetings.

The 49ers rebounded on the road by rallying from a 17-point deficit to defeat the Buffalo Bills 41–24 (Buffalo had changed its name from the Bisons to the Bills) and then scored two late touchdowns at Baltimore to salvage a 28–28 tie with the Colts.

Returning to Kezar Stadium the next week, Shaw's club faced Chicago's Rockets. During the off-season former Notre Dame "Four Horseman" Jim Crowley abdicated his position as AAFC Commissioner to become part-owner and head coach of the Rockets. The luck of the Irish didn't follow Crowley to his new post, for the Rockets came to town winless in six outings. They'd leave winless, too, as the 49ers beat them 42–28. The next week Paul Brown brought his six-win, one-loss Browns to Kezar before a record-setting crowd of 54,325. With his offensive line giving him great protection, Browns' quarterback Otto Graham completed 18 of 24 passes, most of them to either Dante Lavelli or Mac Speedie, for 278 yards and two touchdowns. The Browns won by the same score they had prevailed by at Kezar the previous year: 14–7. Lauding both Lavelli and Speedie after the contest, Shaw confessed, "We're just not good enough to cover ends like that."[6]

As mentioned in Chapter Eleven, Buck Shaw was a forgiving man. After bouncing Dick Bassi from the squad for missing a flight home from Cleveland, Shaw invited Bassi to the 49ers' camp in '47. Unfortunately, the guard suffered a knee injury in August that kept him inactive. Reactivated in late October, Bassi made the trip to Los Angeles for the team's rematch with the Dons. Nearly 54,000 fans saw Frankie Albert throw four touchdown passes as the 49ers rolled to a 26–16 win. Kicking for the Dons that afternoon was Ben Agajanian, who became pro football's first kicking specialist in 1945. He'd kick for over a half-dozen pro teams during the span of three decades. While playing at the University of New Mexico, Agajanian lost the toes on his kicking foot in an industrial accident. After the mishap, Agajanian had a shoemaker fit him with a square-toed shoe so he could still kick.[7] Agajanian had made 71 consecutive extra-points since turning pro. After the Dons scored a meaningless touchdown late in the game, Agajanian aligned to kick number 72. Knowing the extra-point wouldn't affect the game's outcome, several 49ers yelled across the line of scrimmage, "Go ahead, Ben—take your time. We aren't going to rush you." Agajanian did take his time, only to see his kick carom off an upright—no good. Realizing his consecutive string was broken, he covered his face with his hands, fell to his knees, and wailed repeatedly, "My record! My record! What have I done to my baby?" Even reporters in the press box heard Agajanian's agonizing cries. Trotting off the field 49er Dick Bassi quipped to a teammate, "Maybe we made a mistake. I guess we should have rushed the guy. Then he would have made it."[8]

The 49ers then made an ill-fated stop at New York's Yankee Stadium where they were treated to heavy dollops of one Orem "Spec" Sanders. The native Texan's superman performance had the 49ers wondering if he'd dressed for the game in a phone booth. Trailing 16–7 at halftime, the Yankees scored 17 unanswered points in the last 30 minutes to beat the 49ers for the fourth time in four outings, 24–16. Sanders was virtually a one-man show, rushing for 160 yards on 20 carries, completing 11 of 17 passes for 162 yards, and returning kicks and punts for another 115 yards. Sanders alone accounted for 437 of New York's 561 all-purpose yardage.

A week later the Browns eliminated Shaw's club from the Western Division race by hammering them 37–14 before 76,504 fans at Cleveland's Municipal Stadium. Critiquing the game afterwards Shaw bemoaned: "They just had too many fireworks for us. We don't have enough depth of material. This was the best game the Browns have played against us. That gets disheartening."[9] On November 21 the 49ers soothed the pain of their last two beatings by sailing to a 34–0 halftime lead over Chicago's Rockets en route to a 41–16 win. Only 5,791 fans showed up in cavernous Soldier Field to watch coach Jim Crowley's Rockets drop their 11th game in 12 contests.

In a fitting season finale on December 7, the Western Division runner-up 49ers tied the Eastern Division runner-up Buffalo Bills 21–21 at Kezar. The tie gave both teams identical records of eight wins, four losses, and two ties for the 1947 season. On December 15, the Browns defeated the New York Yankees 14–3 at Yankee Stadium for their second consecutive AAFC championship.

* * *

Among the changes to the 49ers organization in 1948 was the signing of its first two African American players, Joe Perry and Bob Mike. Buck Shaw signed 20-year-old Fletcher Joseph Perry, Jr., on October 20, 1947, after watching the 6-foot, 210-pound running back tear up the Stanford jayvee while playing for the Navy's Alameda Air Station team. Today's pro scouts give greater credence to one's 40-yard dash time than they do the 100, but Perry ran the 100-yard dash in 9.7 seconds. His explosive quickness in getting to the line of scrimmage earned him the nickname of Joe "The Jet" Perry. After his discharge from the Navy in March of '48, Perry spent the next 13 seasons with the 49ers. The second Black player signed was 30-year-old rookie Robert Melvin Mike, the 6-foot, 1-inch, 220-pound tackle had played college ball at both Florida A&M and UCLA. Mike played two seasons for the 49ers.

Buck Shaw's long-time assistant Al Ruffo left the 49ers to devote more time to his San Jose mayoral duties. To fill the void Shaw hired Eddie Erdelatz, the former St. Mary's and Navy assistant, to help coach his defense. After two seasons on Shaw's staff, Erdelatz left for Annapolis to become the head coach at Navy. He led the Middies for nine seasons before becoming the first coach of the Oakland Raiders in 1960.

With most of the 49ers returning for their third season under Shaw's guidance, San Francisco joined the Browns as the crème de la crème of the league. Beginning the '48 season with a four-game home stand, the 49ers defeated Buffalo 35–14 in the opener before meeting the Brooklyn Dodgers. Branch Rickey and baseball's Brooklyn Dodgers took ownership of their football namesakes during the off-season and introduced several new concepts to enhance the league's popularity. In *The League That Didn't Exist*, author Gary Webster outlines one of Rickey's outlandish proposals:

> Coming from a baseball background, with games played almost every day, Rickey firmly believed that football players were capable of competing in two games per week. Rickey suggested expanding the AAFC's schedule to an unprecedented 29 games for 1949, and to prove his point, he wanted one team to take on the task of playing three games within an eight-day period in 1948. The league's other owners were willing to humor Rickey, and they chose the AAFC's flagship franchise to be the guinea pig for his grand experiment. When Paul Brown and Mickey McBride got their team's schedule for 1948, it showed the Browns playing the Yankees in New York, the Dons in Los Angeles and the 49ers in San Francisco in an eight-day span in late November. Just two days would separate games in Los Angeles and San Francisco. Brown agreed to the schedule because it meant his team would make only one west coast trip. He hated visiting California twice.[10]

During the 1948 preseason, the innovative Rickey scheduled an exhibition game with the Montreal Alouettes of the Canadian Football League. In the first half they played by

American rules. In the second half they played by Canadian rules, which allowed for a bigger field and a twelfth man. Much to the Alouettes' regret, the Dodgers inserted Tulsa rookie Hardy Brown as their twelfth man.

Brown's unorthodox, but brutal tackling style eventually made him one of the most feared players in pro football. Crouching low as he approached the ball carrier, Brown would leap up and forward into the runner. He never wrapped his arms around the man. With uncanny timing, only his shoulder made contact, usually with an opponent's chin or chest. On this particular afternoon, Brown's punishing tackling technique resulted in seven Alouette players being carried off the field.[11]

However, Brown's tackling didn't deter San Francisco, who handled the Dodgers under new coach Carl Voyles, 36–20. The 49ers made a more compelling statement the following week by pounding New York's Yankees 41–0 before 60,927 delighted fans. The 49ers' first win over the Yanks in five outings cost head coach Ray Flaherty his job. Yankee owner Dan Topping tabbed former St. Mary's Gael coach Red Strader to replace him.

The 49ers finished the home stand against another former Gael head coach, Jimmy Phelan, who had replaced Dud DeGroot as coach of the Los Angeles Dons. On a fog-filled afternoon Frankie Albert threw for three touchdowns and executed a beautiful bootleg run for a fourth as the 49ers overcame a stubborn Dons' defense for a 36–14 win. After the contest Phelan, who praised opponents as often as a miser tipped a silver dollar, was lavish in his praise of the 49ers. "Those 49ers just have too much speed for my team," lauded Phelan. He then declared, "For my money, the Cleveland Browns and the 49ers are the greatest teams in pro football. It's also my opinion that Frankie Albert is the greatest quarterback in the game."[12]

The 49ers won the first contest of a four-game road swing by beating Buffalo 38–28. Undefeated in five games at the end of September, San Francisco was a step ahead of Cleveland, who were undefeated in four outings. While prospects were bright for the 49ers, the same couldn't be said for the league's financial outlook. On September 30, San Francisco owner Tony Morabito announced, "The only teams making a go of it in our league are Cleveland, New York and our own 49ers. But we can't go on supporting the rest of the league."[13] While AAFC teams Brooklyn and Chicago were on financial life support, several NFL teams were losing money as well. The NFL had refused to recognize the AAFC's existence since the league's inception in 1946, and the lack of a common draft continued to bid up players' salaries. With television in its infancy, there were not yet any lucrative television deals to keep financially struggling franchises afloat. Even Buck Shaw weighed in on the precarious situation: "If the two leagues don't get together, and soon, there won't be any more pro football, and the holiday for the players will come to an end."[14]

Putting financial matters aside, Shaw's 49ers continued their winning ways on the gridiron by finishing out the eastern swing with wins over Chicago (31–14), Baltimore's Colts (56–14) and the New York Yankees (21–7). They played the same winning tune over the next two weeks at Kezar, disposing of the Colts (21–10) and coach Ed McKeever's Chicago Rockets (44–21).

The 49ers, undefeated and untied in ten games, then traveled to Cleveland on November 14 to meet the Browns, who were undefeated and untied in nine games. It's believed to be pro football's first meeting of undefeated teams with a combined total of 19 games under their belts. Before a Municipal Stadium crowd of 82,769 fans—the largest crowd ever to see a pro football game to that point—the game's two best teams went head to head. The game started as poorly as a game can start for the visitors when Forrest Hall fumbled the opening kickoff and Cleveland's Lou Saban recovered on the 49er 16-yard line. Two plays later Otto Graham scrambled 14 yards to score. Lou Groza's extra-point kick gave the Browns a 7–0 lead. Answering immediately, the 49ers drove 80 yards to score on Joe Perry's one-yard plunge. Joe Vetrano's kick tied the game at 7. It stayed that way until the Browns took the second-half kickoff and marched 84 yards on a dozen plays to score. One of the key plays on the drive was a 14-yard pass completion to rookie Ara Parseghian, who in 1966 would coach Notre Dame to a national championship. Groza's kick gave the Browns a 14–7 lead. The 49ers missed a great opportunity when the usually reliable Alyn Beals dropped a pass when he was all alone behind Cleveland's secondary. If Beals had caught it, the 49ers might have earned a tie. (Again, the word "if." "If" wishes were horses beggars would ride.) But he didn't and the Browns prevailed 14–7.

The 49ers had two weeks to wait before earning a shot at redemption against the Browns at Kezar. First, however, the 49ers visited Brooklyn's historic Ebbets Field where they took out their frustrations by topping the Dodgers 63–40 in a scoring fest. Only 9,336 fans witnessed the offensive fireworks that saw the teams combine for over 1,000 yards in total offense. While San Francisco was running wild in Brooklyn, the Browns were at New York's Yankee Stadium playing the first of Branch Rickey's three games in an eight-day barnstorming experiment. Cleveland topped the Yankees 34–21 and then hopped a plane to Los Angeles where they met the Dons before 60,000 at the Los Angeles Coliseum on Thanksgiving. A tight contest for the first half, the Browns pulled away for a 31–14 win. The victory was costly, however, as the Browns' star quarterback Otto Graham was helped off the field in the fourth quarter with a knee injury. With only two days to recuperate before meeting the 49ers at Kezar, it seemed unlikely that Graham would play.

Numerous quotes citing Buck Shaw's integrity and gentlemanly conduct are cited in earlier pages. Should the reader still entertain doubts regarding the man's character, perhaps the following incident will put them to rest. The day before the Browns rematch, the Silver Fox overheard several players talking about "taking the injured Graham out" of the game early. Just before the opening kickoff to determine the Western Division championship, Shaw assembled his club in the locker room. "Fellows," Shaw addressed the squad, "Graham will be a sitting duck out there today. I want you to rush him hard and fair. But I don't want anyone to 'get' him. No one is to pile on or twist his leg or rough him up. I want to win this game as much as you do, but there would be no pleasure in victory if we had to cripple Graham in order to win."[15] To a man the 49ers adhered to their coach's request. Shaw's words serve as a clarion for sportsmanship in any era.

Nearly 60,000 fans bought tickets for the 49ers' much-anticipated rematch with the Browns. Cleveland's gutsy Graham—who could barely walk let alone run—convinced Paul Brown to let him start the game. The afternoon began almost as poorly for the 49ers as the one two weeks earlier in Cleveland when Forrest Hall fumbled the opening kick-off. This time the speedy Hall returned the kickoff to the 49ers' 38-yard line, only to see Jim Cason fumble on San Francisco's first play from scrimmage. Tony Adamle recovered it for the Browns. Testing his gimpy knee right away, Graham tossed a 40-yard scoring strike to Dante Lavelli. On San Francisco's next possession 49er Johnny "Strike" Stryzkalski fumbled. This time Cleveland's Forrest Grigg recovered at the San Francisco 22. The 49er defense stiffened and Lou Groza booted a 21-yard field goal to give the visitors an early 10–0 lead.

The 49ers responded by driving the length of the field from their own 34 to score on Joe Perry's two-yard run early in the second quarter. The rules of the day allowed for a tackled ball carrier to get up and continue running if not held down by the defender when the whistle blew. It made for exciting football, but also encouraged tacklers piling on which led to many injuries. Seeking to atone for his earlier fumble, Stryzkalski bounced up from tackles three times during a dazzling 29-yard run later in the quarter. The run set up Frankie Albert's 5-yard touchdown pass to Alyn Beals. Vetrano's extra-point kick gave the 49ers a 14–10 halftime lead.

Gambling early in the second half, the Browns failed to make a first down on fourth-and-one from their own 29-yard line and San Francisco took possession. Going to the air on first down, Albert hit Beals on a scoring strike. Vetrano's extra-point kick upped San Francisco's lead to 21–10. Not for long, however, as a hobbling Graham rifled touchdown passes to Marion Motley, Dub Jones and Edgar "Special Delivery" Jones before the quarter ended. Undeterred by the Browns' aerial tsunami, the 49ers launched a fourth-quarter drive from their own 22 that culminated in Albert's 14-yard scoring pass to Joe Perry. Leading 31–28, the Browns took the following kick-off with seven minutes remaining and began a time-consuming drive. With three minutes left and a third-and-10, it looked like the 49ers might get the ball back with time for one more drive. However, the unflappable Graham completed an 18-yard pass to Edgar Jones to keep the drive alive. The 49ers finally took over on downs at their own 13-yard line with only 48 seconds remaining but couldn't make a miracle happen. Cleveland's 31–28 win earned them the Western Division Championship.

After the game a dismayed Buck Shaw told reporters, "Too many horses and too much spot. You just can't make mistakes with those guys [the Browns], at least not 10 points worth and expect to beat 'em." He then added, "But there's more to it than that. They put pressure on a passer and make life miserable for him. Frankie Albert was no sooner turned around than they were climbing all over him. There's no denying they're a great ball club … they get the pigskin and hang onto it like they own it."[16]

After dispatching the Brooklyn Dodgers 31–21 in the regular season's finale, the Browns confirmed Shaw's claim by pounding the Buffalo Bills 49–7 in the league's championship game. In winning the AAFC's third consecutive championship the Browns finished the 1948 season with a perfect 15-win and 0-loss season.

The 49ers finished the regular season on a high note, defeating the Los Angeles Dons 38–21 before over 51,000 fans in Los Angeles for a final season record of 12 wins and two losses. Both losses, of course, came at the hands of the league champion Browns.

* * *

The All-America Conference fielded only seven instead of eight teams in 1949. After losing an estimated $320,000 in '48, the Dodgers merged with the New York Yankee franchise and played under the Yankee name. With an odd number of teams, league officials opted to have just one seven-team division rather than an Eastern and Western division as in previous years. According to estimates by Cleveland owner Arthur McBride, whose league champion Browns lost $35,000, the 49ers were the only league team to make a profit, although a small one.[17] The struggling Chicago franchise which lost an estimated $100,000 had new ownership. Banker James Thompson was now the club's majority stockholder. By changing the team's name from Rockets to Hornets and hiring Ray Flaherty as its coach, Thompson hoped to change the franchise's fortunes. While most AAFC team owners were affluent and could absorb significant losses, they were also astute businessmen who didn't back losing operations. Prospects for the league's future

FRONT ROW, left to right: Vetrano, Hall, Sullivan, Perry, Albert, Standlee (Captain), Crowe, Susaeff, Elston, Orgich, Lillywhite. SECOND ROW: Cason, Carr, Beals, McCormick, Williams, Wallace, Woudenberg, Matheson, Johnson, Mike, Banducci. THIRD ROW: Shoener, Bruce, Bentz, Howell, Collier, Bryant, Maloney, Cox, Eshmont, Clark, Strzykalski. BACK ROW: Zamlynsky (Equip. Mgr.), Erdelatz (Ass't Coach), "Buck" Shaw (Head Coach), Lawton (Ass't Coach), Kleckner (Trainer).

Shaw's 49ers finished with a 12-win, two-loss record in 1948, both losses coming at the hands of the Cleveland Browns. Shaw later called the '48 Browns the best football team he ever saw (courtesy Sue Healey).

were shaky at best. With most of Shaw's team returning from their 12-win season, San Francisco opened the '49 campaign with three successive home wins over Baltimore (31–17), Chicago (42–7) and Los Angeles (42–14). The Los Angeles win was especially gratifying for the 49ers. Although the home team jumped out to an early 26–0 lead, the Dons' acerbic coach Jimmy Phelan was heckling several 49er players from the sidelines. As a result, Shaw didn't call off the hounds until well into the fourth quarter.

Soaring into Buffalo as a 14-point favorite, the 49ers crashed. The Bills' 28–17 win was their first of the season and totally unexpected as the 49ers had handled the Bills (21–10) in an exhibition game a month earlier. However, Buffalo now unleashed a new arrow from its quiver in quarterback George Ratterman, who completed 15 of 22 passes for 224 yards. A contract hold-out, Ratterman had not been with the Bills for their August meeting. (Instead, quarterback Jim Still was at Buffalo's helm and his lone nine-yard completion in 17 attempts tells all one needs to know about their August performance.) A frustrated Buck Shaw lamented, "We played the worst 60 minutes of football since we've been in existence. We couldn't do anything right. We were all wrong all day."[18]

To exacerbate matters, a heckler got in quarterback Frankie Albert's face as he headed to the locker room after the game. With no police on duty in the stadium, Albert pushed the miscreant aside, knocking him down. Teammate Bob Mike intervened to bring an end to the incident and escorted Albert to the locker room. Minutes later the cheek-marked heckler appeared in the stadium press box threatening legal action against Albert, the 49ers and the Bills. Buffalo general manager Jim Wells quickly defused the issue by offering the heckler tickets to future Bills games.

Shaw's club looked like their old selves the following Friday night. Behind Alyn Beals' three touchdown receptions, the 49ers dumped the Chicago Hornets 42–24. As the players scrambled in the locker room afterwards to catch a flight home, a reporter asked fullback Joe Perry if his injured ankle would keep him out of action the next week. Perry replied, "There's nothing wrong with me. And we'll definitely beat the Browns next week. You can quote me on that!"[19]

Perry was true to his word. The next week the 49ers pasted the Browns 56–28 before 59,770 fans at Kezar. In a brilliant performance southpaw Frankie Albert completed 16 of 24 passes for 242 yards and threw five touchdown passes. Taking a 35–21 lead into the locker room at halftime Buck Shaw told Albert, "Play the second half just like it was scoreless."[20] Albert did just that. Leading by the final score of 56–28, the scrappy quarterback called for a fake field goal late in the game only to throw an interception in the end zone. Defensively, rookie end Hal Shoener sacked Browns' quarterback Otto Graham twice for big losses. Playing superb football, San Francisco broke the Browns' 29-game undefeated streak dating back to 1947. With its four-win and one-loss record, the victorious 49ers vaulted into first place with the Browns right behind them with three wins, a loss and a tie. Team captain Norm Standlee awarded the game ball to defensive coach Eddie Erdelatz. Elated, Erdelatz planned to have the team autograph the pigskin and mount it in a glass display case. Playing all 32 men on the roster, Shaw told reporters afterwards, "It was a great team effort and it would be unfair to single any one out."[21]

Seeking revenge for their earlier loss to Buffalo, the 49ers mauled the injury-riddled and dispirited Bills 51–7 on October 16. A week earlier Bills owner Jim Breuil, disillusioned with his team's lone win in six outings, fired head coach Red Dawson and replaced him with line coach Clem Crowe. Breuil wasn't doing Crowe any favors. With three-quarters of Buffalo's starting backfield sidelined with injuries, Crowe had a better chance of taking out a Panzer tank with a can-opener than he did beating the high-flying 49ers. San Francisco rushed for 311 yards with Joe "The Jet" Perry scoring three touchdowns and Frankie Albert tossing three scoring passes, two to end Paul Salata and one to Alyn Beals.

Buck regretted Buffalo's dismissal of Red Dawson. The two had met while serving as assistants on the 1940 College All-Star staff in Chicago and got along well. Dawson saw league meetings as a devilish opportunity to rattle the cage of Cleveland's priggish Paul Brown. At one meeting he turned to the stodgy Brown and asked him which one of Shaw's plays he was going to use next.[22] Buck had other regrets upon leaving Buffalo. Starting halfback Johnny Stryzkalski suffered a broken leg that ended his season, while Eddie Carr was carried off the field with a knee injury forcing him to miss several games.

The 49ers fell from the penthouse to the outhouse in New York on October 23. After Joe Vetrano's field goal gave San Francisco a 3–0 halftime lead, Coach Red Strader's Yankees totally dominated the second half to earn a 24–3 upset win. The Yankees did not allow the 49ers a first down in the second half and limited them to four yards rushing. Their huge, aggressive defensive line pressured Frankie Albert so often that he sometimes seemed to be throwing passes in self-defense. Running for his life, Albert completed only three of 17 second-half passes for 17 yards. Shaw moaned that his team's performance was "worse" than its pitiful showing against Buffalo a month earlier. "We weren't right by a long shot today," groaned Shaw. "Sure, you've got to give the Yankee line a lot of credit … but there wasn't one kid on our squad who played his normal game."[23] Now in third place in the league behind the Browns and Yankees, the 49ers had their work cut out for them as they headed to Cleveland.

The 49ers gave the Browns all they could handle in front of 72,189 fans at Municipal Stadium but came up on the short end of a 31–28 score. While Otto Graham had his usual effective passing performance, completing 14 of 25 passes for 271 yards and two touchdowns, it was his unexpected runs that repeatedly killed the 49ers in crucial situations. He carried five times for 43 yards with his longest run being 20 yards for a touchdown. Across the field, Graham's doppelganger, Frankie Albert, completed 14 of 27 passes for 254 yards and two touchdowns. He carried five times for 57 yards with one touchdown. The difference in the game came down to the teams' kickers: the 49ers' Joe "The Toe" Vetrano and Cleveland's Lou "The Toe" Groza. Depending on one's perspective, Groza's toe was either more accurate or luckier than Vetrano's. Each kicker had one field goal attempt. Groza booted his through the uprights from 37 yards away, while Vetrano's barely missed from 24 yards out.

An emerging star for San Francisco that afternoon was rookie halfback Sam Cathcart, whose 116 yards on 11 carries made him the game's leading rusher. Cathcart also caught a pass good for 72 yards. A 25-year-old rookie, Cathcart found playing pro football easier and certainly more enjoyable than his G.I. experience. As a 21-year-old squad leader assigned to the 75th Infantry Division, Cathcart fought at the Battle of the Bulge. His scariest moments, however, came later on February 4, 1945, when his company approached the town of Wolfgantzen in the so-called Colmar Pocket. With his squad halted by intense enemy fire, Cathcart knew his outfit could advance no further until a German machine gun nest hindering their advance was taken out. Alone, he jumped into the gun emplacement and began fighting with its four occupants. In the chaos, several of the defenders fled and Cathcart caught shrapnel in his right arm. As his company advanced, the bloodied Oklahoma native carried a severely wounded buddy to an aid station. For his gallantry Cathcart received the Silver Star as well as the Purple Heart. His gridiron performance with the 49ers earned Cathcart the AAFC's "Rookie of the Year" honors in 1949.

Now in third place behind New York and Cleveland, the 49ers took their six-win, three-loss record to Baltimore. Sportswriters hailed Baltimore's Colts as the "best last place team in the history of professional football" when the 49ers came to town. Despite their lone win against eight losses, the determined Colts were spoiling for a fight. When quarterback Y.A. Tittle's one yard sneak gave the Colts a 10–7 lead, it awakened the 49ers, especially veteran fullback and captain Norm Standlee, whose 38-yard scamper led to Sam Cathcart's three-yard touchdown run. Standlee later added an eight-yard scoring run and Alyn Beals caught a touchdown pass giving the 49ers a 28–10 win.

Shaw's 49ers returned west on November 13, where on a sweltering 90-degree afternoon, the 49ers kept their undefeated record against their California "cousins" intact by defeating Jimmy Phelan's Dons 41–24 at the Los Angeles Coliseum. Frankie Albert's passing was just as hot as the temperature, throwing four touchdown passes for the day. San Francisco then had two weeks to prepare for regular season's finale against the always dangerous New York Yankees.

The 49ers trailed 14–7 in the third quarter when Yankee kicker Harvey Johnson missed a 35-yard field goal try. The failed kick suddenly brought the home crowd of 44,000 to life. The spirited cheering and enthusiasm usually reserved for Bay Area college games now reverberated throughout Kezar Stadium. Buck Shaw heard it, so did his players. Unaccustomed to such rabid support, the 49ers quickly responded to the crowd's zeal by scoring three touchdowns in an eight-minute blitz to take the lead for good. When the smoke cleared the 49ers had a 35–14 win. Finishing the season in second place with nine wins against three losses earned Shaw's club the right to host the same Yankees in a conference playoff game the following Sunday. Meanwhile, the first-place Cleveland Browns would host the fourth-place Buffalo Bills.

After the game reporters asked Shaw about the crowd's enthusiasm. "It gave us a helluva lift," the Silver Fox answered. "It was one of the finest things I've seen in professional sports."[24]

* * *

While the spirited crowd may have been one of the finest things Buck Shaw witnessed in professional football—and his players relished the rapture of the moment—it was still "pro" football. Players expected to be compensated for both their performance and their pain. After most players had signed their contracts the previous June, the league announced that players would not receive a share of the gate receipts from first-round playoff games. The announcement's content and timing left 49er players disgruntled. Anticipating both their teams would make the playoffs, several 49ers met with Browns players during their October visit to Cleveland to discuss petitioning the league to get paid for their semi-final playoff game. The meeting generated little interest among the Browns. Unanimous in their belief that they should be compensated for playing an additional game, the 49ers selected team captain Norm Standlee and halfback Len Eshmont to meet with team owners Tony and Vic Morabito before the November 30 practice. The pair asked that each player be paid a $500 bonus for the playoff game or else they would strike. The brothers summarily dismissed the players' request and issued their own ultimatum. "We've given them until 9:30 tomorrow morning to show up for practice in uniform at Menlo Park. If they do not do it, they are to turn in their suits, the season is over, we will forfeit our game to the Yankees and that is the end of it. This is not a bluff. We're not kidding."[25]

Upon hearing the Morabitos' response, the players left the field without practicing. Loyal to his boss while sympathetic to his players, Buck Shaw tried to intercede without success. "I feel terrible about this," Shaw said. "A lot of people are going to get hurt."[26] Later that night all 32 players met with coaches Shaw, Eddie Erdelatz and Jim Lawson at Lawson's Palo Alto home to discuss the situation. Because Tony Morabito had withheld 25 percent of players' salaries for the season and could levy fines against that money, Morabito had the players by the "short hairs" and they knew it. When the late-night meeting adjourned, the team released a statement that included the following:

> It is the unanimous decision of the 49er football team that our first and most important obligation is to the fans who have supported us so loyally. We feel the same gratitude toward the coaching staff. "We have, therefore, elected to enter next Sunday's contest with a determined will to win…."
>
> We still feel our principle involved in requesting remuneration for Sunday's game was most fair and sound since all of us were under the impression at the time we signed our 1949 contracts that compensation for this game would be forthcoming.[27]

Football's "bonus marchers" gave it their all against the Yanks before 41,000 fans at Kezar. The home team scored first on the ol' Statue of Liberty Play when Vern Lillywhite plucked the ball out of Frankie Albert's cocked passing arm and scooted 40 yards around left end to score. Joe Vetrano added a field goal and Albert tossed a six-yard touchdown pass to Don Garlin as the 49ers notched a 17–7 win and a trip to the championship game against Cleveland on December 12.

However, the championship game lost much of its luster with the announcement on December 9 of the All-America Conference's merger with the National Football League. While final details remained to be worked out, the new league was supposed to be called the National-American Football League. The AAFC's Baltimore, Cleveland and San Francisco franchises would remain intact, while the Buffalo Bills, New York Yankees and Los Angeles Dons would be consolidated with the Cleveland Browns, New York Bulldogs and Los Angeles Rams, respectively.

Buck Shaw said the merger was a "damn good thing for professional football."[28]

Reasons for the AAFC's demise are well documented. Many claim the biggest reason was Cleveland's domination of the league and its overall lack of competition. In the league's four-year existence, the Browns won all four championships while compiling an incredible overall record of 52 wins, four losses and three ties. The next closest teams were Shaw's 49ers with 39 wins, 15 losses and two ties, and the New York Yankees with 35 wins, 20 losses and two ties. The lack of a common draft between the two leagues resulted in bidding wars for talent that strained teams' financial resources. Abysmal attendance in several cities also doomed the AAFC's survival as a separate entity.

On a bitterly cold, damp day at Cleveland's Municipal Stadium the Browns won the AAFC's fourth and final championship. Played on a soggy, slippery field, Cleveland's larger line and bigger backs gained better traction than the 49ers. Cleveland rushed for 217 yards to San Francisco's 122, and controlled the contest from the outset. Scoring first on Edgar Jones' two-yard run, the Browns jumped to a 14–0 third-quarter lead when Marion Motley bolted 67 yards for a score. Each team added a fourth-quarter touchdown as Paul Brown's gridiron machine captured the league's last championship with its 21–7 win. Considering the Browns played their inaugural home-season opener before a crowd of 60,135 fans on September 6, 1946, and won its fourth and final AAFC championship game before a hometown crowd of only 22,550, one could accurately say that the league started with a bang and ended with a whimper.

FOURTEEN

The NFL:
A New Beginning

As the 49ers prepared for their maiden NFL season in 1950, Shaw's coaching staff underwent one significant change. In early January, Eddie Erdelatz was named head football coach at the U.S. Naval Academy. Buck quickly signed Stanford freshman coach Chuck Taylor to replace him. Named an Associated Press All-American guard in 1942, Taylor played on Stanford's 1940 undefeated Rose Bowl–winning "Wow Boys." A Navy veteran, Taylor commanded an LCT (landing craft tank) at Normandy during the invasion. He took over Stanford's freshman team after the war. and his undefeated Cardinal frosh won 15 games and tied one.

Opening the 49ers' training camp for their inaugural NFL campaign on July 29, Shaw might have been overly confident about his squad's capabilities and the level of competition they'd soon be facing. Most league teams had opened camp almost two weeks earlier. When a local reporter asked about the 49ers' late starting date Shaw replied, "I don't like a long practice season. It's tiring on the players. A few weeks is all we need. We'll be ready."[1]

Sixty candidates reported to the team's Menlo Park training facility. With NFL rosters limited to 32 men, Shaw had some difficult and painful decisions to make. One of the most distasteful was having to release halfback-kicker Joe Vetrano. An original 49er, Vetrano had never missed an extra-point kick during his 107 attempts in four years with San Francisco. However, Vetrano's lack of speed limited his playing time. Shaw painfully gave the New Jersey native the bad news. Taking it like the man he was, Vetrano said he understood and wished Buck and the squad the best of luck. After Vetrano left the room Shaw glumly told a waiting reporter, "I feel rotten inside."[2] Having to release guys who worked years to fulfill a dream of playing pro ball but are just a step "too slow" or inexperienced to make it is a gut-wrenching task for any coach. Other 49er cuts, as in the cases of Bob Celeri and Herman Wedemeyer, proved unpopular with local media and Bay Area fans and drew harsh criticism from both camps. Celeri, a rookie, had starred at quarterback for California's Golden Bears in '49, and Wedemeyer had previously been an All-American running back at St. Mary's. Fans of the original *Hawaii Five-O* television show might remember Wedemeyer as Lt. "Duke" Lukela. Wedemeyer appeared in over 300 episodes during the show's 10-year run.

The 49ers found gold that year with their first-round draft pick in Leo Nomellini. Leo was born in Tuscany, Italy, and his family immigrated to Minnesota when Leo was a toddler. The family later moved to Chicago, where the 6-foot-2-inch, 230-pound Nomellini bypassed football at Crane High School to work after school to help support his family. In 1942, he joined the Marines and participated in his first football game playing for the Cherry Point Marines. He later saw action at both Saipan and Okinawa. After the war he enrolled at the University of Minnesota, where he became a four-year varsity starter and two-time "All-American" as well as the Big Ten Heavyweight Wrestling Champion. Nicknamed "Leo the Lion," Nomellini would play 15 seasons for the 49ers (six as first team All-Pro) and be inducted into the Pro Football Hall of Fame in 1969 and the College Hall of Fame in 1977. He played offensive tackle for his first three years with the 49ers before switching to defense.

In the 22nd round of the 1950 draft, Shaw selected San Jose State end Billy Wilson as a future pick. Although Wilson didn't join the club until '51, he would be a standout receiver for the 49ers for a decade. An end who joined the 49ers that year was Gordy Soltau, who had been Nomellini's teammate at Minnesota. Green Bay selected Soltau with their third pick in the 1950 draft and promptly traded him to Cleveland. While playing in the 1950 College All-Star game, Soltau impressed Buck Shaw, who was serving as an assistant to Eddie Anderson. Later that summer Cleveland coach Paul Brown gave Soltau the choice of either staying with the Browns as a backup or being traded to San Francisco, which needed an end and a place-kicker. Soltau opted for the trade. However, upon arriving at Menlo Park he initially wondered if he was joining a rag-tag outfit. Buck Shaw had only two assistants, while Paul Brown had one for every position. Things at the 49ers' training camp were also looser than the Browns' strict regimen. Soltau soon realized that Shaw knew his football and was a good man.

A native of Duluth, Minnesota, Soltau joined the service right out of high school and became a member of the Navy's first class of frogmen, the predecessor of today's Navy Seals. Trained in underwater demolitions, he served for the Office of Strategic Services (OSS) in both the Pacific and Europe. The OSS, of course, evolved into CIA.

* * *

Training camp is for evaluating personnel, conditioning players, and honing fundamentals and play execution. Yet the 49ers didn't seem to be improving as the exhibition schedule progressed. Dropping four of five exhibition games, the 49ers' toughness and temperament were soon called into question. After an early exhibition loss to Washington, a Redskin player said of San Francisco, "They played like a lot of little Lord Fauntleroys." After another exhibition loss to the defending champion Philadelphia Eagles, an anonymous Eagle told a Bay Area reporter, "They have spirit. They just aren't mean enough and act like schoolboys. They were so polite and courteous. I could hardly believe they were pros."[3] If not hitting after the whistle or refusing to take "cheap shots" meant playing like Lord Fauntleroys or schoolboys, Shaw didn't mind the analogy. However, if it implied a lack of effort or courage, Buck didn't keep those types around.

Two days before the season's opener, Shaw signed a four-year contract extension at $25,000 annually that would carry him until July of 1955. By 1950, only six of the original 49ers still manned spots on the roster. They included quarterback Frankie Albert, fullback Norm "Chief" Standlee, pass-catching phenom Alyn Beals, guard Bruno Banducci, guard Visco Grgich and halfback Johnny "Strike" Stryzkalski. Stryzkalski had rebounded from a broken leg sustained the previous season against Buffalo.

The 49ers hosted the New York Yankees in the season opener at Kezar Stadium before 29,600 fans. These New York Yankees were not the same Yankees that played in the AAFC between 1946 and '49. These Yankees had formerly been the NFL's Boston Yanks. In 1949, team owner Ted Collins moved the club to New York and changed its name to the Bulldogs. In 1950, they dropped the Bulldog moniker in favor of the Yankees. Oddly enough, Red Strader, the man who coached the AAFC's Yankees in '49, now coached the NFL's 1950 version of the Yankees.

With less than two minutes remaining and the Yanks leading 21–17, the 49ers took possession on New York's 40-yard line. However, as he'd admit later, Buck Shaw took too much time sending in a play with end Hal Shoener. As Shoener ran into the game to relay the play, the 49ers had already broken the huddle and began aligning at the line of scrimmage. Realizing he was too late, Shoener turned and sprinted back to the sidelines. However, the ball was snapped before Shoener made it, resulting in the 49ers being penalized 15 yards for having too many men on the field. The penalty killed the 49er drive and the Yanks held on for the win. The following week a Kezar crowd of 35,550 turned out to see George Halas' Chicago Bears. The home team grabbed a 14–12 halftime lead but couldn't hold it. Behind the passing of Johnny Lujack, the "Monsters of the Midway" scored 17 third-quarter points to beat Buck's boys 32–20. Afterward, 49er fullback Norm Standlee muttered, "the Bears just had too many horses."[4] The following week got no better, as Los Angeles' powerful Rams steamrolled over San Francisco 35–14.

The struggling 49ers dropped their next two contests as well—one against the Lions at Detroit (24–17), the next to the Yankees at New York (29–24). Elsewhere in the league, the former AAFC-turned-NFL Baltimore Colts were also winless. However, the four-time AAFC champion Cleveland Browns had won four of five games. Their lone defeat was a 6–0 setback at the hands of the New York Giants. Yet the Browns had dismantled the NFL's defending champion Philadelphia Eagles 35–10 in the season's opener. Not only did the Browns' overwhelming performance stun 71,000 fans at Philadelphia's Municipal Stadium, but they showed the entire sporting world that Cleveland was the real deal.

On the weekend of October 21–22, winless San Francisco returned home for a rematch with Detroit's Lions. In an interview with *San Francisco Examiner* sports editor Curley Grieve before the game, 49er quarterback Frankie Albert assessed the NFL: "I have to admit it is considerably faster. In the old AAFC, we'd have a tough game and then two easy ones. In the NFL they're all tough…. There isn't a breather."[5] Albert thought that NFL teams were better organized and did a better job of scouting than the AAFC teams had. Over the season's first five contests, he added, the 49ers confronted a "new look" defense every week, with no two defenses being identical. Compared to the AAFC, said Albert, the NFL teams were more "deep pass" conscious and more skilled at jamming tight ends on the line of scrimmage to keep them from releasing on pass patterns.

Publicly identifying the league's differences—as well as a bit of luck—may have helped the 49ers break into the win column on October 22. Trailing the home team 28–21 late in the game, Detroit scored on a 19-yard halfback pass from Bob Hoernschmeyer to Dick Rifenburg to pull within a point. However, on Detroit's previous possession, 49er Norm Standlee laid a crushing tackle on the Lions' Doak Walker. Walker, Detroit's regular place-kicker, was helped off the field with a severely sprained ankle. Walker's injury left quarterback Bobby Layne to attempt the tying point. Layne missed and the 49ers ran out the clock to earn their first regular season NFL win, 28–27.

The following week Lowell Wagner's touchdown-saving tackle on Hal Crisler in the game's last 30 seconds helped the 49ers stave off a late Baltimore Colt rally for their second win, 17–14. Grateful for consecutive victories, Shaw was still a realist. Winning one game on a missed extra point and another over a winless Colt team coming off a 70–27

49ers Sam Cathcart (83) and Frankie Albert (63) pin Rams halfback Paul Barry to the goalposts in San Francisco's 28–21 loss at the Los Angeles Coliseum on Nov. 5, 1950. Barry scored on the play (Library of Congress).

loss to the Rams was nothing to write home about. Injuries to key players like Joe Perry, who played several games on a heavily taped sprained ankle before suffering what was initially diagnosed as broken ribs against the Colts, certainly hurt the 49ers. Buck also believed his team was fumbling too much and continually getting "beat deep" on passes. Unfortunately, not much changed during San Francisco's month-long November road swing. Playing before a Rams season-high crowd of 33,234, the 49ers held a 14–7 lead early in the third quarter only to have the Rams explode for three touchdowns and prevail 28–21. The 49ers then traveled to Cleveland to meet their old AAFC nemesis, the Browns. With the halftime score tied at 14, San Francisco hosted a fumble festival in the second half, with the Browns converting two fumbles and an interception into touchdowns. On the day the 49ers fumbled seven times. Joe Perry, playing with specially designed pads to protect severely bruised (not broken) ribs, lost four fumbles alone.

Afterwards, a frustrated Shaw sighed, "You just can't make that many mistakes against a team like that!"[6] The Browns had now won seven games and lost two, while the 49ers' record stood at two wins and seven losses.

With an injury to a key player or a game-changing fumble always just a play away, coaches know things can always get worse. Things got worse for Shaw and the 49ers the following week against the Bears in Chicago, when the team endured its first shutout loss in its five-year existence, 17–0. The road swing came to an agonizing end on November 26 at Green Bay. San Francisco led 21–19 with only three minutes remaining when Paul Christman, subbing for Packers quarterback Tobin Rote, faced a fourth-and-ten on San Francisco's 44-yard line. Unleashing a desperation heave, Christman connected with wide-open rookie Floyd "Breezy" Reid for a touchdown. The final score read: Green Bay 25, San Francisco 21.

In the post-game locker room a visibly upset Shaw growled, "We've been playing like that all year.… We get a bulge on another team and make mistakes at critical times—get a penalty that puts us out of business."[7]

On December 2, 1950, Shaw elaborated on the frustrating season in an interview with the *San Francisco Examiner's* inquisitive Curley Grieve.

> GRIEVE: Should any blame for the 49ers showing be attached to the coaching staff?
> SHAW: Put it a different way. The coaching staff received more credit than it deserved when we were winning. It's only right that we should be saddled with some of the responsibility when we are losing.
> GRIEVE: How do you analyze the unexpected collapse of the club?
> SHAW: I just can't help but believe that it has been due in a large measure to critical mistakes we made. It seemed we were forever offside, holding or had backs in motion at crucial times. Time and again when we were inside a team's 20-yard line and driving, the whistle would blow to stop us cold.
> GRIEVE: Are other coaching staffs outfoxing you? Are they shooting new stuff at you?
> SHAW: No—on both counts. But because the clubs have been in business longer, they have better organizations. As for what happens on the field, there's little that's new. Coaches steal our stuff and we grab anything they have that seems worth it.
> GRIEVE: How would you classify this season?
> SHAW: As the worst I've ever experienced and one I'll never forget.
> GRIEVE: Suppose USC sent a quick call for you—would you consider the job?
> SHAW: No. Here I have only a couple on my back. Down there I'd have 200,000.

One point neither Grieve nor Shaw mentioned was the performance drop-off in the Albert to Beals passing combination. Playing in 12 games each year, Alyn Beals caught 44 passes for 678 yards and 12 touchdowns in 1949. In 1950, Beals caught only 22 passes, for 315 yards and three touchdowns. Joe Perry, who rushed for 647 yards on 124 carries for a 5.2-yard average, was the only 49er to finish in the top five of any major statistical category for the season.

San Francisco enjoyed an off-week before hosting the same Green Bay Packers in the season's finale. In a pregame ceremony the club honored Captain Norm Standlee, one of the original 49ers. With lovely wife Cleo and daughter Shirley by his side, the humbled Standlee received dozens of gifts, including a new automobile. The game itself started in spectacular fashion when the Packers' Tobin Rote flipped a swing pass to halfback Billy Grimes who rambled 96 yards for a touchdown. Stunned by the Packers' lightning score, the 49ers rebounded with a vengeance. Frankie Albert threw scoring passes to Joe Perry and Johnny Stryzkalski before Perry bolted 76 yards to score. Gordy Soltau added a field goal to give the 49ers a 24–7 halftime lead. Albert later tossed a fourth-quarter scoring pass to Fred Gehrke as San Francisco ended the disappointing season on a high note with a 30–14 win. Finishing the season in a tie for fifth place with Green Bay in the National Conference, the 49ers' final record of three wins and nine losses undoubtedly affected attendance. In 1949, San Francisco's home attendance averaged 41,000. It dropped to 30,000 in 1950.

Meanwhile, the Cleveland Browns thumbed their noses at all the so-called football savants who ridiculed the AAFC's quality of play by defeating the Los Angeles Rams 30–28 to win the 1950 NFL Championship. The Browns finished the regular season with a record of 10 wins and only two losses.

* * *

In January 1951, the *San Francisco Examiner*'s Prescott Sullivan wrote a column claiming the working relationship between team owner Tony Morabito and coach Buck Shaw grew strained during the '50 season—so much so that at one point Shaw considered quitting and at another came close to getting fired. Obviously, fielding a losing pro team often results in less fan interest, which leads to fewer paying customers on game day and a dip in revenue. Neither Shaw nor Morabito was pleased with the 1950 season's outcome. However, if their association had been stressful or acrimonious that year it never came to light. Both now focused on making the 49ers the best team it could be in '51—beginning with the NFL player draft on January 18.

The 1951 draft was unusual. Abe Watner, owner of the Baltimore Colts, became so disgruntled when NFL owners refused his request for a supplemental draft to help bolster his hapless club that he pulled his franchise from the league and disbanded the team. As a result, NFL teams could now draft players off the Colts' 1950 roster as well as college players. With their first-round choice, the 49ers selected Baltimore's Yelberton Abraham (Y.A.) Tittle. A native Texan, Tittle played his college ball at LSU before being drafted in 1948 by both the NFL's Detroit Lions and the AAFC's Cleveland Browns. Tittle signed with the Browns. That year, in an attempt to increase the league's overall competitiveness, owners implemented a "share the wealth" program in which the AAFC's stronger teams agreed to bolster the weakest teams, Baltimore and Chicago, by sending each team several players from their rosters. (The 49ers' owner Tony Morabito refused to participate in the plan.) "For the good of the league," the Browns sent Tittle to Baltimore.[8] In 1948, Tittle led the Colts to a seven-and-seven record while being named the AAFC's "Rookie of the Year." However, the Colts only won two games total during 1949 and '50, losing several hundred thousand dollars in the process and forcing Watner to pull the franchise's plug.

There were several reasons why San Francisco opted for Tittle. He threw the long ball as well as anyone and with three years of pro ball under his belt, he'd make a suitable backup for Frankie Albert. Furthermore, due to injuries he suffered in football, the draft board classified Tittle as 4-F. With the Korean War escalating, Albert, who served in the Naval Reserves, could possibly be called to active duty. Tittle didn't have that problem. (The 49ers lost halfback Sam Cathcart for the entire '51 season when the Army recalled him to duty.) Another reason was financial. Following their three-win, nine-loss season, Morabito asked Albert, the team's highest salaried player at $20,000 annually, to take a 25 percent pay cut to $15,000. Having Tittle waiting in the wings gave Morabito better leverage in upcoming salary negotiations with Albert. However, Albert was no babe in the woods when it came to negotiating. When still unsigned in early May, Albert revealed to the local press that he had been contacted by one Lou Hayman, a representative of the Montreal Alouettes of the Canadian Football League, about playing north of the border. When asked what it would take for Albert to join the Alouettes, the southpaw quarterback quoted a figure a few thousand dollars above his 1950 salary with the 49ers.[9] Hayman said he'd get back to him. When the financial dickering ended in late May, owner and quarterback agreed to split the difference and Albert signed again with the 49ers for $17,500.

Another player the 49ers plucked from the Colts roster with their 21st pick, linebacker Hardy Brown, drew little attention at the time. After earning small college All-American honors at Tulsa playing for Coach Henry Frnka, Brown signed with the AAFC's Baltimore Colts in 1948. He spent 1949 with the Chicago Hornets before joining the NFL's Baltimore Colts in '50. Brown's traumatic childhood reads like something out of a Stephen King novel. At age four he witnessed two men murder his father. Several months later he watched a family relative avenge his father's death by blowing both men away with a shotgun. When his mother abandoned the family, Hardy, two older brothers and a sister were sent to the Masonic Home Orphanage in Fort Worth, Texas. Hardy learned to play football there under Coach Rusty Russell. During his 49er years, Brown's punishing hits made him one of the most feared men in the NFL. In a 1983 interview with NFL Films' Steve Sabol he explained his unique tackling technique: "take one step forward, keeping your back straight and eyes open, and like a boxer throw that shoulder up into the man."[10] Years before anyone ever heard of Chronic Traumatic Encephalopathy (CTE), and football outlawed targeting and spearing, Brown's aiming point was either the ball carrier's jaw or shoulder. Brown looked awkward when he missed, but when he made contact, players standing on the sidelines felt the jolt. Opponents nicknamed Brown "The Thumper." Rams quarterback Norm Van Brocklin compared Brown to a Western gunslinger who notched his gun handle for every man he killed. In Brown's case, it was for every man he knocked cold.[11] Feared and hated league-wide, Brown by his own admission believed he knocked out between 75 to 80 men during his pro career with his brutal tackling style. The Los Angeles Rams once offered a $500 bounty for any team member who "took Brown" out of the game.[12]

Another 49er find in the '51 draft was 5-foot, 11-inch, 180-pound halfback Joe Arenas. Their eighth pick, Arenas never played high school football. At age 19, he earned a Purple Heart and 20 months of visits to Veterans' hospitals when a fist-size piece of shrapnel penetrated his body during the Battle of Iwo Jima. After the war Arenas enrolled at Omaha University (today's University of Nebraska at Omaha) and, lacking any football experience, went out for varsity team. Not only did he make it, but he was named the squad's "Most Valuable Player" in 1948. In his rookie season with the 49ers, Arenas led the league in both punt and kick returns.

Other draftees who made the club as rookies and played for several years were guard

Nick Feher (University of Georgia), tackle Al Carapella (University of Miami, Florida) and end Bill Jessup (University of Southern California).

On February 3, the 49er coaching staff underwent another change when line coach Chuck Taylor was named head football coach at Stanford. Taylor succeeded Marchie Schwartz, who resigned unexpectedly. One of Schwartz's assistants was Phil Bengston. Having served as Stanford's line coach for a dozen years, Bengston had coached Taylor during his Cardinal playing days. Besides the hurt of being passed over for the head job, Bengston felt it might be uncomfortable for both him and Taylor if he stayed on to assist a player he had coached. Bengston resigned and several days later joined Buck's 49er staff. A happy Shaw claimed, "I could probably look the country over before finding a better man than Phil."[13]

A college teammate of quarterback Bud Wilkinson at the University of Minnesota, Bengston coached for several years under Don Faurot at Missouri before joining Clark Shaughnessy's staff at Stanford in 1940. Bengston would serve as an assistant with the 49ers through the 1957 season. In 1959 he joined Vince Lombardi's staff at Green Bay, eventually succeeding him as head coach in 1968.

* * *

In 1950 Shaw opened training camp on July 29, nearly two weeks later than other NFL clubs. Realizing that may have contributed to the 49ers slow start and overall poor showing, Shaw opened the '51 Menlo Park camp on July 16 for quarterbacks and a select group of receivers. All others reported on July 21, with the first full team practice on July 23. A common sight in camp was that of team members carrying playbooks with them when not on the practice field. When reporters asked Shaw about it, the Silver Fox replied, "Here we ask that our players learn football." Then half-jokingly added, "They can be as dumb as they want on any other subject and they often are."[14]

There was some early grumbling among the players who lived nearby about having to sleep overnight in camp with lights out at eleven rather than spend evenings at home with their families. The policy really raised eyebrows when a local sports columnist reported that at day's end, head coach Shaw drove home to Atherton to snooze in his own bed. Whether the report was true or not, there was neither a team rebellion nor reports of players going AWOL or breaking curfew.[15] On the contrary, the camp ran smoothly with the 49ers winning four of their five exhibition games.

With high hopes, 52,219 fans turned out at Kezar for the 49ers' season-opener against their archrival, the Cleveland Browns. The home team wouldn't disappoint. Trailing 7–0, Frankie Albert connected with rookie Billy Wilson on a 52-yard touchdown pass to tie the score at 7. Gordy Soltau's 35-yard field goal gave the Niners a 10–7 halftime lead. Sparked by fullback Verl Lillywhite's 145 rushing yards on 17 carries, San Francisco scored twice more on Joe Perry runs for a 24–10 win. In the post-game locker room an ecstatic Shaw claimed, "It was our greatest game ever! [Be]cause we had to use so many rookies and had so many men injured and still came through!"[16] Against the powerhouse Browns the 49ers played a near perfect game.

However, the magic didn't last. The following Saturday night at Philadelphia's Shibe Park the 49ers dropped a 21–14 decision to the Eagles. Employing a single wing formation that he jokingly called his unbalanced T Formation, the Eagles' venerable coach "Bo" McMillan had quarterback Adrian Burk take direct snaps 10 yards deep. From that depth he threw completions to receivers Bobby Walston and Pete Pihos for most of the game.

In another solid performance, 49er fullback Verl Lillywhite ran 60 yards for a touchdown and out-wrestled Eagle defender Russ Craft in the end zone for a touchdown pass from Y.A. Tittle. But it wasn't enough. After the game a glum Buck Shaw only muttered, "We've got ten more to go."[17]

Throughout the '51 season San Francisco seemed to play to the level of the competition. After nine games their record stood at four wins, four losses and a tie. Besides their dominant win over the Browns in week one, the 49ers played lights out against the first-place Los Angeles Rams in week five at Kezar. Before the start of the regular season, Buck Shaw stated, "Soltau has made the biggest year's improvement of any man on the squad."[18] Soltau proved it against the Rams by catching three touchdown passes, kicking five extra-points and a 22-yard field goal for a total of 26 points. (It would stand as a 49er single game scoring record until Jerry Rice broke it by scoring 30 in a game 39 years later.) Joe Arenas and Johnny Strzykalski also scored on short runs while Leo Nomellini recovered a Norm Van Brocklin punt he had blocked in the end zone to give the 49ers a convincing 44–17 win over their California rivals.

Afterwards Buck Shaw sat sipping a pint of milk to calm his newly developed ulcers. Shaw enthusiastically told reporters, "This was just as good a game as our boys played when they beat the Cleveland Browns. These two stand out as our best efforts. No, I take it back, I guess this was the best effort. We scored more points in this one."[19]

Sporting a four-win, four-loss record, the Niners flew to New York for their rematch with the Yankees. With the 49ers holding a 10–0 lead entering the fourth quarter, Yankee coach Jimmy Phelan substituted Bob Celeri at quarterback for George Ratterman. The 49ers had cut the former California Golden Bear the previous year. Capitalizing on a poor punt that gave the Yankees possession on the San Francisco 31, Celeri's 20-yard completion to Buddy Young put the ball on the 49er 11-yard line. Two plays later Yankee Sherman Howard scored from a yard out. With a minute and 51 seconds remaining, Celeri's 38-yard completion to Young put the ball on the 49er 15-yard line. Celeri then threw three errant passes into the end zone before Yankee Harvey Johnson came on to boot a game-tying field goal, 10–10.

The 49ers then headed to Detroit, where before 52,000 fans they once again assumed the role of giant-killers. Leading 6–3 at halftime, Shaw started Y.A. Tittle at quarterback for Frankie Albert in the second half. Tittle connected on touchdown passes to Bill Jessup and Joe Arenas while the defense played stellar football in holding the Lions to one touchdown for a 20–10 victory. The win knocked Detroit out of first place, and the angry hometown crowd reacted by heckling and pelting the 49ers with trash as they left the field.

Tittle started at quarterback the following week. Although Tittle was a little off his game, the 49ers managed a 13–10 halftime lead. Shaw started Frankie Albert for Tittle in the second half, and he responded by leading the 49ers to three touchdowns to defeat Green Bay 31–19. For the first time all season the 49ers enjoyed back-to-back wins. That same day the Lions defeated the Rams in Los Angeles to regain first place in the National Conference.

Before a Kezar crowd of nearly 38,000, the 49ers again reverted to their role of giant-killer in their season finale rematch with Detroit. The Lions jumped to an early 10–0 lead before Lowell Wagner's interception of a Bobby Layne pass set up Joe Perry's 33-yard halfback pass to rookie Billy Wilson for a touchdown. Minutes later Wagner returned another interception 18 yards to the Lion 34-yard line. Tittle then tossed a

27-yard scoring pass to Gordy Soltau and the Niners led 14–10 at halftime. Trailing 17–14 late in the fourth quarter, 49er Joe Arenas returned a punt 51 yards to the Detroit 18. With second-and-goal from Detroit's 2-yard line Tittle perfectly executed a bootleg run that fooled the entire Lion team for the score. Soltau's extra-point made the final score 21–17. The 49ers once again knocked the Lions out of first place.

The hometown crowd went berserk, rushing the field after the game to hug and slap the backs of their local giant-killers. In the post-game locker room Tittle responded to questions about his winning bootleg touchdown run, "You know, you can't stick around Frankie [Albert] for a year and not pick up something."[20]

The 49ers' season ended on a joyous note, just like it began. However, it was a season of what could have been. Their seven-win, four-loss and one-tie record earned them a tie for second place with Detroit's Lions in the division. The Rams won the division title with eight wins and four losses. The 49ers beat the Lions twice and split with the Rams. They also gave the American Conference champion Cleveland Browns, who finished 11 and one, their only loss. However, a 27–21 upset loss to the Cardinals and their tie with New York's Yankees cost San Francisco a trip to the championship game. As it was, the Rams defeated the Browns 27–24 for the 1951 NFL Championship.

Fifteen

Making a Dent in the NFL

In 1952, the 49ers acquired another great football player with their number-one draft pick in University of Washington running back Hugh McElhenny. A Los Angeles native, McElhenny could have attended almost any college in the nation coming out of high school. However, he chose to attend Compton Junior College before heading to Seattle to play for the Huskies. Why the Huskies? Because they gave him the best deal. Besides the $75 per month stipend permissible for scholarship athletes, Washington boosters gave McElhenny a monthly $300 check under the table. They also provided his wife Peggy with a legitimate job as a medical receptionist. Between the monthly checks and Peggy's salary, the McElhennys grossed about $10,000 annually during the halfback's three years at UW. Although the McElhennys paid the rent on their apartment, boosters furnished it. Before Hugh arrived on campus, boosters paid for the couple's honeymoon in Palm Springs and flew them to Seattle—both of which were illegal. For years players and friends whispered that McElhenny took a pay cut when he signed his rookie contract with the 49ers for $7,000.[1]

At 6 feet, 1 inch and 195 pounds, McElhenny was an electrifying open-field runner who ran 100 yards in 9.6 seconds. In college, he nearly gave coach Howie Odell a stroke when he fielded a USC punt on his own goal line, but Odell's fright turned to delight when McElhenny returned it 100 yards for a touchdown. Hugh's other collegiate feats included returning a kick-off 96 yards for a touchdown against Minnesota and a 91-yard scoring run versus Kansas State. Against archrival Washington State in 1950, he rushed for 296 yards on 20 carries. Unfortunately, McElhenny's college experience ended on a sour note. After his senior season Hugh played in a Honolulu All-Star game. Having exhausted his athletic eligibility, he returned to Washington with every intention of earning the remaining credit hours he needed for a degree in business administration. Unfortunately, McElhenny learned that he was no longer enrolled and that Washington had made no provisions for his return. Unknowingly, he had agreed to a scholarship that ended once his athletic eligibility did. His $75 a month stipend was now going to another chap, with three years of eligibility remaining, for sorting out the athletic department's mail once a day.[2]

With the second-round pick, the 49er's selected 6-foot, 2-inch, 260-pound tackle Bob Toneff out of Notre Dame. Toneff would play both offensive and defensive tackle for the 49ers through 1958 and then spend six years with the Washington Redskins. Shaw, however, sometimes went off the beaten path to find talented players; such was the case with Charlie Powell.

A great athlete at San Diego High School, Powell earned 12 varsity letters in four different sports: football, basketball, baseball and track. By his senior year he stood 6 feet, 4

Hugh McElhenny and wife Peggy during their days at the University of Washington, November 2, 1949 (University of Washington Libraries, Special Collections, UWC8706) (University Libraries, University of Washington Special Collections).

inches, weighed 230 pounds, and ran the 100-yard dash in 9.6 seconds. He threw the shot 57' 9¾" and could high jump six feet. A power-hitting outfielder, he signed a contract out of high school to play for the Stockton Ports, a Class B affiliate of the American League's St. Louis Browns. As Powell sat on his front porch one day trying to play *Sentimental Journey* on an old saxophone, Buck Shaw pulled up in a gold Cadillac convertible. Shaw asked, "Excuse me. Which one of these houses does Charlie Powell live in?"

POWELL REPLIED, "You're talking to him."
SHAW: "Can I come up and join you on the porch?"
POWELL: "Yes, sir."[3]

At the time the NFL couldn't sign a player until his class graduated from college. However, because he had already signed a professional contract to play baseball the rule didn't apply to Powell. When Shaw discovered that, he asked the 19-year-old if he'd be interested in trying out for the 49ers. With his parents' approval, the 49ers sent him an airline ticket to fly to their Menlo Park training camp. There the coaches pitted him early against the 6-foot, 3-inch, 270-pound veteran Leo Nomellini. In a clash of titans in a one-on-one drill, the teenager more than held his own. Powell played for the 49ers in '52 and '53, and then again from '55 through '57. Powell bypassed football in 1954 to concentrate on a boxing career—something he would do again in 1958 and '59, before making his football comeback with the AFL's original Oakland Raiders in 1960 and '61. During that time he relished playing against his younger brother, Art Powell, who was a pass-catching ace for the New York Titans, and later had productive years with both the Oakland Raiders and Buffalo Bills. Hanging up his cleats with the Raiders, Powell again pursued his boxing career, and at one time was the fourth-ranked heavyweight in the world. His quest for the heavyweight title went "lights out" when he lost to Muhammad Ali (then known as Cassius Clay) in 1963 and later to Floyd Patterson, both by knockouts.

Powell's professional boxing career record was 25 wins and 11 losses.

* * *

In January 1952, Shaw added a long-time coaching adversary to his staff: Red Strader. The first St. Mary's football player to earn All-American recognition, Strader served as an assistant to Slip Madigan at his alma mater from 1935 through 1939. He succeeded Madigan as head coach in 1940, where he and Shaw first crossed coaching swords. They matched wits again when Strader coached the AAFC's New York Yankees in 1948, and again in 1950, when Strader bossed the NFL's New York Yanks. Strader would serve Buck as a scout and backfield coach.

The 49er organization suffered a scare in March of 1952 when team owner Tony Morabito suffered a major heart attack. Doctors worked through the night to save him. Morabito recovered, but family doctors advised him to avoid all excitement and strongly recommended he quit the football business for health reasons. In May, Morabito, who owned 75 percent of the 49ers, and his brother Vic, who owned the remaining 25 percent, put the team up for sale. (Original co-owners Al Sorrell and Ernie Turre sold their interests in 1949.) They had a few nibbles, but no serious offers and after a few months pulled the team off the market.

Shaw's staff weathered another medical scare in April when assistant coach Jim Lawson experienced severe stomach pain while vacationing in Carmel. Rushed to a Palo Alto hospital, Lawson underwent emergency abdominal surgery. Listed in critical condition for several days, he fully recovered in time for the start of quarterback rookie camp on July 22.

Attempting to reduce injuries to his own players, Shaw opted to play a local semi-pro team, the San Francisco Broncos, instead of hosting an intra-squad game. Played at Kezar before 8,700 fans, the exhibition was a laugher. Every man on Shaw's squad saw significant action as the 49ers steamrolled to a 79–0 win. Hoping to keep the score down, Buck inserted 270-pound tackle Leo Nomellini at fullback in the third quarter. Nomellini carried three times for a total of three yards and dropped two passes. Later, the former Minnesota All-American declared, "I've a new respect for backfield men."[4]

Despite winning all five of their exhibition games against league opponents, the preseason took a heavy toll on the team. In their third exhibition contest on September 3 the 49ers defeated the Rams 17–7 in the L.A. Coliseum before 68,000 rabid fans. Fierce rivals, both teams played with the intensity and ferocity of a championship game. Immediately afterwards the 49ers flew to Pittsburgh for another exhibition game against the Steelers four days later. The team left without star end Gordy Soltau, who flew home to San Francisco on crutches for medical treatment on a swollen left heel and aching right knee. In another brutal contest, the 49ers earned a 29–14 win over the Steelers at a high price. Captain Norm Standlee suffered a fractured and dislocated wrist while defensive end Gail Bruce sustained a fractured ankle. Both were expected to miss six to eight weeks of action.

Afterwards Shaw lamented to reporters, "If we're going to play league games from the start, we ought to call them league games and count them in league standings. As it is, we'll be playing 17 games, all of them against league teams and that's too many. These exhibition games can be rough on a club. I've never been in favor of them."[5] Shaw was ahead of his time in regard to exhibition games. Today, preseason exhibition games are limited to four and there's serious discussion about reducing them further. At the time, NFL players weren't paid for exhibition games and wouldn't be for years. Exhibition gate receipts went directly into the pockets of team owners.

After their opening exhibition win over the Redskins, co-owner Vic Morabito made a point of walking through the 49er locker room thanking the players for their efforts. After he passed, one key player quipped, "He should say thanks. He got a helluva lot of football out of us for nothing."[6]

San Francisco won their fifth and final exhibition game—a hard-fought 28–24 squeaker over Cleveland at Akron's Rubber Bowl. The team gave the game ball to a surprised but delighted Buck Shaw.

* * *

The 49ers began the '52 season at a whirlwind pace by winning their first five games. With stellar play from veterans and several rookies doing their bit, San Francisco was running on high octane. Shaw's men opened the season before nearly 58,000 at Kezar with a 17–3 win over Detroit. The club then hit the road for three games. The first stop was Texas on October 5, where they met the league's newest franchise, the Dallas Texans. The Texans were really the transplanted New York Yankees of 1951. Before a disappointing crowd of only 12,566, 49er rookie Hugh McElhenny made his presence known with an 89-yard touchdown run and by snagging a 33-yard scoring pass from Y.A. Tittle in a 37–14 win. The Niners then visited the Motor City for a rematch with Detroit before 56,822 fans—a new attendance record for the Lions. Starting his first game for the 49ers, rookie Charlie Powell, now a grizzled 20-year-old, was a terror at defensive end. In an era before the NFL officially kept statistics on quarterback sacks, Powell sacked Lion quarterback Bobby Layne 10 times on the afternoon for 67 yards in losses. The 49ers held the Lions to four first downs while piling up 21 of their own en route to a 28–0 shutout win. After the contest Buck Shaw proudly proclaimed, "This is the greatest game the 49er defense has played in its seven-year existence."[7]

Being pummeled into the sod at Brigg's Stadium made an impression on Bobby Layne, because he and Powell became good friends during their playing days. Years later Powell recalled,

> He [Layne] was such a great guy. When we played Detroit he would take me out and we'd go nightclubbing. We would just get through playing and either the Lions would whip our butts or we'd whip their butts and he would say, "Charlie, get dressed. I'll wait for you outside your dressing room." And it seemed like any place we went, everybody knew him.
>
> He would take me to the nicest clubs in Detroit and they would roll out the red carpet for him. He would even take me to the Black clubs in Detroit and everybody there knew him, too. They loved him in Detroit. Bobby Layne was a character and a beautiful person. We had a hell of a relationship.[8]

On October 19, San Francisco visited Wrigley Field where they pounded out their first-ever win over the Chicago Bears, 40–16. Leading 14–2 behind Joe Perry's two short touchdown runs, 49er rookie Hugh McElhenny broke the game open with a beautiful

94-yard punt return for a touchdown. Perry and Bob White later scored touchdowns, Soltau added a field goal, and linebacker Bob Momson tackled Bear quarterback Bob Williams in the end zone for a safety to ring up 40 points.

A thrilled Buck Shaw was more loquacious than in most post-game interviews. He raved that McElhenny's 94-yard punt return was the "greatest solo act" he'd ever seen on the gridiron. "It was magnificent!" Shaw exclaimed. "I can't understand how he does it and I can explain it by saying he has unique vision. He can see 'sideways.' I mean out of the corners of his eyes [peripheral vision]. And so quickly can he size up the position of tacklers that he can chart his course almost infallibly."[9]

During the locker room celebration an elated Frankie Albert approached the scoring machine running backs Perry and McElhenny sitting on adjacent benches. Albert told Perry, "Joe, you're still the Jet," before turning to inform McElhenny, "but Hugh, you're the King!"[10] The name stuck.

In the Bears' locker room head coach George "Papa Bear" Halas angrily declared, "They not only outscored us, but they out-charged, outran, out-passed, out-tackled and out-classed us." Halas then added ominously, "It'll be a different ball game in San Francisco."[11]

The Niners returned home for a rematch with the Dallas Texans on October 26. Although winless in four games, the Texans had quality players in Buddy Young, George Taliaferro, Art Donovan, Dick Hoerner and Gino Marchetti. Although Dallas had plenty of fight (Texans Marchetti and tackle Joe Campanella were both ejected for fighting), they couldn't stop the high-flying 49ers. Joe "The Jet" Perry scored on a 77-yard run while Hugh McElhenny bolted 83 yards for another. Gordy Soltau caught five passes for 50 yards and a touchdown while converting on six of seven extra-point attempts, and Notre Dame rookie Bob Toneff blocked Hank Lauricella's punt and returned it 20 yards for another score in San Francisco's 48–21 win. Afterwards, Texan coach Jimmy Phelan told reporters, "I honestly think they [the 49ers] have a good chance to become the only pro team to go through a season undefeated in a long while. I say that realizing that it's a tough trick to pull and don't want to put Buck on the spot. But he has the boys who can do it!"[12]

Phelan may not have wanted to put Buck on the spot, but his prediction may have jinxed the 49ers. Before a standing room only crowd of 60,000 at Kezar the following week, the visiting Bears ended the Niners' winning streak, 20–17. The knockout blow— or kick—came on George Blanda's 48-yard field goal with over five minutes remaining. Blanda had signed with the Bears out of Kentucky in 1949, and except for a brief stint with the Baltimore Colts in 1950, played for the Bears through 1958. He stepped away from football in '59, and it was rumored that George Halas kept him on salary that year so he wouldn't sign on as a kicker with any other club. With the birth of the American Football League (AFL) in 1960, Blanda re-ignited his career with the Houston Oilers. In 1971, the 44-year-old Blanda came off the bench for his trailing Oakland Raiders in five consecutive weeks to either quarterback or place-kick his team to a victory or a tie. Blanda's amazing feat garnered national headlines and made him the hero of middle-aged men everywhere in America, prompting many to rise from their living room couches and take to city streets and playgrounds on weekends to toss footballs with their sons.

The Bear-49er game was a rough-and-tumble affair with Chicago's George Connor and Joe Perry briefly exchanging punches. There was a near bench-clearing brawl when the Bears' Ed Sprinkle attempted to twist Hugh McElhenny's head off when the running back was clearly out of bounds on the 49er sideline. Leading 17–10 at the start of the fourth quarter and in control of things, 49er quarterback Frankie Albert opted to run for a first down on a fourth-and-one from his own 33-yard line. When dropping back to punt, the cagey Albert had a propensity for running towards the line of scrimmage after receiving the snap. If the defense fell asleep and he thought he could make the first down running, he would. Skilled at punting on the run, Albert punted if he saw there was no chance of making it. Believing he could pick up the first down, Albert ran, but Ed Sprinkle stopped him inches short of the mark. Taking possession on the 49ers' 33-yard line, Bears quarterback Steve Romanik hit end Bill Wightkin on an 18-yard touchdown pass and Blanda's point after tied the score at 17. Minutes later Chicago's Herman Clark intercepted an Albert pass that set up Blanda's winning field goal.

One of the reasons the 49ers regarded their head coach so highly was that he rarely, if ever, bad-mouthed his players to the press. In the post-game locker room Buck Shaw staunchly defended Albert's fake punt decision. "We have taken chances in the past and gotten away with them. I could have instructed Frankie specifically," he said. "Since I didn't, it's my fault. You look good when you win one of those gambles and you look horrible when you don't. I'll not second guess Albert. He'd have been all right if he had won. I repeat, we've gambled many times and have been successful more times than not."[13]

The Niners' post-game locker room resembled a morgue. The sporadic crack of a helmet being hurled against a locker was all that broke the dead silence. With bowed heads, several burly linemen hid their tear-swollen eyes with taped hands. A sense of heartache hung over the locker room like the heavy fog that frequently covered San Francisco Bay. The defeat had a special unsavory sting for Buck Shaw—not because it toppled his team from the undefeated ranks, he'd experienced that before, but because it came at the hands of Bears owner/coach George Halas. Several days before the rematch, a concerned Shaw asked NFL officials to enforce league rules mandating that coaches remain within the 40-yard lines during games. Shaw claimed that Halas' roaming sideline antics between end zones during their October 19 game in Chicago were an attempt to influence game officials. Buck stated: "I don't care if Halas is an old hand in this business. The rules apply to him the same as they apply to any one else. If he doesn't observe them Sunday, there'll be a beef from me. So far as I am concerned, Halas' so-called diplomatic immunity is a thing of the past." Shaw then charged: "He works every angle. Whenever the ball is kicked or carried out of bounds, Halas designates himself to mark the spot. He never fails to give the Bears a break of a yard or more and all too frequently the officials take his word for it. On tackles made close to the sidelines by the other team, he'll holler 'out of bounds' and demand that a foul be called…. The officials should resent his interference. Instead, they encourage him to 'take over' more and more by listening to his squawking."[14]

Halas responded to Shaw's complaint several days later, "I'm not changing my style on Shaw's say-so. The rule he mentions is one that has always been liberally interpreted, and I'll be surprised if it is suddenly enforced to the letter…. I've got to see what's going on. If Shaw wants to sit on the bench, that's his business. Personally, I'm not that lazy. I like to get up and walk around."[15]

* * *

Despite the loss, the 49ers retained first place in the National Conference when they departed for a three-game road swing. Among the walking wounded accompanying the team east was fullback Joe Perry. Nursing an extremely sore toe, Joe neither practiced all week nor wore a shoe on his swollen foot. Hindered by an aching back, safety Jim Cason made the trip but was sidelined for the game against the New York Giants on November 9. Over 54,000 fans jammed into the Polo Grounds to witness a punishing contest between two seemingly powerhouse teams. Suffering a broken bone between his ear and cheek, quarterback Frankie Albert left the game early. Shortly after knocking Giants halfback Frank Gifford silly and out of the game with his shoulder "thumper," Hardy Brown exited the contest with a separated shoulder. Joe Perry left for the sidelines after only five carries, while a knee injury sidelined 49er tackle Ray Collins. Injuries hospitalized the Giants' Bob Wilkinson and John Amberg. While both teams' trainers were busy tallying the body count, Giants coach Steve Owen jettisoned his T Formation at the end of the opening quarter in favor of the anachronistic "A" Formation. It paid dividends. New York's Eddie Price rushed for over 100 yards and Ray Poole's three field goals proved to be the difference in the Giants' 23–14 victory. Playing rock-solid defense, the Giants held the 49ers to a mere 35 yards rushing, while pilfering four San Francisco passes.

The Giants' upset win was the talk of the town on Monday, especially at the weekly luncheon of football sportswriters. Giants head coach Steve Owen was engaged in a lively conversation about the game with Columbia football coach Lou Little and former Colgate coach Andy Kerr. Congratulating Owen, Little said, "That was as good a game to watch as I ever saw, Steve." He then added, "Your boy, Gifford, was hit by the hardest tackle [Hardy Brown's 'thumper'] I ever saw."

Kerr then chimed in, "I'm just an old fashioned guy, but it did my heart good to see the Giants using an old-fashioned running attack."

"I don't like to disagree with you gentlemen," said a serious voice, "but I didn't enjoy that game one bit."

The trio turned to see a wryly grinning Buck Shaw. Shaw, whose team was spending the week at the Bear Mountain Inn about 50 miles north of the city before departing to Washington, D.C., moaned, "Maybe we just don't like your climate here, because we've come to New York seven times and never turned in a great performance."[16]

* * *

The following week San Francisco turned in a great performance during the last seven minutes of their game with the Redskins at Washington's Griffith Stadium. Trailing the upset-minded Redskins 17–9 on a soggy field midway through the fourth quarter, Hugh McElhenny broke lose on a 46-yard scoring run. Gordy Soltau's extra-point cut Washington's lead to 17–16. With just over four minutes to play the Redskins had a third down-and-two with the ball on their own 34-yard line when quarterback Eddie LeBaron shunned grinding down the clock and gambled with a pass to Hugh Taylor. He lost. San Francisco's Sam Cathcart picked off the aerial and returned it to Washington's 33-yard line. Two plays later Tittle connected with Billy Wilson on the Redskin 16, where the San Jose State grad broke two tackles en route to the end zone giving the 49ers a 23–17 victory. Now sporting a record of six wins and two losses, the Niners gained a tie for first place with Detroit for the conference lead. They then traveled to Los Angeles for the first of back-to-back games with the Rams.

In a television interview days before meeting the Rams, Buck Shaw stated that he thought Hugh McElhenny was the best runner he'd seen in 30 years. When asked if that included Notre Dame's legendary George Gipp, Shaw replied, "Absolutely." He then added that while Gipp was not quite as dangerous a runner as McElhenny, he was one of the best passers and kickers football ever saw. Unbeknownst to Shaw, his innocuous comment would create a stink.

Heavy rains hit Los Angeles that Saturday turning the Coliseum's field into a quagmire. In an attempt to dry the field and improve traction the grounds' crew spread tons of sawdust across it. As the 49ers headed down the tunnel entry for the opening kickoff, they learned that Detroit had lost earlier in the day. They now knew that by beating the Rams they would gain sole possession of first place in the National Conference. The slow track hindered both teams to start. The game's initial score came when Woodley Lewis brought the crowd of 78,000 to its feet with an 82-yard punt return for a touchdown to give the home team a 7–0 halftime lead. They built the lead to 21–0 by the fourth quarter. Only then did the Niners bare some teeth. Charlie Powell sacked Van Brocklin for a safety and on the subsequent possession Tittle hit Gordy Soltau on a five-yard touchdown pass to cut the lead to 21–9. However, that was all the visitors could muster while the Rams' Vitamin Smith scored two touchdowns to give Los Angeles a 35–9 win.

Immediately afterwards Shaw gathered his players behind closed doors, out of earshot of reporters, and let 'em have it. Chagrined, he related that they had just endured the worst defeat in San Francisco's seven-year existence. After administering a tongue-lashing, the Silver Fox gathered what remained of his dignity and left to address the media.

"I can't say much after a performance like that. The Rams deserved to win. There was a mental drop after the Chicago Bears beat us a month ago at Kezar. We haven't played a good game since. I can't figure it out."[17] Before leaving the press conference, however, he did commend rookie Charlie Powell on his exceptional effort and the Rams' pass-blocking and receiving corps for their fine game.

Later in the week, numerous Niners expressed agreement with Shaw's post-game address telling reporters that "Buck ripped us good and we deserved it."

Again, coaches know things can always get worse. Exacerbating the beatdown, the next day Frank Finch's article in the *Los Angeles Times* claimed the 49ers were a team torn by dissension. Finch based his claim on supposed conversations with two anonymous, but key, San Francisco players an hour after the loss. According to Finch, one 49er complained, "We no longer are a team; we are a bunch of individual stars." He then added, "A lot of players resented it when Coach Buck Shaw on a recent television program compared McElhenny to George Gipp. Sure, McElhenny is a great player, but some of us think Joe Perry, the fullback, is the key to our offense. Some of the older players don't like a rookie being called 'the King.'"[18] According to the article, the second player voiced concerns that the team was losing its confidence.

The 49er coaching staff was indignant over Finch's story. Addressing the article, Shaw said: "If there's dissension among the players it's news to me. It is true that my team has lost its spark which carried it to 10 straight victories (including exhibition games) earlier this season, but I just can't believe there's dissension. And I'll stand on my statement that McElhenny is the greatest runner I've seen in football."[19]

The 49er players interviewed about the veracity of Finch's article were adamant in their opinion that the story was flapdoodle. John Strzykalski, an original 49er who lost his starting job to McElhenny, emphatically declared: "McElhenny is one of the nicest guys on the squad. He's a ball player who's always trying. You've seen the gang get up off the bench to whack him on his back after one of his long runs. Do you think we'd do that if we didn't like the kid?"[20]

Hugh McElhenny, the focus of the so-called dissension, said, "It was a surprise and a shock to me. I've never had words with anyone. It's rough when you lose, but I've never heard any grousing, either in the huddle or on the sideline."[21]

Niner defensive back Lowell Wagner had his own theory on the story. "I don't know Finch," he said. "I think he got the story from the Rams. They're trying to stir things up. The only thing for us to do is to go out and beat the hell out of them."[22]

With the advent of 24-hour cable news, sports radio talk shows and Twitter, today's pro athletes come under more public scrutiny than the 49ers ever experienced in the '50s. However, locker room gossip, true or not, is detrimental to any team's welfare because it diverts owners, coaches and players from their major task of preparing to win games. Dealing with it can be a distraction lasting for days, weeks or an entire season. The entire Niner organization quickly shunted aside the Finch article to focus on a real problem. On Friday morning, November 28, 49er team captain Norm Standlee was admitted to the Children's Hospital where he was diagnosed with poliomyelitis. On Saturday morning, 49er team physician Dr. William Wagner issued the following statement: "We know Standlee has polio. As of this moment he has no paralysis. This is what Dr. E.B. Shaw, who is handling the case, has told me. But the prognosis of the disease will manifest itself within the next 24 to 28 hours. At the moment we are hopeful that the disease has reached its height and that Norm will improve from here on in."[23]

Having missed the team's first eight games of the season due to a broken wrist sustained in the exhibition season, Standlee returned to action against the Rams the previous Sunday, playing linebacker and carrying the ball twice for eight yards. Standlee was an active participant when the 49ers resumed practice on Tuesday. That evening he complained of a terrific headache. When he was feeling weak and vomiting on Wednesday, his wife Cleo continually pleaded to call an ambulance, but the 6-foot, 2-inch, 235-pound fullback refused. When he could barely lift his feet two inches off the ground, Norm finally agreed to allow a neighbor to drive him to the hospital.

The news staggered Shaw's 49ers and the entire Bay Area community. Norm "Chief" Standlee had been a local favorite since his playing days at Stanford. Upon graduating he played for the World Champion Chicago Bears in 1941. When Uncle Sam went to war in 1942, Standlee joined the Army and served as a captain in the Engineering Corps in India. Since the 49ers' inaugural season, Standlee had been a steadfast linebacker and punishing blocking fullback.

Hoping to win the game ball for their ailing teammate, the 49ers charged onto the field at Kezar intent on fulfilling safety Lowell Wagner's earlier words of "going out and beating the hell out of the Rams." In the first half it seemed like the football gods might be rooting for San Francisco when the Rams' "Tank" Younger carried the ball from his own three-yard line 96 yards before being tackled on the 49er one-yard line. The play was nullified, however, when officials ruled that the Rams were illegally in motion. Amused, the gods intervened again on behalf of the 49ers. This time they targeted Elroy "Crazy Legs" Hirsch's seemingly impossible acrobatic 53-yard catch from Norm Van Brocklin that had also put the ball on the Niners' one-yard line. An offensive holding call negated Hirsch's spectacular catch. After that, however, the football gods turned their attention elsewhere, for early in the fourth quarter the Rams held a 27–7 lead. It was then that the 49ers, thinking of the hospitalized Standlee listening to the radio broadcast of the game, made their move. Tittle's touchdown passes to Bill Jessup and McElhenny cut the Rams' lead to 27–21. When 49er Jim Powers recovered a Ram fumble on the visitors' 13-yard line, it looked like San Francisco might win it for the "Chief" after all. It didn't happen. With 51,000 hometown fans on their feet yelling "Go, go, go!" Joe Perry's first down run lost two yards. Dropping back to pass on second down, Tittle slipped and fell losing eight more. After a timeout, Tittle's third down pass was incomplete. On fourth down Tittle threw to Bill Jessup who—with the ball in mid-air—collided with a Ram defender, the pigskin falling harmlessly to the ground. No call! When the Rams took possession on their own 23-yard line, Woodley Lewis' 52-yard run set up Dan Towler's second rushing touchdown of the day and the Rams prevailed 34–21.

In the 49ers' tomb-like locker room players dressed silently before heading to St. Mary's Hospital for gamma-globulin shots hoping to ward off polio. As the devastated players gathered to leave, safety Jim Cason succinctly stated, "Men, let's face it. We got handled." No one disagreed.

A depressed Buck Shaw reiterated to reporters: "There's no question in my mind that in early season we were [playing] over our heads. We started winning and kept going until we hit the Chicago Bears here. We dipped and stayed there and we haven't been able to get up since." He then added, "On the other hand, the Rams got away to a slow start and now they're up where they belong. They're a helluva an outfit."[24]

Prospects for turning the season around didn't get any better when they learned that their upcoming opponent, the Pittsburgh Steelers, hammered the New York Giants 63–7 earlier in the day. Only 14,886 steadfast fans turned out the following week to see the Steelers mathematically eliminate the 49ers from playoff contention with a 24–7 win. Home attendance increased slightly to 17,579 for the season finale at Kezar on December 14, when the season ended on a positive note with a 24–14 win over Green Bay. The game was the swansong for original 49ers Frankie Albert and Johnny "Strike" Strzykalski. Although Albert and Tittle had shared quarterbacking duties throughout the season, Tittle graciously offered to "ride the pine" for Frankie's finale. Albert played a strong game—completing 16 of 26 passes for 213 yards and tossing a touchdown pass to Joe Arenas.

In the game's waning moments, a joyous Albert sat on the bench and began shedding his equipment. As adoring fans approached the retiring hero, Albert began giving his equipment away to wide-eyed kids. It started with his chinstrap, but progressed to his helmet, shoulder pads, cleats and jersey. Unaware of the circumstances, equipment manager Frank Clark (who took over for Ziggy Zamlynski in '51) chased two of the kids down, retrieving both the helmet and shoulder pads. Upon learning that Albert had given them as gifts, Clark returned them to both boys. When the game ended a grinning and shivering Albert left the field wrapped in a blanket and wearing only his football pants.

Afterwards, Shaw paid tribute to his retiring star, "It's sure going to seem very strange around here without that little guy. We're going to miss him for a lot of reasons, but most of all because he has always been a tremendous lift to the team." He then added, "There were times he drove me crazy. But he did that to the defense, too."[25]

After their whirlwind start, the 49ers experienced a frustrating finish, dropping five of their last seven games to finish third in the division with seven wins and five losses. The Rams and Lions finished tied for first place in the National Division with identical nine-and-three records. In a playoff game, the Lions defeated Los Angeles 31–21 to win the division title, and then whipped the Browns in Cleveland 17–7 for the 1952 NFL Championship. Interestingly enough, San Francisco beat the Lions twice that season. Individually, 49er Gordy Soltau led the league in scoring with 94 points and finished tied for third in receptions with 55. Joe Perry and rookie Hugh McElhenny finished third

After defeating Green Bay at Kezar Stadium on December 14, 1952, retiring quarterback Frankie Albert gave away his equipment to young fans after his last game for the 49ers (OpenS FHistory/wnp14.2835.jpg).

and fourth in league rushing with 725 and 684 yards respectively. McElhenny averaged a whopping seven yards per carry.

With the season's end the Morabito brothers announced that due to continuing concerns over Tony's health the team was again up for sale. Off the field, the 49ers received some holiday cheer when Palo Alto Hospital released team captain Norm Standlee to spend Christmas at home with wife Cleo and daughters Shirley and Susan. The determined Standlee would gradually recover, but his famed gridiron career was over.

* * *

News that the 49ers were again on the auction block sprouted rumors that Buck Shaw would return to Santa Clara University as head football coach, succeeding Dick Gallagher who resigned in late November to join Paul Brown's coaching staff at Cleveland. Despite Shaw's claims to the contrary, rumors bubbled until Santa Clara's December 29 announcement that the school was dropping football. The Jesuit school's decision hammered the final nail in the coffin of a once colorful, but short-lived era of independent football on the Pacific Coast. Its heyday was in the '30s, with fierce rivalries such as the Little Big Game detailed in earlier chapters. The death spiral started during World War II when Gonzaga dropped the sport. Portland University gave up the gridiron ghost in '49, with Saint Mary's following in '50. Both Los Angeles' Loyola University and the University of San Francisco jettisoned the game after the '51 season. The independents' demise was attributed to the Pacific Coast Conference schools' reluctance to schedule them and the higher price tag that accompanied the advent of two-platoon football.

Sixteen

Hi-Lo Country

Although too late to help Santa Clara, on January 14, 1953, the National Collegiate Athletic Association's (NCAA) rules committee voted to outlaw free substitution and end two-platoon football. The ruling pleased college presidents who saw it as a necessary cost-cutting measure, but irked the vast majority of college coaches, who believed free substitution made for a better-played game with fewer injuries. Buck Shaw agreed with the coaching majority. When he coached at Santa Clara, Shaw's "two-unit" system of playing 11 men (the Buckaroos) for six or seven minutes and then substituting another 11 (the Shawnees) proved to be advantageous. He viewed the elimination of free substitution as a revival of "iron man" football which he thought dead. He also believed that returning to single-platoon football provided fewer kids chances to play. Shaw explained, "If a boy can only do one thing well—like throw or catch a pass, kick or run back a kick—he isn't going to play football in college. A fellow like Y.A. Tittle of the 49ers wouldn't get off the bench."[1]

* * *

With Frankie Albert's retirement most football prognosticators believed the 49ers would select a quarterback with their bonus pick in the 1953 college draft, but the 49ers threw them a curve by selecting Harry Babcock, a 6-foot, 2-inch, 193-pound receiver out of Georgia. Shaw defended the decision, "I'm convinced that a 'six-point' end is more important than anything else in pro football today. Babcock fills that bill to perfection."[2] Reaffirming his belief, Shaw selected Texas receiver Tom Stolhandske with San Francisco's first-round pick. Unfortunately, the Silver Fox's aspirations for the pair never materialized. Babcock, whom teammates felt lacked aggressiveness in going after passes, could never beat out either Soltau or Wilson at end. He only caught 16 passes in three seasons with the 49ers. Stolhandske rebuffed the 49ers and signed with the Canadian Football League.

The gem of the Niners' 1953 draft turned out to be tackle Bob St. Clair. The 6-foot, 9-inch, 265-pound San Francisco native finished his collegiate career at Tulsa when the University of San Francisco dropped football after the '51 season. Team captain Bruno Banducci nicknamed St. Clair "the Geek." St. Clair spent his entire 11-year pro career with the 49ers. Because of his height the coaches often inserted him on defense when opponents attempted field goals and extra-points. During the 1956 season alone he blocked ten kicks. Unfortunately, on one attempt he blocked Norm Van Brocklin's foot with his mouth, losing five front teeth in the process. The giant tackle trundled to the sidelines momentarily to have his bloody mouth stuffed with cotton before returning to finish the rest of the game. In another testament to his toughness, he once played an entire quarter with a broken shoulder. St. Clair could literally be described as a "meat-eater," for he ate raw meat—steaks, chicken, fish, dove hearts, whatever. Named an All-Pro over a half-dozen times, St. Clair was voted into Pro Football's Hall of Fame in 1990. Shortly before the induction ceremony, an interviewer asked him if he thought players in his generation could play in the modern NFL. "I don't think the question should be 'Could we play today?'" replied St. Clair. "The question is, 'Could these candy-asses have played with us?'"[3]

In January of 1953, Abe Saperstein, owner of the Harlem Globetrotters, led a Cleveland syndicate in offering the Morabito brothers $375,000 of their $425,000 asking price for the club. For a while it looked like the deal would materialize, but to Saperstein's surprise and disappointment the Morabitos backed out. That March, William D. Cox, acting as an intermediary on behalf of Dallas' Murchison brothers, Clint and John, offered to buy the 49ers. (Cox had once been president of Major League Baseball's Philadelphia Phillies, but league commissioner Kenesaw Mountain Landis banned him for life for betting on his own team.) The deal collapsed, however, when the Morabitos stipulated that as part of the sale the Murchisons would have to keep both Tony and Vic Morabito on the payroll at an annual salary of $12,000 each.[4] Before the year ended, Los Angeles swimsuit mogul E.W. Stewart offered the Morabitos $500,000 for the 49ers, but the brothers declined. That refusal had the Bay Area media openly questioning if the Morabitos were indeed serious about selling the team or merely seeking publicity. The brothers, however, continued to claim that they'd sell when the "price was right."

As usual the 49er organization underwent off season changes. In March, Red Strader resigned as a full-time scout and assistant coach to take an executive position with a construction firm. To replace Strader the Silver Fox hired the 49ers' original kicker, Joe "the Toe" Vetrano. On May 31, safety Jim Cason left the 49ers to sign with the Saskatchewan Rough Riders of the Canadian Football League. The Canadian League pulled an even bigger coup on June 3, when its Calgary Stampeders signed recently retired 49er quarterback Frankie Albert. Albert told shocked 49er fans that Calgary general manager Bob Robinett "made me an enticing offer I couldn't resist."[5] The Stanford grad reportedly signed for $31,000 with the opportunity to buy into a lucrative oilfield. (By all accounts, to say that Albert had a less than stellar season with Calgary would be generous.) Just before the start of the training camp, Bruno Banducci became the only original 49er remaining on the squad when guard Visco Grgich announced his retirement. Grgich had missed most of the '52 season with a knee injury.

After a restful Hawaiian cruise with wife Marge and family friends in March, Shaw did some off-season soul searching and re-evaluated both the game of pro football and his 49er team. As a result, he opened training camp in late July with several new ideas. Shaw believed that his 49ers had had the best ground game in football for several years. Yet it hadn't earned them a championship. He felt his team needed to put a greater emphasis on the passing game if it hoped to grab the league's brass ring. Shaw still wanted a strong ground game, but now saw it as a way of keeping the defense honest while setting up the passing attack. Frankie Albert had been an effective short-and middle-range passer, but Shaw felt Tittle was both, and had the added advantage of throwing the long ball as well as anybody. Buck also deducted that the key to the Cleveland Browns' tremendous success was the steady play of quarterback Otto Graham, a true pocket-passer. In the first days of training camp, Shaw confided to reporters, "I've just about decided that ball handling, while a valuable asset, is a lot more important in college than it is with the pros. After examining all the evidence, I've reversed my thinking. As between ball han-dling and the pass, I'll take passing."[6]

Shaw also had a new outlook on exhibition games. In previous years, he thought it important to win as many as possible to maintain team morale and generate fan interest. However, with the recent loss of veterans Albert, Norm Standlee, Jim Cason, Visco Grg-rich, Johnny Stryzkalski and Ray Collins, the 49ers had numerous holes to fill. In late July, Shaw announced that the prime aim of the exhibition season was "the development of the new kids, a whole flock of whom we're just getting to know by name."[7]

With dozens of newcomers in camp and so many positions to fill, the initial week of practice had heavy dollops of contact drills and scrimmages. After a week of camp, Shaw told reporters, "We're a helluva lot tougher now than we were last year at this time."[8] The rookies saw plenty of game action when, instead of an intra-squad game, the 49ers played an exhibition game in Sacramento against the Army's Fort Ord team for the bene-fit of Sacramento's Crippled Children's Society. Playing in the backfield for Fort Ord was former University of San Francisco great and Olympian Ollie Matson. Matson immedi-ately got the 49ers' attention when he bolted 75 yards for a touchdown on the game's first play from scrimmage. The shocked pros responded quickly and with a vengeance, scor-ing four touchdowns to take a 28–7 first-quarter lead. Shaw played only rookies and new-comers the last three quarters as San Francisco rolled to a 42–7 win.

In the next exhibition contest against Cleveland's powerhouse Browns, Shaw felt compelled to play more regulars because he believed the rookies would be over-matched. Nevertheless, quite a few saw playing time in a 20–7 loss. Afterwards a pleased Shaw told reporters, "I have a nice feeling about this being a squad with a lot of ceiling, because there are so many kids. Looks to me as if, with a little experience, some of them are going to be mighty good. It's a helluva lot better than starting with a bunch of vets with a limited ceiling."[9] For the remaining exhibition games Shaw adhered to his primary preseason aim of evaluating rookie talent. The 49ers won two, lost three and tied one against NFL teams.

* * *

With a dozen rookies on the squad, Shaw's 49ers opened the 1953 season against the Philadelphia Eagles before 27,819 hometown fans. In an impressive performance, quar-terback Y.A. Tittle threw three touchdown passes in leading San Francisco to a 31–28 vic-tory. What caught everyone's attention, however, was a seven-minute brawl that erupted with five minutes remaining in the game. *San Francisco Examiner* sportswriter Bill Mulli-gan wrote that he'd never seen anything like it in his 30 years of covering sporting events. To spectators and sportswriters alike the game manifested no ill will until Eagle end Bobby Walston and Charlie Powell began having heated words. As the two jawed at one another, Joe Perry came off the sidelines and belted Walston. (Being the only other Afri-can American 49er, Perry may have felt a duty to protect the 21-year-old Powell.) Then all hell broke loose as both benches emptied. Fans threw bottles and cans onto the field. Two dozen players were grouped together at midfield punching, pushing and swing-ing helmets, while 25 yards away Hugh McElhenny was hammering Philadelphia's Pete Pihos with his helmet. On the opposite side of the midfield cluster, Hardy Brown and Eagle Al Pollard were exchanging roundhouse punches. Attempting to restore order, the 49er band began playing the "Star Spangled Banner." When tempers cooled and police restored order, the officials ejected both Walston and Powell.

Eagle coach Jim Trimble blamed Perry's incursion onto the field as the spark that ignited the donnybrook. However, underlying stimuli may have been at play. Earlier in the game, Hardy Brown delivered a "thumper" to Eagle halfback Toy Ledbetter that sidelined him with a depressed cheek fracture requiring surgery two days later. Also, on the 49ers' last extra-point try, Eagle tackle Mike Jarmoluk unleashed a savage uppercut that raised a colorful mouse under the eye of San Francisco center Bill Johnson. Either act may have lit the fuse.

The teams finished the game with no further incidents. Afterwards Eagle coach Jim Trimble called the melee an "embarrassment to the league," and letters to local papers castigated the players for their lack of sportsmanship. If the NFL investigated the matter, nothing came of it. In the post-game locker room, numerous 49ers were sporting shiners and bloody lips. Despite the swollen-shut eyes and facial welts, the rumble produced one positive—the 49ers drew closer as a team.

Preparing for the visiting Rams the following week, Shaw put his charges through drills and meetings daily from 10 a.m. until 6 p.m., with a break for lunch. By the end of the first quarter, 49er fans wondered if Shaw had practiced them at all as the explosive Rams raced to a 20–0 lead. Later in the quarter, Hugh McElhenny thrilled the fans when he returned a punt 91 yards for an apparent touchdown. Unfortunately, the officials flagged Bob St. Clair on the play for clipping Andy Robustelli, which nullified the score. Unshaken, McElhenny, Perry, Billy Wilson, Tittle and company rallied to take a 28–27 lead late in the fourth quarter. A Ben Agajanian field goal gave the Rams a 30–28 lead with only three minutes remaining. With many of the 43,922 fans now slumped in their seats thinking the 49ers' heroic rally had been for naught, San Francisco went to work. From their own 20-yard line Tittle hit McElhenny on a quick flare pass. The "King," flashing his inimitable open-field running, bolted 71 yards before Dick "Night Train" Lane and Woodley Lewis dragged him down at the Ram nine-yard line. Four plays later Gordy Soltau booted a 13-yard field goal with six seconds left to give the 49ers a dramatic 31–30 win.

Shaw blamed his team's poor start on youthful inexperience and being too keyed up, just as they had during the first quarter against the Eagles. He explained, "We looked awful and I know most of the fans may have given up hope for a San Francisco victory. But when we settled it was for keeps and the results showed. We are coming of age."[10]

Ram coach Hampton Pool called it a "great game." He then added, "That McElhenny is just plain great! I've never seen anything like him."[11]

On October 11, Shaw's 49ers traveled to Detroit. A record crowd of 58,079 fans turned out at Briggs Stadium to witness the undefeated teams battle. With five straight regular season wins over the Lions, San Francisco seemed to have the defending NFL champions' number. As in their first two games, the 49ers found themselves trailing early. Refusing to wilt, the visitors briefly took a 14–10 lead. However, Lion quarterback Bobby Layne was red-hot and Detroit regained the lead 24–14 in the third quarter. The 49ers then drove to inside the Lion 10-yard line. On third-and-goal from the four, Tittle ran a bootleg and dove into the end zone to score. In doing so, however, Lion corner back Jim David's knee caught him in the face, fracturing Tittle's cheek bone in three places. Jim Powers replaced Tittle at quarterback. Despite Tittle's absence, the 49ers still had their chances to win, but McElhenny fumbled the ball away twice—once on Detroit's 17-yard line late in the third quarter and again on the Detroit 22-yard line in the fourth quarter—and the Lions held on to win 24–21.

True to form, the next week at Wrigley Field the 49ers trailed the Bears 21–0 after

11 minutes of play. With Jim Powers at quarterback for the injured Tittle, the 49ers—also true to form—fought their way back. Joe Perry's 51-yard touchdown burst made the half-time score 21–7. Joe Arenas' 60-yard third-quarter touchdown run cut the Bears' lead to 21–14, before the Niners tied it at 21 on Powers' 22-yard pass to Billy Wilson. The gutsy Wilson, who suffered a broken nose in the first quarter, told team trainer Bob Kleckner not to tell Buck Shaw of the injury, for fear the Silver Fox would sideline him. Kleckner acquiesced and packed Wilson's nose with cotton gauze. A little luck and Jim Powers' quick thinking led to the Niners' fourth touchdown. With Powers holding, Gordy Soltau attempted a field goal from Chicago's 37-yard line. However, the Bears blocked the kick which Powers caught on the fly before advancing it 23 yards to the Bear 13. Three plays later Perry scored from three yards out. Perry scored again in the fourth quarter giving the 49ers a come-from-behind 35–28 win, and propelling Shaw's club into a three-way tie for the Western Conference lead with the Lions and Rams.

Afterwards, an excited but humble Powers, who completed 11 of 31 passes for 128 yards, lavished praise on his teammates for the win. Crediting Tittle's understudy on his solid performance Shaw declared, "Powers did an excellent job of directing the running attack in the second half. He showed a lot of poise when we were three touchdowns behind." He then added, "Boy, a couple of more games like this one and they'll carry me out in a box!"[12]

In their rematch with the Lions at Kezar before 53,000 fans, the 49ers deviated from their standard operating procedure by jumping out to a 10–0 lead. But Detroit's Bobby Layne hurled touchdown passes of 49 and 12 yards to Dorne Dibble and Ollie Cline respectively to give the Lions a 14–10 win.

A grueling defensive struggle, Shaw's strategy to twice go for first downs instead of attempting field goals deep in Detroit territory drew harsh criticism from sportswriters and fans alike. When asked about it, Shaw explained, "It was early in the third quarter when we were down in Lion territory with a choice between kicking or going for a touchdown on fourth down. I did not know whether we would have other such opportunities. On the second opportunity, I followed the same reasoning. As it turned out, Detroit did get a touchdown and seven points. That put them ahead 14–10. From then on we had to go for the big seven to win."[13]

The fact that the 49ers missed two first-half field goal attempts may have influenced Shaw's thinking. Unlike the coach on the sideline who has all of 30 seconds to make a decision, sportswriters and talk show analysts—whose livelihoods are not on the line—and have the benefit of hindsight are quick to second guess those in the arena.

The next week Tittle returned to the lineup and San Francisco knocked off the Bears 24–14. For the first time in eight years it rained during a 49er game at Kezar. However, the weather didn't hinder the aerial duel between Chicago's George Blanda and Tittle. Nearly 28,000 fans saw the pair combine to complete 55 of 94 passes, breaking the previous NFL record of 91 passing attempts in a single game.

With a record of four wins and two losses, San Francisco headed south for a rematch with their California rival, the Rams. Several Ram players told reporters that the 49ers were lucky to win their first meeting at Kezar, and confidently predicted the Rams would settle the score in Los Angeles. A shirt-sleeved crowd of 85,865 fans baked in 100-degree temperatures, hoping the hometown team would deliver on its promise. With Tittle again donning a protective mask to protect his cheek, the LSU grad threw a 17-yard scoring pass to Gordie Soltau with 72 seconds remaining in the game to give the 49ers a heroic

31–27 win. The key to the contest, however, came early in the fourth quarter when the Rams had a first-and-goal on the Niners' seven-yard line. Art Michalik, a 6-foot, 2-inch, 225-pound 49er rookie out of tiny St. Ambrose College in Davenport, Iowa, made his presence known by making four successive tackles of Ram running backs to prevent Los Angeles from scoring. Michalik's efforts on this crucial goal line stand probably saved the game for the 49ers. Buck Shaw certainly thought so and praised Michalik afterwards.

In the Rams' post-game locker room, Coach Hampton Pool lauded Buck to reporters, "I've never seen a coach get a team mentally ready as well as Shaw does. He's a master."[14]

Detroit, Los Angeles and San Francisco were now all tied for first place in the Western Conference with identical records of five wins and two losses.

* * *

The schedule makers didn't do the 49ers any favors. Up next came the Eastern Conference Champions and their old AAFC nemesis, the Cleveland Browns. Stoical Cleveland coach Paul Brown declared after the contest, "The bodily contact out there was the most brutal I have ever seen in our series."[15] Any of the 80,698 fans in attendance would agree. Late in the half with Cleveland facing a third-and-long, Otto Graham dropped back to pass. Spying no open receiver, he tucked the ball and scampered 19 yards for a first down before being knocked out of bounds by three 49er defenders. While lying on the ground, Graham caught Art Michalik's elbow, which opened a gash on the corner of his mouth. George Ratterman subbed at quarterback for Graham, who was bleeding profusely. Without the benefit of anesthesia, Graham received 15 stitches on the sidelines to close the cut.

With a face mask added to his helmet to protect his swollen and aching mouth, the courageous, but light-headed Graham returned to the lineup for the second half. Thanks to Joe Arenas' 43-yard kick-off return the 49ers soon found themselves at Cleveland's seven-yard line with a fourth down and three yards-to-go. Trailing 10–7, Shaw found himself in the same situation he had faced against Detroit three weeks earlier. Buck now made the same decision he did then. Eschewing the field goal attempt, he went for the first down with the same outcome. Tittle threw a quick swing pass to Joe Perry, who dropped the ball when Cleveland's Tommy Thompson arrived at the same time. The Browns took over on downs.

Lou Groza's three field goals turned out to be the difference as the Browns edged the 49ers 23–21. The narrow margin of defeat resulted in the *San Francisco Examiner's* next day headline: "S.F.'s Failure to Try for Three is Costly." Sportswriter Harry Borba again dredged up the previous Detroit game with the same scenario, revitalizing the Bay Area's second-guessing of Shaw. Nevertheless, Shaw had the courage of his convictions.

In the post-game locker room Graham, who threw a 34-yard touchdown pass to Ray Renfro in the second half, said, "This is the worst I've ever been cut. I don't know who hit me, but he [Michalik] came up after the game and apologized."[16]

The loss now left the five-win, three-loss 49ers a game behind the Lions and a half-game behind the Rams. Having already played both Detroit and Los Angeles twice, the 49ers needed help to catch them. In the meantime, San Francisco couldn't afford a loss.

Taking care of business, the 49ers clubbed the Packers 37–7 in a raging snowstorm the following week at Milwaukee's County Stadium. Shaw's boys finished their four-game road swing at Baltimore, where former Colt Y.A. Tittle received a greater applause than any Baltimore player during team introductions. Tittle received even more applause that afternoon in leading San Francisco to a 38–0 lead, before Shaw substituted for him. The Colts rallied for three touchdowns to make the final score San Francisco 38, Baltimore 21. After the game the 49ers learned the uplifting news that "Papa" Halas' Bears beat the Rams in Chicago. By winning their last two games, the 49ers would finish ahead of Los Angeles and tie Detroit if the Lions lost one of their two remaining games.

Returning to Kezar on December 6, the hungry Niners faced Green Bay. The Packers, who had fired head coach Gene Ronzani the week before, were now being co-coached by Hugh Devore and Ray "Scooter" McLean. The change didn't help as the 49ers rolled over Green Bay 48–14. During the game 49er fans were on the edge of their seats, anxiously listening to the public address system reporting scores from Detroit. Unfortunately, Detroit dashed their hopes by beating the Bears 13–7.

The 49ers were confident they'd hold up their end in the season finale against the visiting Colts. In an interesting individual matchup, the 49ers' Bob St. Clair often found himself battling the Colts' Gino Marchetti. The two giants had been teammates and major cogs on the University of San Francisco's undefeated 1951 team. The 49ers had little trouble in defeating Baltimore 45–14. That same afternoon, however, the Lions defeated the New York Giants to clinch the Western Conference title with twelve wins and two losses. The 49ers finished in second place with nine wins and three losses. Detroit, the Western Conference champion, went on to edge Cleveland for the 1953 NFL Championship, 17–16.

In the 49ers' post-game locker room team owner Tony Morabito was asked if he was happy with the season. "Are you kidding?" replied Morabito. "Hell, yes, I was satisfied! It was a great season. We fear no team now. What I liked about the 1953 team is that no one held any hope for us at the start. Some said we'd be lucky to win three games. Instead, we should be playing for the championship."[17]

Morabito had reason to be happy. Besides his team's terrific record, his club cleared a profit of over $100,000 for the second consecutive year. Morabito had also recently enhanced his club's future championship hopes by signing former St. Mary's running back John Henry Johnson to a contract on December 2. A punishing runner, Johnson spent the '53 season playing football in Canada.

Individual kudos went to Joe "the Jet" Perry, who led the league in rushing with 1,018 yards for a 5.3-yard average per carry. Gordy Soltau again led the league in scoring with 114 points, while Y.A. Tittle finished third in the league in passing, throwing for 2,121 yards and 20 touchdowns.

On December 14, the day after the season ended, the *San Francisco Examiner*'s Curley Grieve interviewed Buck Shaw:

> GRIEVE: What made the 49ers so successful this year?
> SHAW: There's only one answer to that—spirit. You can't play football successfully any other way except with heart.
> GRIEVE: Then it wasn't a case of great players?
> SHAW: Sure, we had great players. Men like Tittle, Joe Perry, Hugh McElhenny—ends, tackles and guards. But behind that was something else—desire. And it was desire that brought success to the season and pushed the team to the heights in every game.
> GRIEVE: Every game?
> SHAW: That's right. From the start of the season, the 49ers never turned in a bad

performance. The hallmark of greatness in a team is consistency. That's why I say—this was a great team.

GRIEVE: Aren't you going to give yourself a little credit?

SHAW: Not very much. Why should I? Every coach in the league has as much football knowledge as I do. I don't think I out-coached any of them. The difference was in the players. They wanted to win—not one game or one Sunday. But every game and every Sunday.

* * *

Unbeknownst to the Silver Fox, when Coach Frank Leahy informed Notre Dame of his intention to resign in January of 1954, school officials had only two candidates in mind: Terry Brennan, the young coach of the Irish freshman team, and Buck Shaw.

Administrators wrestled with whether they should give the job to Shaw for three to five years and assure Brennan that the job would eventually be his. Ultimately, the Rev. Theodore Hesburgh, Notre Dame's president, decided to go with Brennan. He offered the post to Brennan with the admonition that if he felt he were too young, the job almost certainly would be offered to him sometime in the future.[18] Brennan accepted immediately.

* * *

The 49er organization believed it was on the threshold of winning its first league championship in 1954. Signing running back John Henry Johnson added to an already explosive offense. The Bay Area media would tag the 49er quartet of Tittle, Perry, McElhenny and Johnson as the "Million Dollar Backfield." (However, their collective career salaries as active players would never come anywhere near a million dollars.) Shaw and his staff believed tightening the defense, especially the secondary, could yield a championship. In search of the missing pieces, San Francisco selected University of Maryland's Bernie Faloney with its first-round pick. Shaw hoped to play Faloney, a solid two-way player, at defensive back where the team needed immediate help, while having him understudy Y.A. Tittle at quarterback. However, Faloney let it be known that he wanted a shot at quarterback first and foremost. Faloney then asked for a salary that 49er General Manager Lou Spadia was unwilling to meet. Rebuffed, Faloney signed with the Canadian League.

The Niners also lost their third-round pick, George Washington University center/linebacker Steve Korchak, who signed a minor league contract to play baseball for the Washington Senators. On a positive note, disillusioned expatriates Jim Cason and tackle Ray Collins, who skipped north of the border to play in Canada in '53, re-signed with San Francisco for the '54 campaign. A proven performer at safety, Cason would help immediately. Still seeking to solidify the secondary, the 49ers traded Collins to Washington for defensive back Johnny Williams.

The first sign of the injury tsunami that would wash away the club's title hopes occurred off the gridiron. Morgan Williams, the team's 13th-round draft pick out of Texas Christian, played for the College All-Stars' in their victory over the Detroit Lions that August. En route from Chicago to the 49ers' Menlo Park training camp, Williams' younger brother Scott fell asleep at the wheel outside of Little Rock, Arkansas. Veering off the road the car flipped throwing Morgan from the vehicle. The linebacker sustained a fractured skull ending his hopes of becoming a 49er. His brother and another passenger were not seriously injured.

While it's difficult to comprehend today, the 49ers played seven exhibition games in 1954. The expansive preseason delighted team owners who pocketed the gate receipts. San Francisco won all seven exhibitions, which catapulted the expectations of both the Morabito brothers and Bay Area fans. In an interview shortly before the regular season's opener, Buck Shaw told quarterback-turned-newspaper columnist Frankie Albert, "I feel we have the necessary horses to field our greatest team ever. Barring injury—which is a determining factor—we are capable of winning it all."[19] Shaw had no inkling just how much of a determining factor injuries would play.

In the regular season's opener against the hapless Washington Redskins, the 49ers cruised to a 41–7 victory at Kezar. Filling in for the injured Gordy Soltau, the versatile Joe Perry kicked five extra-points. An omen came in the fourth quarter, when backup quarterback Arnold Galiffa broke a bone in his right hand forcing him to miss the next six weeks. The injury prompted the team to sign former San Francisco State quarterback Maury Duncan as insurance.

On October 4, the Niners headed south to meet the Rams. A zealous crowd of 93,553 witnessed an exciting contest. Hugh McElhenny's dazzling 28-yard scoring run gave the visitors a 24–17 lead midway through the fourth quarter and seemingly made him the game's hero. However, McElhenny fumbled a punt return minutes later, and the Rams recovered on San Francisco's 34-yard line. It took five plays before "Deacon" Dan Towler's one-yard plunge and Les Richter's extra-point kick tied the score at 24. With less than a minute remaining the 49ers' newly acquired Johnny Williams intercepted Van Brocklin's pass and returned it to the Rams' 38. The 49ers' rushed out the field goal team with Gordy Soltau to attempt it. However, time expired before the visitors could get the snap off, and the game ended tied at 24.

If there was ever such a thing as a Pyrrhic tie, this was it. Quarterback Y.A. Tittle suffered a broken left hand while Art Michalik and linebacker Don Burke both sustained torn knee ligaments requiring season-ending surgery. In Burke's case, it ended his pro career. Fortunately, X-rays taken of Joe Perry's bruised ribs were negative. While Tittle could still throw, his left hand was placed in a cumbersome cast that affected his ball handling and gripping the ball when dropping back to pass.

Disappointed and frustrated with the tie, 49er team owner Tony Morabito publicly accused the Rams of playing "dirty football." He angrily declared, "If that's the kind of football they want, that's what they'll get. You can put that on record and I'm not going to apologize to anyone for saying it."[20]

Team captain Bruno Banducci supported Morabito's claim spewing, "I never saw a dirtier bunch of guys in my life. The next time we play them we are going to be rougher and dirtier—and you can put that in print."[21]

Buck Shaw refused to comment on the matter.

The following week Shaw's men journeyed to Milwaukee to battle Lisle Blackbourn's Green Bay Packers. Opting to sit the broken-handed Tittle out of the contest, Shaw started Jim Cason at quarterback. Experimenting to find a suitable backup for Tittle, Shaw had played Cason at quarterback on several occasions during the exhibition season. Buck believed the veteran Cason better prepared to handle the quarterback reins on a rain-soaked field than the newly signed Maury Duncan. Under the circumstances, Cason performed admirably, leading the 49ers to a 10–0 halftime lead. However, behind the pinpoint passing of Tobin Rote, the Packers caught fire in the third quarter and held a 17–10 lead with 12 minutes remaining in the contest. Tittle and ailing veteran center Bill Johnson then entered the game for Cason and center Pete Brown, respectively.

Taking possession on their own 29-yard line, Tittle led the 49ers on a 71-yard touchdown drive, culminating with Joe Perry's eight-yard scoring sprint. Unfortunately, Gordy Soltau's extra-point attempt failed and the 49ers still trailed 17–16. The Niner defense then held, and San Francisco took possession on its own 31. Tittle immediately connected with McElhenny on a 53-yard completion to the Packer 16. After several running plays the gutsy Tittle, ignoring his broken left hand, carried the ball the final two yards to paydirt. Soltau's extra-point kick gave the 49ers a 23–17 victory.

The third game of their road swing took the 49ers to Chicago, where the team stayed at the Hotel Wyndamir East located in Hyde Park. Bob St. Clair prevailed upon Leo Nomellini to show him some of the Windy City's lively nightlife. It was nearly 1:00 a.m. before the two tackles returned to the hotel—well past the team's 11 p.m. curfew. While they were sneaking in the back way to the hotel, traveling secretary Lou Spadia popped out of the bushes with a pen and clipboard asking, "Okay, you guys, where have you been?"

Nomellini answered, "We went to a late show."

"Well," replied Spadia, "I hope you enjoyed it because it's going to cost you!"[22]

When the irate Nomellini threatened to break Spadia's neck, the traveling secretary bolted for the main hotel entrance. Nomellini saw no need to make good on his threat as Spadia fled at "breakneck" speed. St. Clair related the next morning's events in his own words:

> We had a team meeting with Buck Shaw. First thing he said when he came in was, "I'm really disappointed in you guys. I have used the honor system with you guys my whole coaching career. I have never had a problem. But last night I was really concerned!" As he was talking I knew he was talking directly to me. I figured Spadia had told him that Leo and I were the two guys who were out….
>
> I was slumping down in my chair. Then he said, "Last night out of 33 players 28 of you guys were out!" All of a sudden I sat up in my chair. I thought, "Geez, that's not too shabby." He fined us all $50.00…. Later on he said if we beat the Bears he would disregard the fines.[23]

So the 49ers had a little extra motivation when they met George Halas' outfit. The Bears led 17–14 at the start of the second half and caught the whiff of "victory meat" when Maury Duncan trotted onto the field to replace the ailing Tittle at quarterback. Tittle had started the game, but the Bears' relentless pass rush had repeatedly knocked him to the turf. Tittle's aching left hand in the cumbersome cast had severely hindered his ball-handling. Helped by Joe Perry's long runs of 58 and 53 yards, the rookie Duncan calmly directed an efficient running game that scored 17 unanswered points in the third quarter. Grabbing a 31–24 lead late in the game, Hardy Brown's second interception of the afternoon choked off the Bears' last scoring threat to clinch the 49er win. When presented with the game ball in the post-game locker room, the teary-eyed Duncan blubbered, "This is the greatest thrill of my life!"[24]

Twenty-eight of the 49ers were also thrilled that Buck Shaw rescinded their $50 fines for breaking curfew.

Sporting three wins and a tie, the 49ers returned home to meet the defending NFL Champion Detroit Lions on October 24. Believing his team needed a respite, Shaw took the unorthodox step of calling off Friday afternoon's practice and canceling Saturday's customary walk-through. The move appeared to pay dividends when the 49ers jumped to a 17–0 lead before 58,981 delighted fans at Kezar. With San Francisco leading 24–10 in the third quarter, 49er tackle Bob Toneff, who recently rejoined the team after fulfilling his military obligation to Uncle Sam, sacked Lion quarterback Bobby Layne. Layne suffered a concussion on the play, and Tom Dublinski replaced him. However, the Lions weren't the only ones taking casualties. During the course of the afternoon 49er defensive backs Rex Berry, Johnny Williams and Jim Cason left the game—Berry with a fractured jaw, Williams with a sprained ankle and Cason with a knee injury. Bill Tidwell, John Henry Johnson, future California legislator Pete Schabarum and Joe Arenas now manned the 49er secondary. With the starting defensive backfield nearly depleted (Arenas was the only starter), Dublinski threw three touchdown passes to cut the 49er lead to 37–31 in the game's waning seconds. But 49er rookie defensive end Jackson Brumfield snuffed Detroit's last-ditch effort when he sacked Dublinski for a 14-yard loss on fourth down.

Detroit head coach Buddy Parker later growled, "I don't think we got a break all afternoon. But I'll tell you one thing. We're going to beat them when they [the 49ers] come to Detroit."[25]

With their victory over Detroit, the Niners remained the only undefeated team in the NFL. Despite numerous injuries, San Francisco was still favored the following week over the visiting Bears. On Halloween afternoon, Chicago unveiled plenty of tricks, most of them perpetrated by a 6-foot, 3-inch, 200-pound rookie end out of tiny Florence State Teachers College (today's University of North Alabama) named Harlon Hill. Due to the 49ers' injury-riddled secondary, Bill Jessup, ordinarily an end, was forced to play defensive back. Jessup was no match for Hill as the rookie caught touchdown passes of 47, 20 and 11 yards from George Blanda. Nevertheless, with just 39 seconds remaining in the game and the score tied at 24, Gordy Soltau's 17-yard field goal gave the 49ers a 27–24 lead, apparently pulling the 49ers' chestnuts out of the fire. When the Bears' offense took possession at their own 34-yard line with only 26 seconds remaining, former University of San Francisco quarterback Ed Brown aligned at right offensive halfback, while speedy John Henry Johnson replaced Jessup at defensive halfback for the 49ers. On the snap Blanda pitched to Brown, who started to run a sweep. Harlon Hill ran directly at Johnson, now subbing for Bill Jessup on defense, before throttling down as if to stop. Reading a curl pattern, Johnson came up to cover Hill, who turned on a dime and ran past Johnson. At the same time, Brown pulled up and let loose a pass to Hill who by this time was well beyond the fooled defender. Hill caught Brown's pass in full stride for a 66-yard touchdown—his fourth touchdown reception of the game. The Kezar crowd of nearly 50,000 moaned in unison. Blanda's conversion made the final score Chicago 31, San Francisco 27.

No longer undefeated, Buck Shaw lifted the blame from Jessup in his post-game comments. "We didn't have much chance to work Bill into his defensive job," said Shaw. "It was unfortunate that we had to put Jessup on the spot. That Hill hurt us in Chicago and he killed us here."[26]

Then Shaw added confidently, "This loss will take the pressure off the kids. They've been under stress for five weeks and they now can get down to playing football."[27]

That afternoon the 49ers lost more than a ball game. With slightly over three minutes remaining in the contest Hugh McElhenny, who had a 16-yard touchdown run earlier, sustained a separated left shoulder. Team doctor William O'Grady reported the injury required surgery and that "The King" was out for the season.

* * *

Although team captain Bruno Banducci and owner Tony Morabito had made scathing remarks about the Rams' so-called "dirty play" in their earlier meeting, neither man had much to say on the subject when the Rams came to San Francisco for their November 7 rematch. In fact, Banducci publicly apologized for his earlier disparaging remarks. Even with McElhenny in street clothes, the 49ers showed some devastating offensive punch with Soltau's two field goals and Joe Perry and John Henry Johnson's long first-half scoring runs. Nevertheless, the 49ers went into the locker room at halftime trailing the Rams 21–20. Leading 35–34 late in the game, the Rams put the game away on Norm Van Brocklin's 5-yard scoring pass to Tank Younger for a 42–34 win. Van Brocklin enjoyed a magnificent day, completing 16 of 18 passing attempts for three touchdowns.

Afterwards the injured Hugh McElhenny empathized with his head coach: "We have the best offensive team in football. But the defense hurts us. We've just had too many injuries back there." The King continued, "I feel sorry for Shaw. He's one of the finest defensive coaches in the business. How he must be suffering. Our only chance is to outscore 'em. We can't stop 'em."[28]

In the visitors' locker room victorious Rams' coach Hampton Pool lauded, "In my mind the 49ers were quite possibly the greatest team the league ever knew when it all started this year. However, it 'died' under the injury jinx."[29] Pool's well-meant words wouldn't help Shaw in the eyes of the Morabito brothers.

Things grew worse for the 49ers the following week when the Lions made good on Coach Buddy Parker's earlier promise that "we'll beat 'em when they come to Detroit." They certainly did, inflicting the worst-ever defeat on San Francisco by the score of 48–7 before 58,000-plus ecstatic fans. Back in California, a newsman called 49er owner Tony Morabito who had watched the game on television. "I can tell you that I certainly didn't enjoy watching the game," said Morabito.

When asked about circulating rumors that Shaw would not be back next year, Morabito replied, "No comment." He then added, "I think the best thing I can do at this time is say absolutely nothing on that subject."[30] The statement certainly didn't boost Shaw's confidence. "No comment" was the refrain Morabito continually uttered when asked about Shaw's future for the remainder of the season.

Back in the Bay Area the sporting wolves began to howl. It seemed like every guy who ever watched a football game while perched on a neighborhood bar stool had an answer to the question "what happened to the 49ers?" Some claimed that Shaw put too much of an emphasis on winning exhibition games, and that by bringing the team along too fast, they had shot their bolt by mid-season. Yes, the 49ers won all of their exhibition games in '54, but so did the World Champion Detroit Lions and it didn't seem to bother them. Other theorists accused Tittle of lousy play-calling; blaming Shaw for "allowing" too many injuries; criticized the club's failure to develop a second-string quarterback, and other claims that often fell inches short of insanity.

On Saturday night, November 20, Shaw temporarily held the critics at bay when the 49ers beat the Steelers at Pittsburgh's Forbes Field 31–3. It was a brief respite. The following week at Baltimore's Municipal Stadium, heartbreak set in for the 49ers again, when Colt quarterback Gary Kerkorian completed a 78-yard scoring pass to Royce Womble with 77 seconds remaining to give Coach Weeb Ewbank's Colts a 17–13 win. It was Shaw's first loss to the Colts in ten outings. After losing two of the road swing's three games, the Niners flew home to meet the Packers. Team owner Tony Morabito continued to utter "no comment" to inquiries regarding Shaw's future with the organization. Meanwhile, the sporting wolves bayed louder.

The day before meeting the 49ers, Green Bay coach Lisle Blackbourn told a reporter,

"We've been here only a couple of hours, but I bet all of our boys have read already the criticism the 49ers and Coach Buck Shaw have been getting. They're back home now after three games on the road and they've got their backs to the wall. It's always hard to beat a team like that."[31]

Blackbourn's analysis proved correct. The 49ers regained their early season form in blanking the Packers 35–0. Tittle completed 15 of 18 passes for 243 yards, while Joe Perry became the first player in NFL history to rush for over 1,000 yards in two consecutive seasons. When the public address announcer informed the crowd of the record, Perry, in a class move, asked the same announcer to tell the customers how deeply he appreciated the support they had given him during this and other seasons.[32]

Joe Perry was the first African American 49er and the first pro player to rush for over 1,000 yards in consecutive seasons. Here, Perry runs in an exhibition game loss against the Washington Redskins at Kezar Stadium on August 26, 1950 (OpenSFHistory/wnp.14.2379.jpg).

As speculation ran rampant about the Silver Fox's future, during the week of December 4, Bay Area papers began printing excerpts from fan letters expressing support for the embattled Shaw. Rallying behind their beleaguered coach, the 49ers eked out a 10–7 win in a bitterly-contested struggle against the Baltimore Colts to finish the season with seven wins, four losses and a tie.

In the post-game locker room Shaw quietly made the rounds, congratulating each player on the win, while owner Tony Morabito stood at the opposite end of the room, occasionally exchanging greetings with passersby. His only comment to reporters was, "I'm happy we won."[33]

Later that evening, Shaw and wife Marjorie attended the 49ers' annual post-season party held at the Colonial Manor. Players, coaches, team officials and their wives attended the function. The Shaws sat on one side of the room and the Morabitos sat on the other. During the awkward affair, the two never spoke to each other. Although the party lasted until midnight, the Shaws left early.

All the speculation ended on Monday morning, December 13, when Tony Morabito made the following announcement at a press conference at the team's office: "Coach Buck Shaw's contract expires in July 1955. It will not be renewed. He is relieved of his duties as of this day." Morabito then added, "He [Shaw] has been given 100 percent authority, not 99 percent, but 100. Four out of the past five years, the 49ers have either folded completely or lost the big one. I think it's time we tried something else."[34]

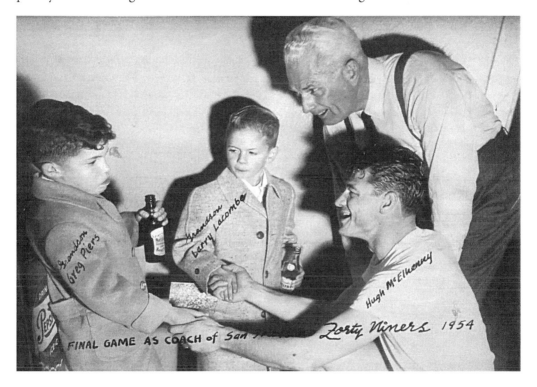

Buck Shaw introduces his grandsons to injured 49er star Hugh McElhenny after the 49ers defeated Baltimore on December 11, 1954. Shaw was fired two days later despite leading an injury-laden squad to a seven-win, four-loss and one-tie record (courtesy Greg Piers).

At a five-minute meeting earlier that morning in Mr. Morabito's office, the owner informed Shaw of his dismissal. Buck did not attend the press conference. After Morabito's announcement, the *San Francisco Examiner's* Don Selby tracked down the fired coach having lunch with Mrs. Shaw in a peninsula restaurant. Calm and dignified, the Silver Fox agreed to Selby's interview request. When asked if he expected to be fired Shaw replied, "I had to surmise this was coming with all that 'no comment' stuff. But Tony didn't talk to me about it until this morning."

Regarding what he thought of the firing, the former long-time coach said, "What can I think about it? I really don't want to comment on it at all. This is my time to say 'no comment." He then elaborated, "It is never pleasant to work under a situation such as existed for the past few weeks, and I feel better that it's over."[35]

To a man, the 49er players regretted their coach's firing. Gordy Soltau said, "I'm sorry to see Buck go. I've never played under a better coach. I don't think he's been given half the credit for the job he's done. I'd like to see any coach in America take our team with the injuries we had and win the championship. They'll have a tough time getting a better man."[36]

Team captain Bruno Banducci declared, "Shaw would be the last man in the world I'd blame for our late season defeats. He did everything humanly possible to build us into a championship team. It wasn't his fault that injuries threw us off stride."[37]

Reflecting on his career with the 49ers, Joe Perry recalled years later, "I don't want to forget Buck Shaw. He was a very good coach and a great person. I got along very well with him the whole time he was there and I thought the 49ers made a mistake when they got rid of him."[38]

Al Carapella, a two-way tackle between 1951 and '55, regarded Shaw as the best coach for whom he'd ever played. "He was an excellent coach. He never raised his voice."[39]

Quarterback Y.A. Tittle offered, "He is the finest gentleman and finest coach I ever played for."[40] In his later book, *I Pass!* Tittle wrote, "I never knew that football could be fun until I played for Buck Shaw."

Tackle Leo Nomellini mournfully stated, "Everybody is disappointed. Buck is a wonderful man and a great coach. I know the entire squad feels as badly as I do."[41]

In the Bay Area, newspaper offices were flooded with phone calls supporting Shaw while vilifying the Morabito brothers. Bay Area journalists and prominent national sports columnists like Arthur Daley of the *New York Times* wrote articles lamenting Shaw's dismissal. All agreed that Shaw was the individual most responsible for pro football's success in San Francisco.

A gentleman in the truest sense of the word, Shaw handled his firing with class and dignity. When conversing with a United Press official by phone at his Atherton residence, Buck said, "I wish the 49ers the best of luck. The dismissal was just one of those things. It's the first time I've been fired in 32 years. Maybe this is the time I should adopt Mr. Morabito's attitude and say 'no comment.'"[42]

Buck Shaw soon discovered that while Tony Morabito no longer wanted him as coach, there were many people in the football world that did.

SEVENTEEN

Buck Joins the Air Force

Only hours after Shaw's dismissal became public, the league office asked Shaw to coach the Western Conference team in the NFL's 1955 Pro Bowl. The game would be played in the Los Angeles Coliseum on January 16. Buck agreed. The West's 29-man All-Star roster included seven 49ers: Y.A. Tittle, Joe Perry, John Henry Johnson, Billy Wilson, Bruno Banducci, Al Carapella and Jim Cason.

Later that afternoon Buck was in his Atherton home, answering the phone and opening telegrams from friends and well-wishers who felt the 49ers gave him a rotten deal when a United Press official called from Denver. He asked if Shaw had applied for the head football coaching position at the new Air Force Academy. When Buck replied he hadn't, the reporter read him a statement Lt. Col. Robert V. Whitlow, athletic director of the air academy, had made earlier in the day: "For my money, Shaw is one of the fine gentlemen in football. He's terrific. His firing came as a big surprise. We don't know if he would be interested or not. We would be extremely fortunate if he is interested in the academy."[1]

Shaw informed the reporter, "I definitely would be interested in the job there. I understand that it is going to surpass even the Army and Navy academies. It would be a wonderful opportunity."[2] Whitlow phoned the next day asking if the two could meet.

Evolving from the U.S. Army Air Corps, the U.S. Air Force was established as a separate branch of the Armed Forces by the National Security Act of 1947. Lt. Gen. Hubert Harmon spent four years working assiduously to get legislative approval to create a United States Air Force Academy. In 1953, President Eisenhower asked Harmon, his old classmate and football teammate at West Point, to come out of retirement to serve on two commissions—one to select the Academy's site, and the other to plan its building and operation. Serving on the site selection commission with Harmon were Brig. Gen. Charles Lindbergh of "Spirit of St. Louis" fame and Gen. Carl Spaatz. Under the direction of Secretary of the Air Force Harold Talbot, the commission flew over 18,000 miles inspecting 67 of the proposed sites before selecting Colorado Springs. When President Eisenhower signed Public Law 385 on April 1, 1954, the Air Force Academy became a reality. On August 14 of the same year, Hubert Harmon was named the academy's first superintendent. With construction of the Colorado Springs campus not expected to be finished until 1957, the academy greeted its first class of 306 cadets at a temporary site on Denver's Lowry Air Force Base on July 11, 1955.

On June 24, 1954, 35-year-old Lt. Col. Robert V. Whitlow was named the Air Force Academy's first director of athletics. A 1943 West Point graduate, Whitlow had played tackle for the Black Knights from 1940 through '42. He also earned varsity letters in basketball and baseball. As a pilot during World War II, Whitlow amassed over 500 hours of combat flying during two tours in Europe. During his first tour Whitlow piloted B-24 Liberator bombers with the 458th Bombardment Group. On his second tour, the Army Air Corps somehow managed to fit Whitlow's 6-foot-5-inch, 230-pound frame into the cockpit of a P-51 Mustang, where he flew reconnaissance missions for 8th Air Force. Among the numerous citations he earned were the Silver Star and four Distinguished Flying Crosses.

Serving as the academy's first assistant athletic director was Maj. Frank Merritt. A West Point teammate of Whitlow's, Merritt earned All-American honors at tackle in 1942 and again in 1943 while opening holes for future Heisman Trophy winner Glenn Davis. His gridiron exploits earned him posthumous induction into the College Football Hall of Fame in 1996. A pilot for 32 years, Merritt served with distinction in Korea, where he earned both the Distinguished Flying Cross and a Bronze Star. Whitlow and Merritt both had a special affinity for football but were determined to build an overall first-class athletic program at the academy. By November 1954, Whitlow was overseeing the transformation of a 24-acre plot of prairie east of Denver into a football practice facility for the cadets.

Although Shaw regarded Whitlow's overture as a lifeline to resume coaching, he was deliberating whether he wanted to return to the sidelines. A sensitive man, his firing hurt him deeply, certainly more than he let on in public. At age 55 he felt like he was at a crossroads. He had always felt that eventually he would go into private business. When accepting the head job at Santa Clara in 1936, he took it with the mindset that if he flopped at it after a year he would do something else. Shaw pondered if continuing to coach only postponed the inevitable. Furthermore, he had always known there was no security in coaching. He had witnessed many of his colleagues, good men and fine coaches, dismissed at the whim of an athletic director or over-zealous alumni. As he'd just learned firsthand, one had no more security in his 32nd year of coaching than he did in his first. In his nine years with the 49ers, Shaw had won 72 games and lost 40 with four ties for a 62 percent winning percentage. Being fired was Shaw's reward for winning seven games while losing only four with an injury-depleted squad. Shaw now needed time to reflect and weigh whatever options might lie ahead.

The 1954 season saw several well-publicized disagreements between Los Angeles Rams head coach Hampton Pool and his staff. All four assistants tendered their resignations in protest the day after the season. Team owner Dan Reeves backed Pool in the dispute. Nevertheless, days after Shaw's firing, Pool resigned as Rams head coach for "the good of the team." Several Los Angeles sportswriters immediately wrote columns campaigning for Shaw to become the Rams' next coach. One local paper's poll had Shaw as the fans' overwhelming favorite to succeed Pool.

* * *

On December 23, 1954, owner Tony Morabito introduced Norman "Red" Strader as the 49ers' new head coach. Strader had served as an assistant coach and scout on Buck Shaw's staff in 1952 but resigned to enter the construction business before the start of the '53 season. In 1954, however, he scouted the Rams for Shaw and presented scouting reports on his findings to the team. When speculation circulated about Buck's future during the waning weeks of the '54 season, several Bay Area columnists predicted Strader would replace Shaw. At Strader's introductory press conference Tony Morabito claimed Strader would provide the "inspirational direction and leadership" the team needed.

Taking a swipe at Shaw, Morabito added, "He [Strader] doesn't suffer from the occupational disease that some in the coaching fraternity suffer from. He is not afraid of his job, not afraid to make decisions and not afraid of criticism."[3]

When asked if the 49ers would retain Strader if the incoming coach did not win the NFL Championship in 1955, Morabito guaranteed that Strader would return in '56. In selecting his assistants, Strader retained line coach Phil Bengston and Joe Vetrano as chief scout from Shaw's staff. However, in a private meeting with end coach Jim Lawson on December 27, he informed the Stanford graduate that he'd be letting him go as ends coach. On December 29, Strader replaced Lawson with Red Hickey. A recent Rams assistant, Hickey played a role in the turmoil leading to head coach Hampton Pool's resignation. Upon learning of Hickey's hiring, the fired Lawson told reporters, "It's only natural for Strader to want to hire his own coaches, those men he has worked with and knows."[4] In a surprise move, Strader filled out his staff by hiring former 49er quarterback Frankie Albert.

* * *

The week of January 9, 1955, was a hectic one for Shaw. Not only was he preparing the West team for the upcoming All-Star game, but between and after practices he met with several perspective employers regarding coaching opportunities. On January 13, the Vancouver newspaper *The Province* reported that Don Mackenzie, owner of the British Columbia Lions, had a meeting scheduled with the Silver Fox to discuss his coming to Vancouver as a backfield coach. Mackenzie told *The Province,* "I have an appointment with him. He has told me he will not accept any other offer until we have had our talk." Only a stupendous offer could have persuaded Shaw to jump north of the border as an assistant.

The same day *The Province* article appeared, Lt. Col. Robert V. Whitlow flew to Los Angeles to pitch Shaw on the Air Force Academy. Together, Whitlow and Maj. Merritt had waded through over 200 resumes of applicants expressing interest in the Air Force job. Two of the more impressive applicants were Vince Lombardi and Ara Parseghian, but Whitlow had his sights set on the Silver Fox.[5] On January 16, the Associated Press reported on their meeting. "Whitlow didn't make a specific offer but I suppose it amounted to that," said Shaw. Although Buck stated that he thought "something could be worked out," he was uncertain about returning to coaching college football. He added, "I don't know if I want to stay with the pros or get out of coaching altogether. I just haven't made up my mind."

Whitlow declared that the academy couldn't make a definite offer to anyone until "our financial situation improves." He explained, "The Air Force Academy Athletic Association simply doesn't have enough money at this time to pay for a coach."[6]

The day before the Pro Bowl, Rams owner Dan Reeves phoned Shaw asking if they could meet that evening at the Knickerbocker Hotel. It was the first contact between the two since Pool's resignation. The meeting was amicable. When asked how their talk went, Reeves downplayed it. "It was simply routine. I talked with Shaw as I have at least a dozen other prospective coaches."[7]

Shaw's take on the meeting may have been more optimistic: "I told him [Reeves] before any terms were discussed I would have to make up my mind whether I wanted to stay in coaching. I will have to make up my mind about that in a few days. If I do remain a coach, I would prefer to live here in Los Angeles."[8]

Reeves never did offer the position to Shaw, and it wasn't until late January that he hired Sid Gillman as the Rams' new head coach.

* * *

The Pro Bowl game itself was an exciting, but often sloppily played event due to intermittent cold rain and soggy field conditions. The Philadelphia Eagles' Jim Trimble coached the East squad with Otto Graham and Adrian Burke sharing the quarterbacking duties. Eagle linebacker Chuck Bednarik and Cleveland guard Abe Gibron captained the East. Other stalwarts included the Cardinals' Ollie Matson and Dick "Night Train" Lane; New York's Eddie Price and Kyle Rote; Cleveland's Dante Lavelli, Lou Groza and Frank Gatski; and Philadelphia's Lum Snyder and Pete Pihos. Besides the seven 49er players, Shaw's big guns included the Rams' Norm Van Brocklin, Bob Boyd, Duane Putnam, Dan Towler and Leon McLaughlin; the Lions' Joe Schmidt, Doak Walker, Luke Creekmur and Lavern Torgerson; the Colts' Buddy Young, Art Donovan and Gino Marchetti, and Chicago's Harlon Hill and Ed Sprinkle.

Although a three-and a-half point favorite, the West found themselves trailing 19–3 at halftime. Shaw had selected longtime coaching cronies Phil Bengston and Jim Lawson to serve as his assistants. Between halves, Shaw and Bengston implemented several blocking changes that jump-started the West's ground game in the second half. Manning the phones upstairs, Jim Lawson relayed several pass patterns that were always open—so much so that 49er Billy Wilson, who caught 11 passes for 157 yards and a touchdown, was named the game's most valuable player. Tittle threw a long scoring pass to Harlon Hill, while Doak Walker kicked another field goal and Joe Perry plunged two yards for the winning score as the West rallied for a 26–19 victory.

Although Billy Wilson had been voted the game's most valuable player, West captains Bruno Banducci and Art Donovan, at the squad's insistence, presented the game ball to a grinning Buck Shaw. One Ram player, who preferred to remain anonymous, commended Shaw on the "simple, but effective" blocking changes he made at halftime, adding, "He's a great coach! It was swell working for him."[9] Each West player received a check for $700, which was $200 more than the losers' take.

Meanwhile, across the way, an East team player remarked, "They [the West] were really out to show Tony Morabito that he was a sap ever to fire Shaw. And it kind of looks like they succeeded!"[10]

* * *

While pondering his future, Shaw arrived at one cogent decision. If he were to return to coaching, it wouldn't be on a 12-month basis. He would be willing to spend up to six months annually coaching football, but no more. He'd spend the remaining months pursuing outside business opportunities. Shaw was confident in his coaching abilities, but also cognizant of the profession's precarious nature. He wanted something to fall back on. If he was to reenter the coaching ranks it would be on his terms, not those of an athletic director or team owner.

In today's world of professional and major college football, Shaw's conditions would be regarded as totally unrealistic. The advent of pro football's scouting combine, along with the millions of dollars involved, competitive recruiting and social media, have raised the stakes. If Shaw submitted a resume today with such a demand, it'd receive a hearty belly laugh before either being deleted or fed into the paper shredder. But football—pro and major college—was not the billion-dollar industry in 1954 that it is today.

Fortunately for both the Silver Fox and the Air Force Academy, Shaw's conditions paralleled what academy superintendent General Hubert Harmon was looking for in the school's first coach. Harmon wanted a part-time coach who would lend prestige to the academy football program without signaling a concerted effort to build a football factory.[11] Shaw, in turn, did not want a full-time coaching job that required year-round recruiting trips across the fruited plain.

On February 11, 1955, Air Force Academy superintendent Harmon announced, "We are extremely fortunate that one of the most respected and admired men in the sports world has agreed to advise and help train our coaches of freshman and intramural football during this initial year."[12] Shaw's appointment as special consultant was taken to mean that he would be named football coach when the academy began varsity play in 1956. Speaking from his Atherton home, Shaw—who was about to become director of trade relations for Juillard, Inc. Wholesale Wine Distributors on March 1—explained, "The job actually fits in fine with my business plans." He then added, "If they like me and I like them, then we'll talk about my taking over the head coaching job."[13]

As Buck was about to discover, the Air Force went first-class. In unveiling the future of Air Force football to the general public, its military brass sponsored a gala luncheon at San Francisco's elegant Sheraton-Plaza Hotel on February 23. To ensure a successful premiere, Maj. Merritt enlisted the services of his stepfather, Christy Walsh, as toastmaster. A longtime agent for sports celebrities like Babe Ruth, Walsh had an inimitable knowledge of public relations and the press. The noted writer, one-time cartoonist and renowned sports agent knew how to keep an event lighthearted and fast paced in his role as emcee.

Buck Shaw, looking both sartorial in his well-cut suit and distinguished with his wavy gray hair, gave eloquent and brief remarks. The afternoon's major address came from Athletic Director Robert Whitlow. Speaking with both pride and a sense of urgency, Whitlow informed the audience that the first class of 300 cadets selected from 6,000 nominees would step onto a newly constructed $126 million campus within a few years. "Our problem is unique," said Whitlow. "West Point has been in existence 153 years. Annapolis' roots go back more than 110 years, and Harvard has more than 300 years of history behind it. We haven't the time for slow development. In four years, or less, we must convert 16,000 acres of prairie land into the finest institution of its kind, so we have to work fast—in all things."[14]

Whitlow presented convincing data from the recent Korean conflict showing that football players and other athletes engaged in contact sports made better fighter pilots than non-athletes. Thus, the academy was recruiting athletes who had engaged in contact sports. He then elaborated on what the academy could offer perspective student-athletes: "We can offer these advantages—the equivalent of a college degree in science, flight training, $81.12 a month, plus $1.42 a day in ration money while they're in school, a commission as a second lieutenant and $5,000 a year upon graduation and, above all, a chance for advancement in the Air Force."[15]

His words and their delivery impressed the audience. Whitlow also explained that the academy would field only a freshman team in 1955 against frosh squads of Big Seven Conference schools. In 1956, the school intended to play a varsity schedule against small colleges in the Rocky Mountain area. The academy hoped to play larger schools in '57, and with four full student classes on campus in 1958, undertake a major college schedule against the likes of Army, Navy and Notre Dame. In his role as consultant, Shaw would serve full-time at the temporary Lowry Field site from July 1 through September, training the freshman coaches, planning practice schedules, assessing talent and advising the administration and staff on purchasing equipment.

At publicity junkets for Air Force football over the following months, Athletic Director Whitlow continually sang the praises of the academy's special consultant. "We were told by many authorities on the subject," lauded Whitlow, "that Buck Shaw knew more about the fundamentals of football than any one else and that he was the very finest teacher."

"On top of that Buck is held in such high esteem as a gentleman on and off the football field that he fitted the description of the man we needed."[16]

With Shaw as a consultant, Lt. Col. Whitlow served as head coach of the Academy's 1955 freshman squad. Air Force personnel stationed at Lowry Air Base comprised the staff. This included Lt. Jesse Bounds, a former Tulane lineman; Lt. Marvin Jenkins, an Alabama standout in the late '40s; Lt. Byron Gillory, who as a Texas Longhorn played in three New Year's bowl games; and Lt. Tom Brookshier, a former defensive back at the University of Colorado, who played for the Philadelphia Eagles in 1953 before fulfilling his military obligation. Brookshier would later play for Shaw in Philadelphia.

Of the 306 freshman cadets enrolled in the academy's first class, 77 tried out for football on the first day of practice on September 7, 1955. The day was primarily devoted to meeting the coaches, the press and posing for pictures. The highlight came when the squad ran through a giant paper banner held by Whitlow and Shaw that read "Here Comes the Air Force." To a man, the squad reported in excellent condition as all had undergone intense physical conditioning since reporting on July 11. Since academic classes began a few days before the start of practice, the squad's workout time was limited to two hours a day, six days a week.

While all the players were classified as freshmen, several had transferred in after having played previously at other colleges. Quarterback Eddie Rosane had played on the University of Washington freshman team the previous season, while center Robert Delligatti played two years at Washington & Lee. Brock Strom, who would become the academy's first All-American football player, had previously played three seasons at Indiana. Because the academy did not yet have four full academic classes (freshman through senior), NCAA rules regarding transfers having to "sit out" a year did not apply. Like all of the cadet corps, the football players were smart, disciplined and eager to succeed.

"I was confident if we exposed Buck to our fine young men they'd do a better selling job than I could," said Whitlow.[17]

"This was an entirely new kind of deal for a coach," confessed Shaw. "It's rare that one has the opportunity to stay three months to look over a proposition."[18]

What coach wouldn't enjoy working with such fine young men? Buck Shaw certainly liked what he saw and, on September 29, signed a five-year contract to become the head coach of the Air Force Academy beginning in 1956.

That same week the first class of cadets voted to adopt "Falcons" as the school's official nickname. As the Colorado Springs campus was still a few years away from becoming a reality, and the team didn't have its own stadium, city officials nationwide approached Athletic Director Whitlow about hosting future Air Force games. In August of 1955, the city of Shreveport offered to host a football game between Air Force and Louisiana Tech

Upper photograph. Special consultant Buck Shaw holds banner that reads: "Here Comes the Air Force" on September 7, 1955. It was the inaugural day of football practice for the first freshman team at the Air Force Academy. *Lower left*. Buck Shaw in Air Force coaching attire. *Lower right*. Col. Bob Whitlow, the first Air Force Academy athletic director (courtesy United States Air Force Academy Archives).

at the Louisiana State Fair Stadium on November 10, 1956. With the support of Louisiana Congressman Overton Brooks, the city hoped to make it an annual extravaganza. Explaining that the city of Pueblo, Colorado, had already guaranteed the Academy $18,000 per game, Whitlow asked Shreveport to provide a guarantee of $25,000—$18,000 to match Pueblo's guarantee and an additional $7,000 to pay for air travel and lodging expenses.[19] Responding to Whitlow's request, *The Shreveport Journal* initiated a fund drive to raise the necessary amount. Shreveport's businesses and citizens met the challenge by raising over $50,000 and contractual negotiations began. Before the contract was signed, however, Louisiana Tech president Dr. R.L. Ropp withdrew from negotiations in March of 1956, effectively canceling the game.

The immediate catalyst for Ropp's decision was a provision in the game contract the Air Force submitted that read, "*no player of the U.S. Air Force Academy will be barred from participating in this game because of creed or race.*" In canceling the game Ropp announced, "While we believe the possibility of Negro personnel on the Air Force Academy squad is remote, we do not want to risk placing our visitors and our thousands of alumni and friends of the college into any position which might cause them embarrassment.… In view of prevailing conditions in Louisiana, we feel that we would be lending ourselves to the creating of a more serious problem in inter-racial relations by scheduling an athletic contest in Louisiana in which a member or members of the Negro race might take part."[20] Ropp elaborated that committing his school's team to a game in which it might have been required to oppose a racially-integrated squad would threaten the good race relations which had existed in Shreveport throughout the years.[21] The South's resentment of the Supreme Court's 1954 *Brown vs. Board of Education* decision outlawing segregation in public schools also influenced Ropp's action. The cancellation disappointed academy officials and many Louisianans.

With Shaw observing as a spectator from the stands, and Whitlow and his staff calling the shots from the sidelines, the Air Force Academy fielded its first football squad on October 8, 1955, when its freshman battled the University of Denver frosh at the University of Denver stadium. Despite being stung on the game's first play from scrimmage on Don McCall's 65-yard touchdown pass to Dick Stevens, the Falcons rebounded behind the play-calling of quarterback George Klitinoty to defeat Denver 34–18. The contest was played before 17,785 paying customers, believed to be the largest crowd ever to witness a game between two college freshman teams at the time. The afternoon also saw the unveiling of the school's first mascot: a peregrine falcon named "Mach I."

In October and November, Shaw took care of business for Juillard Wines in San Francisco and flew to Colorado on weekends to watch the freshman games. When doing so, he never told the academy coaches what to do, but enjoyed witnessing the spirit the cadets demonstrated on the field. His new academy job revitalized the Silver Fox. When the *San Francisco Examiner*'s Curley Grieve paid Buck a weekday visit at his Atherton home in early November he was surprised by what he saw. Lost was that gaunt, haggard look Shaw had during his last weeks as coach of the 49ers. He now seemed like a man without a care in the world.

"Why, Buck!" Grieve declared. "You look like a new man!"

"Feel like a new man, too," Shaw replied.

As if to prove it Shaw shinnied up a tree in his backyard, and as he sat with feet dangling from an upper branch, proclaimed, "Life can be beautiful."

At that moment Mrs. Shaw appeared and demanded that he descend from his perch.

"You'll have to excuse Buck," she said. "He's been acting like a kid ever since he got his new job."[22]

Competing against other freshman squads in '55, the Falcons defeated the University of Denver, and both Colorado St. and Wyoming by identical scores (21–13); and won a 7–6 squeaker over the University of New Mexico, while suffering losses to Colorado (32–0), Kansas (33–0), Oklahoma (48–12), and to Utah (a tough one, 12–6) to finish with a four-win and four-loss record.

Like at Annapolis and West Point, Congress appropriated no funds to support the academy's athletic program. It proved to be no obstacle for the hard-driving Robert Whitlow, who organized the Air Force Athletic Association and successfully appealed to 15,000 Air Force officers to donate $10 a piece to provide an operating budget for 1955. Gate receipts eventually replenished the athletic war chest. However, the question of where the academy would play its future games was still undecided. The Air Force Academy Foundation, formed by business and civic leaders to promote the academy's location, pledged $3.2 million to build a 40,000-seat stadium on the academy grounds. However, influential politicians wanted the stadium built in Denver, the state capital, with a population 10 times that of Colorado Springs. Both factions had an opening target date of 1958. After lengthy political haggling, the decision was made to build the stadium on campus. However, it wasn't completed until 1962.

In a foreshadowing of things to come, Philadelphia Eagles general manager Vince McNally approached Shaw after the Falcons' '55 season about taking his club's head coaching reins. McNally knew Shaw from his days as an assistant coach at St. Mary's under Slip Madigan. Furthermore, he had heard great things about the Silver Fox while serving as an assistant to Clipper Smith at Villanova. When asked about Philadelphia's overture, Shaw replied, "I told them I had accepted a five-year contract with the Air Academy and expected to carry it out."[23]

* * *

As Shaw flew to Denver on weekends to watch the Air Force freshmen games, lethargy and indifference characterized the San Francisco 49ers' 1955 season under Shaw's successor, Red Strader. In his first major act as coach, Strader moved the team's training camp from Menlo Park to the St. Mary's campus in Moraga. Many veteran players, who lived in or near Menlo Park, bristled at the move. Team morale took another hit when team owner Tony Morabito and Strader refused to invite nine-year veteran and team captain Bruno Banducci to camp after a brief salary dispute. Team morale deteriorated as the season progressed. After winning three of their first six games, the listless 49ers dropped five of their last six to finish the season with a disappointing record of four wins and eight losses. The team that many expected to win the Western Conference title finished in fifth place. Despite Morabito's pledge when he hired Strader a year earlier that the new coach would have more than a year to win an NFL Championship, Morabito fired Strader on December 20, 1955.

When asked what he thought of Strader's firing, Shaw replied that he didn't know enough about the situation to comment, but added, "I do know this: There isn't money enough in the world to make me take the job back."[24]

On January 13, 1956, San Francisco hired Frankie Albert as its new head coach. In introducing Albert to the media, owner Tony Morabito referred to his former quarterback as "Mr. T Formation" and called him an inspirational leader. Then, perhaps taking another swipe at Shaw, he declared, "He [Albert] has done more for the 49ers than any other one man."[25]

* * *

Back home in Atherton, taking care of business for Juillard Wines and numerous speaking engagements kept Buck quite active. In late January he joined a list of Bay Area celebrities at the Santa Rosa Hotel as guests of the annual March of Dimes Sports Celebrity Banquet. It was an event Buck attended through the years and a cause he strongly supported.

That April Buck returned to Denver for the start of spring practice. Because several team members were participating in other sports, only 26 cadets participated in spring football. Due to injuries or disciplinary infractions, Shaw and his staff often found themselves working with only 20 players at practice. Working with so few players limited what Shaw could accomplish. However, he was extremely optimistic about the academy's football future.

"Right now, we're in temporary quarters, and the academy still is something new to most youngsters." Shaw predicted, "As soon as we get into permanent quarters [at Colorado Springs] by 1958, and when our name will have more appeal, I'm sure we'll be able to hold our own in major competition."[26]

On July 31, just before Buck's maiden season at the Air Force helm, Gen. Hubert R. Harmon, in failing health, retired as the Academy's superintendent and from the Air Force. Harmon had been one of Shaw's most ardent supporters. Maj. Gen. James E. Briggs succeeded Harmon as superintendent on August 1. His arrival soon led to a change in attitude about Air Force football.

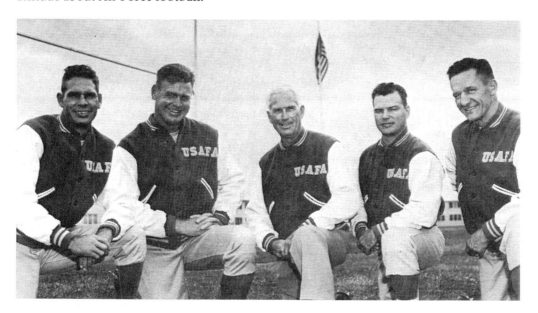

The first Air Force varsity football coaching staff. Left to right: Lt. Marvin Jenkins, Lt. Jesse Bounds, Buck Shaw, Lt. Byron Gillory and Maj. Casimir Myslinski (courtesy United States Air Force Academy Archives).

EIGHTEEN

Climbing into Air Force's Football Cockpit

Practice for the 1956 season officially began at Lowry Field on September 10. One hundred candidates came out for football: 60 freshmen and 40 sophomores. Cadet life was demanding both physically and academically. Of the 306 freshmen admitted in the fall of 1955, only 240 returned for the fall semester of 1956. Because of limited facilities at Lowry, the academy could only admit another freshman class of 300, which brought the institution's total enrollment to 540 that fall. The academy would have to wait until the Colorado Springs campus was finished in the fall of '58 before admitting the targeted class size of 700.

After several weeks of preseason practice and scrimmages, Buck named a 35-man traveling varsity squad consisting of 14 sophomores and 21 freshmen. Lt. Col. Whitlow, now coaching the jayvee, inherited the other candidates. As the season progressed Shaw recruited several jayvee players so that by mid-season the varsity dressed out 41 cadets. There may not have been a younger college varsity team in all of America. Of the 41 squad members only six were 20 or older. Fielding just freshmen and sophomores, the Falcons played a full slate of four-year colleges, most from the Rocky Mountain area. The future flyboys had speed but not much size. Only seven of the 41 players weighed 200 pounds or more. Gene Vosika, a 215-pound guard from Bellevue, Nebraska, was the heaviest man on the squad.

The starting backfield consisted of quarterback Eddie Rosane of Pasco, Washington, halfbacks Mickey Gouyd of Anaheim, California, and Steve Galios of Napa, California, as well as fullback Larry Thomson from Billings, Montana. Other key players included sophomore guard Charles Zaleski, who in his freshman year won the 177-pound Rocky Mountain A.A.U. Wrestling Title. Air Force coaches said that Brock Strom could have played on anybody's team. Hailing from Ironwood, Michigan, Strom played center in high school, but became a 203-pound guard in college. Extremely bright, Strom's score on the academy's entrance exam was one of the highest in the initial class of 306 to arrive at Lowry in July 1955. After graduating from the academy, Strom went on to earn a Ph.D. in astronautical engineering from Arizona State University and later served as the Director of Engineering for the Global Positioning System (GPS), an invaluable technological advancement for the nation and the world. Prior to that he flew 90 missions in Vietnam as a navigator. Strom became the Air Force Academy's first All-American and was inducted into the College Football Hall of Fame in 1985. Another standout two-way player was end Tom Jozwiak. Hailing from Detroit, Jozwiak led the Falcons in receptions in both 1956 and '57. Quarterback George Pupich and fullback Charlie May were also solid performers.

That season the academy introduced a concept to reduce both injuries and dental expenses. Academy dentists made every player an individual mouthpiece custom-fitted to the grooves of one's teeth. Any cadet participating in a contact sport was required to wear one.[1] Before that time few collegiate or pro players wore mouth pieces and schools certainly didn't issue them as standard equipment.

"Our sophomores have a year of valuable experience and we expect some help from the freshmen, so we should be improved over 1955," Buck predicted. "I am optimistic about winning a fair share of our games."[2]

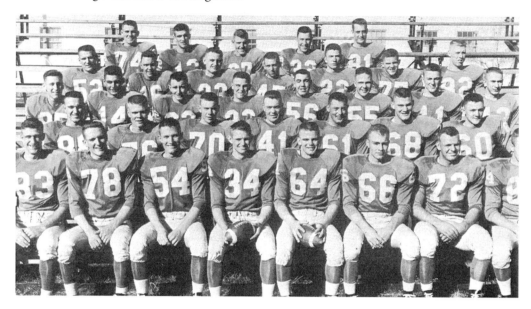

First Varsity Air Force Academy Football Team, 1956: won 6, lost 2, tied 1. Front row, right to left: Rodgers (partially obscured), Cwach, Mitchell, Zaleski, Thomson, Gulledge, Dolan, Jozwiak. Second row, right to left: McCullough, Van Inwegen, Wideman, Kerr, Bronson, Phillips, Holmes. Third row, right to left: Zersen, Kuenzel, Brost, Loh, Clark, Murphy, Pupich, Hendricks. Fourth row, right to left: White, McLain, Galios, Goud, May, Rosane, Strom. Fifth row, right to left: Taylor, Scher, Elsbernd, Oaks, Vosika (courtesy United States Air Force Academy Archives).

Whether one is coaching at the pro, major college, small college or high school level, coaches all share many of the same challenges and frustrations. The demands at any level can work on one's nervous system and are often the sole focus of one's attention. Buck Shaw was no exception. The academy's first varsity football game was against the University of San Diego at Balboa Stadium on September 29. Buck was returning to the same stadium where ten years earlier he coached the San Francisco 49ers in their first-ever football game, an exhibition contest against the Los Angeles Dons. Since then he had coached before crowds of over 80,000-plus in the Los Angeles Coliseum, Cleveland's Municipal Stadium and Chicago's Soldier Field while matching wits against the likes of Paul Brown and George Halas. After coaching squads at such famed venues with so much on the line, one would think that coaching what virtually amounted to a junior college team against a small Catholic college would have no effect on such a battle-hardened coach. Yet, while attending a reception of sorts on the eve of the San Diego game he bumped into the wife of a friend of his.

"Why, Mr. Shaw," she inquired, "what are you doing here?"

Shaw then explained about the game.

"Are you nervous about the game?" she asked. "I mean, are you nervous about returning to the West Coast where you were a coach for so long?"

"Naw," replied Shaw, "Just another game."

"Sure you're not nervous?"

"Naw. All games are alike to me."

"Then Mr. Shaw," said the amused lady, "what are you doing here in the ladies' powder room?"[3]

As it turned out, Shaw had no reason to be nervous. Despite completing only two of 14 passing attempts, his Falcons rolled to a 46–0 win in their inaugural varsity game. Shaw's young squad only gave up 66 yards in total offense to San Diego. Upon returning to Denver, Shaw told reporters, "We don't know what we have yet, but we sure liked what we saw Saturday."[4]

How the University of San Diego came to be the academy's first varsity opponent is an interesting story. The small Catholic college was only two years old and didn't have a football team before September 5, 1956, except in the mind of Gil Kuhn. Kuhn, an executive vice president of a fish packing company and former USC football player, volunteered to coach the school's non-existent football team. With the aid of several boosters, Kuhn hastily organized a squad of 40 students. In need of a game, he phoned Col. Robert Whitlow with whom he flew missions from England during World War II and simply challenged Air Force to a game. Whitlow accepted his old buddy's challenge.

The following week the cadets traveled 75 miles south from Lowry Air Base to Colorado Springs, the future site of the Air Force Academy, to play Colorado College. Over 9,000 spectators, the largest crowd to see a game at Washburn Field since 1943, turned out to see if the nation's newest military academy could block and tackle. The Falcons showed they could by hammering the Tigers 53–14. Air Force fullback Larry Thomson carried 18 times for 167 yards while scoring four touchdowns on runs of 46, eight, four and one yard. He also kicked two extra-points. After building a 35–0 halftime lead, Shaw emptied the bench.

Hosting Western State College from Gunnison, Colorado, at the University of Denver Stadium next, the Falcons rolled up 485 yards in total offense en route to a 48–13 victory. It was more of the same the following week when Air Force quarterbacks completed 10 of 17 passes for 222 yards in a 49–6 win over Colorado Mines. Afterwards Shaw said his young team was "undefeated, untied and untested."[5]

On the Monday following the Mines game, William B. Hoffman, the Managing Director of the annual East-West Shrine game, phoned Shaw asking if he would coach the West Squad in the December 29 contest. Nostalgic to roam Kezar Stadium's sidelines again, the Silver Fox agreed. That same week he consented to something else. For months members of his coaching staff had pestered the civilian about taking a ride in an Air Force jet. On October 26, Shaw finally accepted the invitation. His line coach, Lt. Jesse Bounds, who flew combat missions in Korea, piloted the plane. Wearing flight gear, Buck strapped himself into the jet's back seat. The jet headed south from Lowry Field, over the site of the future campus in Colorado Springs and then on to Pueblo and back to Denver by way of Boulder. Posing for a post-flight publicity photo Buck told a newsman, "You're as young as you feel and I felt like a kid up there." Then plugging the academy he added, "I wish I was 18 again so I could enter the academy as a cadet."[6]

Air Force tacklers Brock Strom (52), Eddie Rosane (16) and Larry Thomson (34) close in on Colorado College running back Dave Fletcher in the Falcons' 53–14 win at Washburn Field on September 26, 1956 (courtesy United States Air Force Academy Archives).

The next day Shaw's Falcons continued their high-flying ways by beating Eastern New Mexico University 34–7. Fullbacks Larry Thomson and Charlie May each scored two touchdowns while quarterback Ed Rosane added another. The Greyhounds from Portales scored when Joe Wood, a 150-pound scatback, returned a punt 96 yards to pay-dirt. Despite the seemingly lopsided score, Shaw was far from pleased with his squad's performance. "It's obvious we need more scrimmage work to correct some mistakes and get back on the right track," Shaw said. "We're darned lucky we got almost every break or we would have been in a bad way."[7]

Shaw followed through by canceling Monday's customary film session for contact drills and a brief chalk talk. The Falcons then held a short scrimmage on Tuesday to prepare for their next opponent, Colorado State College at Greeley (today's Northern Colorado University). The Bears came to Denver with five wins and two losses, and the most points scored against them came in a 13–0 loss to Montana State University. Injecting more contact drills into that week's practice schedule paid off for the Falcons as they jumped to a 21–0 halftime lead. Larry Thomson stung the Bears in rushing for 106 yards on 11 carries and kicking two extra points in the game's first 30 minutes. However, the Bears stymied the Falcons in the third quarter, and penalties and fumbles plagued both teams in the fourth as Air Force prevailed for their sixth straight win, 21–0.

While admittedly playing small colleges, Air Force's six-game winning streak with only freshmen and sophomores generated national attention. Besides creating

Falcon fullback Larry Thomson plunges toward Colorado State College's goal line (today's Northern Colorado University) in a 21–0 Air Force victory on November 3, 1956. The game was played at Denver University's Hilltop Stadium (Archives and Special Collections, University Libraries, University of Northern Colorado, Greeley, Colorado).

excitement, Air Force football also generated human interest stories. One dealt with cadet Gerry Elsbernd from Calmar, Iowa, who never played high school football. When Elsbernd arrived with the first class of Air cadets in 1955, he tried out for the team. Teammates had to show the novice how to put on shoulder pads and lace up his football pants. The Iowan stayed with it, however, and when a first-string varsity guard went down with an injury Elsbernd, seeing his first game action, filled in admirably at the position.

Unfortunately, not all football seasons have a Cinderella ending. On November 10, Air Force flew to Los Angeles to meet Whittier College. While their nickname "the Poets" didn't strike fear into the future flyboys, the 1956 Whittier team was a pretty good outfit. A major reason was their head coach, George Allen. Allen would leave Whittier after the '56 season for an assistant's job with the Los Angeles Rams before joining George Halas' Chicago Bears staff. While serving as defensive coordinator, the Bears awarded Allen the game ball after defeating the New York Giants for the 1963 NFL Championship. In 1965, he became head coach of the Los Angeles Rams where he served until taking the coaching reins of the Washington Redskins in 1971. Intense and slightly eccentric, Allen adopted the motto "The Future Is Now" and traded away numerous future draft choices for proven veteran players. Although critics often decried the veterans Allen acquired as being "over-the-hill," most became revitalized under Allen, whose Redskin squads never experienced a losing season. Redskins owner Edward Bennett Williams once joked that he gave Allen an unlimited budget and he overspent it in just two weeks. After winning nine games and losing five in 1977, the Redskins fired Allen, whose overall NFL head coaching record was 116 wins, 47 losses and five ties.

When the cadets aligned for the opening kickoff before 9,000 fans at East Los

Angeles Junior College Stadium, they found the temperature to be 50 degrees warmer than what they had left in snowy Denver. With each team squandering a scoring opportunity, the game remained scoreless at halftime. Allen's Poets drew first blood in the third quarter when tailback Gary Campbell tossed a 26-yard touchdown pass to end Dick Beam. In the fourth quarter the duo connected again on a 33-yard paydirt pass. Trailing 14–7 with six minutes remaining, the Falcons, determined to remain undefeated, launched a 63-yard ground offensive culminating in Larry Thomson's one-yard scoring plunge. George Pupich's second extra-point kick of the game made the final score 14–14.

The next week the Falcons faced stiffer competition in hosting Idaho State University in Pueblo, Colorado. Limiting the cadets to only two first downs and 28 yards of total offense in the game's first 30 minutes, the Bengals led 7–0, when quarterback Ken Peterson threw a 21-yard touchdown pass to Jim Wagstaff with only 30 seconds remaining before halftime to boost their lead to 13–0. Air Force only scored once in the second half, on Larry Thomson's two-yard run, suffering their first loss of the season, 13–7.

The season's finale against Brigham Young at Denver University Stadium also ended on a sour note. After battling to a 7–7 halftime tie, a plethora of third-quarter Falcon fumbles led to Cougar quarterback Carroll Johnston throwing his second touchdown pass of the day to Raynor Pearce. Johnston later scored on a one-yard run before tossing a four-yard scoring pass to Steve Campora. Down 27–7, the Falcons rallied for two scores on Charlie May's 85-yard pick-six and Ed Rosane's one-yard sneak but came up on the short end of a 34–21 score. The Falcons finished their first season of varsity football with a record of six wins, two losses and a tie.

* * *

Because of a temporary Congressional appropriations freeze, construction at the institution's Colorado Springs site fell behind schedule. Due to Lowry Field's limited facilities, incoming classes for the next two years were reduced by half of what the academy had initially planned. Instead of four classes totaling 2,496 cadets by 1958, the four classes would now only contain 1,200. Unfortunately, when Colonel Whitlow scheduled football games for 1958 and beyond, he did so with the understanding of an enrollment of 2,500 in mind. The '58 schedule now seemed overly ambitious.

In December, Buck Shaw was home in Northern California readying to coach the West Team for the upcoming Shrine Bowl game on the 29th. During game week sportswriters fired numerous questions at Buck regarding the Falcons' '56 season and the future of Air Force football. While proud of what his freshmen and sophomore squad accomplished, he admitted that the academy's '57 season would see a major upgrade in competition. Facing significantly tougher opponents, Shaw predicted the flyboys might take some beatings. When asked if a contractual provision freeing him from any off-season duties hindered the institution's athletic recruiting, Shaw replied, "It wouldn't do us any good if I did find some football players. Chances are 1,000 to one that anybody I found couldn't get in anyway."[8] Buck was obviously referring to the academy's strict admission standards. Ensuring its academic house was in order, the academy posted grades every Monday. Cadets receiving a grade less than 70 percent in any class were immediately ruled ineligible for athletic participation and stayed ineligible until the grade improved significantly. At other colleges, athletes could be failing a class throughout the semester, but were only declared ineligible at the semester's end. (On October 3, 1956, Athletic Director Whitlow wrote the academy's superintendent asking if this stipulation could be lifted or lessened as it severely hurt the institution's athletic teams, to no avail.) Another restriction confronting the academy that other colleges didn't face were the height and weight requirements for admission. Because of jet cockpit specifications no cadet could be admitted if he were taller than 6 feet, four inches and weighed more than 216 pounds.

* * *

Shaw and his assistants for the East-West Shrine game, "Cactus" Jack Curtice of Utah and San Jose State's retiring Bob Bronzan, greeted the West All-Stars when they reported to the Stanford campus on December 16. Future pro stars comprising the West roster included Stanford quarterback John Brodie and guard Paul Wiggin, halfbacks Dean Derby (University of Washington), John Arnett (USC), and guard John Nisby (College of the Pacific).

Notre Dame's Terry Brennan coached the East Squad with Penn State's Rip Engel and Kentucky's Blanton Collier serving as his able assistants. Heisman Trophy winner Paul Hornung (Notre Dame) and Milt Plum (Penn St.) would handle the East's quarterbacking chores, with Abe Woodson (Illinois) and Terry Barr (Michigan) lending strong backfield support. Ohio State's massive Jim Parker led the East's offensive line.

Good luck smiled on the West squad the morning of December 21, when quarterback John Brodie and USC halfback Jon Arnett were involved in an auto accident. Brodie fell asleep at the wheel when driving on the Bayshore Freeway shortly before 4 a.m. The '56 Chevy hit a sign reflector and caromed into a nearby ditch. Both players awoke covered in broken glass, but neither had any significant injuries. The two then hitch-hiked to the Redwood City police station where they reported the accident. When finished they took a cab to the Stanford campus. Police claimed that no alcohol was involved and later told newsmen that the matter was closed.

Coach Shaw had granted Brodie permission to stay out beyond the team's 11 p.m. curfew. However, he later admitted, "I gave permission to be out late, but I didn't think he'd stay out that late."[9] That morning Shaw addressed the squad about having pride in what they do, and that perhaps the auto accident would have a sobering effect on their future actions. Shaw took no disciplinary action against either Brodie or Arnett because he believed their consciences would dictate how to conduct themselves in the future.

A relieved Brodie told newsmen, "From now on the only place I'm going to be after 9 p.m. is in the West team dormitory in bed!"[10]

As it turned out Brodie was named the Shrine game's Most Valuable Player. His 26-yard touchdown pass to UCLA's Pete O'Garro produced the West's only touchdown in their 7–6 win over the East. The East scored on Paul Hornung's 35-yard screen pass to Abe Woodson in the second half. Fortunately for the West, Utah's Jerry Liston blocked the East's extra-point attempt, while Dean Derby made his extra-point for the West.

Besides the gratification of knowing that he played an integral role in raising over $250,000 for the Crippled Children's Hospital of San Francisco, the afternoon's personal highlight for Buck may have been when Kezar Stadium's 60,000 fans stood as one and gave him a thunderous standing ovation when the public address announcer introduced him.

In the victor's locker room after the game several West players praised their coaching staff. "They made us feel like we've been playing together for years," said hero Pete O'Garro. "They [Shaw, Curtice and Bronzan] gave us formations so simple a baby could understand them. That's why all went so well. We all knew what we were doing."[11]

Dean Derby, who kicked the winning point for the West, complimented Shaw. "He's a real gentleman," said Derby. "He's quiet. He never bawls anybody out, but a player knows when Buck thinks he should be doing better."[12]

* * *

The new year promised to be a busy one for Buck. On January 22, 1957, the Royal Container Company in San Francisco named Shaw a vice president of the firm. The announcement came weeks after the Silver Fox bought an interest in the company. Five days later, Shaw was again a featured guest at the fourth annual March of Dimes Banquet at the Santa Rosa Hotel. Other guests included former Yankee baseball star Joe Gordon, Hugh McElhenny, Gordy Soltau, Jim Lawson, Joe Perry, Bob St. Clair and Ernie Nevers. Upon taking his turn at the podium, the audience gave Shaw the longest and warmest applause of the evening. During his brief address he recounted a dark period in his coaching career, when a friend attempting to bolster his spirits told him, "Cheer up, it could be worse."

In one of the better lines of the night Buck told the audience, "I cheered up and sure enough it got worse."[13]

In mid–March, Shaw began spring football drills for the academy's upcoming season. The squad finished only 13 practices when several back-to-back snowstorms paralyzed Denver. With no field house or suitable indoor facilities of any type at Lowry Air Base, Shaw postponed practices for over a week. When the adverse weather continued into mid–April prohibiting outdoor work, Shaw canceled the remainder of spring practice.

In June, the Air Force re-assigned Col. Robert Whitlow, and Col. George Simler succeeded him as athletic director. Commissioned an officer in the Army Air Corps in 1942, Simler was awarded the Distinguished Flying Cross for skillfully leading a squadron of B-26 Bombers on a successful mission despite having lost an engine to enemy ground flak. During his ninth mission of a second European tour in July of 1944, Simler's plane was shot down behind enemy lines. The cunning Johnstown, Pennsylvania, native successively eluded capture for over two months before rejoining his old outfit in England that September. Via a special Army program Simler finished his college degree at the University of Maryland where he played football for Clark Shaugnessy in '46 and captained Coach Jim Tatum's 1947 Gator Bowl team.

After his initial meeting with Air Force's head football coach, Simler said of Shaw, "He impressed me as the type of man you'd like to have your own son play under." He then added, "I'm terrifically interested in the Air Force Academy being a winner. But I'm not interested in winning unless it's under a good code of ethics. I think we have that type man in Buck Shaw who'll play to win, but who'll do it ethically."[14]

In August, Shaw accepted an invitation to coach a team of mainland College All-Stars in Hawaii's Hula Bowl on January 5, 1958. Shaw's squad would meet an All-Star team comprised of the best college, military and pro players from the Hawaiian Islands.

Due to the Congressional appropriations freeze, the academy's enrollment at the start of the 1957 academic year was slightly over 700. As previously mentioned, when Colonel Whitlow compiled the '58 football slate against the likes of Iowa, Tulane, Stanford and Colorado, he did it believing the academy would have an enrollment of approximately 2,400. It was now apparent that cadet enrollment for 1958 would actually be 1,200, half of the original projection. That fact had both Superintendent James Briggs and new athletic director Simler concerned that the academy might be hopelessly outmanned playing those schools. In concert with Coach Shaw, all three agreed to make the October 5 meeting against the University of Detroit the test game to see if the academy would finalize contracts to play those four big-time opponents in 1958. Should the Cadets make a presentable showing, then it'd be full speed ahead.

In the meantime, Shaw and his staff greeted 106 football candidates on August 29. The coaches soon divided the group into both a varsity and "B" squad. However, they let it be known that the division was not binding and the personnel could change. By mid–September junior Eddie Rosane had re-established himself as the squad's starting quarterback with southpaw John Kuenzel in a backup role. With the cadets' practice time limited to 90 minutes daily, Shaw's staff faced a stiff challenge getting the team ready for the season opener against Occidental on September 28. However, a situation arose that presented an even more formidable challenge.

The University of Florida was scheduled to open the season against UCLA on the evening of September 20, at the Los Angeles Coliseum. Unfortunately, a case of Asian flu felled 65 members of the Gator squad during the second and third weeks of September, forcing Florida to cancel its trip to California. Learning of UCLA's predicament, Shaw saw a tremendous opportunity to publicize Air Force football. On September 11, he phoned his good friend Red Sanders and asked the Bruin head coach if UCLA would be interested in having the Falcons fill the September 20 date. While Shaw and Air Force officials knew the cadets might be out-manned, Buck was eager to see how his club stacked up against a major power. Since the federal government allocated no funds to finance Air Force's athletic programs, academy officials welcomed the $25,000 guarantee UCLA offered. Although UCLA was the overwhelming favorite, the teams had one similarity. Neither squad had any seniors. The Pacific Coast Conference had barred UCLA's seniors for accepting illegal aid, while the academy, in only in its third year of existence, had no senior class. Both UCLA athletic director Wilbur Johns and coach Red Sanders were extremely grateful that Air Force volunteered to step into the "breech" on such short notice.

The game went as predicted. Bolting to a 26–0 halftime lead over the out-classed Falcons, Sanders cleared the Bruin bench in the game's last 30 minutes as UCLA cruised to a 47–0 win. Before 33,293 fans, the home team rolled up 418 yards in total offense to Air Force's 130. In doing so, the Bruins handed Buck Shaw the worst defeat in his coaching career, surpassing the Detroit Lions' 48–7 pasting of his 49er squad in 1954. Despite the lopsided loss, the game drew national attention for the Falcons, while giving the cadets a reality check on their need to improve if they hoped to compete with the big boys.

Following their ill-fated foray into major college football, Air Force rebounded the following week by thumping Occidental College at home 40–6. Up next came the crucial October 5 date with the University of Detroit. Coming to Denver University Stadium off a 12–0 win over Marquette in their season-opener, Coach Wally Fromhart's Titans were a solid favorite to ground the airmen. As previously mentioned, the Air Force brass considered this game a litmus test to determine whether the academy should sanction or renege on playing several big-time schools tentatively scheduled for 1958.

Although unaware of the contest's significance, Shaw's players seemed tense at the final practice before the Detroit encounter. Their apprehension may have partially stemmed from six teammates reporting to sick bay that afternoon with the flu. Among the ailing were four starters, including quarterback Eddie Rosane. Sensing his squad's tension, and hoping to lighten the mood, the Silver Fox joked, "We're going to put your IQ in the program alongside your name, weight and height. We'll beat 'em to death with brains."[15]

Shaw's quip seemingly failed to ease cadet anxieties when an errant Air Force snap from center sailed over the punter's head, giving Detroit possession on the Falcons' 11-yard line early in the game. On the next play Dan Collins bolted untouched off-tackle to give the visitors a 6–0 lead. Retaliating immediately, Air Force drove 89 yards on 14 plays and scored on Steve Galios' 23-yard run off a "razzle-dazzle" double reverse tying the score at 6. With quarterback Rosane and his ailing mates watching in street clothes from the sidelines, the Falcons, with John Kuenzel quarterbacking, scored two more touchdowns to upset Detroit 19–12 before 6,700 surprised, but ecstatic fans. (Kuenzel played so well that he took over the starting position from Eddie Rosane for the season.)

Local scribes and Marshall Dann of the *Detroit Free Press* hailed the outcome as the biggest win in the academy's brief history. Impressed with the Falcons' performance, superintendent James Briggs and athletic director George Simler decided to play the likes of Iowa and Stanford in 1958. In what turned out to be bad timing, Col. Simler announced the decision publicly on October 11, prior to the Air Force–George Washington University game. In doing so he cautioned, "We might be a little out of our league playing some of them so soon, but I'm sure we'll make a representative showing." He then declared, "We have the greatest coach in the country, bar none, in Buck Shaw. And we have some really first-rate players."[16]

Sitting in a box seat on the 50-yard line while enjoying a hot dog was the nation's commander-in-chief, President Dwight D. Eisenhower. Ensconced among officials from both schools, the hero of Normandy seemed to thoroughly enjoy the contest. The career military man tried mightily to remain neutral, even cheering lustily when the Colonials scored. At halftime, the Air Force unveiled its best act of the night when a cadet keeper released the academy's live falcon mascot, "Mach I," from midfield. To Ike's utter delight and that of the other 12,000 fans in attendance, Mach I soared and swooped about the upper deck of Washington, D.C.'s Griffith Stadium before returning to its keeper. The academy's precision drill team then marveled the crowd with its intricate maneuvers before giving way to the Falcon bagpipe band, which received a standing ovation as it brought down the halftime curtain.

Unfortunately, the academy's disappointing gridiron performance let the air from Colonel Simler's pregame announcement. Behind halfback Mike Sommer's two touchdowns, one on a 68-yard punt return, the Colonials blanked the Falcons 20–0. The loss evened the flyboys' record at two wins and two losses, with a bye week to prepare for the Tulsa Hurricanes.

* * *

After four games the Falcons' performance was as balanced as a team's could be. Sporting an even record, offensively the team ran 54 percent and passed 46 percent of the time. They now traveled to meet winless Tulsa. His team having lost all five of their previous games, Hurricane coach Glenn Dobbs greeted the visitors with a "coach's lament" of how the severe physical pounding North Texas State administered to his boys a week earlier left his squad crippled. Dobbs moaned that nine starters, including quarterback Benny Davis, would be sidelined for the academy game. With Air Force favored to win, it's possible Coach Dobbs was "sandbagging" in hopes of injecting a dose of over-confidence into the cadets. It certainly seemed that way when several of the so-called disabled, among them quarterback Benny Davis, aligned for the opening kickoff. With Air Force clinging to a 7–6 lead late in the fourth quarter, Davis engineered a 44-yard drive, culminating in his own six-yard touchdown run to give the Hurricanes a 12–7 win. The victory turned Tulsa's season around, as they won four of their last five games.

* * *

The day after the Tulsa loss, Buck Shaw's former boss, Tony Morabito, watched his beloved 49ers tangle with the Chicago Bears from Kezar Stadium's press box. Since his near-fatal heart attack in 1952, family physicians had advised him to get out of the pro football business for health reasons. With Chicago leading 14–7 just before halftime, the 47-year-old Morabito collapsed and was rushed to St. Mary's Hospital, where he died 30 minutes later. Morabito never lived to see the 49ers win a league championship.

* * *

The flight plan didn't get easier for Shaw's airmen the following week traveling to meet the defending Skyline Conference Champions, the University of Wyoming. Laramie's weather was a balmy 28 degrees with a 15 mph wind at kickoff. Bob Devaney, who would later win 101 games against 20 losses during an enviable 11-year run at Nebraska, was in his first season as the Cowboys' head coach. Before a crowd of 7,600 Wyomingites bundled in blankets and sporting earmuffs, Air Force played its best football of the season for 30 minutes. The Falcons' ball-control offense limited Wyoming to just four offensive plays during the first quarter. Defensively, cadet Phil Lane snuffed Wyoming's only first-half scoring threat with an end zone interception. Quarterback John Kuenzel's 16-yard scoring toss to Tom Jozwiak and George Pupich's conversion gave the Falcons a 7–0 halftime lead.

However, the contest's momentum flip-flopped in the second half. The frigid temperature must have numbed cadet hands, for they lost five fumbles. Cowboy Larry Zawada's one-yard scoring plunge and Mike McGill's extra-point kick were the only points tallied in the last 30 minutes, and the game ended in a 7–7 tie. Air Force's record now stood at two wins, three losses and a tie.

Although disappointed, Shaw hoped his club's stellar first-half showing against a solid Wyoming squad might lead to four well-played quarters in the upcoming game against Denver University. The contest not only pitted two neighborhood schools against one another, but it also matched landlord against tenant as the academy paid rent to the University of Denver to play their home games at Denver's Hilltop Stadium. By this time, however, academy officials and the Air Force Academy Athletic Association had committed to building a permanent stadium on the 28-square-mile Colorado Springs campus. A well-publicized fundraising drive was already underway.

In a lighter moment, Glenn Wright, a nine-year-old boy from Annville, Pennsylvania, mailed the Air Force Athletic Association $2 to help pay for the stadium's construction. When informed of the youngster's donation, Buck Shaw, in a classy move, wrote young Glenn a heart-felt thank you, asking if he might some day want to join the cadet ranks. He also informed the boy that Lt. John Gurski, an Air Force freshman coach, would soon deliver a package to his home containing an Air Force t-shirt, pennant, shoulder patch and decals.[17]

That Saturday, Denver's Pioneers afforded neither Shaw nor the Falcons too many light moments. "Landlord" and "tenant" knocked each other in the dirt for 60 minutes. Shortly after he scored the game's first touchdown, Air Force knocked Pioneer Danny Loos groggy, forcing the rubbery-legged fullback to the sidelines. Loos returned briefly in the second quarter only to suffer the same result. George Colbert added a three-yard scoring run to give Denver a 13–0 halftime lead. Rebounding on short touchdown runs by Phil Lane and Larry Thomson, the Falcons cut the Pioneer lead to 21–14. With Air Force driving deep into Denver territory late in the game, the twice-kayoed Danny Loos re-entered the Pioneers' lineup. Straight out of what could have been a Hollywood script, Loos saved the day by intercepting a pass on Denver's own nine-yard line and then navigating a circuitous 91-yard course through an array of would-be cadet tacklers to paydirt. Loos' heroic "pick-six" gave Denver a 26–14 win.

It could have been the best of times or the worst of times for Air Force to visit Salt Lake City on November 16. Why the paradox? On the day the Air Force cadets and Pioneers were battling to determine who would be king of Denver's football hill, the University of Utah was also battling cadets—those of the Army. Coach "Cactus" Jack Curtice, who served as Buck Shaw's assistant in the 1956 East-West Shrine Game, took his 30-point underdog Utah team to West Point's Michie Stadium to meet the famed Black Knights of the Hudson. Coached by the legendary Earl "Red" Blaik, Army entered the

Buck Shaw, seated on bench with sunglasses, watches as Denver University defenders Melvin Johnson (43) and Al Yanowich (17) break up a pass intended for an unidentified Falcon receiver during the academy's 26–14 loss at Hilltop Stadium on November 9, 1957 (courtesy Denver University Special Collections and Archives).

contest ranked eighth in the nation with five wins and one loss. Their defeat came at the hands of Notre Dame, 23–21. Football savants predicted that Utah would hold up as well as a snowflake in summer when faced with Army's explosive running game. The experts were right in that regard, but what they hadn't counted on was the pinpoint passing of Utah quarterback Lee Grosscup. Behind the running of consensus All-American Bob Anderson, Army—marching over hill and dale—took an early lead. Then Utah moved through the air to tie things up. The scenario played out several times and as the game progressed, the action grew hotter and faster. The fourth quarter alone saw five touchdowns scored. Grosscup completed 13 of 24 passing attempts for 316 yards, several on the famed "Utah" or "shovel" pass. Halfback Bob Anderson personally accounted for 214 of Army's 396 rushing yards while scoring three touchdowns as Army held on for a 39–33 win.

The game had the sell-out crowd of nearly 28,000 holding their collective breath until the game's last play. Eastern sportswriters hailed Utah's valiant effort. Coach Curtice was so proud of his team's gallant showing that he shed tears of joy afterwards. The near upset drew national attention.

More than 5,000 cheering fans greeted the team upon its arrival at the Salt Lake City airport on Sunday afternoon. United States Senator Arthur Watkins and Salt Lake's mayor were among the attendees. Two local television stations aired a replay of the entire game on Monday night. Even in defeat, Coach Curtis, his staff, the team and the entire Beehive State felt like world-beaters. All Utahans were agog over their football team.

By all accounts, the Utes had just earned a "moral victory" over a top-ranked team in the biggest intersectional game in school history. Why, then, might the following week have been "the best of times" for Air Force to visit Salt Lake? Because after playing a great game teams often can't continue riding the emotional wave. They frequently suffer a letdown after such a contest. Whether the success goes to their head and they overlook their next opponent or they now feel that they have nothing else to prove, who knows? After a strong performance against a superior foe many teams often founder against a lesser opponent the following week.

Conversely, the following week could also have been the "worst of times" for Air Force to visit Salt Lake. Why? Because a great win or strong performance sometimes awakens a team to its potential. Instead of resting on newly won laurels, the team grows hungrier and wants to become the best it can be. With this newborn confidence and "fire in the belly" the team attempts to soar to new heights. If a great performance and public acclaim result in a team adopting this "hungry" attitude, watch out! Unfortunately for the Falcons, Utah adopted this outlook after its moral victory over Army.

Buck Shaw, attempting to gain a psychological edge for his Falcons, named Bob Brickey as an Air Force captain that week. Although only a freshman, Brickey was a talented end, who had been an All-State player at Salt Lake City's East High School the previous season. Furthermore, Brickey's dad was once an assistant football coach at Utah. Shaw's ploy wasn't enough. While the determined Falcons never quit or shied away, the Utes just had too much firepower. Utah rolled up 509 yards in total offense with Lee Grosscup completing 13 of 16 passes, eight of them to 147-pound Stuart Vaughn. When the home team took a 27–0 lead only three minutes into the second half, gentleman Jack Curtice sat Grosscup down for the day and mercifully emptied his bench. The Utes blanked the Falcons 34–0 and went on to win the Skyline Championship with a conference record of five wins and one loss.

Returning to Denver on November 23, the Falcons hosted the University of New Mexico. After a strong start, coach Dick Clausen's Lobos slumped and entered DU Stadium with a four-win and four-loss record. Only 5,000 fans showed up on a chilly, but sun-splashed afternoon to watch the cadets dominate New Mexico 31–0. Freshman halfback Phil Lane, who during the last few weeks of the season made his presence known, rushed for 133 yards and scored two touchdowns. Perhaps throwing one of the shortest passes on record, quarterback John Kuenzel tossed a touchdown pass to Tom Jozwiak from the 6-inch line. From 21 yards out, Falcon George Pupich etched his name into the academy's football annals by kicking the first field goal in Air Force history. Defensively, the cadets held Lobo running back Don Perkins to 32 yards on 12 carries. Perkins later enjoyed a lengthy and productive career with the NFL's Dallas Cowboys.

While the few Lobo fans making the trip to Denver bemoaned their team's play, they raved about the halftime show. Cadet keeper John Melacon now had a second falcon, Mach II, to accompany Mach I on his 100 mph dives and swoops throughout DU Stadium.

After their strong showing against New Mexico, the Falcons' season finale against Colorado State was a disappointing denouement. Only 4,500 fans turned out at Denver University's Stadium to watch the scrappy Aggies (as they were known at the time) overcome Air Force's 7–6 halftime to earn a 21–7 victory. Air Force finished the 1957 season with three wins, six losses and a tie.

* * *

Early December found Buck Shaw in his Atherton, California, home resuming his duties as vice president of the Royal Container Company. After the '57 football season Stanford head football coach Chuck Taylor resigned to become the school's athletic director. His resignation sparked rumors that Shaw would be the Cardinals' next head coach. A strong and vocal contingent of Stanford alumni certainly wanted him. When asked about his interest in the Palo Alto job, Shaw told newsmen, "I'd be flattered if I were among those being considered, but I would not be interested in a full-time coaching position."[18]

Days afterward, on December 10, the Associated Press broke a story that Philadelphia Eagles coach Hugh Devore would be fired after the season. The story claimed that Eagles general manager Vince McNally had compiled a short list of leading candidates to succeed Devore. Supposedly, the candidates were Jim Tatum of the University of North Carolina, Wally Butts of Georgia and Buck Shaw of Air Force. Responding to inquiries about the story's accuracy, Shaw said he was very happy at the Air Force Academy and planned to stay.

On December 11, in his column "The Low Down," the San Francisco Examiner's Prescott Sullivan claimed that Buck Shaw looked healthier than he did with the 49ers three years earlier and doubted that he'd return to coaching pro football. He added, "Buck is emphatic that he has had it where pro football is concerned. Besides, even if he did want to return to the business, Mrs. Shaw wouldn't stand for it."[19]

On Sunday, December 29, Buck arrived in Honolulu with wife Marge and their two married daughters, Mrs. Joan Lacombe and Mrs. Patricia Piers. Assisted by local coaches Bill Wise and Allen Nagata, Shaw set to work coaching the mainland College All-Stars. Shaw had only six days to prepare for the January 5 meeting, but he had great talent with which to work. The list of All-Stars included Heisman Trophy winner John David Crow and tackle Charlie Krueger, Texas A&M; Tackle Alex Karras and end Jim Gibbon, Iowa; Lou Michaels, Kentucky; quarterback Jim Ninowski, Michigan State; Clendon Thomas, Oklahoma; and former West Point All-American end Don Holleder. (Tragically, Holleder would be killed leading a rescue mission at the Battle of Ong Tanh in Vietnam in 1967. Today, the basketball and hockey arena at West Point bears his name: The Donald W. Holleder Center.)

Elroy "Crazy Legs" Hirsch served as the player/head coach for the Hawaiian All-Stars. While Hawaiian collegians and military personnel comprised half of the squad, 14 NFL players complemented the roster. Some of the pros included: Tobin Rote (Lions), Kyle Rote and Frank Gifford (Giants), John Simerson (Eagles), Herman Clark (Bears) and R.C. Owens and Dickie Moegle (49ers). The game constituted a reunion of sorts for Buck, who would again see some of his old charges from the 49ers—Joe "The Jet" Perry and Bob St. Clair. Only this time, he'd view them from the opposing sideline.

There's a distinct difference between collegians and pros, one that can't be matched with only six days of practice. Before a near capacity crowd of 25,000 at the Hula Bowl the first quarter was a nightmare for Buck's All-Stars. At the end of the first 15 minutes of play the Hawaiian All-Stars led 33–0. Heisman Trophy winner John David Crow scored for the mainlanders in the second quarter and the Hawaiians took a 40–7 lead into the locker room at halftime. Perhaps overcoming a case of stage fright, Buck's boys out-played and out-scored the pros in the second half. The final score might have been closer than the 53–34 outcome had the collegians not turned the ball over on downs twice in the fourth quarter—on the Hawaiians' nine- and seven-yard lines. But the pros showed why they were pros. Detroit's Tobin Rote threw five touchdown passes, one of 51 yards to Elroy Hirsch, while Joe Perry scored four touchdowns. The wide-open contest had 38 total first downs.

Despite the loss, the Shaw family had a wonderful and memorable time in Hawaii.

* * *

By the start of the 1957 season the men who had originally hired Shaw as Air Force's head coach, Gen. Hubert Harmon and Col. Robert Whitlow, were no longer at the academy. Harmon had retired and Whitlow was re-assigned. Gen. James Briggs was now the academy's superintendent and Col. George Simler, the athletic director. Both wanted to spotlight Air Force at center stage of major college football. To do so, they believed the school had to have a full-time coach—one who could meet prospective recruits visiting the campus on weekends or travel the country during the off-season, recruiting and promoting Air Force football. Buck Shaw didn't fit the bill. Shaw's original five-year contract, signed in September of 1955, still had three years remaining. It stipulated that Buck be at Air Force for spring practice and for the period of September 1, through the close of the football season. The academy brass now wanted Shaw at the academy from mid–January through spring practice and from August 1 through December 1.

Both parties met and attempted in earnest to work something out. Talks were frank and civil. While a contract was a contract, and Shaw enjoyed coaching the cadets, he'd feel uncomfortable remaining if academy officials really wanted a full-time coach. Also, as vice president of a successful container corporation in San Francisco, he couldn't just walk away from such a lucrative business. After lengthy talks the parties reached a mutual agreement. Shaw agreed to be released from his contract and the academy agreed to pay him half of his annual salary (believed to be in excess of $15,000) for the remaining three years. Colonel Simler announced the mutual agreement on January 28, 1958. It was an amicable ending to a productive and enjoyable relationship.

On January 31, Col. Simler announced the appointment of 37-year-old Ben Martin as the new head coach of the Air Force Academy.

NINETEEN

The Silver Fox Becomes an Eagle

A month after the *Philadelphia Inquirer* predicted it, the Philadelphia Eagles fired Hugh Devore as head coach on January 11, 1958. In his two seasons in the City of Brotherly Love, Devore's teams compiled an overall record of seven wins, 16 losses and a tie; finishing in the Eastern Conference basement in '56 and next to last in '57. A Notre Dame graduate, Devore established himself in the coaching profession as line coach of Fordham's famed "Seven Blocks of Granite" from 1935 through 1937. Beginning in 1938, Devore held head coaching positions at Providence, St. Bonaventure, NYU and Dayton. He also served as interim head coach at Notre Dame in 1945 while Frank Leahy served in the Navy. Though he was a kind, good man who fathered seven children, the rap on Devore was his inability to take charge. Critics claimed the Eagles' losing ways were directly attributable to Devore's lack of discipline and poor organization.

Just before Devore's dismissal, Philadelphia's general manager Vince McNally sent feelers to both Oklahoma University's Bud Wilkinson as well as the University of Mississippi's Johnny Vaught. Neither expressed interest. When the Eagles finally pulled the plug on Devore, their search for a successor went into high gear. Compiling a list of 20 possible candidates, McNally vowed that he'd take however long it took to find the right man. A front-runner was Hampton Pool, the ex–Rams coach who was now coaching the Toronto Argonauts in the Canadian Football League. Other candidates included ex-Cleveland Brown tackle and Packers assistant Lou Rymkus, Dartmouth's Bob Blackman, Cleveland Browns assistant Dick Gallagher and Steelers assistant Nick Skorich.

McNally was at the NFL draft meeting when he learned of Buck Shaw's resignation from the Air Force Academy on January 28. Asked if Shaw was a candidate for the Eagles' job, McNally responded, "I'm sure he didn't resign on my account." He then added that he doubted Shaw wanted to return to the NFL: "I understand he has a thriving nuts and bolts business in San Francisco."[1]

McNally had approached Shaw about the Eagles' job in 1955, shortly after Buck had signed his five-year deal to coach Air Force—and he was still the man McNally wanted. He decided to make another run at Shaw now that he was available. Knowing he had to act fast to beat other NFL suitors, McNally phoned Buck, scheduled a meeting and then flew secretly to California, hoping to close the deal. As he later recalled, "Believe me, I broke all speed records in shoving a contract under his nose."[2] McNally signed his man, but on Shaw's terms. As with his Air Force employment, Shaw contracted to spend only five and a half months annually coaching football—from July 1, through the end of the football season. He'd spend the rest of the year working at his container company in San Francisco. Buck signed a one-year contract at a reported $20,000 annually.

The Eagles' management wanted to keep their new hire's identity secret until club president Frank McNamee could formally introduce him. On the morning of February 13, the club sent a telegram to the press saying they were going to hold a news conference at the Warwick Hotel the next day at noon. *Philadelphia Inquirer* sportswriter Herb Good, suspecting Shaw might be the team's next coach, called all the airlines in Philadelphia. He asked each one to check the passenger lists out of San Francisco for the next 24 hours to see if anyone named Shaw was on board. One airline said that a passenger named Shaw was on a flight that night. A few minutes after the flight was scheduled to land, the sleuth Good called the airport and had McNally paged. The airport worker answering the phone replied, "Hold on, Mr. McNally was just here."[3] That's all Good needed. He wrote an article for the *Inquirer*'s morning issue declaring that the Eagles would introduce Buck Shaw as the team's new head coach at the luncheon.

Good's scoop eliminated the Eagles' element of surprise but didn't diminish the fans' delight at Shaw's hiring. As the Eagles' sixth head coach in nine years, Buck was jumping onto a coaching hot seat. At age 59, he was no longer a young man. Why would he undertake such a precarious and formidable challenge? As vice president of a profitable corrugated box firm in San Francisco he didn't need the money. Running a business has its share of headaches. Why did he need to compound it with the strain, pressure and frustration that often accompanies coaching? Shaw had just finished laying the foundation for a major college football program from scratch—a program whose success would be a marvel of the national football scene in 1958. In an '80s radio interview coach Hank Stram, whose teams played in two Super Bowls, told former Atlanta Falcon Tommy Nobis something to the effect of "If you can live without coaching, you're probably better off not getting into it." A coach's life is an emotional roller coaster ride of extreme highs and heart-breaking lows, sleepless nights and truckloads of criticism. Yet there's nothing quite as rewarding as building and guiding a winning football team, and the unique camaraderie that blossoms from it. It can be addicting. Perhaps Buck wanted one more shot at grabbing the brass ring—winning a league championship. In his nine seasons with the 49ers, his clubs were often bridesmaids, but never a bride. The farm kid from Stuart, Iowa, had grown into a darn good football coach, one of the best in the nation. He just wasn't ready to hang up his whistle.

One might ask if the Eagles wanted Shaw so badly, why did they only sign him to a one-year contract? Because Buck only wanted a one-year deal. He later shared with newsmen, "I have a one-year contract. I'll do the best I can. If they are not happy with me or I'm not happy with them at the end of the year there will be no hard feelings. We'll part company."[4]

* * *

Shaw's first task was to assemble a coaching staff. Since Buck planned on spending six months of the year in California, he needed a loyal, dependable, communicative assistant in the team's Philadelphia office to handle the daily matters necessary for running an efficient operation. He needed a trustworthy individual who'd watch his back and not undermine him. For this trusted role, Shaw selected 34-year-old Jerry Williams. A star halfback at Washington State University from 1946 through '48, Williams had spent six seasons as an NFL player—four with the Rams and two with the Eagles. The high light of his pro career came in 1951 when he returned a field goal attempt 99 yards for a touchdown against the Green Bay Packers. Before Shaw hired him away, the father of four had been the head football coach at the University of Montana since 1955. Williams, like Shaw, believed in emphasizing the passing game and a wide-open offense.

On February 27, a week after bringing Williams on board, Shaw hired his former 49er captain Bruno Banducci as line coach. Banducci quit the NFL before the start of the 1955 season after a salary dispute with owner Tony Morabito. Since retiring from the gridiron, Banducci was making a lucrative living as a car salesman in San Francisco.

Believing he'd need more coaching help when training camp started, the Silver Fox rounded out his staff by hiring Bob Bronzan as a part-time assistant on June 20. The former head football coach at San Jose State, Bronzan had previously served as Shaw's assistant in the East-West Shrine game after the 1956 season. Still a full-time physical education instructor at San Jose State, Bronzan would assist Buck throughout the preseason before returning to his faculty duties in September.

One stipulation Vince McNally agreed to when he signed Shaw was to procure a seasoned veteran quarterback for the start of training camp. Although promising to do so, he had no idea who that quarterback might be. An opportunity arose that spring when Rams quarterback Norm Van Brocklin announced that he'd retire before playing another season for coach Sid Gillman. The disgruntled Van Brocklin felt Gillman was grooming Billy Wade to become the club's starting quarterback. Van Brocklin asked the Rams to trade him to either Cleveland, New York or Pittsburgh in the Eastern Conference. Knowing Van Brocklin possessed all the traits Shaw had requested in a quarterback, McNally rolled the dice. On May 26, he offered to trade offensive tackle Buck Lansford and defensive back Jimmy Harris to the Rams for the 32-year-old Van Brocklin. His gambit paid off; the Rams agreed. The trade surprised Van Brocklin. But having enjoyed playing for Shaw's West squad in the 1954 Pro Bowl, Van Brocklin approved the deal.

Known throughout the league as the "Dutchman," Van Brocklin broke into the NFL with the Rams in 1949. During his early years in Los Angeles, he watched and waited in starting quarterback Bob Waterfield's shadow. When Van Brocklin had the chance to start for the injured Waterfield in the '51 season opener against the New York Yanks, "Dutch" made the most of his opportunity. He passed for a record-setting 554 yards in leading the Rams to a 54–14 victory—a single-game record that still stands nearly seventy years later. The Oregon graduate and gifted understudy influenced Bob Waterfield's decision to retire at the top of his game after the 1952 season. With the acquisition of Van Brocklin, the Eagles got a superb passer as well as an excellent punter, who averaged 42.9 yards per punt during his 12-year pro career. However, the greatest asset Van Brocklin brought to Philadelphia was his fiery leadership. Years after Van Brocklin's retirement, former New York Giant Dick Lynch said of the Eagle quarterback's leadership, "Dutch was the reincarnation of General Patton. He went at every game as if he were leading his men across the Rhine, and God help anybody who let him down. Patton slapped his troops. Dutch kicked his in the rear end."[5]

In the weeks leading up to the start of training camp, Shaw spent many evenings reviewing 1957 Eagles game films with his new assistants Bruno Banducci and Bob Bronzan. Meanwhile, back in Philadelphia, Jerry Williams studied game film until he didn't know who his mother's son was. When not cloistered in a dark film room, Williams assembled dossiers on each returning Eagle player. Shaw, Banducci and Bronzan arrived in Philadelphia on July 1, and the staff spent the next three weeks planning for the season. Several days before the July 28 opening of camp in Hershey, Pennsylvania, Van Brocklin flew in from his Portland, Oregon, home and spent a weekend planning strategy with Shaw.

Van Brocklin made his presence known on the first day of camp. After taking physicals, the players gathered for an informal workout during which Van Brocklin threw passes to anyone who cared to run a pattern. A speedy blond kid with shoulders as wide as the back of a bus caught his eye. When the Dutchman asked who he was, a team official replied, "Pete Retzlaff. We tried him as a running back, but he fumbled a lot. We tried him at end, but he had bad hands. We figure we'll give him one more look at corner back, and if he doesn't cut it there, we'll let him go."

"The hell you will," snarled Van Brocklin. "That big stud is going to be my split end. All we have to do is teach him how to soften up his hands."

Then Van Brocklin inquired about Tommy McDonald. He was told that the former Oklahoma Sooner was too small to make it as a running back and too undisciplined at running patterns to make it as a flanker. The Dutchman again offered his two cents: "With his speed and those hands, he's gotta be our flanker. I don't give a damn if we have to put a bell around his neck. It's his job to get clear and my job to find him."[6]

* * *

The Silver Fox's soft-spoken, calm demeanor and organizational skills impressed the Eagle veterans from day one. Within a week they knew Shaw had a command of every aspect of the game of football. Furthermore, he knew how to relate to his team, not only as players, but as men. At practice he never screamed, derided players or launched into profanity-laced tirades. His assistants took their cue from Buck in this regard. Hard-core veterans like Chuck Bednarik and relative newcomers such as halfback Billy Ray Barnes often related that throughout their college and professional playing days Buck Shaw was the only coach who never cursed at them.

The exhibition season started well with the Eagles coming from behind to beat the Baltimore Colts 30–28 in Hershey. Shaw recognized immediately that the squad was blessed with some very talented second-year men, among them Billy Ray Barnes out of Wake Forest; Clarence Peaks from Michigan State; and Tommy McDonald from Oklahoma. The fleet-footed McDonald caught one of the three touchdown passes and returned a punt 83 yards for another score.

By the end of August, Shaw had won over the squad. He only had praise for the Eagles' newly acquired quarterback. "Not only is Van Brocklin one of he best passers ever to play in this league," lauded Shaw, "but he gives this club confidence. You can see the effect he has on the rest of the squad. They respect him."[7]

In late August it sounded like a mutual-admiration society when Van Brocklin told reporters, "I hope I can play 10 years for Buck Shaw. He's my kind of coach, a player's coach."[8]

For Buck and the Eagles, the preseason highlight came on September 21, in the team's final exhibition game against the 49ers at Kezar Stadium. The week of the game, Shaw scoffed at reporters questioning whether the upcoming contest against his former team would be a grudge match. "This game is no more important than any other to us," Shaw replied. "And it's between the Eagles and the 49ers, not the coaches. As for the grudge angle, nothing to it. Life's too short."[9] While Shaw may have meant what he said, only a five-star milquetoast would ever believe that Buck wouldn't reap a dollop of extra satisfaction from whipping a team that had previously fired him.

Pro sports fans are often as classy as a loud belch in church. The verbal abuse they can heap on players, coaches, officials and even nearby fans merely clapping for the visitors can be appalling and downright intimidating. The most venomous catcalls are often aimed at either former hometown players, who were traded away or coaches who took a job elsewhere and then return to compete against their former team. This game was Buck's first trip back to Kezar Stadium as an opposing coach. Bill Campbell, who was the Eagles' color analyst for the game's radio broadcast, remembered one poignant moment from that afternoon.

"There was a big tunnel at the far end of the field through which the players had to come. We were busy preparing for the broadcast when he [Shaw] began his walk up that tunnel," recalled Campbell. "I remember it because we were so engrossed in our work, and we suddenly heard this rumble within the stadium. I looked up. I thought maybe the President had come to the game. The people stood and cheered and applauded him all the way to the Eagles' bench."[10]

It must have been a gratifying and humbling experience for Shaw. Bay Area fans still remembered, respected and appreciated all that the gentleman coach had done to popularize pro football in San Francisco. Although it wasn't immediately apparent because the hometown 49ers glided to a 21–0 halftime lead, the outpouring of sentiment affected the Eagle players as well. Van Brocklin, who played erratically in the first 30 minutes, led the Eagles on an 80-yard drive culminating with a 38-yard scoring pass to end Bobby Walston to start the second half. The 49ers quickly retaliated as rookie Fred Dugan made a miraculous 48-yard touchdown catch with Eagle defender Lee Riley (the brother of famed basketball coach Pat Riley) draped all over him. The 49ers seemed firmly in command. However, trailing 28–7 at the start of the fourth quarter, the Eagles came to life. Taking advantage of an eight-yard 49er punt and a blocked kick, the Eagles rallied to score 24 fourth-quarter points—the last three coming on Walston's 19-yard field goal with just 30 seconds remaining. In those last 30 seconds the 49ers, determined not to lose to their old coach, frantically drove to the Eagles' 15-yard line. With time left for just one play, Y.A. Tittle conferred with 49er coach Frankie Albert during a timeout. Both decided that since it was an exhibition game they'd go for the win rather than the tie. Sending receiver R.C. Owens to the corner of the end zone, Tittle floated him their patented "Alley Oop" pass. The "Alley Oop" consisted of throwing a sky-scraping pass into the end zone and letting Owens outleap the defenders to make the catch. On this last gasp Alley Oop, however, Eagle defender Eddie Bell knocked the ball away and the Eagles earned a 31–28 win.

Threading his way past well-wishers, accommodating autograph seekers and shaking hands with old friends resulted in Buck being the last man into the locker room. While reporters anxiously awaited the winning coach with pen and pad at the ready, Norm Van Brocklin gave them something to write about. "All the boys wanted to win this one for Buck on his old stomping grounds," the quarterback declared. "Also, Frankie [Albert] was riding me unmercifully in that second half. That made me want to win all the more. It acted as a spur."[11]

When Shaw finally arrived the players greeted him with a resounding cheer that shook the rafters before presenting him with the game ball. It was a memorable day for the Silver Fox.

* * *

As previously mentioned, a coach's world is a roller coaster ride of extreme highs and lows. One week you're viewing the world from a majestic mountain top, and the next you're a troglodyte stumbling in a deep cave looking for a crevice of light. Losing seems to be tougher on coaches than players. When a loss is imminent, a player can gain some degree of physical or emotional satisfaction by extending more energy into the next play's block or tackle. A coach in the same situation can only watch the seconds tick off the scoreboard clock while musing how he'll get his team ready for the next game.

Before 36,853 hopeful fans at Franklin Field, Buck Shaw's regular season debut afforded no mountain top view. In the first-ever regular season NFL game played on a college campus, the Washington Redskins erased the Eagles' 14–10 lead by scoring two fourth-quarter touchdowns to win 24–14. Calling the offensive shots for Washington that afternoon was their gutsy field general, 5-foot, 7-inch, 160-pound quarterback Eddie LeBaron. An excellent ball-handler, nifty runner and exceptional passer, LeBaron completed 10 of 15 passes for 134 yards. A graduate of the College of the Pacific, LeBaron was invited to play in the 1950 College All-Star game against the then world champion Eagles. While at the All-Stars training facility in Delafield, Wisconsin, the Marines Corps notified him that he was being called to active duty. Not only did LeBaron quarterback the All-Stars to victory over the Eagles, but sportswriters voted him the game's Most Valuable Player. After playing two exhibition games for Washington, 2nd Lt. LeBaron spent the next year leading a rifle platoon in Korea. Wounded twice, he was awarded the Bronze Star for gallantry in action and a Purple Heart. Leaving the Marines with the rank of major, he returned to pro football in 1952. LeBaron would play seven seasons with the Redskins before becoming the first quarterback of the Dallas Cowboys in 1960, where he played four years.

After the disappointing loss against the Redskins, Shaw remarked, "We were on Cloud Eight the last two weeks. We just hit bottom against Washington. That was our worst exhibition so far…. Nobody had a good day."[12] It was a disappointing start to what would be a disappointing season for Buck and the Eagles. But there were a few bright spots. One came the following week when the Eagles hosted the New York Giants.

After the Eagles' lackluster performance against Washington, only 23,178 fans came out to watch the Eagles draw first blood on Van Brocklin's 13-yard scoring pass to Clarence Peaks. On their next possession, the Giants tied the score on 37-year-old Charley Conerly's touchdown pass to Frank Gifford. With the score later tied at 10, the most spectacular play of the afternoon came on Van Brocklin's 91-yard touchdown pass to speedy Tommy McDonald. The moonshot pass play not only gave the Eagles a short-lived 17–10 lead, but was, and still is, the longest reception in Eagles history. (DeSean Jackson has since tied it.) The Giants' Phil King scored on a two-yard run to tie the game at halftime 17–17. Then Charley Conerly's 16-yard touchdown toss to Kyle Rote gave the Giants their only lead of the game, 24–17. Trailing 24–20, Van Brocklin led the Eagles on a 66-yard touchdown drive that ended with Billy Ray Barnes' one-yard scoring plunge. Lady Luck then smiled on the Eagles when a wide-open Alex Webster dropped Conerly's pass on the Eagle five-yard line. That forced Pat Sumerall to attempt a game-tying field goal from the Philadelphia 35-yard line. With 2:48 remaining, Sumerall's kick wobbled off to the right, and the Eagles ran out the clock for a 27–24 win.

A standout that afternoon, like he was throughout his 14-year career with the Eagles, was Chuck Bednarik. Shaw had originally hoped to play Bednarik at center, but due to injuries Bednarik played both ways—at center and linebacker—in the upset win, a feat he had performed dozens of times as an Eagle. The son of a Czech immigrant born into poverty, Bednarik grew up in Bethlehem, Pennsylvania. As a boy his aspiration was to grow up and work in the steel mills. After graduating from Bethlehem's Liberty High School, where his play proved instrumental in Liberty going undefeated in 1942, Bednarik enlisted in the Army Air Corps. While serving as a waist-gunner on a B-24 bomber, he flew 30 missions over Germany. Surviving the war changed his goals. Upon returning Stateside he decided to attend college. He matriculated at the University of Pennsylvania on a football scholarship. Graduating in 1949, Bednarik became the first and only Ivy League player to be selected as the NFL's overall number-one draft pick. His punishing bear hug-like tackles and extreme toughness earned him All-League linebacker status from 1951 through 1957. He had already been voted All-League center in 1950. In the years he played for Buck Shaw, Bednarik led by his intense style of play.

The following week at Pittsburgh, however, the Eagles reverted to their season-opening form against the Redskins—only the Eagles never led in this contest. Two weeks earlier Philadelphia gave up 212 yards rushing against Washington while only rushing for 60. Against the Steelers they gave up 214 yards rushing while only rushing for 59. The Eagles' only points came on Bobby Walston's 36-yard field goal, while Pittsburgh's Tom Tracy and Tank Younger tallied touchdowns in the Steelers' 24–3 win.

While Buck Shaw was gentlemanly and soft-spoken, his patience had its limits. In an interview with this author former Eagle halfback Billy Ray Barnes shared that Buck once became so upset that he fired a player on the practice field. That player might have been defensive back Rocky Ryan, who days after the Steeler loss reportedly had a biting, sarcastic reply to Shaw's constructive criticism. Immediately after the blowup, the Eagles placed Ryan on waivers. Chicago's Bears picked up Ryan where he played four games. However, 1958 was his last year in the NFL.

The 49ers came to Franklin Field on October 19, looking to avenge their exhibition loss to the Eagles several weeks earlier. Trailing 30–24, the Eagles recovered a 49er fumble on San Francisco's 28-yard line with three minutes remaining in the contest. Several plays and a roughing the passer penalty gave Philadelphia a first-and-goal on the 49ers' eight-yard line. On third down Van Brocklin tossed what looked like the tying touchdown to Bobby Walston. However, officials negated the catch, ruling that Walston's foot came down an inch out of bounds. On fourth down Tommy McDonald slipped flat on his face while trying to run down Van Brocklin's pass to the corner of the end zone. Shaw then watched in silent agony as the 49ers ran out the clock for a 30–24 win.

Heartbreak accompanied the Eagles to Green Bay the following week where Packer quarterback Babe Parilli tossed four touchdown passes to give the home team a 38–14 lead at the end of the third quarter. In the fourth, the Eagles rallied for three touchdowns while holding "the Pack" scoreless. However, it wasn't enough. Paul Hornung's first-quarter 30-yard field goal turned out to be difference in Green Bay's 38–35 win. The Eagles ended their four-game losing streak against the Cardinals on November 2, at Chicago's Comiskey Park, when Van Brocklin flipped a one-yard touchdown pass to end Dick Bielski with just 18 seconds remaining in the game. Bobby Walston's extra-point kick ended the game in a 21–21 tie. At the season's halfway point, the Eagles' record stood at one win, four losses and a tie.

* * *

One bright spot for the Eagles was the play of 6-foot, 1-inch, 208-pound flanker Pete Retzlaff, who was tied with Baltimore's Ray Berry for the league lead in receptions with 29. Detroit's Lions drafted Retzlaff out of South Dakota State in 1956, and Vince McNally picked him up after the Lions cut him in preseason. Retzlaff played offensive end for the Eagles in 1957 before being benched for dropping too many passes. However, on the first day of practice Norm Van Brocklin noticed Retzlaff running patterns. "I owe it all to

Dutch [Van Brocklin]," Retzlaff admitted. "The first day he threw to me he told me what was wrong. I was cradling the ball, catching it in my arms. He made me use my hands. Even in positions where an arm catch would be easier, he insisted I use my hands."[13]

By mid-season Buck Shaw was sold on Retzlaff. "Pete did it himself," Shaw told reporters. "Every day after practice he and Dick Bielski spend at least 20 minutes throwing to each other. While the other fellows are showering, they're out there on Franklin Field firing that ball back and forth at every angle you can think of."

Shaw then added, "He has wonderful endurance and he's strictly a team man. I just wish I had 33 more Retzlaffs."[14]

The following week Retzlaff caught an 18-yard touchdown pass from halfback Billy Ray Barnes in a losing effort before 26,306 fans at Franklin Field. Behind newly acquired quarterback Bobby Layne's four touchdown passes—three to halfback Tom "The Bomb" Tracy—the Steelers edged the Eagles 31–24.

Only 18,315 faithful followers showed up the following week to see the Eagles explode for the most points they had scored since 1954. Fullback Clarence Peaks did most of the damage, scoring four touchdowns in a 49–21 win over the Chicago Cardinals. Walt Kowalczyk, Tommy McDonald and Bobby Walston also scored touchdowns in what would be the Eagles last win of the season. The following week at Cleveland the Eagles played a solid game but lost 28–14. The difference was the sparkling play of rookie halfback Bobby Mitchell, who returned the opening kickoff 98 yards for a touchdown and later ran back a punt 69 yards for another score. After Mitchell's two scores put the Eagles behind 14–0, Philadelphia outplayed Cleveland the rest of the game.

The Dutchman hated to lose and during the second half the frustrated Van Brocklin began firing verbal zingers at Cleveland. "So you are the mighty Browns," the quarterback taunted as he aligned under center before calling signals. "You're just a bunch of lucky stiffs. You couldn't carry the water bucket for some of the good Brown teams I played against. Try to stop this play, you bums."[15]

While unleashing a barrage of insults may have alleviated some of the quarterback's frustrations, the barbs bounced off the Browns like a dribbled basketball off hardwood, for Cleveland coach Paul Brown repeatedly preached to his players to avoid reacting to verbal taunts and chippy insults. Instead, he preached that if one really wanted to hurt an opponent, the nastiest thing one could do was to beat him on the scoreboard, something the Browns often did to opponents.[16]

Several Eagle players were just as upset at Cleveland Coach Paul Brown's post-game refusal to shake hands with Buck Shaw as they were with the loss itself. In the locker room Norm Van Brocklin growled to a reporter, "I can't understand that kind of thing. Why should that so and so snub a guy like Buck Shaw."[17]

Philadelphia end Dick Bielski added, "When I first came in here [the locker room] I was so mad I couldn't talk. I wanted to go out there and get Brown. What a thing to do!"[18]

Paul Brown defended his actions by saying that two years previously one of the Eagles had flattened one of the Browns from behind after the game and nearly started a riot. Because of that, Brown just wanted to get off the field in a hurry. For his part Shaw did his best to gloss over the incident, saying it didn't matter.

* * *

While Shaw was enduring an agonizing season in Philadelphia in 1958, the Air Force program that Buck had an integral role in building was making a tsunami-like wave in major college football. The only blemish on their record was a 13–13 tie against heavily favored Iowa at Iowa City. Attempting to explain the academy's phoenix-like rise from their 1957 record, Denver sports columnist Chet Nelson suggested that as a part-time coach Buck Shaw's heart may not have been in it. He also stated that the pro offense Shaw had implemented was too much for college kids to assimilate. He then credited Coach Ben Martin with instilling "a lot of fundamentals and hard-nosed football into the attack and defense."[19] However, when the *Salt Lake Tribune*'s John Moody asked Larry Amizich and Evert Jones, two Utah graduate assistants who had played for the Utes against Shaw's 1957 Air Force team, how they'd rate Buck's squad, they had a different take.

"The score did not tell the true story," Amizich claimed. "The team [Air Force] blocked and tackled real well last year. We thought it was one of the best-coached teams in fundamentals we met. They blocked and tackled hard and crisp."[20]

Adding his two cents, Jones supported Amizich's assessment: "We played several Skyline games, with the score much closer, and the opponents weren't as tough as the Falcons."[21]

Brig. Gen. Benjamin B. Cassidy, Jr., was the deputy commandant of cadets at the academy from 1955 through 1959. While serving on the five-man board that hired Ben Martin to replace Shaw, Cassidy was the only dissenter. "I thought that Buck should stay on another year,"[22] recalled Cassidy.

The Falcons finished the 1958 season undefeated, with nine wins and two ties. One of the ties was a scoreless deadlock against heavily favored Texas Christian in the Cotton Bowl. Reflecting on that successful season, Brig. Gen. Cassidy added, "In my mind, the reason we did so well was because we had Buck Shaw as a starting coach. But Ben [Martin] brought a spirit to the team that Buck Shaw in his gentlemanly and quiet manner really didn't manifest with the team. He was a professional coach, whereas the coach at the college level had to have the 'fire and brimstone follow me boys' attitude. That early Air Force team would not have done as well under anybody else but a man like Ben Martin, with the previous training that a man like Buck Shaw had given in basic fundamental football. So put the two together and we had a winning team."[23]

A common thread ran through the comments of cadets who played on Shaw's Air Force teams. They regarded him as a "fantastic gentleman," whose profound knowledge of the game gave Air Force football a great start. While they all revered him, the players never got close to Buck. They felt that it wasn't in his nature to deliver a "give 'em hell" speech—a sentiment that echoed Cassidy's. An edge that Ben Martin had over Shaw in relating to the cadets was that Martin was a graduate of the U.S. Naval Academy, which helped him understand and empathize with what the players were experiencing in their daily military regimen. As an assistant to Coach George Sauer at Navy in 1948, Martin formulated a defensive game plan that allowed the winless Middies to tie Earl Blaik's powerhouse Army team 21–21. Martin's role in Navy's stunning performance that day resulted in Blaik strongly recommending him for the Air Force job in '58.

Martin did a terrific job implementing a double-wing offense emphasizing a belly series and bringing a rousing spirit to the program. Even though Shaw wasn't around to take any bows for the Falcons' success in '58, the Silver Fox needs to be recognized for crafting a solid foundation that allowed Martin to pilot Air Force football to soaring heights.

* * *

In New York's frigid Yankee Stadium on November 29, the Giants avenged their early season loss to Philadelphia with a 24–10 win. In temperatures just as frigid at Franklin Field the following week, the Eagles extended a solid performance in their rematch with Cleveland but came up on the short end of a 21–14 score. This time 228-pound fullback Jim Brown, who carried 21 times for 138 yards, and halfback Lew Carpenter, who gained 100 yards on 21 carries, provided the knock-out blows.

Most coaches sporting a two-win, eight-loss record while working on a one-year contract would be keeping their fingers crossed that they'd be re-hired. On December 10, with one game still remaining, Eagle President Frank McNamee announced that the Eagles had signed Buck to another one-year contract to coach in 1959. In doing so McNamee declared that Shaw had "given Philadelphia its most exciting football and we are confident that with a little more help and luck, Buck will be back to his winning ways."[24]

Unfortunately, neither Buck nor the Eagles returned to their winning ways in the season finale against Washington. The grounds crew had to dig out the field from under a blanket of snow before kickoff. Then the 22,600 die-hard fans who braved the elements witnessed the Redskins bury Philadelphia 20–0. Washington possessed the football for 43 of the contest's 60 minutes. Van Brocklin completed only two of 10 passes before giving way to backup Sonny Jurgensen in the second half. The loss gave Philadelphia a final record of two wins, nine losses and a tie for the 1958 season, which tied them for last place with the Chicago Cardinals. It was the Eagles' worst record since 1942.

After the game Shaw followed his sullen team into the locker room below Griffith Stadium. Locking the door behind him, the soft-spoken coach addressed his players. They all sensed the determination in his voice's tone. "This has never happened to me before. It will never happen again. If you don't have pride, I do. I'll be here again next year, but some of you may not. We'll win if I have to use three teams—one coming, one going and one playing."[25]

* * *

As the Cleveland Browns and New York Giants prepared to meet in a playoff game to determine who would be the 1958 Eastern Conference Champions, Buck Shaw was back at his Menlo Park, California, home. In an Associated Press interview he said that if he wasn't successful with the Eagles in 1959, he just might "hang it up."[26] When Buck originally signed with the Eagles he thought he might only coach through the '58 season, but after all of his successful years on the sidelines, his pride wouldn't let him walk away from the game after a two-win and nine-loss season. In Buck's mind only a dozen members of the '58 squad possessed championship talent. For the Eagles to compete for the Eastern Conference title, Shaw knew they had to strengthen the running game, the defensive secondary, and improve the pass rush.

Shaw made several coaching changes during the off-season. Bob Bronzan and Bruno Banducci would not return in 1959. Jerry Williams would continue to oversee the defense while Shaw brought in Chuck Gauer to work with ends and backs, Nick Skorich to coach the lines, and Frank "Bucko" Kilroy to handle the scouting. Kilroy and Gauer had both previously played and served as assistant coaches for the Eagles. Skorich had played and worked as an assistant for the Pittsburgh Steelers. Confident and unconcerned with his public perception at this stage of his career, Shaw adopted a CEO's posture, delegating specific tasks to his assistants with the authority to execute them.

Believing that a savvy veteran like Van Brocklin could see more from behind center than Shaw could from the sidelines, the Silver Fox continued to let the "Dutchman" call his own plays. The two discussed strategy during timeouts, and Shaw occasionally sent in a play, but Van Brocklin called the shots in the huddle. Regarding Van Brocklin as another coach on the field, Shaw gave the fiery quarterback the authority to send any player out of the game that he didn't feel was doing his job. When later asked how he felt about his coach giving him such a free hand, the quarterback explained, "Buck likes to operate that way. He puts his confidence in you and you feel obligated to do a job for him."[27] Van Brocklin took his role as field general/coach seriously. When the team scrimmaged the "Dutchman" often asked Shaw, "Buck, why don't you put the kid in?" The kid was the young back-up quarterback, Sonny Jurgensen. As Jurgensen broke the huddle, Van Brocklin would stand about 15 yards behind the offense and bark instructions to the "kid" as the play developed, "Stay in that pocket! Don't let 'em chase you out of there!"[28]

Shaw and Van Brocklin melded like peanut-butter and jelly. In team meetings Shaw might spend 10 minutes diagramming a play on the chalkboard and when finished inevitably turn to Van Brocklin and query, "Is that all right with you, Dutch?"[29] Just as inevitably, Van Brocklin would consider the play for a moment before nodding in agreement.

Only 24 veterans from the '58 squad returned for the start of the Eagles' training camp in Hershey, Pennsylvania, in late July. The coaching staff expected some heated competition for the remaining 11 spots. Anticipating the start of training camp, Shaw told reporters, "There's nothing like competition to bring forth the best in a man and we believe we will have competition this year."[30] The numerous fistfights that erupted during intra-squad scrimmages gave credence to Shaw's opinion.

For the most part, his team's performance during the exhibition season pleasantly surprised Shaw. The Eagles won three of six games defeating the defending NFL Champion Baltimore Colts, the New York Giants and, in the last exhibition, the Rams in Los Angeles.

After playing well in their win over the Rams, the Eagles spent the week in Northern California getting ready for the season-opener against the 49ers. A Kezar crowd of over 41,000 gave Shaw a two-minute standing ovation just before the opening kickoff. It was the highlight of the afternoon for the Silver Fox. San Francisco built a 21–0 lead after three quarters. Abe Woodson's dazzling 65-yard punt return gave the 49ers the ball on the Eagle 5-yard line setting up fullback J.D. Smith's one-yard scoring plunge. Lightning struck again later in the quarter when 49er Eddie Dove returned another punt 62 yards, giving the home team possession on Philly's 13-yard line. Two plays later Tittle passed 10 yards to R.C. Owens for another score. Ineffective in the first half, Van Brocklin rallied to throw fourth-quarter touchdown passes to Dick Bielski and Bobby Walston. The game ended with the Eagles' offense still fighting, on the 49er one-yard line. The 49ers spoiled Shaw's homecoming with a 24–14 win.

At the football writers' luncheon the following Tuesday, Shaw said of his Eagles, "They were all steamed up for the Ram game—but it didn't count. Then we go to San Fran. We heard reports about how good we're becoming and that the 49ers weren't a football team. By game time we weren't a football team."[31]

When asked if Van Brocklin's shabby first half performance was to blame Buck replied, "I just didn't feel it was altogether his fault. We only had one receiver free the whole first half. Another quarterback wouldn't have helped."[32] Then contradicting his previous year's statement that playing the 49ers was just another game, he conceded that the loss was especially painful because he had spent nine years in San Francisco. Shaw concluded his remarks by intimating that players who failed to improve over their '58 performance might soon find themselves as ex-Eagles. He promised his squad would spend a lot of time in the upcoming week on punt coverage.

But the next week, just as they had done in '58, the Eagles upset the New York Giants at Franklin Field. Speedy Tommy McDonald's whirlwind performance sparked the Eagles' victory by catching touchdown passes of 35 and 55 yards from Van Brocklin, and a 19-yard scoring pass from Sonny Jurgensen. He also returned a punt 81 yards to paydirt. Another thrilling moment came when Eagle rookie Art Powell (Charlie's little brother), returned the second half kick-off 95 yards before stumbling down at the Giants' two-yard line. When the final gun sounded, the Eagles had walloped New York 49–21.

McDonald, the third-year pro, was born in the small town of Roy in northeastern New Mexico. His family moved to Albuquerque for his junior year of high school, where McDonald shined in three sports and earned All-State honors in football. Numerous colleges recruited him, but Oklahoma's Bud Wilkinson was the only coach who asked about his educational goals. That proved to be the decisive factor in McDonald choosing to become a Sooner. In McDonald's three varsity seasons, from 1954 through 1956, Oklahoma never lost a game. In his senior year he finished third in the Heisman balloting behind Notre Dame's Paul Hornung and Tennessee's Johnny Majors. One of four future Philadelphia Eagles invited to play in the 1957 College All-Star game against the New York Giants, McDonald saw game action only in holding for Paige Cothren's two field goal attempts and a couple of kick returns. After the All-Stars' 22–12 loss, the fiery McDonald gave Otto Graham, his position coach during the three-week practice session, a piece of his mind. He and fellow All-Stars Billy Ray Barnes, Clarence Peaks and Jim Harris all made the cut with Philadelphia. Thinking McDonald too small to be a running back, Eagle head coach Hugh Devore delegated him to returning punts and kickoffs for the first half of the season. On November 24, with the Eagles trailing Washington, Devore inserted McDonald into the game at offensive end, where he promptly caught a 61-yard scoring pass from fellow rookie Sonny Jurgensen. Later in the contest McDonald made his second catch, a 25-yard touchdown reception. From that moment on, McDonald was no longer a running back, but a wide receiver.

Because of McDonald's zany personality many of his teammates considered him to be a flake. One might want to check out McDonald's 1998 NFL Hall of Fame Induction speech online and make one's own judgment. Although game programs listed him at 5 feet, 9 inches, 175 pounds, teammates swore he stood no taller than 5 feet, 7 inches. He claimed to have honed his eye-hand coordination by catching ping pong balls people fired at him. Because of his diminutive size, Van Brocklin called him "Squeaky." The "Dutchman" soon learned, however, that whenever "Squeaky" said he could get open, Van Brocklin had a completion waiting to happen. In his 12 pro seasons McDonald snagged 495 passes for 8,410 yards and 84 touchdowns. Buck Shaw hailed McDonald as one of the three greatest receivers he'd ever coached. The others were Pete Retzlaff and 49er Billy Wilson, neither of whom are in the NFL's Hall of Fame.[33]

McDonald spoke nostalgically of Shaw years later, "I can still remember that [game] program drumming against the palm of his hand. His greatest asset was the psychology he used, the philosophy he believed in. He knew plenty of football…. But he knew how to put players together, to make 'em feel like a family. I played for lots of coaches in the NFL, but Buck Shaw is the man at the top of the ladder, for me the best of 'em all."[34]

The following week against Pittsburgh, McDonald made a great leaping grab of a Van Brocklin pass in the end zone while surrounded by three defenders. His acrobatic catch was the clinching touchdown in an exciting 28–24 Eagle victory. The last few minutes of the game were so gut-wrenching that they may have caused NFL Commissioner Bert Bell, a spectator in Franklin Field's south stands, to collapse from a heart attack. Bell died within minutes of his arrival at University Hospital.

The Eagles took their two-and-one record to New York's Yankee Stadium on October 18 for a rematch with the Giants before 68,783 zealous fans in their home-opener. Because baseball's New York Yankees were riding the crest of their dynasty in the '50s and early '60s, and playing almost annually in the World Series, the football Giants played on the road until mid–October. During this time New York's football fans loved the Giants, and home games always sold out. Because the NFL blacked out television broadcasts in cities hosting games, thousands of New Yorkers who couldn't purchase tickets drove to Connecticut and rented motel rooms beyond the "blackout" range to watch Giant home games on the tube. In 1958, the Giants lost the NFL Championship game to the Baltimore Colts in overtime in what many have called "the greatest game ever played." The two clubs would play for the championship again in 1959.

Chagrined over their lopsided loss to Philadelphia two weeks earlier, the Giants were determined to take no prisoners in the rematch. On the afternoon, Giant quarterbacks Charley Conerly and George Shaw combined to complete 13 of 19 passes for 277 yards. Meanwhile, the Giants' pass rush led by Andy Robustelli and Jim Katcavage put constant pressure on Van Brocklin, and safety Jimmy Patton covered McDonald like a blanket. When the dust settled, the Giants had again regained first place in the Eastern Conference with a convincing 24–7 win.

Playing the Chicago Cardinals the next week in the neutral site of Minneapolis' Municipal Stadium, the Eagles appeared to be suffering a hangover from their Giant loss as the Cardinals raced to a 24–0 third-quarter lead. Suddenly, a 71-yard Van Brocklin to McDonald completion woke the Eagles from their comatose state and set up the first of Billy Ray Barnes' two touchdown runs. With the aid of a couple of fourth-quarter interceptions, the Eagles caught fire and with 3:12 left in the game, McDonald made a diving catch of Van Brocklin's 18-yard pass to give Philadelphia their only lead of the game and a 28–24 win.

While Shaw was thrilled with the win, he was even more enthused about his team's chemistry. The Silver Fox attributed it to the rapport between the squad's veterans and rookies. "The rookies behave like the veterans," claimed Shaw.

> If the veterans are indifferent, if they are lacking in spirit, the rookies adopt the same attitude. They think, "This is the way this pro game should be played."And they become indifferent.
> Fortunately, our veterans aren't that way. Fellows like Bednarik, Walston, Jesse Richardson and Tom Brookshier have a winning spirit. And they are lifting up the rookies, and our other new men. Van Brocklin's the same way. He never quits.
> And our team can win a lot of games, as long as our veterans keep their spirit. Because the new men will hustle along with them.[35]

Hosting the Washington Redskins the following week, Shaw's squad vaulted to a 30–9 halftime lead, before gutsy Eddie LeBaron led Washington on an amazing second-half comeback. With the Eagles holding on to a 30–23 lead in the game's waning moments, LeBaron connected on a 49-yard pass to Bill Anderson. Only the efforts of a hustling Tom Brookshier who caught him at the three-yard line, prevented him from scoring. Making a courageous goal line stand, the Eagles repulsed Redskin fullback Don Bosseler from reaching paydirt on three successive carries to preserve the 30–23 win. The victory gave the surprising Eagles a four-win, two-loss record at the season's halfway mark.

Visiting Cleveland the next week, the Eagles encountered one Brown too many. Jim Brown rushed for 125 yards and Cleveland engineered three long scoring drives to take a 21–0 halftime lead. The Eagles defense stiffened significantly in the second half, but Cleveland still prevailed 28–7.

The Eagles bounced back the following week at Franklin Field, winning a 27–17 seesaw contest over Chicago's Cardinals. The win gave Philadelphia a five-win, three-loss record, just a game behind the conference-leading Giants and Browns.

With the game tied at 20 the following week against his former team, the Los Angeles Rams, the fiery Van Brocklin worked his passing magic by leading Philly on an 81-yard drive in the game's last 90 seconds. With just 16 seconds remaining, Paige Cothren, cut by the Rams earlier in the season, booted a 14-yard field goal to give the Eagles a 23–20 win. Improving their record to 6–3, the Eagles now shared second place with the Browns, only a game behind the Giants.

Unfortunately, the runner came off the Eagles' sleigh in snowy Pittsburgh on November 29. The Steelers intercepted four Van Brocklin passes and blocked two Paige Cothren field goal attempts to snow-blind Philadelphia 31–0. Whatever luck the Eagles may have had in the whirling snow was all bad, as typified by Tommy McDonald having his apparent second-quarter touchdown catch knocked from his hands as he ran full speed into the goal post. (In those days the goal posts were placed on the goal line.) Meanwhile, Pittsburgh's venerable veteran Bobby Layne was at the top of his game, passing for four touchdowns and kicking all four extra-points as well as a field goal.

Venturing to Washington's Griffith Stadium on December 6, Van Brocklin and McDonald had a great day. McDonald caught nine of the Dutchman's passes for 141 yards including three touchdowns for a 34–14 win.

Sporting a seven-win, four-loss record and a game still remaining against Cleveland, Shaw signed a one-year contract to coach the Eagles again in 1960. In signing he told the press, "This Eagles team has great potential and is a championship team in the making. When you get so close to the top you don't want to quit until you reach it. We have a wonderful group of boys and it's been a pleasure to coach them. They have tremendous spirit and give all they have. No coach can ask for more."[36]

Shaw could have had a longer contract but informed club president Frank McNamee and Vince McNally that he planned to retire from coaching after the 1960 season.

Two days later the Eagles hosted the Browns in the season's finale. In a bitterly-fought contest, Philly battled from behind to take a 21–14 halftime lead. However, the Browns made a great goal line stand in the third quarter and then proceeded to drive 99 yards, culminating on Jim Brown's one-yard scoring plunge. Aided by a windswept Eagles punt in the fourth quarter, Cleveland took possession on the Eagles' 44-yard line and marched the distance to score on Brown's four-yard run for a 28–21 win. The victory earned Cleveland a seven-win, five-loss record and a second-place tie with the Eagles in the Eastern Conference. New York's Giants won the 1959 division title but would again lose to the Baltimore Colts in the championship game.

TWENTY

Winning the 1960 NFL Championship

In some respects, a coach gambles in announcing that the upcoming season will be his last, especially if the team gets off to a slow start. In such cases players might come to view the coach as a "short-timer" or "lame duck." A couple of early season losses might induce some to adopt an attitude of "Oh, well, coach won't be around next year, let's just play out the string." Such a situation would certainly undermine a coach's decision-making and disciplinary authority. If Buck ever entertained such thoughts, and it's highly unlikely he did, he might have taken some comfort that the team's undisputed leaders, Norm Van Brocklin and Chuck Bednarik, announced that 1960 would be their last season as active players as well. (Bednarik eventually changed his mind.) Knowing the competitive nature of both men, Shaw knew they would do all they could to go out winners. The fact is that Shaw had taken the reins of a Philadelphia squad going nowhere and by his second season had turned them into legitimate contenders. He firmly believed that now, in his third year, the Eagles were on the verge of becoming conference, if not league, champions.

The 1960 exhibition season went well, as the Eagles won four of six contests, with several promising rookies seeing plenty of action. Among them were running back Ted Dean out of Wichita State and linebacker Maxie Baughn from Georgia Tech. A real surprise was speedy halfback Timmy Brown. Green Bay drafted him in '59 out of Ball State in Indiana. He saw very little action with the Packers before joining the Eagles in '60.

For Buck Shaw, history strangely repeated itself when Philadelphia traveled to San Francisco for an exhibition game with the 49ers at Kezar Stadium—only this time he was standing on the Eagles' sideline, not the 49ers'. The reader may remember the 1953 back-alley brawl between both clubs that began with harsh words between the Eagles' Bobby Walston and the 49ers' Charlie Powell. The donnybrook lasted seven minutes and needed police intervention as well as a rendition of the national anthem to restore order. This time the brawl began when Eagle linebacker John Nocera decked 49er rookie Fred Williamson with a blindside block on a kickoff. Irate, the rookie jumped up and kicked the prone Nocera in the ribs. (For fans old enough to remember, this was the same vaunted Fred Williamson who dubbed himself "The Hammer" because his clothesline-type tackling kayoed numerous ball carriers. As a member of the Kansas City Chiefs prior to Super Bowl I, Williamson claimed he was going to drop "The Hammer" on the Packer receivers. On game day, however, Green Bay's Donny Anderson knocked Williamson cold while running a sweep, resulting in the Hammer being carried off on a stretcher. The play prompted Packer Willie Wood to inform teammates, "The Hammer got nailed.")

Back to San Francisco: After kicking Nocera, Williamson was immediately flattened by Eagle tackle Don Owens before all hell broke loose. Both benches emptied and nearly

80 players began a frenzied barrage of roundhouse rights, uppercuts and kicks. On the edge of the melee the crafty 34-year-old Van Brocklin grabbed 49er veteran Joe Perry (who was one of the instigators of the '53 brawl) by the jersey sleeve and suggested that due to their age, perhaps they should sit the dance out. Perry agreed and both sported big grins while watching their respective teammates go at it hammer and tongs. It took 13 minutes for both teams to punch themselves out, after which officials ejected the 49ers' Abe Woodson and Philly's Billy Ray Barnes and Jerry Wilson.

Shortly before the start of the regular season the Eagles made two key acquisitions. First, they traded a future draft choice to the Rams for 6-foot, 4-inch defensive back Don Burroughs. Then just days before the opener, they picked up defensive back Bobby Freeman from Green Bay for another high draft pick. Both would play critical roles in the upcoming season.

Unfortunately, the Eagles began the 1960 season the same way they ended the '59 season: by hosting the Cleveland Browns at Franklin Field and losing. Only this time the 41–24 beatdown before 56,000 fans was more severe than the loss in '59. Behind Jim Brown and Bobby Mitchell, Cleveland unleashed a punishing ground game that rushed for 329 yards. Brown rushed for 153 yards on 24 carries while Mitchell carried 14 times for 156 yards. Most of Mitchell's carries were outside sweeps executed with speed and moves that left Eagle defenders picking up their jocks. Mitchell scored on runs of 30 and 31 yards and on an 11-yard pass from Milt Plum.

Asked about the performance of Cleveland's Brown and Mitchell, an astonished Chuck Bednarik told reporters, "I've never seen anything like them. The only way to stop them is to break their legs."[1]

Afterwards, Shaw remained optimistic. "We were trounced," the coach confessed. "Walloped. Slaughtered. I've never been beaten in so many ways. But I know we're not that bad. It's just that there's not a single fellow I can point to and say, 'He gave us a good game.'"[2]

Assistant coach Jerry Williams sat dejectedly in the locker room and assistant Nick Skorich told reporters that the team was too tight before the game.

When asked about Mitchell's "will-of-the-wisp" open field runs, Shaw replied, "I didn't see one shoulder tackle. It's a wonder we didn't lose an arm out there."[3]

A simmering Shaw told the team the following Tuesday, in so many words, "if we don't turn it around, we're not going anywhere." Those words didn't sink in immediately. That Friday night Philly traveled to the Cotton Bowl as heavy favorites over the expansion Dallas Cowboys. Thanks to Bobby Freeman's two extra-point blocks, the Eagles managed to escape with a 27–25 win. When the Eagles aligned for the kickoff against the St. Louis Cardinals (who had moved from Chicago) at Franklin Field on October 9, Shaw's message had reached the squad. In a game that saw them battle from behind on three separate occasions, the Eagles went ahead for the last time on Van Brocklin's 11-yard touchdown pass to McDonald with just over six minutes to go. Eagle defender Don Burroughs then scaled the Cardinals' fate with a timely interception deep in Philadelphia territory to give the home team a 31–27 win.

Hosting the Detroit Lions the next week, the Eagles' newfound pass rush made life miserable for quarterback Jim Ninowski. After being sacked numerous times and completing only five of 16 passes, Coach George Wilson benched him in favor of Earl Morrall, who fared no better. The Eagles prevailed 28–10.

Before medical professionals became cognizant of the dangers of chronic traumatic encephalopathy (CTE) resulting from repeated blows to the head, coaches, trainers and athletes occasionally joked about one getting one's "bell rung" or getting "dinged." Even sportswriters found it amusing. Midway through the second quarter, Eagle defensive back Tom Brookshier made an explosive hit on Detroit tight end Dave Middleton. Middleton got up. Brookshier didn't. Here is how *Philadelphia Daily News'* writer Larry Merchant described the incident:

> In a while the defensive man was led off the field doing a splendid imitation of Charlie Chaplin, legs wobbling crazily. (They "turned to putty," Brookshier said later.) On the next set of plays he was back at his post. The putty was not in his legs. It was in his helmet.[4]

Brookshier continued playing, but his mental daze didn't clear until late in the third quarter. He usually called the defensive signals, but now he couldn't remember them. He asked teammate Chuck Weber to call them, but Brookshier didn't know what they meant. On each play another teammate, Gene Johnson, had to tell him what to do.

In the game's last minute, the Lions' Dick "Night Train" Lane tackled Eagle fullback Clarence Peaks. In the process Peaks caught an elbow to the jaw, that left him literally out on his feet. Although he didn't remember it, he walked to the locker room on his own steam. While Peaks was sitting alone on a bench, a trainer recognized that the former Michigan State Spartan wasn't quite right. For a few seconds he waved smelling salts under the fullback's nose.

THEN PEAKS ASKED, "Where am I?"
TRAINER: "The game's over."
PEAKS: "What game? Who'd we play?"
TRAINER: "Detroit."
PEAKS: "Did I just talk to a reporter from Detroit? How'd I get up here?"
TRAINER: "You probably walked. Your name is Clarence Peaks. You play fullback for the
     Philadelphia Eagles. That's a football team."
PEAKS: "Who did we play last week?"
TRAINER: "The Cardinals."
PEAKS: "What's our record?"
TRAINER: "Three and one."
THEN HALFBACK BILLY BARNES WALKED BY AND SAID: "Nice game!"
PEAKS: "What'd I do?"
BARNES: "You played a helluva game."
PEAKS: "I don't remember none of it."[5]

Both Peaks and Brookshier were in the Eagles lineup for the next game.

* * *

Jesse Richardson, a 6-foot, 2-inch, 260-pound tackle, was the last NFL lineman not to don a face mask. After breaking his nose for the ninth time he stopped counting. Richardson became a major contributor to Eagles effective pass-rush against the Lions. After the Lions' game he predicted, "We're working together now and I think we're on our way to a championship."[6] For Richardson's prediction to materialize, Philly would have to win its next game, a rematch with the Browns at Cleveland. Since taking over at Philadelphia, Buck Shaw and his Eagles had lost five straight to Paul Brown's powerhouse squads.

On October 23, a gloomy afternoon before 64,580 raucous Cleveland fans the two contenders squared off. The Eagles showed they meant business when Van Brocklin hit Bobby Walston on a 49-yard touchdown on the team's first play from scrimmage. It set the tempo for a contest filled with long runs and exciting pass plays. The Eagle defense played with more vigor and toughness than they did in their season-opener, but Philly still trailed at halftime 15–7. Cleveland extended its lead to 22–7 four minutes into the third quarter on Jim Brown's explosive 71-yard run. Then Clarence Peaks, hopefully recovered from the concussion he sustained a week earlier, sparked the Eagles with a 57-yard run on a draw play, putting the ball on the Browns' seven-yard line. Two plays later Billy Ray Barnes plunged a yard to paydirt making the score 22–14.

On Philly's next possession Van Brocklin uncorked a 57-yard scoring bomb to the nimble Tommy McDonald, making it 22–21. With the Eagles defense now playing lights out, they held Cleveland again and got the ball early in the fourth quarter. Completing four passes on a 64-yard drive, the final being an eight-yard touchdown toss to Barnes, the Eagles took a 28–22 lead. But like all of Paul Brown's teams, Cleveland was a disciplined, efficient machine. On their next possession the Browns launched a punishing, time-consuming 88-yard drive culminating in Bobby Mitchell's three-yard scamper into the end zone. Sam Baker's extra-point kick gave the Browns a 29–28 lead.

The Eagles responded by marching to the Browns' 19 when a Cleveland interception halted the drive. Then the Eagle defense held, forcing Cleveland to punt, and Philly got the ball back on their own 10-yard line with 90 seconds remaining in the game. With his team's back to the wall, Van Brocklin was at his best. He completed a 27-yard pass to Retzlaff. Three plays later he completed another to McDonald at the Browns' 48. Another pass failed. But on second down the Browns were called for pass interference and Philly had a first-and ten on Cleveland's 31-yard line with only 10 seconds remaining.

At this point Buck called a timeout. Unwilling to risk another pass play with such little time remaining, the Silver Fox called upon kicker Bobby Walston to attempt a 38-yard field goal. Walston had missed an earlier try from the Cleveland 45. Eagle end Pete Retzlaff recalled his thoughts at that moment: "I thought this isn't going to end well. Bobby's leg isn't that strong."[7] The ball was snapped and the Eagles' sideline held its collective breath. Walston's kick was straight and true clearing the crossbar by a couple of feet. The Eagle sideline erupted with players running onto the field to congratulate the 32-year-old kicker. Walston's timely boot gave the Eagles a 31–29 victory and a four-win, one-loss record to put them in second place behind New York's Giants. The last-second win proved to be the turning point in the Eagles' season.

Depending on what newspaper or eyewitness account one believes, somewhere between 1,000 to 10,000 fans awaited the Eagles' return flight into Philadelphia's airport later that night. One cheering throng of people rushed the gate and carried Bobby Walston to the parking lot on their shoulders.[8]

* * *

During the 1959 season, Shaw had lauded the great spirit of the club's veterans and how the rookies were taking their cue from it. The social bonding on the club grew even stronger in 1960—partly due to the informal Monday meetings that Norm Van Brocklin organized. Although Monday was a non-practice day during the season, it was payday. The Eagle players usually picked up their checks that morning and then headed to a "watering hole" called Donoghue's near the Walnut Park Plaza, where many of them lived during the season. There they played cards or shot pool and discussed Sunday's game at Van Brocklin's table.

Defensive back Tom Brookshier vividly recalled those informal Monday gatherings:

"He'd [Van Brocklin] drop his kids off at school, then he'd tell the hotel switch board operator, 'OK, get 'em up.' She'd start calling every guy on the team. My wife would literally drag me out of bed. She'd say, 'C'mon. Dutch wants you at Donoghue's.' Can you imagine, a wife telling her husband to go to a bar at nine o'clock in the morning? That's the kind of power Dutch had. We'd drink beer all day, talking things over. If a guy had a beef, he aired it. Any problem we had, we settled right there. There were no cliques; nobody whispered behind anyone's back. We developed an intense team feeling and that's what won the title for us."[9]

When talking about the 1960 Eagles years later, a nostalgic Tommy McDonald said, "We were a family."[10]

Pete Retzlaff added, "We weren't 36 or 38 individuals, we were a team."[11]

In 1960, the citizens of Philadelphia rallied behind their team. After a bye week the Eagles returned to Franklin Field to host Pittsburgh before a crowd of over 58,000. In their home game three weeks earlier against Detroit, they drew 38,000. The turnout for the Pittsburgh game was the largest crowd to attend an Eagles game in 10 years. The home team dominated play from the opening kickoff until the final gun for a 34–7 win—a win that gave them sole possession of first place in the Eastern Conference. An elated Shaw said, "It's the best game we've played in three years."[12]

With eight minutes left in the game against the Redskins the following week and Philly trailing 13–9, the Eagles were faced with a fourth-and-ten on Washington's 28-yard line. Shaw was faced with the dilemma of attempting a field goal or going for the first down. Gambling, Shaw went for the first down. Van Brocklin's pass found Walston open on the Skins' 12-yard line and the Georgia alumnus ran it into the end zone to give the Eagles a 16–13 lead. With 40 seconds remaining, Walston kicked a 10-yard field goal to make the final score: Eagles 19, Washington 13. However, the Eagles suffered a major setback that afternoon when fullback Clarence Peaks was lost for the season with a fractured leg.

* * *

During the '50s and '60s, pro football players didn't earn the multi-million dollar salaries that so many of them make today. Not only did most players have full-time off-season jobs, but some worked other jobs during the season to provide for their families. Philadelphia linebacker Chuck Bednarik was one such player. The Eagles would practice most days until noon. Then Bednarik showered, changed, grabbed a quick lunch and hustled off to sell cement mix for the Warner Concrete Company. Sometime during the 1960 season a radio broadcaster claimed that Bednarik's tackles were as "hard as the concrete he sold." Local media and fans tapped into the phrase and began referring to the linebacker as "Concrete Charlie" Bednarik. Bednarik relished the moniker and did his best to live up to it, like when the Eagles ventured to New York's Yankee Stadium to meet the Giants on November 20. With the Eagles record of six wins and a loss against the Giants' five wins, one loss and a tie, it was a key game in the Eastern Conference race.

A sellout crowd of 63,571 were on hand to see the Giants dominate play in the first half. Limiting Van Brocklin to one completion in six attempts, the overwhelming pass rush of the Giants' front four of Andy Robustelli, Jim Katcavage, Dick Modzelewski and Rosey Grier sacked the Dutchman for 33 yards in losses and once forced the trapped quarterback into an intentional grounding penalty. A knee injury limited Charley Conerly to holding for extra points and field goals, so the Giants started backup George Shaw at quarterback. Shaw performed admirably in leading New York to a 10–0 halftime lead on Joe Morrison's one-yard scoring plunge and Pat Summerall's 26-yard field goal. Shortly before halftime the Eagles' defense behind Tom Brookshier, Joe Robb and Jim McCusker rose to the occasion by stopping the Giants' Frank Gifford on a fourth-and-goal from the one-yard line. The critical goal line stand seemed to bolster the Eagles' confidence and turned the game's momentum.

The Eagles broke the scoring ice in the third quarter when Van Brocklin connected with a twisting, falling Tommy McDonald covered closely by Lindon Crow and Jimmy Patton for a 35-yard touchdown. Walston's extra point cut the Giants' lead to 10–7. Early in the fourth quarter, Walston attempted a 17-yard field goal that New York's Dick Lynch blocked. Unperturbed, on Philly's next possession Van Brocklin led them on a 68-yard drive. Now the Giants' gritty defense dug in at the half-yard line, forcing Walston to kick a 12-yard field goal to tie the score at 10 with 4:24 remaining in the contest.

Chuck Bednarik started the game at center, with John Nocera playing left linebacker. But after Walston's game-tying field goal, Shaw removed Nocera and had "Concrete Charlie" play both ways. The move immediately paid dividends. With 2:37 left in the

Chuck Bednarik (60) celebrates teammate Chuck Weber's recovery of Frank Gifford's (16) fumble that saved Philadelphia's 17–10 win over the Giants on November 20, 1960, at Yankee Stadium. Bednarik's blindside tackle of Gifford caused the fumble. At the moment this photograph was snapped the jubilant Bednarik was unaware that Gifford was unconscious and seriously injured (Library of Congress).

game, Bednarik's jarring tackle of fullback Mel Triplett at the line of scrimmage, forced a fumble, which Eagle defensive back Jimmy Carr snagged in midair and returned 36 yards for a touchdown. Walston's extra point gave Philly a 17–10 lead.

George Shaw had the Giants moving on the their last possession when he passed to a wide-open Frank Gifford at the Eagles' 30-yard line. As the USC grad snagged the pass and ran across the field, Bednarik caught him from the blindside with a vicious tackle, causing Gifford to fumble. Eagle linebacker Chuck Weber recovered it. Realizing Weber's recovery had sealed the win for Philly, an ecstatic Bednarik threw his fist in the air and yelled, "This @#% game is over!"[13] At that very moment a photographer snapped a picture of Bednarik's celebratory gesture. From the angle of the shot it looks like Bednarik is taunting a prone and unconscious Gifford. But at that precise moment, "Concrete Charlie" was unaware of where Gifford was or that he was severely injured. Medical personnel carried the fallen New York star off the field on a stretcher. Unbeknownst to Gifford's concerned teammates, a fan had suffered a fatal heart attack during the contest. Medical personnel took his covered corpse on a stretcher to the Giants' locker room to await transport to the morgue. Spotting the covered corpse upon entering the locker room after the game, several stunned and panicked Giants momentarily believed the blanket-covered body on the stretcher was Gifford's.[14]

Fortunately, Gifford was taken to St. Elizabeth's Hospital where Dr. Francis Sweeny reported "that the wet X-rays show no fracture and he's conscious although his memory is hazy. We'll keep him here at least 48 hours. But it's too early to say about next Sunday's game."[15]

Not only did the injury end Gifford's season, but it influenced him to leave the game in 1961, only to return in '62 and experience three more productive seasons for the Giants as a wide receiver. Upon returning to Philadelphia, Bednarik sent the hospitalized Gifford a fruit basket and a get-well telegram. Bednarik's hit was brutal, but clean. After watching the game film, Gifford attested through the years that it was a clean hit.

The 17–10 victory gave the Eagles sole possession of first place in the Eastern Conference. Due to a scheduling quirk, the two teams met again the following Sunday in Philadelphia.

* * *

With Gifford and defensive end Jim Katcavage out for the season with injuries, and Charlie Conerly only expected to hold for Pat Summerall's place-kicks, the Eagles entered the contest a six-and a-half-point favorite. However, the Giants mustn't have read the papers that week, for on their first play from scrimmage, quarterback George Shaw rifled a 71-yard touchdown pass to Kyle Rote, who was playing with a specially designed cast to protect his broken hand. The SMU grad later caught another 11-yard scoring pass. That combined with Pat Summerall's field goal gave the visitors a 17–0 lead at the end of the first quarter. But all that Monday afternoon social bonding at O'Donoghue's, plus their recent wins over both Cleveland and the Giants, gave the spirited Eagles a sense that they were bullet-proof. In the second quarter Van Brocklin got the Eagles on the scoreboard with a 25-yard touchdown pass to rookie Ted Dean. Walston later added a field goal and when halfback Billy Ray Barnes fumbled into the end zone on Philly's next possession, hustling Eagle tackle J.D. Smith outraced two Giants to recover it for the tying touchdown. However, another Summerall field goal gave the Giants a 20–17 halftime lead.

During the week, offensive coach Charlie Gauer confided to Buck Shaw that he thought the Giants might be susceptible to a play-action pass off a fake trap play. Shaw told Gauer to draw it up. Gauer did, and Buck shared it with Van Brocklin the next day. Late in the third quarter, Van Brocklin realized that Giants' middle linebacker Sam Huff was picking up the Eagles' audibles. With that, he called "one-twenty-one" at the line of scrimmage, which was an audible that had halfback Billy Ray Barnes running a trap to Van Brocklin's left. On the snap Giant middle linebacker Sam Huff shot the gap and stopped Barnes cold. Upon returning to the huddle Van Brocklin told the team, "Okay, the trap is set."

As the Eagles huddled for the first play of the fourth quarter trailing 23–17, Shaw called Gauer's new play. But before breaking the huddle Van Brocklin told his teammates, "Look, I'm gonna call an audible, but ignore it. It's just a fake for ol' Sammy boy." On the line of scrimmage Van Brocklin called "one-twenty-one." Taking the snap Van Brocklin quickly faked to fullback Ted Dean through the hole over right guard, then turned and faked to Barnes over left guard, who was instantly met in the hole by Huff.[16] Meanwhile, Dean, who would have been Huff's man on a straight drop back pass, ran down the middle of the field. The Dutchman hit the wide-open Dean for a 49-yard touchdown pass to give Philly a 24–23 lead. The Eagles scored again to earn a 31–23 victory. The eight-win, one-loss Eagles now only needed one more win in their three remaining games to clinch the Eastern Conference title.

* * *

As the Eagle players silently gathered to exit the dressing room for the opening kick-off the following week against the Cardinals in St. Louis, Shaw told them, "Gentlemen, I assume you are all good businessmen. In the next hour, you can make $83.33 a minute."[17] Today's NFL Division champions would undoubtedly laugh at the amount, but it was big money in 1960. Shaw's words resonated with the players. Behind two Bobby Walston field goals and Van Brocklin's touchdown passes of 22 and 25 yards to Walston and Retzlaff, respectively, the Eagles prevailed 20–6. Afterwards, reporters asked Shaw if he delivered an emotional pregame speech to the squad. Shaw replied, "That stuff doesn't go anymore. Nowadays everything you say to kids has to make sense. They'll laugh in your face if you try anything else."[18]

Several other Eagles then shared Shaw's pregame talk with the media: "Men, this is the game to win. We can nail down the title by winning anyone of our next three games. But let's do it today. Then we'll have three weeks to get over injuries before the championship game, if any occur. Besides, it'll be easier on our nerves."[19]

As his victorious squad "hammed it up" and posed for post-game pictures, Shaw lauded the Eagles to newsmen, "I never saw a team with more desire and hustle. There's an old saying that a team that won't be beat can't be beat. This team is the best example of that of any team I've ever had any association with."[20]

Chuck Bednarik then praised the Eagles' head coach. "He's a great leader. He is tough when he has to be tough," said Bednarik. "Some coaches are just too tough on and off the field…. If you're complacent he'll get rid of you. If you do your best to your utmost ability he'll go along with you. If you get beat mentally, like fouling up on assignments, that's out of the picture with him but he understands there are times you'll get beat physically."[21]

Linebacker Bob Pellegrini was one Eagle who was feeling it physically that afternoon against the Cardinals. Seeing his first game action since being injured in Cleveland,

Pellegrini had not practiced much while recuperating. Having gained six pounds during his playing hiatus and not in the best of shape, the huffing and puffing Pellegrini felt like he was dying in the second quarter. Only the constant urging of teammate Jesse Richardson kept him going. Knowing a win over St. Louis would cinch the Eastern Division crown, the former University of Alabama tackle kept cajoling his winded teammate to continue by repeating, "It's money Pelli, beautiful money!"[22]

When the team's return flight landed in Philadelphia at 9:30 p.m. that evening, thousands of appreciative and enthusiastic fans greeted them. Years before the horrific events of 9/11, airport security was nearly non-existent. Jubilant fans amassed on the tarmac and in the terminal. This time there was no uncertainty as to the crowd's size—10,000 strong. It took the players and coaches 90 minutes to weave their way through boisterous celebrants to waiting rides in the airport's parking lot.

In the wake of the massive turnout, Buck confessed days later, "I was warned by friends when I took this job that Philadelphia had the worst fans in the league. I've found them to be wonderful, the most loyal and fair fans of any I've encountered."

He then elaborated, "The fans have been great. They didn't even give us the business when we looked bad three years ago. That's one of the reasons I wanted to come back and redeem ourselves. They deserve a winner. We're grateful for their wonderful support."[23]

* * *

Men in their early or mid-twenties regard people in their late 50s or early 60s as ancient. The young 1960 Eagle players were no different. One former Eagle told the author, "We thought Buck was old as dirt!" But to a man they revered Shaw, regarding him to be a true gentleman. Many of the Eagles chuckled at one of Shaw's idiosyncrasies. Buck perpetually kept his distinguished-looking gray hair impeccably groomed. The players felt the Silver Fox went to extremes to keep it that way, for whenever dark clouds loomed on the horizon, rather than risk getting his wavy hair wet, Buck inevitably either called off practice or moved it inside.

After clinching the Eastern Conference title Shaw shared one of his coaching beliefs with reporters: "One important thing is in trying to show each player by your actions that you have confidence in him. A player doesn't get better by a coach telling him how ineffective he is. Start making them believe they are champions and pretty soon they'll be playing like champions."[24]

Playing in two inches of snow and 27-degree weather the following Sunday, the Steelers ended the Eagles' winning streak at nine games with a 27–21 victory. Shaw gave his backups plenty of game action in the second half, with quarterback Sonny Jurgensen and halfback Timmy Brown playing well. The Eagles bounced back in the season's finale at Washington with a 38–28 win, for a final regular season record of 12 wins and two losses. Tommy McDonald and Timmy Brown each caught two touchdown passes for Philly. However, the Eagles didn't emerge from the Washington game unscathed. Linebacker Bob Pellegrini suffered torn knee ligaments that required surgery. The following Tuesday Buck Shaw informed the press that 35-year-old Chuck Bednarik would start at both left linebacker and center the following week in the championship game against Green Bay.

The day before the December 18 game at Washington, writer Harry Grayson, thought it was as good a time as any to ask the retiring Silver Fox who in his opinion was the best back and lineman he had ever seen. Without a moment's hesitation Shaw replied, "Nello Falaschi and Chuck Bednarik."

Shaw then elaborated on the former Santa Clara Bronco, who would be inducted into the College Football Hall of Fame in 1971: "Nello weighed 200 pounds, had good speed, was absolutely fearless, did everything well and was the most savage blocker I ever saw. Defensively, he was equally as fierce as a middle linebacker. As for an offensive center and linebacker, my vote has to go to Bednarik."[25]

Shaw later told the same reporter that the best football team he ever saw were the undefeated 1948 Cleveland Browns.

When later asked what advice he might give young aspiring coaches, Shaw replied, "You might want to get into high school coaching. There's some degree of security there. [In college] coaching success depends on winning games, regardless of what effect you have on players. It's unfair. It would be wonderful if the coach had the security of professors."[26]

In a prelude of what was to come, on December 22, a United Press International poll of 39 writers named Buck Shaw the NFL's Coach of the Year and Eagle quarterback Norm Van Brocklin the NFL's Player of the Year. Green Bay coach Vince Lombardi was runner-up to Shaw, while the Packers' Paul Hornung finished second to Van Brocklin.

When notified of his selection Shaw humbly replied, "It's very generous of a lot of people. After all, I had very little to do with our success. The people who made that possible were those on the field. Eighty percent of a coach's success depends on his horses. All they need is a little direction."[27]

Unfortunately, amid the honors and exciting anticipation, a tragedy befell the Eagle family.

On the same day Shaw and Van Brocklin won their awards, tackle Jesse Richardson, who after the Detroit game had predicted an Eagles championship, and his wife Dorothy lost their seven-week-old son, Jesse III, to pneumonia.

* * *

Since Sunday, December 25, was Christmas Day, the NFL scheduled the Championship game between the Eagles and the Western Conference Champion Green Bay Packers for Monday, December 26. Kickoff was scheduled for noon because Franklin Field had no lights. NBC would televise the contest. Tony Morabito, the late owner of the 49ers, must have been rolling over in his grave. The coach he had fired in 1954 had just taken the last place Eagles to championship heights in only three years, while his beloved 49ers wallowed in mediocrity.

To accommodate the overwhelming demand for tickets, Philadelphia's ticket manager arranged to have 7,000 temporary seats installed around the field's track to bring the afternoon's seating capacity to 67,000. By kick-off there wasn't a vacant seat in the house. Before the days of artificial turf, intermittent snow and rain earlier in the week left the field's footing treacherous. Although the sun shone brightly, the 28-degree temperature kept fans and players on the sidelines bundled against the chill throughout the game.

Disaster befell the Eagles on their first play from scrimmage when Green Bay's Bill Quinlan intercepted Van Brocklin's flare pass. Taking possession at the Eagle 22-yard line, the Packers drove to the five-yard line where they faced a fourth-and-two. Philly's determined defense snuffed Jim Taylor's rushing attempt for a first down and took possession. However, lightning struck twice a few plays later when Ted Dean fumbled and linebacker Bill Forester recovered for Green Bay again on the Eagle 22. Although not reaching paydirt, the Packers got on the scoreboard with Paul Hornung's 20-yard field

FRANKLIN FIELD PHILADELPHIA
PRIOR TO CHAMPIONSHIP GAME
December 1960

Eagle coach Buck Shaw diagrams a play shortly before the 1960 NFL championship game in Franklin Field's austere locker room on December 26, 1960 (courtesy Pam Hammer).

goal. Hornung added a 24-yard field goal in the second quarter to make Green Bay's lead 6–0.

On Philly's next possession, the "Dutchman" hit "Squeaky" McDonald for a 25-yard gain to Green Bay's 35. In the huddle before the next play, Van Brocklin told McDonald to run a corner route.

Running a great pattern, McDonald beat Packer Emlen Tunnell and hauled in Van Brocklin's pass for a 35-yard touchdown. With Sonny Jurgensen holding, Walston's extra-point gave the Eagles a 7–6 lead. Walston soon added a 15-yard field goal which upped the Eagles' lead to 10–6. On the last play of the half, Philly dodged a bullet when Paul Hornung missed a chip-shot nine-yard field goal attempt.

After a well-deserved 15-minute respite from the bitter cold and savage hitting, the Eagles launched a scoring threat in the third quarter. Sparked by Pete Retzlaff's tremendous over-the-shoulder catch of Van Brocklin's pass for a 43-yard gain, quickly followed by a 25-yard completion to Bobby Walston, the Eagles had the ball on the Packer five-yard line. From there Van Brockin rolled out and fired a pass into the end zone intended for McDonald. However, Johnny Symank saved the day for Green Bay with a crucial interception.

Behind a stellar defense, it looked like Philly would soon get the ball back when Max McGee dropped back to punt on fourth-and-ten with the ball on the Packer 20. Receiving the long snap, the wily McGee quickly assessed that there was no rush and sped off against a napping Eagle return team for a 35-yard gain that gave Green Bay a first down on Philly's 45-yard line. (McGee's fake punt duplicated one the Giants' Don Chandler executed against the Eagles weeks earlier at Yankee Stadium.)

The Packers continued to drive in the fourth quarter, cashing in on Bart Starr's seven-yard touchdown pass to McGee. Paul Hornung, who left the game after in the third quarter with a pinched nerve, returned to boot the extra-point giving Green Bay a short-lived 13–10 lead.

Eagle Ted Dean took Paul Hornung's following kickoff on the three-yard line and set off on a newly devised kick return Buck Shaw had implemented that week. Running through an alley his teammates formed to his left, Dean followed fellow deep back Timmy Brown and kept running until Willy Wood knocked him out of bounds at the Packer 39-yard line. Seven plays later Dean took Van Brocklin's pitch and, behind pulling guard Jerry Huth's block, scampered five yards around left end for the go-ahead touchdown. Walston's extra point gave the Eagles a 17–13 lead with 9:40 remaining in the contest.

Now would it be Green Bay's turn? Johnny Symank returned Ted Dean's kickoff to the Packer 30. With a first-and-ten from their own 40-yard line, Starr connected on a pass to McGee. Hit hard, the Tulane graduate fumbled and Bednarik, playing both ways, recovered on Philly's 48-yard line. After the Packers stymied Billy Ray Barnes' run on a third-and-one, Van Brocklin punted and Green Bay took possession at their own 12-yard line. An exchange of punts led to Green Bay taking possession on their own 35. Under head coach Vince Lombardi, the Packers were a hungry team on the verge of becoming a dynasty. They demonstrated signs of it on the game's last drive.

With 1:05 remaining Starr passed five yards to Jim Taylor to the Packer 40.

With 55 seconds remaining Starr passed four yards to Tom Moore to the Packer 44. Time out Green Bay.

On third-and-one with 45 seconds remaining Taylor carried to the Eagle 47.

With 40 seconds left Starr passed to Gary Knafelc (pronounced Kuh-naf-el) at the Eagle 30.

Time out Green Bay.

With 30 seconds remaining Starr threw incomplete to Boyd Dowler in the end zone.

With 25 seconds remaining Starr passed to Knafelc at the Eagle 22.

With 10 seconds remaining Starr hit a wide-open Taylor at the 17. He ran to the nine-yard line where the oldest man on the field, 35-year-old "Concrete Charlie" Bednarik, met him head-on and took him to the ground. Bednarik held Taylor down until the last second ticked off the clock. He then informed the Packer fullback, "You can get up now. This @#% game is over!"[28]

The victorious Eagle players jumped for joy as Pete Retzlaff and Bobby Walston hoisted Buck Shaw onto their shoulders and carried him off the field, a well-deserved ending to his 39-year coaching career.

* * *

The champions' post-game dressing room was fraught with testosterone. Laughing players hugged, messed each other's hair, smoked stogies and posed for a multitude of pictures. Each delighted in the thought that he'd be receiving an extra $5,116 for winning the championship, $2,000 more than the runner-up Packers. As the revelers joked and regaled reporters with anecdotes, a humbled and deeply emotional Buck Shaw worked his way around lockers congratulating and shaking hands with each player. He gave a special hug and handshake to co-captain Chuck Bednarik, who at age 35 played 58 minutes of the 60-minute contest. When asked if he was still going to retire the Silver Fox replied, "I'm going back to my business. I don't want any more head coaching. I've said all along I was going to retire. I wanted the championship though, and the boys gave it to me."[29]

After learning that he had been voted Most Valuable Player of the Game, retiring Eagles' trigger man Norm Van Brocklin consistently repeated to anyone who would listen, "What a way to go out! I can't think of a better way. Man, there just isn't any better way. This is the climax."[30]

Holding court with reporters, Shaw asserted that the Eagles' ability to hold the Packers in key situations was why Philadelphia won. Over in Green Bay's locker room Vince Lombardi agreed with Shaw's assessment. Regarding the Packers' inability to punch a touchdown across on their first three penetrations, Lombardi said, "I guess you could say there went the ball game. Instead of leading by two touchdowns we were ahead only 6 to 0 and then Van Brocklin came through."[31]

Lombardi then graciously added, "I'm happy for Buck Shaw. If he's going to retire that's a nice way to go out—on top."[32]

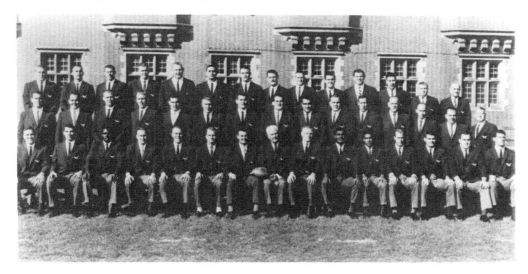

PHILADELPHIA EAGLES
1960 National Football League Champions

Front Row: (L-R): Bobby Freeman, DB; Gene Johnson, DB; Ted Dean, FB; Billy Barnes, HB; Theron Sapp, FB; Bobby Jackson, DB; Norm Van Brocklin, QB; Buck Shaw, Head Coach; Sonny Jurgensen, QB; Clarence Peaks, FB; Timmy Brown, HB; Pete Retzlaff, E; Bobby Walston, E; Gerry Huth, G; Jerry Reichow, QB-E.

Middle Row: Chuck Weber, LB; Jimmy Carr, DB; Howard Keys, T; Riley Gunnels, DT; Jim McCusker, T; Stan Campbell, G; Marion Campbell, DE; Jesse Richardson, DT; Bob Pellegrini, LB; Bill Lapham, C; Gene Gossage, DE; Charlie Gauer, Asst. Coach; Jerry Williams, Asst. Coach; Nick Skorich, Asst. Coach; Ed Hogan, Pub. Dir.

Back Row: Maxie Baughan, LB; John Wittenborn, G; Dick Lucas, E; John Wilcox, DT; J. D. Smith, T; Ed Khayat, DT; Joe Robb, DE; Don Burroughs, DB; Tommy McDonald, FL; Tom Brookshier, DB; Chuck Bednarik, LB-C; John Nocera, LB; Tom McCoy, Trainer; Fred Schubach, Equip. Mgr.

The 1960 World Champion Philadelphia Eagles (courtesy Sue Healey).

TWENTY-ONE

Life After Football

Buck's last official task as Eagles head coach was to attend the NFL player draft held in Philadelphia on December 27–28. While there, reporters repeatedly asked if the 61-year-old might change his mind and return to mentor the Eagles again in 1961. His answer never wavered: "I have a reasonable degree of good health and would like to keep it as long as I can." Buck then added, "I can't soar any higher than being head coach of a world championship professional football team."[1]

Shaw flew home to San Francisco on December 30, where the once-fired 49er coach received a civic reception at the airport before being ushered off to a City Hall ceremony where San Francisco Mayor George Christopher presented Buck with a pair of cuff links with the city's official seal. Reporters again subjected him to a myriad of questions, including if he'd be interested in taking a front office position with the American Football League's Oakland Raiders. Shaw replied, "I would not be interested in a post as advisory coach to the Oakland Raiders or a job as general manager. It requires too much time."[2]

Although officially retired from pro football, Buck still had another obligation to fulfill. In mid–December the NFL had asked him to coach the East All-Stars in 11th annual Pro Bowl to be played in Los Angeles' Coliseum on January 15, 1961. Buck felt compelled to oblige. The game again pitted Shaw against Green Bay coach Vince Lombardi, only this time on a balmy 85-degree afternoon instead of 28-degree Franklin Field. Before 62,000 shirt-sleeved fans, Norm Van Brocklin threw three touchdown passes—two to Eagle teammates Tommy McDonald and Pete Retzlaff—but it wasn't enough as Johnny Unitas led the West to a 35–31 win. (The fiery Van Brocklin had the East en route to another score as the final gun sounded.) Shaw and his Eagle players would undoubtedly have enjoyed winning the All-Star contest, but they had already won the game they wanted most on December 26, in Philadelphia: the NFL Championship.

* * *

Although quarterbacking Philadelphia to a league championship in his last game for the Eagles, Norm Van Brocklin didn't leave the organization with a warm, fuzzy feeling. For weeks speculation ran rampant that the "Dutchman" would succeed Buck Shaw as Eagles head coach. However, meetings with team president Frank McNamee in the first week of 1961 did not go well. Despite Van Brocklin repeatedly stating his intention to retire as an active player, McNamee attempted to talk him out of it. When that failed, McNamee posed the possibility of the Dutchman returning as a player-coach. Van Brocklin's supposed response was that player-coaches went out with Johnny Blood. (Johnny Blood was the alias for one John McNally. McNally played under the pseudonym to protect his amateur status should Notre Dame grant him reentry after his expulsion. An NFL star in the '30s, Blood was admitted as a charter member to the Pro Football Hall of Fame in 1963.) In any case, McNamee neither offered Van Brocklin a salary boost to remain an active player, nor told him what his actual coaching position might be if he returned as player-coach. Talks ended on January 5, without McNamee offering the Dutchman the Eagles' head job.

Afterwards Van Brocklin told reporters that in 1958 the late Bert Bell, former NFL commissioner, told him that if he approved his trade from Los Angeles to the Eagles, he would become the next Eagle coach when Buck Shaw retired. Bell, who had been the owner and head coach of the Eagles from 1933 to 1940, before becoming part owner of the Pittsburgh Steelers from 1941 through 1946, had to give up his interest in the Steelers to become commissioner. While Eagles general manager Vince McNally claimed at the time they couldn't promise Van Brocklin anything, the quarterback believed it to be a strong possibility due to Bell's history with Philadelphia and the influence he wielded as commissioner. However, with Bell's death in 1959, Eagle management felt no obligation to keep the late commissioner's word. The chagrined Van Brocklin told reporters that despite Bell's role in the trade, the Eagles "never intended to name him to succeed Buck Shaw."[3]

Van Brocklin wouldn't be out of football long. Two weeks later, on January 18, 1961, the Dutchman signed a three-year contract to be the first head coach of the expansion Minnesota Vikings, who would begin NFL play that fall. Van Brocklin coached the Vikings through 1966. In 1968, he became the first head coach of the expansion Atlanta Falcons, a post he held for seven seasons. During his 13 years as a head pro coach Van Brocklin compiled an overall record of 66 wins, 100 losses and seven ties.

On January 23, 1961, the Eagles named 39-year-old assistant Nick Skorich to succeed Shaw as head coach. In three seasons at Philly's helm Skorich won 15, lost 24 and tied three before being fired after the 1963 season. However, Skorich later experienced greater success as head coach of the Cleveland Browns where he served from 1971 through 1974. His overall NFL head coaching record was 45 wins, 48 losses and five ties. After his stint with Cleveland, Skorich became the head of NFL officials.

* * *

When not tending to his box business, Shaw received numerous awards and honors in his post-coaching years. Just weeks after leading the Eagles to the NFL Championship, Shaw was voted into the Helms Football Hall of Fame. In February of 1961, the Phoenix Press Box Association named Buck Shaw the "Sports Personality of 1960." Shaw received the award at a dinner before more than 1,000 Arizonans.

Traveling to the Big Sky country of Bozeman, Montana, two months later, Shaw served as guest speaker at a sports banquet emceed by his former Air Force Academy boss, Col. Robert V. Whitlow, who was stationed at Malmstrom Air Force Base near Great Falls, Montana. After retiring from the Air Force in 1963, Whitlow served as the first and last so-called "athletic director" of Major League Baseball's Chicago Cubs. To better get to know the players, Whitlow shagged outfield fly balls at team practices. He also implemented new physical conditioning techniques and introduced more nutritious diets for players. In his two years in that role, Whitlow ended the Cubs' unorthodox practice of rotating coaches to serve as field bosses in favor of a designated manager. Upon leaving the Cubs he retired to Arizona and became heavily involved in a futile attempt to bring an American Football League franchise to the Grand Canyon State in the mid–'60s.

In April 1962, the Rev. Patrick A. Donohue, president of Santa Clara University, announced construction plans for an 8,000 seat multi-purpose stadium on campus. The facility would be named Buck Shaw Stadium. The Bronco Bench Foundation, a booster group, financed the $125,000 project. That same year Santa Clara University inducted Shaw into the school's Hall of Fame.

In July 1965, Buck attended a luncheon paying tribute to members of the original 49ers, the first team ever to represent San Francisco in major league sports. Twenty years earlier they had convened at Menlo Park to prepare to do battle in the All-America Conference. Attendees included Kenny Casanega, Norm Standlee, Johnny Strzykalski, Frankie Albert, Bob Titchenal, Bruno Banducci, Visco Grgich, Eddie Forrest, Alyn Beals and Al Ruffo. During his turn at the podium, former 49er quarterback and coach Frankie Albert turned to Shaw and said, "After him, the mold was broken. But he had to leave us to win a championship. I wish that I had coached like him. I got bad advice. That fellow [name not mentioned] isn't here either."[4]

In 1966, Shaw briefly tested football's waters again when he agreed to scout for his former Eagle general manager Vince McNally. By then McNally headed the Central Personnel Organization (CEPO), which scouted college talent for six NFL teams. Shaw's task included scouting in six Southwestern states.

Reporters often sought Buck out for his opinion regarding changes affecting football. In 1967, the *Des Moines Register* interviewed him regarding the influence of television on the sport. "It seems to me the television tail is beginning to wag the dog," warned Shaw. "Pretty soon TV officials will be drawing up sports schedules the way things are going."

> Don't get me wrong. A lot of good has come from television. It was TV money that saved professional football when payrolls got so high that gate receipts alone couldn't match them.
>
> But anymore the TV people swarm around an event like ants. They're right next to you on the sidelines when angry things are said that shouldn't be heard, and they even take their cameras into the dressing room occasionally.
>
> They grab a coach right after a game (today, on his way to the locker room at halftime) for an interview before he's had a chance to cool off and collect his thoughts—something he wouldn't do except for the power of TV to make him.[5]

Shaw believed that television should be on hand to report what transpires but not run the show. He recognized, however, with all the money involved it was becoming more difficult to keep things balanced. Witnessing today's sideline reporters interviewing quarterbacks during the game, the choreographed end zone celebrations, and players kneeling during the national anthem show the Silver Fox was prescient on the matter.

In 1970, Shaw joined his former Notre Dame teammate Eddie Anderson as an inductee into the *Des Moines Register*'s Iowa Athletic Hall of Fame. Perhaps Buck's most prestigious honor came in December 1972, when the National Football Foundation's Hall of Fame inducted Buck for his coaching accomplishments.

As a prelude to the induction ceremony in New York, the University of Santa Clara Alumni Association and friends sponsored a testimonial dinner for Shaw at San Francisco's Fairmont Hotel on November 11. As the event's emcee, former 49er pass-catching great Gordie Soltau ran the evening's scheduled agenda with the same precision with which he ran his pass patterns in the '50s. The guest speaker was Paul Laxalt, former Nevada governor and Santa Clara alumnus. Shaw took a good roasting from former

In 1970, Buck Shaw reunited with former Wolf Pack associates at the Nevada governor's mansion. Left to right: Raymond "Corky" Courtright, who gave Shaw his first coaching job in 1922, Shaw, and Jake Lawlor, a stalwart player on Shaw's Nevada teams, who later became Nevada's long-time athletic director (courtesy University of Nevada Reno Special Collections and Archives).

players and friends that night. However, among the good-humored barbs directed at the Silver Fox, the words "gentleman" and "class" echoed throughout the evening as speakers described Shaw.

In his retirement years Buck and his lovely wife Marge aged gracefully and became quite the partygoers. At one social function Hugh "the King" McElhenny, upon learning the Shaws had recently celebrated their 50th wedding anniversary, declared, "Isn't that something. I only hope I look as good when I'm Buck's age."[6]

Buck also became a highly-sought-after public speaker at dinners and luncheons. During his talks he spoke mostly about others, rarely about himself. He often raved about the Santa Clara teams that won the 1937 and '38 Sugar Bowls. "If it hadn't [have] been for those Santa Clara teams, I'd never have coached the Philadelphia Eagles."[7]

About his old coach, the legendary Knute Rockne, Shaw said, "Rock had every kid playing above his capabilities all the time. He knew how to get the best out of them. Fight talks? He used to give 'em to car salesmen and have those guys up on their chairs hollering."[8]

Commenting on his own career the Silver Fox told an audience, "I thought that when I entered pro ball the pressure would be less because of no alumni, but I found the pro fans more rabid than college alumni."[9]

The Santa Clara Alumni Association and friends honored Buck's induction into the National College Football Hall of Fame with a celebratory dinner in November 1972. Buck gave a dinner publicity photograph to his grand nephew with the inscription, "To Jim, With all best wishes for greatness in your future athletic endeavors. And don't forget the schooling. All the best from your ancient granduncle, 'Buck' Shaw" (courtesy Pam Hammer).

San Francisco Examiner sports columnist Well Twombly once wrote, "old football coaches never die, they just change jobs until nobody wants them anymore."[10] Had Buck Shaw lived to have read those words, he probably would have agreed. Shaw never encouraged young men to go into coaching. But for those who refused to heed his words he offered this advice: "You're a teacher without tenure. The history teacher doesn't have to send his class out before 64,000 people on Saturday to compete against classes from other schools, classes which may have much better material than he has. But you send your class out and your status keeps changing, according to what happens to it out there."[11]

In October of 1976, during a routine physical, Buck was diagnosed with cancer that had spread into his lungs and other parts of his body. As it continued gnawing at his body, the Silver Fox suffered a harsher blow when the same dreaded disease took the life of his 50-year-old daughter, Patricia, in February of 1977. In early March, Buck was admitted to University Branch Convalescent Hospital. With his death imminent, members of his 1937 Sugar Bowl team visited him in his hospital room just days before he passed. According to a hospital administrator, a smiling and alert Shaw visited with each and called each by name. "It was pretty hard to take," the administrator said later, "watching all these big men crying."[12]

Lawrence Timothy 'Buck' Shaw" died on March 19, 1977. He was survived by Marge, his wife of 55 years; his daughter, Joan; six grandchildren; and one great grandchild. On March 23, St. Raymond's Church in Menlo Park conducted a requiem mass for Shaw, a devout Catholic all his life, which was followed by a private burial.

Buck was honored posthumously in February 1985 when his former assistant coach at Santa Clara, Len Casanova, inducted Shaw into the San Francisco Bay Area Hall of Fame. Then 49er head football coach Bill Walsh accepted the Buck Shaw Award for Shaw's family.

* * *

Marion Campbell was a defensive end who played his 1954 rookie season for Buck Shaw in San Francisco. He later played three seasons for Buck during his coaching tenure in Philadelphia. Upon hearing of Shaw's passing he recalled, "He never asked or demanded respect from any of us, he just got it."[13]

Jim Murray was general manager of the Philadelphia Eagles when Buck Shaw died in 1977. When learning of Shaw's death he professed, "I didn't know him, but it feels like I did. For as long as I've been with the team, the single most-referred-to thing is our history in 1960 … the championship that Buck Shaw won. From what everyone tells me, championship is synonymous with Buck Shaw. He must have touched a lot of people."[14]

Hopefully, Buck Shaw's story has touched the reader as well.

Appendix

Shaw's Career Head Coaching Record

164 Wins, 105 Losses, 17 Ties

North Carolina State, 1924 (Won 2, Lost 6, Tied 2)

	Win	Lost	Tied
1924	2	6	2

University of Nevada, 1925–28 (Won 10, Lost 20, Tied 3)

	Won	Lost	Tied
1925	4	3	1
1926	4	4	0
1927	2	6	1
1928	0	7	1

Santa Clara University, 1936–42 (Won 47, Lost 10, Tied 4)

	Won	Lost	Tied	
1936	8	1	0	(Sugar Bowl Winners)
1937	9	0	0	(Sugar Bowl Winners)
1938	6	2	0	
1939	5	1	3	
1940	6	1	1	
1941	6	3	0	
1942	7	2	0	

University of California, 1945 (Won 4, Lost 5, Tied 1)

	Won	Lost	Tied
1945	4	5	1

San Francisco 49ers, 1946–54 (Won 72, Lost 40, Tied 4)

AAFC	Won	Lost	Tied
1946	9	5	0
1947	8	4	2
1948	12	2	0
1949	10	4	0
NFL			
1950	3	9	0
1951	7	4	1
1952	7	5	0
1953	9	3	0
1954	7	4	1

Air Force Academy, 1956–57 (Won 9, Lost 8, Tied 2)

	Won	Lost	Tied
1956	6	2	1
1957	3	6	1

Philadelphia Eagles, 1958–60 (Won 20, Lost 16, Tied 1)

	Won	Lost	Tied	
1958	2	9	1	
1959	7	5	0	
1960	11	2	0	(NFL Champions)

Chapter Notes

AP: Associated Press
NSJ: Nevada State Journal
OT :Oakland Tribune
PDN: Philadelphia Daily News
PI: Philadelphia Inquirer
RGJ: Reno Gazette Journal
SFE: San Francisco Examiner
SH: Stuart (Iowa) Herald
UP: United Press International

Chapter One

1. *Stuart* (Iowa) *Herald* (*SH*), Mar. 24, 1977.
2. *Ibid.*
3. *SH*, Nov. 30, 1917.
4. *Des Moines Register*, Jan. 1, 1937.
5. *Philadelphia Daily News* (*PDN*), Dec. 22, 1960.
6. For a detailed account of the 1918 influenza outbreak see John M. Barry, *The Great Influenza* (2004).
7. *Omaha Daily Bee*, Nov. 10, 1948.
8. Anthony J. Kuzniewski, S.J., *They Honored Name: A History of the College of the Holy Cross, 1843–1994* (1996), 239.
9. *SH*, Apr. 19, 1918.
10. *SH*, Nov. 14, 1918.
11. *Omaha Daily Bee*, Nov. 17, 1917.
12. *Omaha Daily Bee*, Nov. 29, 1917.
13. *SH*, May 2, 1919.

Chapter Two

1. *PDN*, Dec. 22, 1960.
2. Frank Maggio, *Notre Dame and the Game That Changed Football* (2007), 206.
3. *Chicago Tribune*, Oct. 26, 1965.
4. *SH*, Jan. 4, 1935.
5. *Notre Dame Scholastic*, Dec. 16, 1919.
6. Mark Maxwell, *From Notre Dame to Georgia, Harry Mehr, The Legend* (2017), 195.
7. Kevin Carroll, *Dr. Eddie Anderson: Hall of Fame College Football Coach* (2007), 25.
8. *San Francisco Examiner (SFE)*, Apr. 5, 1931. *(Rockne may have gotten his years mixed-up, for Gipp's greatest single game performance came in its 27–17 win over Army in 1920.)
9. Ray Robinson, *Rockne of Notre Dame* (1999), 72.
10. Carroll, *Dr. Eddie Anderson*, 26.

11. *Ibid.*
12. Murray Sperber, *Shake Down the Thunder: The Creation of Notre Dame Football* (1993), 108.
13. *SH*, Oct. 22, 1920.
14. *Ibid.*
15. Carroll, *Dr. Eddie Anderson*, 27–28.
16. Jim Beach and Daniel Moore, *The Big Game* (1948), 52.
17. Robinson, *Rockne of Notre Dame*, 84.
18. Carroll, *Dr. Eddie Anderson*, 29.
19. Robinson, *Rockne of Notre Dame*, 87.
20. *Ibid.*, 88
21. Carroll, *Dr. Eddie Anderson*, 36.
22. *South Bend* (IN) *Tribune*, Oct. 27, 1921.
23. Carroll, *Dr. Eddie Anderson*, 43
24. Robinson, *Rockne of Notre Dame*, 108.
25. Rockne's relationship with Joe Byrne, Jr., is also detailed on 137–139 of Robinson's *Rockne of Notre Dame* and 203–205 of Sperber's *Shake Down the Thunder*.
26. *SH*, Dec. 16, 1921.
27. Robert Cook interview, Stuart Town Historian, Dec. 15, 2019. **(Coxswain Daignon was one of eight sailors who volunteered for a virtual suicide mission to detonate the *Merrimac* in the channel of Santiago Bay. The mission's aim was to block the channel so the Spanish fleet couldn't exit the bay. However, the ship drifted as it sank and the channel remained clear. Spanish sailors plucked the eight-man crew from the water and held them captive until July 5, 1898, when they were released. When Americans learned of the incident, all eight crewmen became national heroes.)

Chapter Three

1. Carroll, *Dr. Eddie Anderson*, 47–48.
2. *Ibid.*, 48.
3. Johanna Tinnea, "The Game That Never Was," *Taylorville Breeze Courier* (Sesquicentennial Issue), June 18, 1989.
4. *Ibid.*
5. *Ibid.*
6. Carroll, *Dr. Eddie Anderson*, 50.
7. *Ibid.*
8. Associated Press (AP), Jan. 29, 1922.
9. Carroll, *Dr. Eddie Anderson*, 50.
10. AP, Nov. 7, 1958

11. AP, May 14, 1972.

12. Jim Anderson interview (Jim Anderson was the son of Dr. Eddie Anderson), Mar. 20, 2000.

13. Carroll, *Dr. Eddie Anderson*, 51.

14. Scott Hoover, *Touchdown Taylorville!* (1967), copyrighted but unpublished manuscript appearing in Sesquicentennial Issue of *Taylorville Breeze Courier,* June 18, 1989.

15. *New York Times,* Jan. 28, 1922.

16. AP, Jan. 31, 1922.

17. *Ibid.*

18. AP, May 14, 1972.

19. *Des Moines Register,* Mar. 22, 1922.

20. *PDN,* Dec. 22, 1960.

21. Dave Newhouse, *The Incredible Slip Madigan* (2018), 52.

22. *Reno Gazette Journal (RGJ),* Nov. 13, 1922.

23. Gregory Couch, *The Bonanza King* (2018), 336.

24. *RGJ,* Feb. 15, 1923.

25. *Ibid.*

26. *NSJ,* Oct. 10, 1923.

27. *SFE,* Dec. 14, 1934.

28. *NSJ,* Oct. 6, 1923.

29. *RGJ,* Nov. 3, 1923.

30. *RGJ,* Nov. 5, 1923.

31. *NSJ,* Nov. 6, 1923.

32. *Ibid.*

33. *RGJ,* Nov. 5, 1923.

34. *NSJ,* Nov. 6, 1923.

35. *RGJ,* Oct. 26, 1938.

Chapter Four

1. Allison Danzig, *The History of American Football* (1956), 62–63.

2. *Ashville* (NC) *Citizen Times,* Oct. 14, 1924.

3. *North Carolina State University Alumni News,* November 1924.

4. *RGJ,* Oct. 26, 1925.

5. *RGJ,* Nov. 17, 1925.

6. *RGJ,* Oct. 13, 1926.

7. *Los Angeles Times,* Sept. 13, 1957.

8. *RGJ,* Oct. 22, 1926.

9. Dave Newhouse, *The Incredible Slip Madigan,* xviii.

10. *SFE,* Oct. 21, 1926.

11. *SFE,* Nov. 14, 1926.

12. Glenn "Jake" Lawlor, *Oral Autobiography of an Iowa Native with a Close-Up View of Nevada Athletics, 1926–1971* (1971).

13. *RGJ,* Jan. 24, 1928.

14. *Ibid.*

15. AP, Oct. 27, 1928.

16. *RGJ,* Nov. 19, 1928.

17. *Ibid.*

18. *RGJ,* Oct. 26, 1938.

19. *SFE,* Aug. 15. 1936.

Chapter Five

1. *SFE,* Feb. 16, 1929.

2. *Oakland Tribune (OT),* Sept. 15, 1929.

3. *SFE,* Sept. 5, 1929.

4. *SFE,* Oct. 10, 1929.

5. *SFE,* Sept. 22, 1929.

6. *SFE,* Sept. 18, 1929.

7. *SFE,* Apr. 25, 1931.

8. Mvictors.com, Michigan Football, George Philbrook.

9. *SFE,* Nov. 3, 1930.

10. *Ibid.*

11. *Chicago Tribune,* Apr. 1, 1931.

12. AP, Apr. 1, 1931.

13. *Ibid.*

14. *SFE,* Apr. 1, 1931.

15. *Ibid.*

16. JoAnn Wilcox interview (Hunk Anderson's daughter), June 29, 2006. *(Jack Chevigny would be killed in action serving as a Marine officer on the first day of the Battle of Iwo Jima, Feb. 19, 1945.)

17. *Pittsburgh Post,* Nov. 27, 1926.

18. *Pittsburgh Daily Press,* Nov. 29, 1926.

19. *SFE,* Feb. 20, 1931.

20. *SFE,* Apr. 1, 1931.

21. *Ibid.*

22. *SFE,* Sept. 27, 1931.

23. *SFE,* Oct. 30, 1931.

24. *SFE,* Nov. 2, 1931.

25. *SFE,* Sept. 25, 1932.

26. *SFE,* Oct. 27, 1932.

27. Dave Newhouse, *The Incredible Slip Madigan,* 79.

28. *SFE,* Oct. 28, 1932.

29. *SFE,* Oct. 31, 1932.

30. *Ibid.*

31. *OT,* Sept. 25, 1933.

32. *SFE,* Oct. 8, 1933.

33. *Ibid.*

34. *OT,* Nov. 20, 1933.

35. *OT,* Nov. 24, 1933.

36. *Ibid.*

37. *SFE,* Dec. 5, 1933.

38. *Ibid.*

39. *Honolulu Star Bulletin,* Jan. 3, 1934.

40. *SFE,* July 26, 1934.

41. *OT,* Nov. 5, 1934.

42. *OT,* Sept. 19, 1934.

Chapter Six

1. *PDN,* Dec. 22, 1960.

2. *SFE,* June 24, 1936.

3. *OT,* June 21, 1936.

4. *SFE,* Aug. 15, 1936.

5. *SFE,* Aug. 23, 1936

6. *Napa* (CA) *Journal,* Sept. 16, 1936.

7. *SFE,* Sept. 15, 1936.

8. *SFE,* Sept. 25, 1936.

9. *OT,* Sept. 27, 1936.

10. *SFE,* Sept. 27, 1936.

11. *SFE,* Oct. 5, 1936.

12. *The Birmingham News,* Nov. 1, 1936.

13. *SFE,* Nov. 1, 1936.

14. *SFE,* Nov. 16, 1936.

15. *Ibid.*
16. *Ibid.*
17. *Ibid.*
18. *Ibid.*
19. *Ibid.*
20. *Ibid.*
21. Newhouse, *The Incredible Slip Madigan*, 138.
22. *SFE*, Nov. 22, 1936.
23. *Los Angeles Times*, Nov. 23, 1936.
24. *SFE*, Dec. 12, 1936.
25. *OT*, Dec. 9, 1936.
26. *SFE*, Dec. 12, 1936.
27. *SFE*, Dec. 13, 1936.

Chapter Seven

1. *OT*, Dec. 14, 1936.
2. *Selma* (AL) *Times*, Dec. 18, 1936.
3. *Shreveport Journal*, Dec. 13, 1936.
4. *Shreveport Journal*, Dec. 16, 1936.
5. United Press International (UP), Dec. 25, 1936.
6. *Ibid.*
7. AP, Jan. 1, 1937.
8. *OT*, Jan. 2, 1937.
9. Chuck Hillebrand, "Sweetness," *Santa Clara Magazine*, Dec. 18, 2012.
10. *The Tennessean* (Nashville), Jan. 3, 1937.
11. *OT*, Jan. 2, 1937
12. *Ibid.*
13. *Shreveport Journal*, Jan. 2, 1937.
14. International News Service (INS), Jan. 8, 1937.
15. *SFE*, Feb. 3, 1937.
16. *The Lincoln* (NE) *Star*, Feb. 10, 1937.
17. *SFE*, Oct. 31, 1937.
18. *OT*, Nov. 3, 1937.
19. *OT*, Nov. 9, 1937.
20. *SFE*, Nov. 11, 1937.
21. *OT*, Nov. 14, 1937.
22. *SFE*, Nov. 29, 1937.
23. *Ibid.*
24. *SFE*, Dec. 1, 1937.
25. AP, Dec. 1. 1937
26. AP, Jan. 2, 1938. *Naval LTJG Young Bussey was killed while serving in the Philippines in January 1945.
27. *Ibid.*
28. *SFE*, Jan. 4, 1938.

Chapter Eight

1. *SFE*, Jan. 26, 1938.
2. Chuck Hillebrand, "Sweetness."
3. *SFE*, Nov. 9, 1938.
4. *SFE*, Oct. 5, 1938.
5. SFE, Oct. 23, 1938.
6. *SFE*, Oct. 22, 1938.
7. *OT*, Nov. 3, 1938.
8. *SFE*, Nov. 6, 1938.
9. *SFE*, Nov. 7, 1938.
10. *Ibid.*

11. *SFE*, Nov. 10, 1938.
12. *Ibid.*
13. *SFE*, Nov. 14, 1938.
14. *Ibid.*
15. *OT*, Nov. 14, 1938
16. *Ibid.*
17. *Ibid.*
18. *Ibid.*
19. *SFE*, Nov. 16, 1938.
20. Joe Neis with Gus Dorais, *Gus Dorais* (2018), 188.
21. *OT*, Nov. 22, 1938.
22. *OT*, Nov. 28, 1938.
23. *Ibid.*
24. *Ibid.*
25. *Sacramento Bee*, Nov. 28, 1938.

Chapter Nine

1. UP, Sept. 28, 1939.
2. *OT*, Oct. 16, 1939.
3. *SFE*, Oct. 20, 1939.
4. *SFE*, Oct. 23, 1939.
5. *Ibid.*
6. *OT*, Oct. 23, 1939.
7. *SFE*, Oct. 23, 1939.
8. *SFE*, Oct. 29, 1939.
9. *SFE*, Nov. 5, 1939.
10. *Ibid.*
11. *Los Angeles Times*, Nov. 19, 1939.
12. *Ibid.*
13. *SFE*, Jan. 8, 1940.
14. Carroll, *Dr. Eddie Anderson*, 176.
15. *Gallup Independent*, Oct. 9, 1940.
16. *Cedar Rapids* (IA) *Gazette*, Aug. 16, 1940.
17. *Chicago Tribune*, Aug. 30, 1940.
18. Al Moss, *Pac 10 Football* (1987), 75.
19. *SFE*, Oct. 13, 1940.
20. *Ibid.*
21. *Montana Standard* (Butte), Nov. 4, 1940.
22. *NEA Sports Services*, Nov. 5, 1940.
23. Newhouse, *The Incredible Slip Madigan*, xvi.
24. *SFE*, Nov. 12, 1940.
25. *SFE*, Nov. 25, 1940.
26. *SFE*, Nov. 23, 1940.
27. *SFE*. Nov. 25, 1940
28. *Des Moines Register*, Dec. 18, 1940
29. *SFE*, Dec. 1, 1940.

Chapter Ten

1. *SFE*, Mar. 30, 1977.
2. AP, Feb. 11, 1941.
3. AP, Feb. 13, 1941.
4. *SFE*, Feb. 24, 1955.
5. *SFE*, Sept. 29, 1941.
6. *SFE*, Oct. 12, 1941.
7. *OT*, Oct. 12, 1941.
8. *SFE*, Oct. 12, 1941.
9. *SFE*, Oct. 19, 1941.
10. *Sooner Spectator Magazine*, Feb. 23, 2006.
11. *Daily Oklahoman*, Oct. 26, 1941.

12. *SFE*, Aug. 22, 1942.
13. *SFE*, Oct. 2, 1942.
14. *SFE*, Sept. 26, 1942.
15. *Salt Lake Telegram*, Sept. 2, 1942.
16. Jonathan Gold, "NFL Trailblazer Tom Fears Came Full Circle with Return to Mexican Hometown," ESPN.com, Nov. 19, 2018, https://www.espn./com/nfl/story_/1d/25288408/tom-fears.
17. *SFE*, Sept. 28, 1942.
18. *SFE*, Oct. 4, 1942.
19. *SFE*, Oct. 11, 1942.
20. *Los Angeles Times*, Oct. 25, 1942.
21. David Eskenazi, "James Marlin Phelan," Wayback Machine (column), SportsPressNW.com, Oct. 30, 2012.
22. *SFE*, Nov. 15, 1942.
23. *SFE*, Mar. 18, 1943.
24. *OT*, May 23, 1943.
25. *SFE*, July 7, 1944.
26. *Lincoln* (NE) *Star*, July 17, 1944.

Chapter Eleven

1. *Los Angeles Times*, Feb. 8, 1945.
2. AP, Apr. 14, 1945.
3. *Ibid.*
4. *OT*, Mar. 6, 1945.
5. *Los Angeles Times*, Oct. 19, 1945.
6. *OT*, Aug. 22, 1945.
7. *OT*, Sept. 13, 1945.
8. *OT*, Oct. 10, 1945.
9. *Los Angeles Times*, Oct. 14, 1945.
10. *SFE*, Oct. 15, 1945.
11. *SFE*, Oct. 17, 1945.
12. *OT*, Nov. 4, 1945.
13. *SFE*, Nov. 16, 1945.
14. *OT*, Nov. 18, 1945.
15. *SFE*, Nov. 30, 1945.
16. *SFE*, Dec. 4, 1945.
17. www.sfgate.com/sports/article/funeral service, Apr. 29, 2003.

Chapter Twelve

1. *SFE*, Dec. 25, 1945.
2. *SFE*, Jan. 29, 1946.
3. *SFE*, Nov. 24, 1946.
4. *San Jose Mercury News*, Nov. 24, 1996.
5. Al Ruffo Oral History interview, uploaded to YouTube Oct. 1, 1992, updated by History of San Jose, 24 October 2016, https://youtube.com/watch?v=d_H8WdOHjY.
6. Barbara Titchenal interview, May 17, 2009.
7. *Ibid.*
8. *SFE*, Aug. 28, 1946.
9. *SFE*, Jan. 3, 1982.
10. *SFE*, Aug. 27, 1946.
11. *San Jose Mercury News*, Nov. 24, 1996.
12. *Chicago Tribune*, Sept. 26, 1946.
13. *Chicago Tribune*, Oct. 1, 1946.
14. *Chicago Tribune*, Oct. 2, 1946.
15. *Chicago Tribune*, Jan. 28, 1953.
16. *SFE*, Sept. 29, 1946.
17. *North Valley Hollywood* (CA) *Times*, Oct. 13, 1946.
18. Gary Webster, *Just Too Good: The Undefeated 1948 Cleveland Browns* (2016), 14.
19. Charlie Hennigan interview, Dec. 10, 1993.
20. AP, Oct. 28, 1946.
21. *SFE*, Nov. 11, 1946.
22. *SFE*, Dec. 9, 1946.

Chapter Thirteen

1. *SFE*, Sept. 7, 1986.
2. *Ibid.*
3. *SFE*, Jan. 3, 1982.
4. *Ibid.*
5. Barbara Titchenal interview.
6. *SFE*, Oct. 26, 1947
7. Carroll, *Dr. Eddie Anderson*, 96.
8. *SFE*, Nov. 5, 1947.
9. *Cleveland Plain Dealer*, Nov. 17, 1947.
10. Gary Webster, *The League That Didn't Exist*, 133–34.
11. Kevin Carroll, *Houston Oilers: The Early Years* (2001), 66, 172.
12. *SFE*, Sept. 20, 1948.
13. *Cleveland Plain Dealer*, Sept. 30, 1948.
14. *Ibid.*
15. *New York Times*, Dec. 21, 1960.
16. *SFE*, Nov. 29, 1948.
17. Webster, *The League That Didn't Exist*, 174.
18. *SFE*, Sept. 26, 1949.
19. *SFE*, Oct. 1, 1949.
20. *SFE*, Oct. 10, 1949.
21. *Ibid.*
22. *SFE*, Jan. 3, 1982.
23. *SFE*, Oct. 24, 1949.
24. *SFE*, Nov. 28, 1949.
25. AP, Dec. 1, 1949.
26. *Ibid.*
27. *Ibid.*
28. AP, Dec. 10, 1949.

Chapter Fourteen

1. *SFE*, Aug. 23, 1950.
2. *SFE*, Aug. 18, 1950.
3. *SFE*, Aug. 29, 1950.
4. *SFE*, Sept. 25, 1950.
5. *SFE*, Oct. 19, 1950.
6. *SFE*, Nov. 13, 1950.
7. *SFE*, Nov. 27, 1950.
8. Webster, *The League That Didn't Exist*, 141.
9. *SFE*, May 4, 1951.
10. "Top Ten Most Feared Tacklers in NFL History," *NFL Top Ten*, NFL Films, uploaded to YouTube by Isaac Green, Apr. 27, 2020, https://www.youtube.com/watch?v-1ZWq7m4M2Ac.
11. *Ibid.*
12. *Ibid.*
13. *SFE*, Feb. 5, 1951.
14. *SFE*, Aug. 8, 1951.

15. *Ibid.*
16. *SFE*, Oct. 1, 1951.
17. *SFE*, Oct. 7, 1951.
18. *The Minneapolis Star,* Sept. 11, 1951.
19. *SFE*, Oct. 29, 1951.
20. *SFE*, Dec. 17, 1951

Chapter Fifteen

1. Dan Raley, "The Untold Story of Hugh McElhenny, the King of Montalla," *Seattle Post Intelligencer,* Sept. 1, 2004.
2. *Ibid.*
3. Andy Piascik, *Gridiron Gauntlet* (2009), 137–38.
4. *SFE,* Aug. 11, 1952.
5. *SFE*, Sept. 11, 1952.
6. *SFE*, Sept. 9, 1952.
7. *SFE*, Oct. 13, 1952.
8. Piascik, *Gridiron Gauntlet,* 140.
9. *SFE*, Oct. 20, 1952.
10. Dan Raley, "The Untold Story of Hugh McElhenny."
11. *SFE*, Oct. 20, 1952.
12. *SFE*, Oct. 27, 1952.
13. *SFE*, Nov. 3, 1952.
14. *Ibid.*
15. *SFE*, Nov. 7, 1952.
16. *New York Times,* Nov. 11, 1952.
17. *SFE*, Nov. 24, 1952.
18. *Los Angeles Times,* Nov. 25, 1952.
19. *SFE*, Nov. 27, 1952.
20. *Los Angeles Times,* Nov. 25, 1952.
21. *SFE*, Nov. 26, 1952.
22. *Ibid.*
23. *SFE*, Nov. 29, 1952.
24. *SFE*, Dec. 1, 1952.
25. *SFE,* Dec. 15, 1952.

Chapter Sixteen

1. AP, Jan. 15, 1953.
2. *New York Times,* Jan. 23, 1953.
3. *San Francisco Gate,* Apr. 20, 2015.
4. *SFE*, Apr. 6, 1953.
5. *SFE*, June 3, 1953.
6. *SFE*, July 28, 1953.
7. *SFE*, July 27, 1953.
8. *SFE*, Aug. 2, 1953.
9. *SFE*, Aug. 24, 1953.
10. *SFE*, Oct. 5, 1953.
11. *Ibid.*
12. *SFE,* Oct. 19, 1953.
13. *SFE*, Oct. 26, 1953.
14. *SFE*, Nov. 9, 1963.
15. *SFE*, Nov. 16, 1953.
16. *Ibid.*
17. *SFE*, Dec. 14, 1953.
18. *Chicago Tribune,* Jan. 4, 1961.
19. *Daily Independent Journal* (San Rafael, CA), Sept. 15, 1954.
20. UP, Oct. 4, 1954.

21. *Ibid.*
22. Kristine Setting Clark, *St. Clair: I'll Take It Raw!* (2005), see Bedcheck.
23. *Ibid.*
24. *SFE*, Oct. 18, 1954.
25. *SFE*, Oct. 25, 1954.
26. *SFE*, Nov. 1, 1954.
27. UP, Nov. 1, 1954.
28. *SFE*, Nov. 8, 1954.
29. *Ibid.*
30. AP, Nov. 13, 1954.
31. *Green Bay Gazette,* Dec. 4, 1954.
32. *SFE*, Dec. 6, 1954.
33. *SFE*, Dec. 12, 1954.
34. AP, Dec. 13, 1954.
35. *SFE*, Dec. 14, 1954.
36. *Los Angeles Times,* Dec. 14, 1954.
37. *SFE*, Dec. 14, 1954.
38. Piascek, *Gridirion Gauntlet,* 65–66.
39. John Vorperian, "Quick Hits with Al Carapella," *Coffin Corner,* July/Aug. 2019.
40. *SFE*, Dec. 14, 1954.
41. *Los Angeles Times,* Dec. 14, 1954.
42. UP, Dec. 14, 1954.

Chapter Seventeen

1. UP, Dec. 14, 1954.
2. *Ibid.*
3. AP, Dec. 23, 1954.
4. *SFE*, Dec. 31, 1954.
5. Phillip S. Meilinger, *Hubert R. Harmon: Airman, Officer, Father of the Air Force Academy* (2009), 288.
6. *Los Angeles Times,* Janu. 17, 1955.
7. *Ibid.*
8. *SFE*, Jan. 17, 1955.
9. *Long Beach Independent,* Jan. 12, 1955.
10. *Ibid.*
11. Meilinger, *Hubert R. Harmon,* 288.
12. AP, Feb. 12, 1955.
13. *Ibid.*
14. *SFE*, Feb. 24, 1955.
15. *Ibid.*
16. UP, Mar. 2, 1955.
17. *Chicago Tribune,* Nov. 7, 1956.
18. *Ibid.*
19. *The Shreveport Journal,* Sept. 5, 1955.
20. *The Shreveport Journal,* Mar. 20, 1956.
21. *Ibid.*
22. *SFE*, Nov. 2, 1955.
23. *SFE*, Dec. 22, 1955.
24. *SFE*, Dec. 26, 1955.
25. *SFE*, Jan. 13, 1956
26. AP, Apr. 15, 1956.

Chapter Eighteen

1. *The Eugene (OR) Guard,* Sept. 26, 1956.
2. AP, Sept. 30, 1956.
3. *The Parsons (KS),* Oct. 30, 1956.
4. AP, Oct. 2, 1956.

5. AP, Oct. 23, 1956.
6. AP, Oct. 26, 1956.
7. *Greeley* (CO) *Daily Tribune*, Oct. 31, 1956.
8. *SFE*, Dec. 7, 1956.
9. *SFE*, Dec. 22, 1956.
10. *Ibid.*
11. *SFE*, Dec. 30, 1956.
12. *Ibid.*
13. *The Santa Rosa* (CA) *Press Democrat*, Jan. 28, 1957.
14. *Knoxville Sentinel News*, June 2, 1957.
15. *New York Daily News*, Oct. 17, 1957.
16. AP, Oct. 12, 1957.
17. AP, Nov. 7,1957.
18. *SFE*, Dec. 11, 1957.
19. *Ibid.*

Chapter Nineteen

1. UP, Jan. 28, 1958.
2. *SFE*, Sept. 17, 1958
3. *Philadelphia Inquirer* (PI), Aug. 31, 1967.
4. AP, Sept. 6, 1958.
5. *Philadelphia Daily News* (PDN), May 3, 1983.
6. *PDN*, June 20, 1973.
7. AP, Sept. 7, 1958.
8. *Lancaster* (PA) *News*, Aug. 24, 1958.
9. AP, Sept. 16, 1958.
10. *PDN*, Mar. 21, 1977.
11. *SFE*, Sept. 22, 1958.
12. *PI*, Oct. 1, 1958.
13. *Sioux Falls* (SD) *Argus-Leader*, Nov. 9, 1958.
14. *Ibid.*
15. *New York Times*, Nov. 26, 1958.
16. Paul Brown with Jack Clary, *PB: The Paul Brown Story* (1979), 211.
17. *Dayton Journal Herald*, Nov. 24, 1958.
18. *Ibid.*
19. *Salt Lake* (UT) *Tribune*, Oct. 21, 1958.
20. *Ibid.*
21. *Ibid.*
22. *50th Anniversary Oral History of United States Air Force Academy, 1954–2004* (2005), 155.
23. *Ibid.*
24. AP, Dec. 10, 1958.
25. AP, Dec. 27, 1960.
26. AP, Dec. 19, 1958.
27. *PI*, Dec. 26, 1960.
28. NFL Films: The Top 100 Greatest NFL Players, #83, Norm Van Brocklin (YouTube).
29. Pete Retzlaff Talks About 50th Anniversary of the Philadelphia Eagles' 1960 Championship, uploaded to YouTube by the Mighty EROCK, Sept. 2, 2010, https://www.youtube.com/watch?v=P28YtLC12Qo.
30. *PI*, July 12, 1959.
31. *PI*, Sept. 30, 1959.
32. *Ibid.*

33. AP, Nov. 14, 1960.
34. *PDN*, Mar. 21, 1977.
35. *PI*, Oct. 31, 1959.
36. *PDN*, Dec. 12, 1959.

Chapter Twenty

1. *PDN*, Sept. 26, 1960.
2. *Ibid.*
3. *Ibid.*
4. *PDN*, Oct. 17, 1960.
5. *Ibid.*
6. *Ibid.*
7. A Championship Season, the 1960 Philadelphia Eagles (YouTube).
8. *Ibid.*
9. *PDN*, May 3, 1983.
10. A Championship Season (YouTube)
11. *Ibid.*
12. *PI*, Nov. 7, 1960.
13. 1960 NFL Championship, Eagles vs. Packers (YouTube).
14. *Ibid.*
15. *PI*, Nov. 21, 1960.
16. *PDN*, May 3, 1983.
17. *PDN*, Dec. 5, 1960.
18. *PI*, Dec. 5, 1960.
19. *Ibid.*
20. *Ibid.*
21. *Ibid.*
22. *PDN*, Dec. 5, 1960.
23. *PI*, Dec. 11, 1960.
24. AP, Dec. 6, 1960.
25. NEA, Dec. 18, 1960.
26. *PDN*, Dec. 22, 1960
27. *PI*, Dec. 23, 1960.
28. A Championship Season (YouTube).
29. UP, Dec. 27, 1960.
30. AP, Dec. 27, 1960.
31. *Baltimore Evening Star*, Dec. 22, 1960.
32. UP, Dec. 27, 1960.

Chapter Twenty-One

1. AP, Dec. 28, 1960.
2. UP, Dec. 31, 1960.
3. UP, Jan. 6, 1961.
4. *SFE*, July 9, 1965.
5. *Des Moines Register*, June 8, 1967.
6. *SFE*, Sept. 23, 1972.
7. UP, Oct. 7, 1963.
8. *Ibid.*
9. *Daily Oklahoman*, Jan. 24, 1961.
10. *SFE*, Mar. 21, 1977.
11. *New York Times*, Mar. 20, 1977.
12. *Des Moines Register*, Apr. 1, 1977.
13. *PDN*, Mar. 21, 1977.
14. *Ibid.*

Bibliography

Books

Barry, John M. *The Great Influenza*. New York: Viking Penguin, 2004.

Beach, Jim, and David Moore. *The Big Game*. New York: Random House, 1948.

Brown, Paul, with Jack Clary. *PB: The Paul Brown Story*. New York: Signet, 1979.

Carroll, Bob, Michael Gershman, David Neft, and John Thorn. *Total Football II*. New York: HarperCollins, 1997.

Carroll, Kevin. *Dr. Eddie Anderson: Hall of Fame College Football Coach*. Jefferson, NC: McFarland, 2007.

_____. *Houston Oilers: The Early Years*. Austin: Eakin, 2001.

Cavanaugh, Jack. *The Gipper*. New York: Skyhorse Publishing, 2010.

Clark, Kristine Setting. *St. Clair: I'll Take It Raw!* Novato, CA: Kristine Setting Clark, 2005.

Clary, Jack. *Navy Football: Gridiron Legends and Fighting Heroes*. Annapolis: Naval Institute Press, 1997.

Crouch, Gregory. *The Bonanza King*. New York: Scribner's, 2018.

Danzig, Allison. *The History of American Football*. Englewood Cliffs, NJ: Prentice-Hall, 1956.

Dent, Jim. *Twelve Mighty Orphans*. New York: Thomas Dunne Books, 2007.

Eskenazi, David. "James Martin Phelan." *Wayback Machine*, Oct. 30, 2012.

Hillebrand, Chuck. "Sweetness." *Santa Clara Magazine*, Dec. 18, 2012.

Hoover, Scott. "Touchdown Taylorville!" (1967). Copyrighted but unpublished manuscript appearing in Sesquicentennial Issue of *Taylor Breeze Courier*, June 18, 1989.

Kuzniewski, Anthony J. *Thy Honored Name: A History of the College of the Holy Cross, 1843–1994*. Washington, D.C.: Catholic University of America Press, 1996.

Lawlor, Glen "Jake." Oral Autobiography of an Iowa Native with a Close Up View of Nevada Athletics, 1926–71. University of Nevada Oral History Project, 1971.

Lefebvre, Jim. *Coach for a Nation: The Life and Times of Knute Rockne*. Minneapolis: Great Day Press, 2013.

MacCambridge, Michael. *ESPN College Football Encyclopedia: The Complete History of the Game*. New York: ESPN Books, 2005.

Maggio, Frank. *Notre Dame and the Game That Changed Football*. New York: Carroll & Graf, 2007.

Maxwell, Mark. *From Notre Dame to Georgia: Harry Mehre, the Legend*. Athens, GA: Maxwell & Mehr, 2017.

Meilinger, Phillip S. *Hubert R. Harmon: Airman, Officer, Father of the Air Force Academy*. Wheat Ridge, CO: Fulcrum, 2009.

Moss, Al. *Pac-10 Football*. Greenwich, CT: Crescent, 1987.

Newhouse, Dave. *Founding 49ers: The Dark Days Before the Dynasty*. Kent, OH: Kent State University Press, 2015.

_____. *The Incredible Slip Madigan*. Haworth, NJ: St. Johann Press, 2018.

Niese, Joe, with Bob Dorais. *Gus Dorais: Gridiron Innovator, All-American and Hall of Fame Coach*. Jefferson, NC: McFarland, 2018.

Piascek, Andy. *Gridiron Gauntlet*. Lanham, MD: Taylor Trade, 2009.

Raley, Dan. "The Untold Story of Hugh McElhenny, the King of Montlake." *Seattle Post-Intelligencer*, Sept. 1, 2004.

Robinson, Ray. *Rockne of Notre Dame*. New York: Oxford University Press, 1999.

Sperber, Murray. *Shake Down the Thunder*. New York: Holt, 1993.

Tinnea, Johanna. "The Game That Never Was." *Taylorville Breeze Courier,* June 18, 1989.

Vorperian, John. "Quick Hits with Al Carapella." *Coffin Corner: The Official Magazine of the Professional Football Researchers' Association,* July/Aug. 2019.

Wallace, Francis. *The Notre Dame Story.* New York: Rinehart, 1949.

Webster, Gary. *Just Too Good: The Undefeated 1948 Cleveland Browns.* Jefferso,n NC: McFarland, 2016.

_____. *The League That Didn't Exist.* Jefferson, NC: McFarland, 2019.

Periodicals

Asheville Citizen (NC)
Baltimore Evening Star
Birmingham News
Cedar Rapids Gazette
Chicago Tribune
Cleveland Plain Dealer
Daily Independent Journal (San Rafael, CA)
Daily Oklahoman (Oklahoma City)
Dayton Journal Herald
Des Moines Register
Eugene Guard (OR)
Gallup Independent (NM)
Greeley Daily Tribune (CO)
Green Bay Gazette
Honolulu Star
Knoxville Sentinel
Lancaster News (PA)

Lincoln Star (NE)
Long Beach Independent (CA)
Los Angeles Times
Minneapolis Star
Napa Journal (CA)
Nevada State Journal
New York Daily News
New York Times
News and Observer (Raleigh, NC)
North Carolina State University Alumni News
North Valley Hollywood Times
Notre Dame Scholastic
Oakland Tribune
Omaha Bee
The Parsons (KS)
Philadelphia Daily News
Philadelphia Inquirer

Pittsburgh Daily News
Pittsburgh Post
Reno Gazette Journal
Sacramento Bee
Salt Lake Telegram
San Francisco Chronicle
San Francisco Examiner
San Francisco Gate
San Jose Mercury
Seattle Post Intelligencer
Selma Times (AL)
Shreveport Journal
Sioux Falls Argus-Leader (SD)
Sooner Spectator Magazine
South Bend Tribune
Stuart Herald (IA)
The Tennessean

Documentaries

A Championship Season: The 1960 Philadelphia Eagles. Uploaded to YouTube by Philadelphia Eagles, 1 May 2020. https://www.youtube.com/watch?v=VoUfU31-DCM.

"Chuck Bednarik." *SportsCentury.* ESPN. Uploaded to YouTube by tomjackfuser, 17 November 2017. https://www.youtube.com/watch?v=1WAy2lth2Ac.

Chuck Bednarik: The Last of the Sixty Minute Men. NFL Films. Uploaded to YouTube by Grey Beard, 21 April 2020. https://www.youtube.com/watch?v=xll-cmEaYu8.

"Concrete Charlie Bednarik." *NFL Films Presents.* NFL Films. Uploaded to YouTube by Philadelphia Eagles, 4 April 2016. https://www.youtube.com/watch?v+Qo0WUCcs_gs.

"#83 Norm Van Brocklin." *The Top 100 Greatest NFL Players.* NFL Films. Uploaded to YouTube by NFL Films, 7 June 2016. https://www.youtube.com/watch?v=bchv5lnuQYE.

"1960 NFL Championship Game: Eagles vs. Green Bay." 49 minutes, 36 seconds. Uploaded to by Tarik Dean, 22 March 2015. 46 mins. https://www.youtube.com/watch?v=P28YtLC12Qo.

"#35 Chuck Bednarik." *The Top 100 Greatest NFL Players.* NFL Films. Uploaded to YouTube by NFL Films, 9 June 2016. https://www.youtube.com/watch?v=LsSFUtvknNk.

"Top Ten Most Feared Tacklers in NFL History." *NFL Top Ten.* NFL Films. Uploaded to YouTube by Isaac Green, 27 April 2020. https://www.youtube.com/watch?v=1Zwq7m4Mba4.

Author Interviews

Jim Anderson
Billy Ray Barnes
Robert Cook
Charlie Hennigan

Tom Jozwiak
Brock Strom
Barbara Titchenal
Joann Wilcox

Index

Numbers in **bold italics** indicate pages with illustrations